COMMEDIA DELL'AR

The commedia dell'arte, the 'improvised' Italian theatre that dominated the European stage from 1550 to 1750, is arguably the most famous theatre tradition to emerge from Europe in the early modern period. Its celebrated masks have come to symbolise theatre itself and have become part of the European cultural imagination. Over the past twenty years a revolution in commedia dell'arte scholarship has taken place, generated mainly by a number of distinguished Italian scholars. Their work, in which they have radically separated the myth from the history of the phenomenon, remains, however, largely untranslated into English. The present volume gathers together an international group of scholars to synthesise for the first time this research for both specialist and non-specialist readers. The book is structured around key topics that span both the early modern period and the twentieth-century reinvention of the commedia dell'arte.

CHRISTOPHER B. BALME is Professor of Theatre Studies at the Ludwig-Maximilian University of Munich. His recent publications include *The Cambridge Introduction to Theatre Studies* (Cambridge, 2008) and *The Theatrical Public Sphere* (Cambridge, 2014).

PIERMARIO VESCOVO is Professor of Italian Dramatic Literature at the Ca' Foscari University of Venice and co-editor of *Rivista di Letteratura Teatrale*. He is the author of *Entracte. Drammaturgia del Tempo* (2007) and *A viva voce. Percorsi del genere drammatico* (2015).

DANIELE VIANELLO is Professor of Theatre Studies at the University of Calabria and vice-president of the European Association for the Study of Theatre and Performance (EASTAP). He has published widely on the Renaissance and contemporary theatre. He is the author of *L'arte del buffone* (2005), a study of the early commedia dell'arte.

COMMEDIA DELL'ARTE IN CONTEXT

EDITED BY

CHRISTOPHER B. BALME
Ludwig-Maximilian University of Munich

PIERMARIO VESCOVO
Ca' Foscari University of Venice

DANIELE VIANELLO
University of Calabria

CAMBRIDGE
UNIVERSITY PRESS

CAMBRIDGE
UNIVERSITY PRESS

University Printing House, Cambridge CB2 8BS, United Kingdom

One Liberty Plaza, 20th Floor, New York, NY 10006, USA

477 Williamstown Road, Port Melbourne, VIC 3207, Australia

314-321, 3rd Floor, Plot 3, Splendor Forum, Jasola District Centre, New Delhi - 110025, India

79 Anson Road, #06-04/06, Singapore 079906

Cambridge University Press is part of the University of Cambridge.

It furthers the University's mission by disseminating knowledge in the pursuit of
education, learning and research at the highest international levels of excellence.

www.cambridge.org
Information on this title: www.cambridge.org/9781108994088
DOI: 10.1017/9781139236331

First published 2018
First paperback edition 2021

A catalogue record for this publication is available from the British Library

ISBN 978-1-107-02856-2 Hardback
ISBN 978-1-108-99408-8 Paperback

Contents

v

Notes on Contributors

CHRISTOPHER B. BALME is Professor of Theatre Studies at LMU Munich. Recent publications include, *Pacific Performances: Theatricality and Cross-Cultural Encounter in the South Seas* (2007), *The Cambridge Introduction to Theatre Studies* (Cambridge, 2008) and *The Theatrical Public Sphere* (Cambridge, 2014). He is joint senior editor of the six-volume *A Cultural History of Theatre* (2017). His current research interests focus on the globalisation of the arts; theatre and the public sphere. In 2016 he was awarded an ERC Advanced Grant.

MARCO CONSOLINI is Professor at the Institute of Theatre Studies of the University Sorbonne Nouvelle-Paris III. He leads, with Sophie Lucet and Romain Piana, the Interuniversity Research Group on Theatre (GRIRT). He is the author of *Théâtre Populaire* (1953–1964) and *Histoire d'une revue engagée* (1998). He edited the theatrical writings of Roland Barthes, *Sul teatro* (2002), and (with Jean-Pierre Sarrazac) the book *Avènement de la mise en scène moderne/Crise du drame. Continuités-discontinuités* (2010). He is currently preparing the seventh and eighth volumes of the *Registres* of Jacques Copeau (with Maria-Ines Aliverti).

RICCARDO DRUSI is Professor of Italian Literature at Ca' Foscari University of Venice. His primary interests are in texts from the Middle Ages to the early Baroque period. His recent publications include studies of musical performance during Dante's time, on Latin dialogues at the revival of the Bucolic genre in the fourteenth century and on Renaissance comedy's traces within *Egle* by G. B. Giraldi Cinzio. His current research is focused on dialogic fiction in Petrarch's *Canzoniere* and on vernacular theatrical texts in Renaissance Venice. He is a member of the editorial board of *Rivista di Letteratura Teatrale* and the editorial board of Scena Arborata, a book series devoted to studies of Renaissance *pastorale* and *tragicommedia*.

ANDREA FABIANO is Professor of Italian Studies at Sorbonne University. His research concerns the circulation of Italian actors, singers and authors throughout Europe, as well as the reception of Italian theatre and opera in France in the modern era. Recent publications include: *À travers l'opéra. Parcours anthropologiques et transferts dramaturgiques sur la scène théâtrale européenne du XVIIIe au XXe siècle* (2007), (with M. Noiray) *L'opera italiana in Francia nel Settecento* (2013) and a critical and scholarly edition of Goldoni's scenarios for the Comédie-Italienne in Paris (2017).

SIRO FERRONE is Professor of Dramaturgy and History of Acting and Oratory at the University of Florence. He has taught in Barcelona, Stockholm, Paris III and VIII, at De Paul University of Chicago and at the universities of Saarbrücken (Germany), Montpellier (France) and Aberystwyth (Wales). He created and currently directs the online pro- ject *Archivio multimediale dell'attore Italiano*. His main works include: *Comici dell'Arte. Corrispondenze* (ed.) (1993), *Attori mercanti corsari* (1993; 2011), *Arlecchino. Vita e avventure di Tristano Martinelli attore* (2006; French transl. 2011), *Carlo Goldoni. La vita e il teatro* (2011) and *La Commedia dell'Arte. Attrici e attori in Europa XVI–XVIII* (2013, translated into French and German).

ERIKA FISCHER-LICHTE has been the director of the Institute for Advanced Studies on Interweaving Performance Cultures at the Free University of Berlin since 2008. She is a member of the Academia Europaea, the Academy of Sciences Göttingen, the National Academy of Sciences *Leopoldina* and the Berlin-Brandenburg Academy of Sciences, and is a past president of the International Federation for Theatre Research. Recent publications are *Tragedy's Endurance. Performances of Greek Tragedies and Cultural Identity in Germany Since 1800* (2017), *Dionysus Resurrected. Performances of Euripides'* The Bacchae *in a Globalizing World* (2014), *The Routledge Introduction to Theatre and Performance Studies* (2014) and *The Transformative Power of Performance* (2008).

RENZO GUARDENTI is Professor of History of Modern and Contemporary Theatre at the University of Florence. Recent publications include *Sguardi sul teatro. Saggi di iconografia teatrale* (2008), *L'héroïsme par l'image: Sarah Bernhardt et Eleonora Duse entre vie et théâtre* (2014) and *Da Talma a Morrocchesi: modelli attorici e iconografici tra Sette e Ottocento* (2015). His current research interests focus on theatre iconography, the commedia dell'arte in France and European theatre in the nineteenth century. He is director of the Dionysus Theatre Iconography Archive.

RAIMONDO GUARINO is Professor of Theatre Studies at the University of Roma Tre. His current research fields are: theatre, city and celebration in late medieval and early modern Europe, early modern drama and site-specific contemporary theatre in urban spaces. His recent books are: *Il teatro nella storia* (2005), *Teatri Luoghi Città* (2008) and *Shakespeare: la scrittura nel teatro* (2010). A new, enlarged edition of his book about Renaissance Venice (*Teatro e Mutamenti. Rinascimento e Spettacolo a Venezia*, 1995) is forthcoming.

ROBERT HENKE is Professor of Drama and Comparative Literature at Washington University in St Louis. Recent publications include *Poverty and Charity in Early Modern Theatre and Performance* (2015) and *Performance and Literature in the Commedia dell'Arte* (2002). He is the editor of *A Cultural History of Early Modern Theatre* (2017). His current research focuses on two projects: one on Shakespeare and early modern Italian theatre and another on early modern transnational theatre networks.

BENT HOLM was Professor at Copenhagen University until 2014. He has translated Goldoni, de Filippo and Fo and has published interdisciplinary studies in Danish, Italian, French, English and Polish. Recent publications include *Religion, Ritual, Theatre* (2008), *The Taming of the Turk: Ottomans on the Danish Stage 1596–1896* (2014) and *L'arte dell'attore nel settecento: accuse e apologie* (2015). His research focuses on the relationships between historiography, cognition and dramaturgy. A member of the Scandinavian Institute of North African Studies, he received the Holberg Award in 2000.

STEFAN HULFELD is Professor of Theatre Studies at the University of Vienna. His current research agendas focus on the function of prologues in the *commedia all'improvviso*, the emergence of professional theatre in the German-speaking area and the variety of theatre forms during the Yugoslav Wars. Publications include a study in theatre historiography from the sixteenth to the twentieth century, entitled *Theatergeschichtsschreibung als kulturelle Praxis* (2007) and the 2014 edition of the *Scenari più scelti d'istrioni* (Scenari Corsiniani).

M A KATRITZKY is Barbara Wilkes Research Fellow in Theatre Studies at The Open University, Milton Keynes, and a former holder of Alexander von Humboldt, Herzog August Library and NIAS Fellowships. Recent publications include the Ashgate Performance Practice Reprint Series (2014), *Healing, Performance and Ceremony in the Writings of Three Early Modern Physicians: Hippolytus Guarinonius and the Brothers Felix and Thomas Platter* (2012), *Women, Medicine and Theatre, 1500–1750* (2007) and *The Art of Commedia: A Study in the Commedia dell'Arte 1560–1620 with Special Reference to the Visual Records* (2006).

ANNE MACNEIL specialises in the history of Renaissance music, the commedia dell'arte and digital humanities. She is co-director of the international research consortium *IDEA: Isabella d'Este Archive* (https://isabelladeste.web.unc.edu). She recently received a Digital Innovations Fellowship from the American Council of Learned Societies for *Mapping Secrets*, a project concerning the organisation of the Mantuan chancery in the early sixteenth century. Her current project, *Italian Songs from the Time of Christopher Columbus*, is funded by a Mellon Foundation/National Endowment for the Humanities Fellowship for Digital Editions.

BERNADETTE MAJORANA is Professor of Performing Arts at the University of Bergamo. She graduated in art history at the University of Genoa and obtained her PhD in performing arts at the University of Florence. She was a visiting professor at École des Hautes Études en Sciences Sociales (Paris), Blaise-Pascal University (Clermont-Ferrand) and Lumière University (Lyon). She has published extensively on performance and Catholic religious culture in the modern period and on popular theatre. She collaborated for many years with the CRT – Centro di ricerca per il teatro (Milan).

TERESA MEGALE is Professor in Art and Performance at the University of Florence. Her main areas of study are the comedy of art, the history of actors and dramaturgy from the seventeenth to the twentieth century. Her publications include *Tra mare e terra. Commedia dell'Arte nella Napoli spagnola (1575–1656)* (2017), *Paolo Poli* (2009), *Mirandolina e le sue interpreti* (2008), *Locandiera* (2007) by Goldoni (with Mamone), *Visconti e la Basilicata. Visconti in Basilicata* (2003) and *Il Tedeschino* by Ricci (1995).

SANDRA PIETRINI is Professor of Theatre Studies at the University of Trento (Italy). Her publications include the critical edition *L'Amleto di Cesare Rossi* (2014) and the monographies: *I giullari nell'immaginario medievale* (2011), *L'arte dell'attore dal Romanticismo a Brecht* (2009),

Il mondo del teatro nel cinema (2007), *Fuori scena. Il teatro dietro le quinte nell'Ottocento* (2004) and *Spettacoli e immaginario teatrale nel Medioevo* (2001). Her research interests focus on medieval theatre and acting theories. She directs *Arianna*, the digital archive on Shakespearean iconography (http://laboratorioteatrale.lett.unitn.it/progetto-arianna/shakespeariana.html), containing more than 12,000 items.

PAOLO PUPPA was Professor in History of the Theatre and of the Stage at Ca' Foscari University of Venice. A specialist in modern and comparative theatre, he has written critical works on Pirandello, Dario Fo, Rolland, Ibsen, Rosso di San Secondo, D'Annunzio, Goldoni, Brook and Duse. He published a *History of the Modern Stage* and a *Survey of Italian Playwrights*. He co-edited *A History of Italian Theatre* (Cambridge, 2006) and *Encyclopaedia of Italian Literary Studies*. He is also a prize-winning playwright.

FRANCO RUFFINI is a theatre researcher and was Professor for Theatre Studies at Roma Tre University. His publications include: *Stanislavskij. Dal lavoro dell'attore al lavoro su di sé* (2005), *L'attore che vola. Boxe, acrobazia, scienza della scena* (2010), *Theatre and Boxing* (2014) and *L'Arca di Noèe altre storie di teatro* (2014). His most recent research concerns the work of Jerzy Grotowski.

MIRELLA SCHINO is Professor of Theatre Studies at Roma Tre University. Recent publications include: *La nascita della regia teatrale* (2003), *Il teatro di Eleonora Duse* (2008), *Alchemists of the Stage. Theatre Laboratories in Europe* (2009) and *Odin Teatret Archives* (2017). Her current research interests focus on theatrical archives and on actor training.

VIRGINIA SCOTT was Professor Emerita of Theatre at the University of Massachusetts at Amherst. She was a leading authority on early French and Italian theatre whose books include *The Commedia dell'Arte in Paris, Molière: A Theatrical Life* and *Women on the Stage in Early Modern France*. She was also noted for her translation of Molière's plays, as well as a critical edition of *Tartuffe*.

LAURENCE SENELICK is Fletcher Professor of Drama and Oratory at Tufts University, Fellow of the American Academy of Art and Sciences, Alt-Fellow of the Wissenschaftskolleg zu Berlin and recipient of the St George medal of the Russian Ministry of Culture. His books include *Gordon Craig's Moscow* Hamlet (1982), *The Chekhov Theatre: A Century of the Plays in Performance (Cambridge, 1997), The Changing Room:*

Sex, Drag and Theatre (2000), *Soviet Theatre: A Documentary History* (2014) and *Jacques Offenbach and the Making of Modern Culture* (Cambridge, 2017).

FERDINANDO TAVIANI is Professor Emeritus of the University of L'Aquila. Notable publications are: *Il segreto della Commedia dell'Arte* (in collaboration with Mirella Schino, 1982; French transl. 1984), *Uomini di scena, uomini di libro. Introduzione alla letteratura teatrale italiana nel Novecento* (1997) and Luigi Pirandello, *Saggi e interventi*, curated and with an essay by Ferdinando Taviani (2006).

STEFANO TOMASSINI is a Researcher in Theatre and Dance at IUAV in Venice. He has taught at Ca' Foscari University of Venice and at the University of Lugano. He was Associate Research Scholar at the Italian Academy for Advanced Studies, Columbia University (2011). Among his publications are a critical edition of *Prometo* by Salvatore Viganò (1999), the Italian musical and dance libretti on the figure of *Adone* (2009), *Enzo Cosimi* (2002) and the curation of the written choreosophies of Aurel M. Milloss (2002) and the lessons of Ted Shawn (2008).

MARIA DEL VALLE OJEDA CALVO is Professor of Spanish Literature at Ca' Foscari University of Venice. Recent publications include *Stefanelo Botarga e Zan Ganassa. Scenari e zibaldoni dei comici dell'arte nell Spagna del '500* (2007), the critical edition of *El trato de Argel* by Miguel de Cervantes (2015) and *Bueno es callar* by Mira de Amescua (2012). Her current research focuses on Spanish theatre of the Golden Age, commedia dell'arte and the relationship between the Spanish and Italian theatres.

FRANCO VAZZOLER has taught Italian literature and Italian theatrical literature at the University of Genoa. He is the author of essays and articles on the literature and theatre of the seventeenth, eighteenth and twentieth centuries and a monograph on Carlo Goldoni (2012). He has translated *Memorie del teatro* by Georges Banu (2005), curated an edition of *Teatro* by Moravia (Milano, 1998, together with Aline Nari) and published *di I due Pantaloni / i Mercanti di Goldoni* (2001).

PIERMARIO VESCOVO teaches at the Ca' Foscari University of Venice. He has lectured at the universities Paris-IV, Paris-III, École Normale Supérieure (Paris-Lyon) and Barcelona (Autónoma). Most of his publications concern Italian drama. He has a special interest in the relations between literature and visual arts, theory and history of the dramatic text (*Entracte. Drammaturgia del Tempo* (2007) and *A viva voce. Percorsi del genere drammatico* (2015)). He is co-editor of *Rivista di Letteratura Teatrale* and scientific secretary of the committee of the national edition of Goldoni, Gozzi and Nievo.

DANIELE VIANELLO is Professor of Theatre Studies at the University of Calabria and vice-president of EASTAP – European Association for the Study of Theatre and Performance. He taught theatre studies at Sapienza University of Rome and at Ca' Foscari University of Venice. He has published widely on the Renaissance and contemporary theatre. On the topic of the commedia dell'arte, he published *L'arte del buffone* (2005). He worked for several years at the Teatro di Roma, where he was assistant to Italian and foreign stage directors.

Acknowledgements

This book has been a long time in of the making: perhaps too long. Over the years a number of people have had an involvement beyond the authors included in the final version. Regrettably one author, Virginia Scott, did not live to see the book published. Virginia was a fine scholar and indisputably a leading authority on the commedia dell'arte in France: we are gratified that she could complete her contribution in time. Stefan Hulfeld (Vienna) made important contributions during the planning and conceptual phase.

A key role was played by the two translators of the Italian articles, Emmanuele Bernadini and Manuela Gallo at Langwich, Turin, who applied diligence, patience and determination to find the best solution to rendering academic Italian into a readable English equivalent. A final stylistic polish was undertaken by Lisa Maria Bowler.

Regrettably we were unable to include images in the book. A combination of costs plus an increasingly byzantine legal situation governing reproduction rights forced us to take the unusual step of including URLs for the images rather than providing reproductions.

A number of student assistants have also been involved. In Munich we would particularly like to single out Helene Grebner and Rebecca Sturm, who had the unenviable task of tracking and sorting the extremely varied bibliographical references. Katja Meroth supervised the textual redactions and compilation of the index in the final phase.

At Cambridge University Press, we have been fortunate to have had the guiding hands of Vicki Cooper, Fleur Jones, Kate Brett and Sophie Taylor.

Introduction
Commedia dell'Arte: History, Myth, Reception

Daniele Vianello

Today, the commedia dell'arte is widely regarded as one of the most significant phenomena in the history of European theatre. Its famous stock characters, which have become an integral part of the collective imagination, are widely accepted as the very emblem of theatre.

From the second half of the twentieth century onwards, the commedia dell'arte has been the subject of substantial research, mostly by Italian scholars, who have re-evaluated its characteristic features and constitutive elements. These studies remain largely untranslated in English. Furthermore, there are no publications which provide a comprehensive overview of this complex phenomenon or which reconstruct not only its history but also its fortunes over time and space.

An historical overview was published by Kenneth and Laura Richards in 1990, but this is now considered dated. More recent studies are limited to the discussion of specific issues or to particular geographical areas or periods of time. For example, Robert Henke (2002), Anne MacNeil (2003) and M. A. Katritzky (2006) analyse individual aspects between the late Renaissance and the early seventeenth century. *The Routledge Companion to Commedia dell'Arte* (Chaffee and Crick 2015) has the practitioner rather than the scholar in focus. In Italy, Roberto Tessari (2013) and Siro Ferrone (2014), in their important recent contributions focus almost exclusively on the sixteenth and seventeenth centuries.

The main purpose of this book is to retrace the history of the *improvvisa* in light of its legendary past, with special focus on the theatrical practices and theoretical deliberations in the century which has just ended. This work aims to provide a thorough – albeit not necessarily exhaustive – reconstruction of a phenomenon that has significantly affected world theatre.

Scholars from various countries and with different backgrounds have been involved in this project. Each of them was asked to avoid summarising previous, rigidly monographic contributions, but rather to participate in the implementation of a coherent concept in which themes and a problem-oriented approach are at the forefront.

Although most of the contributions are by Italian authors, the decision to publish the book in English highlights the international character of the team of scholars who have been enlisted. Their task is to reconstruct and analyse a phenomenon which has a unique place in the history of theatre – because of its extraordinary capability of moving and transforming itself through space and time. The influence of the commedia dell'arte, in fact, transcends national boundaries and narrow fields of study and can be regarded as one of the elements that characterise both twentieth-century and contemporary theatrical perceptions.

This book was born of the need, felt by many, to study the history of the commedia dell'arte, its fortunes and legendary past from a comparative European point of view. It is not by chance that Part II bears the title 'Commedia dell'Arte and Europe'. Ample space has been given to the reconstruction of the routes and paths along which this Italian-style theatre travelled, in the sense of a 'traveling invention', in order to become so widely accepted.

The theme of travel, typical of the professional Italian itinerant companies, goes hand in hand with the fortunes and myth of the commedia dell'arte. It is well known that this myth, for the most part, originated and developed in places outside Italy, particularly in France and in German-speaking regions. Here the performances of Italian comedians became a genre just like comedy, tragedy and melodrama. The legendary image of a theatre of stock characters, exuding a talent for boundless improvisation and spontaneity, is the one that was absorbed by the collective imagination and has survived until today. The most fruitful legacy of the commedia dell'arte is the manner in which its image was distorted retrospectively throughout Europe – so much so that, according to Ferdinando Taviani, the history of the commedia is, in essence, nothing but the history of its myth (Taviani 1980; 1982).

Hence, the core of the analysis is the relationship between commedia dell'arte and international theatre cultures. Just as fundamental is the movement in the other direction – which brought a more complex and articulated image of the *improvvisa* back to the Italian theatre scene. To retrace the history of the commedia dell'arte and its myth in Europe means not only to observe its presence in different geographical areas but also to highlight the mutual enrichment of the diverse theatrical experiences encountered in all these places.

The great European success of 'Italian-style' theatre, crystallising in the stereotypes of the stock characters and their performing techniques – characterised by text improvisation and the 'vision' of a spontaneous, popular, folkloric and carnivalesque theatre – all tended to partially obscure the richness of the constituent elements and the complexity of cultural exchanges. In addition, the nineteenth- and twentieth-century myth of the commedia dell'arte revived interest in old Italian theatre, albeit often at the price of ignoring or inaccurately rewriting the history behind it.

One of the objectives of this book is to keep separate those areas which are often confused with one another. As already mentioned, relevant publications are frequently characterised on the one hand by specialised studies which break down a phenomenon into too many parts, making it difficult to grasp the subject in its entirety, and on the other by imaginative reconstructions involving a reinvention of the Italian comedians' past and a free use of experience – which are more typical of modern culture and theatre. In the former case, specialist research remains within the confines of academic studies; in the latter, history is 'flattened' by myth and conditioned by popular stereotypes.

History

The first part of this work aims to reconstruct a map of the history of the commedia dell'arte by exploring cross-thematic paths. The constitutive elements (stock characters, improvisation, actor specialisation, the novelty represented by the presence of actresses in the daily life of professional companies and the entrance ticket bought in some theatres) are analysed as distinctive features of the myth of the commedia itself. They describe a varied and extensive theatre experience which, between the sixteenth and eighteenth centuries, crystallises in a stereotyped performance genre, corresponding to the conventional image of a professional theatre of itinerant companies with stock characters committed to improvisation.

The commedia dell'arte is known primarily for the structure of its professional companies, for the creation of roles (such as the first and second Zanni, the first and second Vecchi, the Innamorati), for the tradition of stock characters with their particular language and theatrical gesturing, and for the presence of both masked and non-masked characters. Even more significant, however, is another element, which represents an absolute novelty in the history of performance: the rise of the professional actress and her role in the world of theatre. Allowing women on stage in the second half of the sixteenth century is probably one of the greatest legacies that the Italian theatre tradition was able to pass on to the rest of Europe.

Parallel to their organisation in professional companies and the appearance of actresses, the Italian *comici* inaugurated a kind of production that was new, both in the sense of drama and of spectacle. It was based on fixed stock characters and free interpretation of text. Especially the latter was revolutionary, given that professional European theatre at the time was limited to fixed roles and pre-defined parts. The myth of the stock characters, of specialisation and of improvisation is addressed by distinguishing between the actual practice of carefully orchestrated performance texts and the modern reinvention of the idea of improvisation, where it is considered mostly in terms of spontaneous extemporaneity.

Crucial for an understanding of the history of the commedia dell'arte are some key terms, starting with 'commedia dell'arte' itself. This term first appeared in the mid-eighteenth century. Compared to older and more widespread equivalents – such as *commedia all'improvviso, commedia mercenaria* and *commedia all'italiana* – commedia dell'arte is a later definition that comes from the jargon used by Italian professional companies. Evidence of this is provided by a few texts from the mid-eighteenth century, in particular in the works of Goldoni. The name always appears in its plural form – *le commedie dell'arte comica* – and refers to the *pièces*, the more common plays in the average repertoire of Italian theatre companies operating both in Italy and in other countries.

It is above all in Carlo Gozzi's theoretical and polemical works dating back to the early nineteenth century that we are able to witness a switch from the plural form (to indicate a repertoire of *pièces*) to the singular. The term is used to indicate a theatrical genre, a tradition considered close to extinction. However, as Taviani points out in Chapter 1, Gozzi's crusade in favour of the commedia dell'arte contributed not so much to its survival as a genre but more to its reincarnation in mythic form, in both the Romantic period and the twentieth century.

There are significant differences as well as some overlap between the writing practice which was widespread in Italy and Europe and the compositional techniques popularised by the *comici* for the construction of the 'backbone' and the 'oral part' of a drama. The 'provisional' and 'definitive' structures of a text created through improvisation are analysed, starting with a few technical terms which are typical of the literature of the *comici*: *soggetto, scenario* and *canovaccio*. These are textual forms whose meanings have often been confused. The analysis, therefore, focuses on the forms of memory and dramaturgical transmission – which are related mainly to specific roles such as the 'generic' collections but also to conventional forms of 'premeditated' or 'spontaneous' text, highlighting the relationship that the *comici* established with the publishing world and the resulting sale of *commedia* plays in book form.

Important topics which have influenced the literature of the commedia dell'arte include the relationship between professional and amateur theatre and the interaction between all forms of academic culture and aristocratic experimentation on the one hand and the vast range of professional performance on the other. An excellent example of this is the genre of the so-called *commedia ridicolosa*, made up exclusively of written texts meant to be recited by amateur actors, but whose actual protagonists are the famous stock characters (Mariti 1978).

On the subject of how the reputation of the commedia dell'arte spread, the works of Ludovico Zorzi (1977) and Siro Ferrone (1993b) are still fundamental. These two scholars have reconstructed a geography of early Italian theatre, starting from the territorial division of the peninsula with its several 'theatre capitals' and focusing their analysis on the 'material' aspects of theatre culture: theatre and city, theatre and celebration and the various functions of performance in the courts, in the republics, in the private theatres and in the first commercial theatres of the major cities – Venice, Naples, Ferrara, Mantua, Rome, Florence and so on. What is important in their view is the reconstruction of the process that led from the *spettacolo di palazzo* (lit. 'theatre in grand houses') to the birth of the commercial *stanze di commedia* (*commedia* halls).

Equally important is the (far from unequivocal) relationship that the *comici dell'arte* established, at different times and in different countries, with the various forms of modern auditoriums – starting with the birth of Italian-style theatre in the period between the second half of the sixteenth and the first half of the seventeenth century.

Moving between these many phenomena, this book aims to outline a concise picture of the paths along which the theatre of the *comici* travelled between the sixteenth and the eighteenth centuries, on its way to becoming widely known. In the interests of preserving the structure of the '*invenzione viaggiante*' (traveling invention) – the term coined by Siro Ferrone (1993) – individual sections are devoted to the different situations in each country. The two main, well-known periods, when the Italian *comici* were in France (1680–1697 and 1716–1731), are reconstructed, and their travels in Spain are illustrated in particular by the activities of the company of Alberto Naselli (also known as Zan Ganassa) and that of

Abagaro Frescobaldi, also known as Stefanelo Bottarga. The sporadic presence of Italian actors on English soil became relevant in the light of the influence the commedia dell'arte had on Elizabethan theatre and dramatic writing. The influence of the Italian *commedia* in the German-speaking world is illustrated by performances held in the late sixteenth century at the court of Munich by the musicians Orlando di Lasso and Massimo Troiano and by the famous frescoes in Trausnitz Castle in Landshut. Furthermore, this influence is also evident in the work of famous actors and their companies at the court of Vienna and all over the Holy Roman Empire in the seventeenth and eighteenth centuries. Testimony has been gathered which confirms that the phenomenon also spread to Northern Europe and to the Slavic countries, in particular to eighteenth-century Russia (where interesting hybrids between performances by Italian actors and local folkloristic and comic traditions emerged).

This work focuses, on the one hand, on the experiences which were characterised by continuity and stability (such as the case of the institutionalisation of the Comédie Italienne in Paris). On the other hand, it also places an emphasis on those – far more common – experiences which are characterised by discontinuity and instability.

Ample consideration is also given to a series of problems that assailed the world of the commedia dell'arte from outside. Its contentious relationship with religious authorities led to the imposition of censorship in Catholic countries and to prohibitions and restrictions in regions of Protestant persuasion. Not only is the condemnation of the theatre by religious institutions examined, but emphasis is also placed on their attempts at 'reforming' and 'moralising' it. The positions taken by the church varied between the issuance of vetoes and restrictions on the one hand and the recognition of the attraction of the theatre on the other (Taviani 1969). They are the subject of a broad literature which emphasises the constant, careful attention paid by the church to actors, actresses and their performances.

The rapid spread of the commedia dell'arte throughout Europe and beyond coincided with the parallel proliferation of poetical and polemic writings on theatre by humanists. Schools and academies became the seats of lively discussions on theatre architecture, rhetoric and classical drama. Simultaneously, a literature started to appear that dealt with the role of the actor in society and documented the tortuous path taken by the *comici* to overcome their initial position of marginality and attain general acceptance. This literature consists of writings in defence of the theatre against the prejudices that branded theatre professionals as mercenary and immoral.

These texts eventually led to the recognition and acceptance of theatre professionals over the course of the seventeenth and eighteenth centuries.

In this volume we will not deal with the more obvious topics, such as the techniques of the comedians, the restrictive, misleading labels – often mutually contradictory – of theatre 'amateurs' and 'professionals' or the rise of the modern theatre industry. Similarly, certain important aspects regarding the history of the *improvvisa* (its demonic and carnivalesque origins, clowning), although often analysed in the course of *commedia* historiography and presented as phenomena that certainly gave rise to important (sometimes mutual) exchanges and influences, are of little assistance in reconstructing the rise of the commedia dell'arte and will not be dealt with here.

Conventional classifications designate clowning (*buffoneria*) as a phenomenon belonging to the court or the public square, typical of the so-called centuries without theatre, and see it as the precondition for other accomplishments (the professional performance of the commedia dell'arte, the circus) which are supposed to mark the limits of its historical importance. While there are undeniable similarities between the performances of the *commedia* actors and those of the Renaissance jesters, and evidence supports analogies between the two, there remain important differences as well (Vianello 2005).

The subject of the mask is linked to the theatrical appearance of the main 'masked characters' (especially Harlequin and the Zanni). The inputs from folklore and carnival refer to the demonic pedigree, the agrarian cults and the final theatrical establishment of the stock characters themselves. Parallel to the development in this direction, theatrical stock characters begin to influence the world of carnival. The analysis offered here is designed to demonstrate the existence of performance forms and content which do not exclude one another, but coexist in a state of mutual interplay and the confluence of the old with the new.

Chapter 18 offers an alternative to the customary way of dealing with what is often defined as the 'illustrative adornment' in many histories of the commedia dell'arte. In this book the figures are analysed rather than used merely as illustrations. The intention is to outline a visual history – above all through generic images – of the modern myth of the commedia dell'arte. Importance is attached both to those images that are more or less directly linked to the various characteristics of the individual actors and to those that can be classified as having created 'eternal' characters, independent of the historical period in which they originated. Space is also given to the iconography that led to the reduction of the Italian comedians' performance to street theatre, typical of itinerant actors, strolling players and circus or street acrobats.

In retracing the history of the European iconography of the *improvvisa* – from the sixteenth-century images of the Zanni to Watteau's 'Italian genre' tradition – we see the gradual invention of conventional stereotypes in the creation of the modern myth. These stereotypes played a central, defining role in the process, more so in Europe than in Italy. One section is specifically devoted to the reinvention of the theatrical genre, brought about by the iconography of the *improvvisa* in the various cultures of the twentieth century.

Myth and Reception

The second part of the book is devoted to contextualising the legacy of the phenomenon in nineteenth- and twentieth-century European culture. It is certainly the most difficult to survey, but also the most innovative in the context of existing research. Ferdinando Taviani observed almost forty years ago:

> It is very strange that the commedia dell'arte still survives. It is a good example of what we may understand when, in the history of the theatre, we talk of 'legacy' or 'influences' and mean an experience that appears to have successors. In reality, it is a phenomenon that has to do with those reverse derivations which lead to statements such as 'masterpieces create their own precursors, not vice versa'. The origin of the term 'influences' is linked to astrology. These constellations, it seems, subdivide time and structure human temperaments, whereas in reality it is human beings, in subdividing time and identifying characters and temperaments, who mentally link various stars, scattered across the sky, in unitary figures and constellations. In this sense – inasmuch as they are constellations – the commedia dell'arte does *influence* (Taviani 1980: 393).

Taviani condenses the profound meaning of the nineteenth- and twentieth-century myth of the *improvvisa* in the evocative image of the 'constellation of the commedia dell'arte'. It is the Romantics, the avant-garde experimenters of the early twentieth century, more generally the moderns, who project expectations on to the commedia dell'arte which go beyond its true history. They regard certain features and constitutive elements of the commedia dell'arte as actual opportunities for their imaginations to create a completely new kind of theatre and in this way to reinvent the tradition. From this point of view, history and myth continually overlap and intertwine, forcing us to 'see double'.

As far as the legend of the commedia dell'arte in the nineteenth century is concerned, our analysis is concentrated on France and Germany. Keeping in mind the nostalgic revival attempted by Carlo Gozzi through the medium of the fable, which conjured up a universe dominated by fantasy and naivety, it is undeniable that there is an echo of the commedia dell'arte in the works of the great European writers, from Goethe via Hoffmann to Gautier.

At the same time – very evidently in the visual arts – the new forms of circus and pantomime performed by the Parisian *funambules* codified the tradition of the *comici dell'arte*. Performances of this kind can act as an interpretative (or distorting) lens, through which the overall image of the theatre performer and the artist generally, whether actor, writer or painter, appears as a 'mountebank'. The myth of the circus, as one of the most important developments of the commedia dell'arte phenomenon, is a crucial chapter in the story of its legacy from the nineteenth to the twentieth century. The influence of this myth – inhabited by clowns and jesters, acrobats and tightrope-walkers – goes well beyond the borders of the theatrical world and finds its way into literature, music and opera, classical ballet and dance, cinema and the visual arts. We may think of the portraits of Toulouse-Lautrec, Picasso, Klee and Chagall, or the colourful world to which Jean Starobinski devoted his famous essay (1970). Theatrical design, visual arts and literature interweave in a continual play of mutual influences.

The definition of the myth as 'tradition', comparable to certain experiences in Asian theatre, came about mainly in the twentieth century. If we look at the experimentation carried out by the European avant-garde at the time, we see the gradual acceptance of a new canon (not least in the didactic, introductory sense), a new legacy of Italian theatre, which shaped the theatre practice typical of the modern age.

The genre of commedia dell'arte, particularly in regions beyond its national borders, became a reference point for many theatre practitioners. In the history of those companies that had achieved professional status, they saw a source of inspiration in their struggle against the tyranny of the author and the dramatic text. It is in this context, which is typical of the avant-garde and of director's theatre, that the idea of a non-textual theatre of the imagination takes root. It is the idea of a non-verbal theatre, closely linked to miming and acrobatic skills, advocating a knowledge of the techniques of dramatic composition based on collective creation and on improvisation and in which all these elements are considered crucial to the art of the actor.

The fortunes of the commedia dell'arte in the twentieth century can be retraced panoramically in the experimental workshops, performances and theoretical deliberations undertaken by the protagonists of inter-national theatre, ranging from the pioneers of director's theatre, Gordon Craig, Jacques Copeau, Charles Dullin, Louis Jouvet, Nikolai Evreinov, Vsevolod Meyerhold, Konstantin S. Stanislavski, Aleksandr Tairov, Yevgeny Vakhtangov, Sergei Radlov and Max Reinhardt, to the great mimes Jean-Louis Barrault and Marcel Marceau and – more recently – to masters of the stage such as Jacques Lecoq, Ariane Mnouchkine, Eduardo de Filippo, Giorgio Strehler, Benno Besson, Giovanni Poli, Dario Fo and Eugenio Barba, to cite some of the most important figures.

In the early twentieth century, interest in the commedia dell'arte coin-cided with a general impetus towards change; it was an 'explosion' that led to the destruction of old canons and the creation of new ones. In the second half of the twentieth century, its persistent influence inspired many performances whose participants had links to the experimental and labora-tory theatre at that time and prompted reflections on the most interesting features of the 'genre', all of which was a prelude to the rebuilding of an authentic 'tradition' of the commedia dell'arte.

This book devotes much space to the way theatre was reinvented, starting from the rediscovery of the centrality of the actor. The importance of body, gesture and movement are explored from three different perspec-tives: laboratory theatre, actor training and theatrical theories.

At the same time, we investigate the relationship between the commedia dell'arte and director's theatre (from the era of the avant-garde to contem-porary theatre), distinguishing in the process two divergent approaches to dramatic literature. In the twentieth century, the decision to stage either Goldoni or Gozzi indicated adherence to one of two fundamentally differ-ent and distinctive conceptions of the commedia dell'arte and the very idea of its *mise en scène*. The phenomenon of director's theatre is therefore investigated according to two precisely defined principles: on the one hand, how Gozzi is to be approached via Meyerhold, Vakhtangov, Brecht and Besson; on the other, how Goldoni is to be approached via Reinhardt and Strehler, with particular reference to the respective stagings of *The Servant of Two Masters*. For many, Strehler's direction was by far the best example of a reconstruction of the commedia dell'arte.

It has already been emphasised that the influence of the myth goes well beyond the boundaries of modern theatre. For this reason, special attention has been paid to the various discoveries of supposed realities or 'secrets' of the commedia dell'arte, which are to be found in dance, in mime and in the visual arts, or in comparison with the various forms of Asian theatre. They are also to be found in certain forms of political theatre produced in the second half of the twentieth century.

The fortunes of the phenomenon of commedia dell'arte in the nineteenth and twentieth centuries are dealt with in two extensive chapters, one covering music and opera (Chapter 16), the other dance and mime (Chapter 17). The imaginative use of masks had enormous success in the field of opera, so much so that a true 'aesthetic of the mask' emerged. Soon a series of subjects and motifs arose that ultimately came to mark an important moment in modern and contemporary musical theatre.

Similarly, there is a chapter dealing with the techniques devised for the 'return' of the movement of the masks and other elements. With constant reference to the available iconography, how the body is to be handled or disciplined, is expressed in a didactic and educational framework for the actor, but also as an independent aesthetic language that permeates the experience of pantomime, classical ballet and dance. The explicit influence of pictorial images of the masks on the techniques directing the bodily movement of the dancer-actor varied a great deal throughout the nineteenth and twentieth centuries. It was at times subtle, at times well defined.

In the second half of the twentieth century, certain elements, especially improvisation and stock characters, were used as instruments to further a cause in political theatre. The typically Romantic idea of the early twentieth century as lost time later recovered gave way to the opposite idea, namely a modern mix of elements of theatrical tradition. The commedia dell'arte, originally a popular genre, was used satirically and polemically as a possible way to renew contemporary theatre. In this sense, the experiences of the 1960s and early 1970s – from Dario Fo to the Théâtre du Soleil to Bread and Puppet – were the most important developments.

If the influence of the commedia dell'arte is to be found in certain important forms of twentieth-century political theatre, in a more general sense it may also be traced to the encounter between Western and Asian theatre. Both Asian theatre and the commedia dell'arte attracted many of the pioneers of twentieth-century theatre. They recognized that the study of both of these convention-based, traditional theatres would make it possible to trace the possible premises of a science of acting, on which many men and women of the theatre were to concentrate their interest in the following decades.

As Mirella Schino writes in Chapter 25

> The great masters of the late twentieth century would follow the same road.
> They would propagate a behaviour which is normally not encountered in
> everyday life. It would consist in a way of holding one's shoulders, of
> stiffening one's neck and back, of walking and resting one's feet on the
> ground. Eugenio Barba would later call all of this 'pre-expressive'. It would
> include a series of tense poses that makes the actor's body come alive,
> appear interesting.

The book ends with reflections on the cultural heritage bequeathed by
the myth of the commedia dell'arte as well as the intercultural impulses
it activated. Special reference is also made to the unsuccessful attempts to
'institutionalize' it in Italy itself as a national performance genre worthy of
recognition as part of the country's intangible cultural heritage. Looking at
it in this way, the myth of the commedia dell'arte is enlarged further, finding
its place between tradition, creative renewal and worldwide dissemination.

Undoubtedly, questions meriting further study emerge from the treatment
of certain topics. For example, we may well ask whether Luca Ronconi's
productions based on texts by Giovan Battista Andreini should be considered part of the retrospective myth. Andreini was a renowned *commedia*
actor, son of the most famous couple of seventeenth-century comedians
and the author of some of the theatrical works that are the most difficult
to stage. The Andreini-inspired productions by Ronconi do not reflect
any of the usual features of the genre. The character of Don Giovanni,
who has an important place in the scenarios of the comedians, is problematic too. In the same vein, there are those who maintain that even
Molière should be seen in the context of the history of the *improvvisa* and
regarded as a *comedian dell'arte*, possibly the greatest of all time, despite his
French nationality.

Some of the remarks made by Luigi Pirandello in the preface to *Storia
del teatro italiano* (D'Amico 1936) make it possible to relate his theatre also
to the commedia dell'arte. Rereading the famous 'play-within-the-play'
trilogy, especially *Sei personaggi in cerca d'autore* (*Six Characters in Search of
an Author*) and *Questa sera si recita a soggetto* (*Tonight We Improvise*), where
the title already seems to echo the tradition and the myth of the *commedia
a soggetto* – improvised comedy – we recognise it as comedy written by the
actors in constant dialectical relation with the universe of authors (Taviani
1980: 33–5 and 77–81).

There are also a number of unexpected analyses of the myth of the
commedia in Part V. The reader may be surprised not to find more reflection on Meyerhold, for whom the commedia dell'arte and the 'schemes of

movements' were an essential reference, providing affirmation of the centrality of the actor, independent of text and dramatist and a vital element in the twentieth-century battle to 'retheatricalize the theatre'. Instead, there is an extended discussion of Stanislavsky's workshop activity. In his first studio and in rehearsal for the 1912 production of Molière's *Malade Imaginaire* Stanislavsky tried out a new method of working with the actors. It was suggested to him by his friend Maxim Gorky and was based on the improvisation of the text, leading to the 'collective creation' of the *pièce* starting from the basic outline.

Gorky wrote about Stanislavsky's first studio and related how the idea of a *collective* play became a new variation on the old Italian tradition of the commedia dell'arte. Stanislavsky was perhaps most influenced by the 'constellation of the commedia dell'arte' and seems to have adopted an actual 'method of improvisation'. This was the outcome of his collaboration with Gorky and is even more interesting because he seems to have taken over the 'secret' of the comedians, not so much the most ostentatious features of the *improvvisa* (masks, gags and improvisation) but rather the techniques and the processes of composition of the action. Stanislavsky is given prominence in this book along with Meyerhold, Vakhtangov, Tairov, Craig, Copeau, Reinhardt and Strehler, all of them protagonists of the myth of the commedia dell'arte in twentieth-century European theatre.

In the light of the broader socio-cultural context within which the commedia dell'arte phenomenon took on form and meaning, the book offers a comparison of the results of research and enquiry in various fields – from insights accrued through theatrical practice to the theories formulated in academic scholarship – which have contributed to a profound revision of many precepts in this field of studies in the past few decades. The most important theoretical deliberations are – and it is not by accident – the result of close collaboration between 'stage people' and 'book people'. We may think of the practical-theoretical work of Vsevolod Meyerhold and Nikolai Evreinov in collaboration with Vladimir Soloviev and Konstantin Miklasevskij and, more recently, research on the dramaturgy of the actor of the improvvisa carried out by Dario Fo and Ferruccio Marotti. Also of significance are the artistic and scientific contributions of Eugenio Barba and the Odin Teatret, realised in collaboration with the scholars of the International School of Theatre Anthropology (ISTA).

PART I

Elements

Knots and Doubleness
The Engine of the Commedia dell'Arte

Ferdinando Taviani

In Italy, in the last decades of the sixteenth and first decades of the seventeenth centuries, a form of theatre developed which was based on the dramatic and the comical, on the union of opposites, like the contrast between dark and light in some paintings of those years. This theatre was based on contradictions in terms: exquisite vulgarity, youthful old age, manly femininity, loving ferocity, intelligent folly, buffoonish tragedy and joy and horror. Joy and horror are not exaggerations; when the contradictions in terms are transferred from words to bodies, from the play of images to physical actions, then they elevate the mind and the heart, with the purpose of making us laugh and scaring us, thus bringing on joy. *Joie*: In Italian the word *spasso* derives from *espandersi*, a momentary expansion of life, like an elixir, which can inspire love as much as sex or power can. We can imagine *spasso* as a higher form of entertainment and pleasure, the difference between *spasso* and pleasure being the same as that between the experience of liberation and the illusion of liberty. This explains why some *spassosi* men – men who could give *spasso* to other people – could be loved and venerated as paragons in life and mourned in death, as Yorick is mourned by Hamlet.

Very little information survives on what might be called the 'lost theatre'. It was a form of theatre based on exception, composed of a small number of groups which excelled in this art and were foreigners everywhere. Excellence, exception and the sense of not belonging anywhere developed from an interplay of coincidences, not from a project or a programme. Only later, and always a little covertly, did the ideas emerge which were identified with a way of thinking and then translated into a libertine, artistic consciousness. This lost theatre was separate from but part of the overall tradition of the commedia dell'arte. It was the yeast in the bread of this genre and a source of popularity.

The commedia dell'arte had a very long-lasting and varied influence on world culture because it nurtured an interacting system of ideas and illusions, reincarnating itself as an image, a dream, a theatrical genre or as myth and the shadow of a tradition. This lost theatre was a spark which was soon buried by the cluttered, complex and restricted world of the commedia dell'arte. On the other hand, it was its quintessence, the secret source of the living contrasts which made the commedia dell'arte into a recurrently alluring episode in the history of theatre – at the same time, elementary and difficult to understand. Those who try to get a general idea of the commedia dell'arte experience, a strange and interesting phenomenon, start to see double.

Nowadays the term most commonly used, 'commedia dell'arte' had many predecessors: *commedia all'improvviso*, because actors seemed to improvise the lines for their roles; *commedia mercenaria*, because people paid for performances sold by professional troupes; *commedia delle maschere*, because it was based on stock characters and some of them wore masks; *commedia degli zanni*, because it featured grotesque servant characters, often masters of laughter; and *commedia italiana* or *all'italiana*, because it travelled across Europe and seemed to represent everything that was considered Italian. Commedia dell'arte, the most recent and enduring term, was originally a derogatory epithet which eventually became a crown. It began to be used frequently in the eighteenth century in a negative sense – as opposed to the more positive, 'art' of the *commedia*.

Commedia dell'arte appeared in Italy in the second half of the sixteenth century and had great success throughout the seventeenth century, while touring in many different places. We find references to it in the Spanish theatre of the Golden Age, in Shakespeare and in the English theatre. Its impact was particularly strong in France, even more than in Italy. Without the *commedia all'italiana*, neither Molière nor Marivaux would ever have written the way they did. It declined during the eighteenth century. If it had not existed, the works of Carlo Goldoni, for example, would not have been what they are. It was Goldoni who gave weight to and popularised the proposition that an authentic art of the *commedia* could exist only by denying that the commedia dell'arte was performed by money-grubbing actors. Nevertheless, it was nourished by what it denied. It may be said that Goldoni extracted the tastiest juice from the theatre performed by professional troupes and threw the skins away. Unexpectedly, new roots sprang up from those skins and bore fruit. Although the history of theatre tells us that after Goldoni the commedia dell'arte declined and although this is to some degree true, nowadays the commedia dell'arte is often discussed as if it were still a living theatrical genre. What can this mean for us? How did it become a legend – not only in the field of theatre? How is it possible that after four and a half centuries it still stands for 'new theatre'?

To these questions, we will attempt to find plausible answers. However, the really crucial question here is: What kind of joy does the commedia dell'arte evoke? Was it a sour and contradictory joy, able to spread because of the existence of pockets of tolerance in substantially intolerant cultures, in a Europe ravaged by religious wars, absolutism, the Thirty Years War and great pestilences? The commedia dell'arte was a libertine institution in an age of bourgeois seriousness and unilateral beliefs. It was a hybrid, which assumed the appearance of an indigenous cultural establishment, as well as a form of prostitution turned into its opposite. Knots and doubleness were its backbone.

Poverty and humiliation created nearly all those striking aspects. It seemed to be fantasy but was in fact audacity; it seemed to be experimentation but was really anxiety. From the distance of our chair on an expensive cruise ship, we can see that world rejoice merrily, like an island of liberty. Yet, for those who inhabited it, that world was often a clever or forced refuge. Just as often it was a prison. The great success, the ovations and immense popularity enjoyed by some actors or actresses existed on a sea of indifference, contempt and threats. The reports of that time emphasise the fortunate cases. History, however, should not forget the precarious 'normality' of the lives of members of those theatrical troupes who often suffered persecution. It is a pity that, seen from a distance, the commedia dell'arte can appear to be a friendly, childish form of theatre, while it is in fact a whole theatre-world, an encyclopaedic summary of the multifaceted forms making up the fragmentary universe of theatre – but only when it is not conceived as the performance of a written text. As we look deeper into the subject – like a vagabond character in a Baroque play who is forced to metamorphose – we have to come to terms with misunderstanding and challenges.

Even a condensed treatment of the commedia dell'arte should not overlook some aspects of doubleness. In particular, this term denotes two different theatrical realities, which overlap but do not coincide: on the one hand, the profession of theatre between the sixteenth and eighteenth centuries in Italy; on the other, a formula, a way of performing based on the use of masks and improvisation. This dichotomy is evident in the list of descriptive terms which have been used: *commedia mercenaria*, which underlines the fact that it is a profession; and *commedia delle maschere*, *all'improvviso* or *degli zanni*, which focus on the formula. *Commedia all'italiana* also emphasises the profession, but does not exclude the formula. As explained earlier, the term commedia dell'arte, originally coined to discredit a declining profession, is today associated mostly with the idea of a formula, used in a genre set to last forever. From the point of view of the formula, the commedia dell'arte stands in sharp contrast to the *commedia erudita*, namely that form of theatre based on a literary text composed by an author. However, from the standpoint of the profession and of theatre as commerce, there is no contrast, because professional *comici* often performed and wrote *erudite commedie*. Theatre as a profession is often juxtaposed with a free form of theatre conceived as a festival and performed in courts, academies, parishes and colleges by merry troupes, by intellectuals and also by aristocrats during Carnival time. However, the stark contrast between the two does not concern genres, because the improvised *commedie*, which were performed in the courts and in the academies, were based on the same scenarios used by professional actors. Therefore, a summary approach may create confusion. As mentioned earlier, there was a time in which the commedia dell'arte was in a state of decline, but then started to flourish again. As a matter of fact, what declined was the predominant use by professional troupes of the formula of improvisation. What flourished again was that same formula, but with its commercial context removed.

When referring to the commedia dell'arte, it is important to take into consideration which of its two sides is being emphasised. This requires patience and the acceptance of nuances. The issue of doubleness also involves the 'popular' nature of the commedia dell'arte: Does 'popular' refer to its content or to its origins? Its characters often speak in dialect, using common or vulgar language. The fact that the poor are placed at the centre of the *commedia* does not mean that they placed themselves there; it was often the *aristocrats* who had fun mimicking characters supposed to represent the common people. In the case of professional actors, performing roles portraying these kinds of characters had a double advantage: The lower-class audiences liked it, because they laughed and cried about people like themselves and not about the traditional heroes of sacred stories, myths or tragedies; the *signori* liked it too, because it was a way of mocking the lower classes.

Despite the misunderstandings which may arise from the presence of doubleness and various nuances, the commedia dell'arte is clearly recognisable, and easy to define in a few words, unlike the 'normal' theatre of modern European culture from the sixteenth century on. In general, theatre was and is done by choosing a text, or having one written expressly for an occasion, learning it by heart and then performing it. In the text there are several characters who have a specific function in relation to the story being related in the performance. The commedia dell'arte is different: First a plot is chosen and then the *commedia* is improvised. There are no real characters, only stock characters who always have the same name, the same costume and the same mask, passing from one *commedia* to the other. The performance, as a whole, does not strive to imitate reality, but tends towards farce, the grotesque and the fairy tale.

In normal theatre, each scene depends on the story which is being related in the performance. There are no identical scenes which are repeated in different *commedie* or in different plays. There might be similar scenes, such as recurring, everyday happenings, but they are never completely identical. By contrast, in the commedia dell'arte there are jokes, comic acts, gags and sketches which always appear in identical form, in the most diverse contexts. If we wanted to be even more concise, we might say that the commedia dell'arte is the kind of theatre that, in the history of the last four or five centuries, has stirred up both the most fascination and the most contempt, one sentiment next to the other, one within the other, to an extreme beyond comparison.

Fascination and Contempt

From a distance, the commedia dell'arte appears as a landscape of masks, laughter – laughter – laughter and improvisation. It is characterised by its indelibly Italian spirit and by its universally known anti-hero, Harlequin. He is so well known that, at first sight, only the Crucified Christ is more easily recognisable. This comparison may reek of blasphemy to some and is undeniably in poor taste. However, it is useful. By means of this incongruous but obligatory comparison between an icon representing a great story, the 'great tale', a source of values, a story which is for many the story of all stories, and the icon of Harlequin – a modest, modern and mundane, but equally (and funnily) universal figure. The latter is revealed as being essentially empty of history. He is so empty that even the body of the character risks being extinguished. It seems impossible to imagine a naked Harlequin. Before being a body, Harlequin is a costume. Nothing but his multicolour costume gives him consistence. That costume and the space surrounding him seem to float beyond time and history. The fascination they engender lies mainly in their radical extraterritoriality, which is also the source of the contempt in which they are sometimes held.

To some it may seem pointless to wonder what actually happened in the times in which the commedia dell'arte had a powerful presence in the imagination of Europe. Apparently, the fairy tale they told was everything, or what they did consisted of nothing but the formula they used. It was as if their theatre – once realistic characters were abolished and replaced by Rosauras, Isabellas, Columbines and fake mad women, Harlequin, Pulcinella, Pantalone, the Captain and the Doctor – was a theatrical vessel in which it did not matter when things happened, which had broken its moorings and which turned at times from its space among the clouds ('pure theatre', as some define it) to sneer at the world considered 'real'. Why did this beautiful fantasy also become an object of contempt? In some periods, this contempt was evident and proverbial. Nowadays admiration prevails and the contempt lies in the dark.

At its peak, the commedia dell'arte seemed to be a culturally arbitrary reality, alien to civic traditions, illegitimate, morally irresponsible and only focused on scraping together money by appealing to the worst instincts of spectators and exploiting the basest tendencies of mercenary actors. For us, centuries later, the commedia dell'arte is an inventive form of theatre which, however, was seemingly incapable of conveying any idea or echo of the terrible times in which it developed. It seems to sail into abstraction, almost as if it did not care about blood being shed and slaughter taking place around it. It laughed, using jokes to turn hunger, humiliation and rape into trifles. The difficulty of identifying bridges between its comic formulas and the mephitic times, which were its operational context, may prove intolerable.

The indolence of the commedia dell'arte in the face of such intense suffering is both an ethical and an aesthetic problem. As a result, some consider this theatre to be a world reduced to formulas, a comedy reduced to a framework or mechanism, impermeable to reality, a cold virtuoso display or just theatre which is an end in itself. Others recognise in those formulas, in those mechanisms, the levers to make life as well as laughter emerge suddenly and open up the mind and the heart. They make a laugh that thinks and leaves its mark not through explicit messages, but through the spiritual metabolism of each spectator. In other words, *spasso*.

Further Doubleness

If we come a little closer, we realise that the land of Harlequin is extraterritorial and beyond history in a contradictory, complex way. In fact, it is divided into two distinct and puzzling narratives – myth and documented chronicle – which are so similar and yet so contradictory as to short-circuit the minds of those who observe them.

It was not only a joyous form of theatre which developed in those foul and pestilent times; it was also an improvised theatre with fixed features and repetitive, unperturbed and long-established characters. It was a synonym for *Guittalemme*, the imaginary town of unattached, low-ranking actors. However, it was also recognised as the invention of excellent actors and actresses, whose names have endured down through the centuries. In fact, the term *arte* – which in the expression 'commedia dell'arte' only meant 'job' or 'profession' – still has a noble resonance to it, as if it denoted something particularly refined, an artistic sense in action. It is theatre according to old Italian customs, but also a symbol of the international 'new theatre'. As previously said, it has been so for four and a half centuries, which may seem like a contradiction; yet, even this contradiction has its justification.

It may seem strange that the commedia dell'arte was regarded as new theatre from the beginning. The adjective 'new', however, did not always have a positive connotation. When in the late sixteenth century or at the beginning of the seventeenth century a 'new way of doing *commedie*' was mentioned, it was associated with the ignorant practices of uncultivated men who, as audacious novices, thought they could enter a cultural territory which they were supposed to recognise as being superior and alien to them. The commedia dell'arte does not exist any longer, having been relegated to the past. It is at the same time a form of theatre which is practised and taught by many people today, as if it were a tradition with its own set of codes. Maybe it resembles a tradition or maybe it is even the 'ghost' of a tradition.

An Italian form of theatre earned acceptance, success and legendary status abroad – in France, Germany, England and Russia – and from there the underlying idea returned to be admired in Italy, where mere contempt had prevailed hitherto. In saying so, we are relating, in just a few lines, a story which extends from the end of the sixteenth century well into the twentieth century. Let us now stop and look at the origins: For instance, we can see its anti-hero, Harlequin, becoming a protagonist in Paris and not in Bergamo, where he was said to have been born, nor in Venice, where he got married. It was in Paris that he first imposed laughter, tears and fear on his audiences. He was interpreted by a continual series of Italian actors, extending over a period of almost two centuries, from the end of the sixteenth century (who was the first Harlequin? Tristano Martinelli?) to Carlo Bertinazzi in the eighteenth century, the time of Diderot, Voltaire and Goldoni.

The actor who, in the role of Harlequin, was to make the greatest impression on the memory of spectators was Domenico Biancolelli, whose name came to be widely known there in its French version: Dominique. Born in Bologna in 1636, Dominique died in Paris at the beginning of August in 1688. The cause of his death was pneumonia; he had sweated excessively while showing the Sun King a parody of a particularly refined dance created by Pierre Beauchamps, ballet master at court. In order to reorganise itself (and in mourning), the Italian theatre in Paris remained closed for one month. Eight years earlier, in a royal decree, Dominique and his wife, actress Orsola Cortesi, had been granted French citizenship. As the king wrote in the decree, both of them 'desire to end their days as our subjects'.

When Dominique died, he was a little over fifty years old, the same age as Molière, who had died in February 1673, fifteen years earlier. In a certain sense Molière died of theatre too: On stage, on what was to be the last night of his life, he had started to vomit blood in the middle of a bout of laughter during the performance of his play, *The Imaginary Invalid*. In 1691, the other great figure of the triad of *comici* in Paris, Tiberio Fiorilli, known as Scaramuccia, or Scaramouche, also died. Of the three, he was the oldest and the one who lived the longest. He kept performing even after he was over eighty years old. This great triad of *comici* – which may be regarded as the greatest not only in Paris but throughout European theatre as well – was composed of two Italians and one Parisian. This, however, is not important. What is really important is that Jean-Baptiste Poquelin, known as Molière, Dominique-Harlequin and Fiorilli-Scaramuccia, or Scaramouche were considered by theatre-lovers of the time to be, in equal measure, geniuses in transmitting the irresistible force of the comic – with its mysteries, as the comic has its mysteries too.

In comparison to Dominique and Scaramouche, who belonged to the small group of the greatest actors of his time, Molière now seems to occupy a totally different place, that of the creator of books for eternity, classics of literature. Yet, when he was alive, he was an actor who also wrote. He was considered an actor-philosopher – the most brilliant, independent, unpredictable, restless and dangerous of the actor-philosophers, among whom Dominique and Scaramouche also had their places. Although this may sound like a silly remark, not belonging in a serious scholarly study, I would nonetheless like to support the thesis that Molière should be included in the history of the commedia dell'arte and be considered a *comico dell'arte* among the others. The philology of influences can be left aside. He was French, but does it really matter? Was he the greatest? Undoubtedly.

The fact that the Italian actors of the commedia dell'arte were supposed to be aliens in the world of literature is one of those legendary tamperings with history. These actors and actresses were at times original and spirited creators of books and experimenters in the fields of both publishing and literary genres. They wrote tragedies, comedies and pastoral plays. Nowadays, even historians of literature are beginning to acknowledge that the actor-poet Giovan Battista Andreini should be regarded as a classic figure in seventeenth-century Italian dramatic literature. Previously, he has always been excluded by academic convention from manuals on the period. It is likewise inexplicable that, even today, his mother Isabella is almost always forgotten in the collections of Italian lyric poets covering the period between Tasso and Marino – a meagre period in which she, however, stands out.

This tampering with history works in two directions. On the one hand, it strengthens the belief that the actors and actresses of the commedia dell'arte had nothing to do with literature; as a result, their rich, illustrious literature has been ignored and has remained in oblivion. On the other hand, the legend of the commedia dell'arte would not otherwise have held together so long. The two hemispheres of the commedia dell'arte – its myth and its history – continuously distort each other in such a way as to stimulate a 'mirror' narration of their story. Thus, there are two stories of the commedia dell'arte.

The First of the Two Stories: The Myth

If we were to imagine that these two stories were to be summarised and printed in two adjacent columns, the column on the left ('myth') would tell us that in Italy, in the second half of the sixteenth century, a more or less illiterate kind of theatre developed, in which folkloric images and procedures were combined and developed. This form of theatre was connected to the magic of the masks, to the comic and underworld characters of popular tales, to the rituals of fertility and to Carnival as an upside-down world. It was a kind of theatre that made faces at everything that was either great, high, solemn, cultivated or close at hand. It stood for a satire of the ruling class, the clergy, academics, aristocratic etiquette and the rules and ideals of bourgeois life.

According to the myth, it was performed in streets and squares, in front of small groups of people or crowds at the markets who were attracted by the grotesque virtues of the itinerant buffoons. In fact, it was performed everywhere. This is not only because it was itinerant, or because its popularity spread and reached the courts, but also because its essence – legend has it – can be found, in different guises, even in the most remote cultures, in Asia, Europe and Africa, among the Mediterranean populations as well as in the distant Russia. Therefore, countless Harlequins and Pulcinellas, with different names, seem to meet and discover their kinship, crossing the expanse of history, beyond times and seas. Is it not true that there was a Harlequin in ancient Rome who mimed and who was called *mimus centunculus* because his costume was made of pieces of cloth with patches? We need hardly mention *mimus albus*, as white as Pulcinella, hatching like a *pulcino* (chick) from an egg and showing its *albume* (white of the egg). Other relatives of Pulcinella can also be found in the farce-genre of the *Atellana* or in the Turkish version, the shadow theatre named after the lower-class stock character Karagöz, who was born in Turkey but later became popular in Greece as well as in parts farther east. It also seems possible to recognise Pulcinella in the features of small prehistoric statues or in the Nahuatl culture of ancient Mexico.

Therefore, the popularity of the commedia dell'arte presumably gave visibility and organisational form to the scattered relics of a representative cultural substratum which, according to the tenets of cultural archaeology, had spread all around the world. As far as the history of modern Europe is concerned, these relics were no longer scattered and unknown, but emerged in a spontaneous, anti-Renaissance, Italian form of theatre. Collectively they formed a theatre genre which was based on improvisation and did not tolerate the burden of literary prescriptions (or pre-scripts). By its own nature, it was not only on a collision course with the dominant social and ideological order, but also drilled through the crust of reason, causing the energy of dreams and what had been slumbering in the collective unconscious to gush out onto the surface and be seen by all. It gained prestige and visibility; it became more refined, entered the salons and inspired a small multitude of porcelain figures, but its roots were deeper.

Its core was the mask and its dual identity, both of a grotesque face covering the real face and of a stock character, characterised by a costume, a name and often a peculiar way of speaking. Both inhabit the upside-down world of Carnival but the mask, as a black face, is typical of demons, shadows, the dead who return and of the faces burnt by the fire of purgatory or hell. The actors identified themselves with the mask, which was intended as stock character to perpetuate the legend. They also changed as individuals; they were no longer themselves, but Mr Harlequin, Mr Pantalone, Mr Brighella, Mr Dottores, Mr Capitano Spezzaferro or Spaccamontagne. In other words, they entered the world of theatre by leaving the real world behind them, almost changing their state (and thus changing their name, as often happens among new members of religious orders and of certain sects and guilds).

How could this theatrical genre characterised by a 'savage mind' relate to the modern world? It related as the shadows relate to the body, the conscious to the unconscious or the repressed to the liberated. In another sense it did not really relate; it was able to coexist with it thanks to the friction generated. It was the alternative face. It preserved its subversive force even within the boundaries of civilised theatre and adjusted to some of their rules while imposing its capricious insolence. It declined in the age of the Enlightenment in the eighteenth century after being almost suffocated by the spirit of that age (the great man who imposed some order was Goldoni, who gave Italy the modern comedy of characters and situations). It soon flourished again (its saviour was Carlo Gozzi, who wrote the ten *Fiabe teatrali*). In unwritten form, relics of the genre were preserved in the lower ('popular') layers of the performing arts, in international mime, in the Italian dialect theatres, in isolated pockets of resistance existing in peasant culture and in a flood of images related to the different facets of the taste for the picturesque and the commonplace – from the seventeenth-century engravings of Jacques Callot to the eighteenth-century canvases and frescoes of Jean-Antoine Watteau and Giovanni Domenico Tiepolo, down to Pablo Picasso and the present day. With the coming of cinema commedia dell'arte achieved new popularity thanks to the comedians who used the medium. In fact, Charlie Chaplin and Totò – with regard to the legend of the commedia dell'arte – can be considered as prime examples of the genre and as its eternal heirs.

A continuous tradition, following different paths, was maintained from earliest times through the period of Italian theatre dominance to the Romantics, especially the German and French varieties, and was incorporated by Hoffmann and Gautier in their short stories and novels. Through them, it reached the reformers of twentieth-century theatre, for whom it was a fertile legend – the theatre of yesterday ready to become the theatre of tomorrow. This was the point of view shared by Edward Gordon Craig and Jacques Copeau, by Vsevolod Meyerhold and Max Reinhardt, by Yevgeny Vakhtangov, Alexander Tairov and Charles Dullin.

The difficulty and fascination of writing the history of the theatre genre under consideration here is similar to the task of depicting a country wholly in the clasp of extremes, where the most depraved realities coexist with the noblest, where the most tepid traditionalism stands next to the ice and fire of the revolution, where the boldest experiments in freedom are not jeopardised by their proximity to the numerous cases of intimate subjection and the most stubborn mediocrity. This is a country composed only of suburbs and outlying territories, with no developed areas. Depending on the way it is looked at, it can be seen as small or extremely vast and some can live or travel there or study it, in the course of an outing, a longer stay or as a career. For others, it is a microcosm permeated with omens and intimations of destiny, suggesting a history and geography of love and honour. It is not only in the commedia dell'arte that the contrasts are alive. Hence the commedia dell'arte can be a symbol of the whole theatre – a theatre-world.

The Non-Mythical Story

Now, let us return to the synoptic stories of the commedia dell'arte and concentrate on the column on the right ('history'), where a kind of theatre which developed in Italy in the second half of the sixteenth century is analysed. One date immediately stands out: 25 February 1545, when in Padua, in a notary's office, the first surviving contract creating a theatrical troupe was drawn up, a profit-sharing venture called a 'fraternal company'. It was composed entirely of professional male actors – eight in all – who aimed to sell comedies between the Easter of 1545 and the Carnival of 1546. Their plays were probably centred on the relationship between the Magnifico and the Zanni or between the Zanni and Doctor Graziano, in other words between masters and servants. 'Magnifico' was a title granted in Venice to wealthy representatives of the middle class (today, it is given to rectors of Italian universities). For instance, Pantalone is 'Magnifico'.

After this first surviving contract, other notary documents creating troupes or settling disputes between them followed. Among these, one contract stands out. It was drawn up in Rome on 10 October 1564 and among the contracting parties, all commonly called *commedianti* (*omnes ut vulgo dicitur Commedianti*), the name of an actress, Lucrezia da Siena, appears for the first time. This column should probably be punctuated by 'yes, but . . .'. Yes, it was the theatre of stock characters, of Zanni, Graziani, Pantalone and servants but, at least in the decades between 1570 and the beginning of the seventeenth century, the popularity of actresses such as Vincenza Armani, Flaminia, Vittoria Piissimi and the actress-poet Isabella Andreini became predominant. It was then that actors and actresses attempted to establish a sense of equality in status between the profession of the actor and that of the poet. To this end, Adriano Valerini published poems, a tragedy and a description of Verona; Isabella Andreini associated herself with Torquato Tasso; Flaminio Scala published a collection of scenarios in an elegant edition, almost venturing to create an independent literary genre, like collections of short stories or of comedies; Francesco Andreini published monologues of and conversations with Capitano Spavento, like one of those books with two faces, one crazy, the other serious, and contained a collection of sayings and anecdotes of bizarre characters.

Yes, the commedia dell'arte incorporated themes and characters from popular and carnivalesque culture; but it also adopted the plots of classical and sixteenth-century comedies and of the short stories of Giovanni Boccaccio and Matteo Bandello as well as episodes from Ludovico Ariosto's *Orlando furioso* or Miguel de Cervantes' *Don Quixote*. These were mostly comic stories that also contained chronicles of blood and revenge and adventures of kings, paladins and *condottieri*. The legend of Don Juan, opening with a duel and ending in hell, was regularly utilised. It was a form of theatre often based on improvisation but precisely for this reason, it was planned in detail – not text by text but actor by actor. In other words, each actor could rely on a constantly updated and improved repertoire of spoken or gestural pieces with which he could make his contribution to the construction of the whole (this is one of the crucial issues of the commedia dell'arte, which will be mentioned here only briefly and only in rough, summary form).

It is true that it was a spontaneous form of theatre, but not because it practised the spontaneity of acting (this would have been horrible to watch!). It was spontaneous in the sense that it was born and developed on its own, as no one asked it to come into being. The actors and actresses were true professionals, who could perform the whole range of theatrical genres, not only comedy: *commedie all'improvviso*, written comedies, tragicomedies, tragedies, tragedies set to music and pastoral plays (the pièce de résistance of the troupes was Torquato Tasso's *Aminta* or Battista Guarini's *Pastor Fido*, the most popular pastoral plays in Europe).

What surprised audiences and above all the literary establishment, was that part of the repertoire which consisted of improvised plays and which was produced and changed quickly, with stock characters and without written texts. It was something radically different from the way plays were always supposed to be performed. It had a distinctive character, because it was improvised and codified. It was also something inherently different from the monologues and comic duets of itinerant actors or buffoons. It looked like 'regular' comedy, but without being ordinary. When professional Italian actors travelled abroad with their small troupes, their quick and characteristic way of performing comedies was highly appreciated. It looked like an Italian genre.

In the eyes of professional Italian actors, however, their troupes stood out in the scene of European commercial theatre during the last decades of the sixteenth century, not so much for their improvisational skills but rather for the versatility of their actors, for their metamorphic talent and for their ability to make do with a small number of company members. By comparison, other theatrical companies could rely on a far larger group when touring abroad. The Italian actors could perform the role of a spectacularly funny Zanni one day and the day after that of a tragic tyrant; the night before the role of a cowardly Capitano and the night after that of a lyrical, sentimental poet. The actor Nicolò Barbieri, known as Beltrame, proudly remembered this in *La supplica,* published in 1634 (Molière's first 'regular' [scripted] comedy, which appeared in 1655, in five acts and in verse, was adapted from the *commedia, L'inavertito,* published by Barbieri in 1629). Barbieri said that the actor who performed the role of Harlequin could take off the mask and play a tragic character. This is what characterised the art of professional Italian actors. Almost a hundred years later, this opinion was shared by Luigi Riccoboni, an actor and literary man who tried to question the identification of the commedia dell'arte with the 'Italian theatre'.

It is true that actors and actresses were often called by the names of the stock characters they played in the improvised plays, but not because the newly adopted names replaced their old ones, nor because the actors identified themselves with the fake characters. The new names became something between a nom de guerre and a nickname; they did not denote fixity, but excellence.

Even in the academies of high culture, which became common in Italy from the sixteenth century onwards, academic men and women chose new names for themselves, to add to their own given name. It was often a funny name, like the stage name of actors. Even in the Arcadia, the academy which, in the eighteenth century, unified literary Italy into a national cultural institution with 'colonies' in various cities, this tradition of adopting a new ironic or funny stage name lasted for a long time. This aspect of how and why names were chosen may seem marginal, but it is not; it shows that troupes of actors and actresses were organised as commercial enterprises and that they considered themselves in their organisation as constituting an academy. In fact, some troupes adopted names which were very similar to those of the literary academies of the various Italian cities: Gelosi, Confidenti, Uniti, Accesi and Desiosi.

It is true that on tour, performances were held in streets and squares, in markets and fairs, on small stages and at the corners of streets or under the monumental bridges of large cities. However, this is not a distinctive feature of the commedia dell'arte. Wherever there were festivals, crowds or markets, there were always itinerant comedians, acrobats, charlatans and farce-actors. Nor is the use of the mask a distinctive feature of the commedia dell'arte. Masks were used everywhere in Italy between the sixteenth and eighteenth centuries: in performances, at parties, at public and private meetings, at Carnival, on walks, on stages and in the upper-tier boxes reserved to high-rank spectators, in brothels and in convents.

The column on the right, 'history', insists that the commedia dell'arte stood out because it consisted of theatrical enterprises which sold perform-ances by persuading spectators to buy tickets. They were not specialist artisans, limited to a specific genre. Rather, they specialised in not special-ising, producing a variety of performances almost on an assembly-line basis, increasing the supply and expanding the range on offer in accordance with demand.

The column of the two synoptic stories entitled 'history' explains why the commedia dell'arte was not a product of popular culture, but rather an eccentric combination of commerce and middle-class entrepreneurship, able to amalgamate old and diverse elements (some of them originating in Carnival or popular performance) into an innovative, saleable product, which was essentially ephemeral, consisting of the entertaining and the superfluous. For this reason, it met with much hostility and disapproval. Therefore, it condensed the separation of the theatrical and dramaturgic work into formulas which facilitated the speedy production of its basic reper-toire and which, from the point of view of intellectuals, could be defined as the routine, ongoing repertoire necessary to ensure daily earnings.

It is of fundamental importance not to forget that the troupes sold all kinds of performances. The improvised production was not, in the first decades, the most important quality from the perspective of winning artistic and cultural prestige. It was, however, the most frequently used and, most of the time, the most profitable. As stated before, the most striking aspect of this improvised production was the difference between it and performances produced on the basis of written texts. Its formulas were devised so effec-tively that they seemed to derive from an old, unknown tradition (while they actually derived from the demands of commerce). These formulas were extremely successful in Paris (this is a crucial chapter in the history of the commedia dell'arte, but would be more conveniently discussed else-where). Furthermore, they conveyed a precise idea of a 'different' kind of theatre to the Romantics, to A. W. Schlegel for his *Lectures on Dramatic Literature*, as well as to Goethe, Schiller and Hoffmann, to George Sand and her son Maurice and to Théophile Gautier. Irrespective of whether these intellectuals identified the difference inherent in the work of the commedia dell'arte with a primitive, popular form of theatre or perceived its refined complexity, the commedia dell'arte seemed to be a different kind of theatre because, unlike the fundamental tendency in European theatre as a whole, it did not depend on the literary repertoire of theatre and on the art of textual interpretation.

Through its fixed formulas, the commedia dell'arte showed that it was possible to give equal recognition and importance to the dramaturgical and gestural repertoire of the actors, to the realistic expression of feelings and to their intensified acrobatic and metaphoric representation through energetic dance. The commedia dell'arte can thus be considered both a traditional source and the noble proclaimer of a variety of genres: of mime, of comedy films, especially belonging to the period of silent cinema, of some forms of Italian dialectal theatre, of the performances of the *café chantant*, of variety shows, in particular, the *avanspettacolo* tabloid variety and of the circus, which the representatives of the twentieth-century artistic avant-garde, starting from the Futurists, anticipated by Alfred Jarry, often cited as an example of the art of the future. It also inspired the innovators of twentieth-century theatre (from Gordon Craig to Jacques Copeau; from Vsevolod Meyerhold to Max Reinhardt; from Yevgeny Vakhtangov to Aleksandr Tairov and Charles Dullin).

Strabismus

If we used images to symbolise the commedia dell'arte, then the column on the left ('myth') would show itinerant actors on a small stage, one of them a masked actor, the audience in a circle and all out in the open. In the column on the right ('history'), the image would be less vivid: It would show an entry ticket and the room of the commedia, a closed space which is somehow the workshop of actors and, at the same time, their rustic-looking academy. On one side, there would be the vault provided by the sky, on the other side, the paper sky typical of commercial stages – cheap imitations of the festive stages of the courts.

The greatness of the commedia dell'arte lies between these two symbolic images which, however, are flawed by the fact that they clash with each other. They do not contrast with one another or provide an alternative to each other. Each of them is autonomous. Nevertheless, in order to have a general overview, we need to consider both of them with a single glance. In other words, we need to practise strabismus. Could the two synoptic columns be considered as two profiles of the same face? It is impossible, they are too different. Can we just erase one and keep the other? This is also impossible, as the column on the right is more authentic, but the one on the left is not really false.

The stories which we have related here are a simplification, a mere outline. In the real world, when the commedia dell'arte is described, things are far more entangled and complicated; crossroads open up within other crossroads. This strabismus must become 'complicated', a method which is similar to diplopia, namely the simultaneous perception of two images of the same object. The commedia dell'arte compels us to transform this visual disorder into a game of patience.

2

Popular Traditions, Carnival, Dance

Riccardo Drusi

Folklore and Carnival

An Interpretative Approach

A hypothesis that frequently resurfaces in specialist literature concerns the 'democratic', popular and carnivalesque origins of the commedia dell'arte. At the end of the nineteenth century, literary critic Lorenzo Stoppato identified in his essays a continuity between the commedia dell'arte and a hypothetical medieval tradition of 'implicit' theatre. This theory is polygenetically connected to the expression *narodnyi balagan*, 'theatre booth of the people', which was coined by Konstantin Miklăsevskij in the twentieth century to describe the commedia dell'arte: According to Miklăsevskij, the commedia dell'arte was characterised by a 'theatrical instinct' that eludes any historical classification, being instead socially determined by its relationship with the lower classes (Miklăsevskij 1981). The strong affinity between Stoppato's and Miklăsevskij's theories, despite the geographical, cultural and political distance between them, is particularly evident in the title that Stoppato gave to his 1887 collection of essays, *La commedia popolare in Italia* (*The Popular Comedy in Italy*). He focuses on the qualitative aspect of the commedia, that is, on its popularity, rather than on its historical circumstances, arguing in effect for an anachronistic overlapping of different theatrical traditions. In Stoppato's view, secular drama had organically developed since Plautus's times, characterised by the constant presence of the same stock characters. The professional commedia dell'arte brought this ancient tradition to unparalleled perfection (Stoppato 1887: 7–8). Furthermore, Stoppato believed that both Plautus and the *comici* of the commedia dell'arte considered their art to be a kind of festive antagonism to the austerity of the authorities, and that they derived their means of expression from the anarchic confusion of the carnival.

This critique lent itself to interventions by disciplines related to anthropology and comparative studies in literature, society and history. Starting with the analysis of expressive techniques that were still alive in the Italian countryside of that period (such as the extemporary versifications of the Tuscan *Bruscelli*), scholars in these disciplines aimed to prove the existence of an extremely long-lasting popular theatre, which was improvisational in nature and aimed for a carnivalesque reversal of values. Paolo Toschi, for example, drew on these disciplines as he made his argument for the carnivalesque nature of Italian theatre, particularly the forms of theatre related to the *commedia*. This was in response to Alessandro D'Ancona's account of the origins of Italian comedy in his *Origini del teatro italiano* (*Origins of Italian Theatre*), which Toschi believed was too focused on lending a false air of dignity to the *commedia:* 'Our comic theatre, and in particular the commedia dell'arte, directly inherits from the Carnival the licentiousness, coarseness and obscenity that too often characterise it' (Toschi 1955: 117).

In the first years of the twentieth century, almost contemporarily with Miklăsevskij's theories and their practical implementation by Vsevolod Meyerhold, Winifred Smith formulated a theory to explain how such approaches risked losing sight of their declared purpose, by focussing solely on popular myth and legend. Smith argued that the specificity of the commedia dell'arte was *also* historical and warned her readers against too nonchalantly combining data from distinct and distant time periods, a practice that she believed would make a consistent analysis impossible (Smith 1912: 21). In Italy, Smith's voice went unheard partly for linguistic reasons and partly because of the growing success of Benedetto Croce's aesthetics, which suggested that one should analyse artistic expression without lingering too much on factual and historical variations. Subsequently, the direct examination of written documents – that is, the research method privileged by D'Ancona in the history of theatre mentioned earlier – went out of fashion among theatre historians.

We know that the experience of the *foire* (fairground entertainment) played a major role in Meyerhold's reinterpretation of the commedia dell'arte (Meyerhold 2009: 356). However, looking even further back, the critical juxtaposition of the *foire* and the Italian *commedia* probably happened earlier, in the nineteenth century, when the subjects and the stock characters of early eighteenth-century Parisian *foire* were reinterpreted by the *opéra-comique* and the *opéra-bouffon*. Arlequin, Pantalon, Scaramouche and other such stock characters were transported from the texts written by Lesage, Orneval and Fuzelier to Planard's and Duport's play *Le Mannequin de Bergame*, 1832, to Scribe and Duveyrier's *Polichinelle*, 1839, and to Luigi Ricci's *Une Aventure de Scaramouche*, 1841. These works rekindled the original polemic flame with particular regard to the Second Empire and its dissipation, as exemplified by Jacques Offenbach's *Le Financier et le savetier*, 1856 (cf. Teulon-Lardic 2008). This kind of theatre, distant enough from the classicist tradition to seem spontaneous and straightforward in both structure and content, was considered by George Sand (1860) to be a paradigm of ancient theatre suspended in time. She rediscovered the tradition of the *Comédie Italienne* of the Renaissance and seventeenth century and in her preface to the two volumes of *Masques et Bouffons* sought support for her theory that ancient forms of theatre such as the Greek Phallophorias or the Latin Atellan farces were not, in fact, irregular occurrences. Sand identified a lineage and historical continuity – discontinuous in its manifestations, but uninterrupted in time – that ended precisely with the commedia dell'arte and its improvisation technique (Sand 1860: vi).

As to the theatrical genre per se, Sand contended that the *commedia* was able, for the first and only time, to stage characters that were not fictitious but real, with a much greater anthropological significance and a much broader historical presence: from the crudely painted faces of the first performers in antiquity to the stages of the present-day Opéra-comique (Sand 1860: vii). These *caractères réels* and the need to crystallise them into a primary set of categories were the foundation out of which the stock characters of the commedia dell'arte grew. According to this school of thought, their origins or the exact moment at which they first appeared on stage were insignificant compared to their importance as representatives of universal categories of mankind.

Mask, Carnival, Comedy: Line or Circle?

George Sand and her son Maurice, who shared her interest in Italian Renaissance and Baroque *commedia*, are both to be credited with highlighting the fact that the masks and stock characters behind them are the true distinctive traits of the commedia dell'arte. Behind a mask – any kind of mask – there is an actor. The title of Maurice Sand's work *Masques et bouffons* perfectly summarises this duality. Each mask/character has a chapter dedicated to it, in which a dual analysis is undertaken: first of the universal element, i.e. the mask, and then of the contingent element – the *bouffon*, i.e. the actor, the person who is wearing the mask at a particular time. This relationship between the concrete and the transcendent, where the transcendent is by definition meta-historical, is characterised by the author as functional rather than being bound to the origins of a specific character. Sand thus reinforces the theory first proposed by Luigi Riccoboni (1730: vol. I, ch. II), which can be seen as an attempt to uncover the noble origins of his trade: The stock characters of ancient comedy have slowly but continually been transformed into their corresponding characters in the Italian *commedia*. Old *Pappus* became Pantalone, the shrewd *sanniones* became the *zanni* in a process of simple phonetic adaptation, and subsequently were given their individual names – Harlequin, Mezzetino and Trivellino. However, Sand had no way of documenting the intermediate phases of this tradition; as a result, when he attempted to investigate the birth of the stock characters of the commedia dell'arte, he was faced with the conceptually ambiguous territory of its carnivalesque side, with its disguises and the ritual inversion that they implied. This process, which took place at the beginning of the twentieth century, was facilitated by the insights that historians were gaining at the time into specific mediaeval *kermesses* (fairs) and their popular roots. The spirits of fertility, remnants of paganism in their vulgar larvae and integral parts of events such as the *festa stultorum* (licentious excursions made by groups of young people during the *kalendae januariae* and for the distorted liturgy of the *festum asini*), were identified as the 'prehistory of the Zanni' and regarded as precursors of the masked dramaturgy which is typical of the commedia dell'arte.

The arguments supporting these hypotheses are of great significance, starting with Lucia Lazzerini's etymological approach (1982: 467–71) to the emblematic characters of the Zanni. The name most probably derives from Diana/Johanna, who used to oversee the Sabbath and, through her, from Janus, protector of passages and gateways and responsible for the annual renewal of crops. As theorised by Driesen (1904), it is now believed that the character of Harlequin, too, is derived, like the Zanni, from ancient mythological figures. Tracing it back via a complex process of adaptation that took place primarily in the late sixteenth century, one arrives at Herla, an eerie spectre who was thought to lead his ghostly family across the whole of Europe, haunting its nights.

It is true that the Zanni, when it comes to comedy, shares some of the characteristics of the Zane/Dianus/Janus of folklore, such as a penchant for devilish tricks or gluttony (with regard to both sex and food), which is reminiscent of the opulence of mediaeval rites. It is also true that Tristano Martinelli's Harlequin by all accounts embodied on stage the uncontrollable dynamism that is a traditional mark of the Devil in his carnivalesque rendition. That said, this kind of folkloric analysis does leave a number of questions unanswered, such as: To what extent was the transition of the demonic archetype from ritual to stage deliberate? And implicitly, why? Uncoupled from its context, the original model loses its ritualistic value to the point that it becomes completely distorted.

Harlequin, Bertoldo, Zanni: From Prototypes to Characters

Even though the origins of other stock characters remained unclear, it was possible to learn about the exact moment at which the comic stock character of Harlequin was born. We know from this that its undoubtedly folkloric roots did not contribute in a very significant way to the creation of the *theatrical* archetype. Ferrone's monograph describes how, towards the end of the seventeenth century, Tristano Martinelli, the first actor to play the part of Harlequin, created the character from pre-existing materials in a very deliberate fashion. Rather than arbitrarily appropriating folkloric elements, he carefully judged the circumstances and situations in which he performed. Martinelli was Italian and knew that performing on the Parisian stages meant competing for attention with a large cast of well-known set characters based on long-lasting festive traditions. If the audience liked archetypes such as *Gros Guillaume* or *Gautier-Garguille*, corpulent theatrical embodiments of the gluttonous king of carnival, he would have to create a similar character, based on similar premises. *Hellequin*, the French archetype of Harlequin, thus developed from a vivacious and nimble aerial demon into a symbol of unruliness, even a representative of hell, and from there into a grotesque tradition of popular *diableries* (Driesen 1904: 58–66; Ferrone 2006: 74–6). In some of the oldest texts there is already a tendency to characterise *Hellequin*'s appearance as excessively artificial and tending towards disguise. In one of the best known sources, the fourteenth-century *Roman de Fauvel* (Långfors 1914: vv. 747–58), he leads a noisy *charivari* whose members wear monstrous costumes. What is more, he is characterised by unnaturally large ears, unsettling gigantism and a bushy beard. Other sources give an indication of how early versions of his name gravitate towards the semantic fields of *fatuitas* and *scurrilitas* (stupidity and buffoonery) (Avalle 1989: 54–5; Driesen 1904: 129). In a nutshell, *Hellequin* was already a buffoon, a stock character, before appearing on stage as Harlequin. All that was needed to fulfil his theatrical potential was someone like Martinelli.

In addition to his adaptation of the traditional figure of *Hellequin*, Martinelli derived other distinctive trains of his new character from the medieval *Herlequin*, most notably a particular garment called the *Hurepiaus*.

It was mentioned as early as the thirteenth century in Adam de la Halle's *Jeu de la feuillée*. Nothing is known about the appearance of the *hurepiaus* to date; in fact, it is never mentioned outside of the tales of the army of the damned led by either Hellequin himself or similar otherworldly figures. Most likely it was either a hood used to hide the unsettling demonic appearance of the wearer, or, conversely, a sort of integral mask used to enhance it (Ueltschi 2008: 111). What is significant about this enigmatic garment is that its demonic component intertwines with onomastic elements that call to mind the rural world of peasants – to which the Harlequin of comedy, a manual labourer (porter) who spoke the rowdy dialect of Bergamo, certainly belonged. The name is made up of two parts, the first of which (*hure*) is related to fear, specifically its effect of making one's hair stand on end (see *hurer* in the *Französisches Etymologisches Wörterbuch*, s.v. **Hura*: 'faire dresser les cheveux sur la tête à qn.'). In Old French, the word was also used to designate the hair of peasants, described as bushy and shaggy just like animal hair (Barillari 2000: 28–9 and n. 36). The old *Hellequin* was clearly affected by the derogatory stereotype of the *rusticus,* which was widespread during the Middle Ages and the Renaissance; this reminds us that such stereotypes implied associations to both the world of beasts and demons, and always offensively so. Domenico Merlini's work on satirical depictions of peasants has become a classic and is still useful today. In it, the author analyses an entire repertoire of symbols of evil and darkness that correspond to the typical stigmas of the living conditions of peasants (Merlini 1894: 153–4, 179–86). According to such legends, the inhabitants of rural areas belong to the lineage of Cain, took an active part in the crucifixion of Christ (Lovarini 1965: 64–5), and are wicked and cunning by nature. Their destiny is to go back to where they came from, so that they will be able to say about themselves: 'Il dì del gran deslubio/a' saron di maliti dal lò zanco' (On the day of the Deluge, we will stand among the cursed, on the left hand of the Father) (Lovarini 1965: 74–5). Moral traits are seen to be imprinted on their exterior form as a sort of interchangeable *facies* whose appearance resembles that of fallen angels: A peasant's face is dark, burned by the sun and dirty because of the work in the fields; and similarly dark is the face of the Devil. He has the large belly of a glutton and thin, goat-like legs, reminiscent of familiar demonic iconographies. Even his beard is shaped 'like a beak', according to the physiognomics of the *rusticus* described in Giulio Cesare Croce's *Bertoldo* – that is to say, at a time in which the commedia dell'arte was beginning to flourish.

From what has been said, it is now clear that the demonic connotation of the stock character of the Zanni has little to do with the survival of popular cults; it can, instead, be read as a deliberate evocation of elements designed to make the character immediately recognisable. By revisiting the French *Hellequin,* Martinelli took advantage of a local code which had already established a correspondence between a demonic appearance and the condition of the plebs, more precisely that of peasants. A similar process probably took place in Italy with regard to the evolution of the Zanni, the purpose of which was to modernise the figure of the servant as encountered in Plautus' and Terence's comedies. It was therefore appropriate to utilise the archetype of the urbanised peasant who is at the service of the highest bidder, but also opportunistically prepared for all kinds of immoral or diabolical retractions of loyalty.

Evidence of the gradual evolution of the stock character can also be found in the non-professional theatre that flourished in the late sixteenth century in the academic context. Plays were being written that imitated the commedia dell'arte but that nevertheless retained a sense of independence. They are valuable because they help to explain a number of creative processes that were so deeply assimilated by the professional theatre companies that they have become too difficult to unpick.

The diabolical traits of the Zanni/rural servant were thus accepted in the context of professional and academic theatre because they corresponded to the archetype of the peasant. At the same time, however, the carnivalesque background that, according to Toschi's hypotheses, was concealed behind the masks of the various infernal spirits, added an important element of novelty.

Music, Dance, Song

Music and Comic Theatre:
A Coupling not to be Taken for Granted

Hypothetically, further proof of the popular origins of the commedia dell'arte lies in the fact that music has an important presence on stage and is organically intertwined with the development of the action. Similarly, there is a marked preference for dance as a form of expression.

As regards the sung and instrumental interventions by actors within the performance, a distinction is necessary between music that was performed either between acts or at the end of the play – a common practice perfectly in line with the sixteenth-century and Renaissance tradition of the intermezzi – and other, less well documented, forms of scenic performance. The availability of, and demand for, actors who were also competent musicians can be traced back to the earliest documents relating to

Italian professional theatre: One of the signers of the contract regulating the fraternal company of comedians established in 1545 in Padua was a *lira da braccio* player (see Vianello 2005: 145). It is evident from such documents that musical skills were integral to the intermezzi, but that there were no expectations of framing them as specific objects of spectacle. The case of Francesco Gabrielli, whose stage name was Scapino and whose success as an actor came from the great number of instruments he played on stage, is the exception that proves the rule. As to the rest, it is important to note that pictures or engravings of the time showing *commedia* stock characters singing or playing instruments are not in fact showing them to be standing on the stage of a theatre, but rather on the wooden boards set up by street charlatans. The music that they played and sang thus served the purpose – as documented by the sources – of attracting audiences to sample the products offered by the charlatans. The book *Piazza universale di tutte le professioni del mondo* (lit. The *Universal Town Square of All the Professions in the World*) includes a chapter that describes precisely this category of performance: *De' formatori di spettacoli in genere, e de' ceretani o ciurmatori massime* ('Conventions of Performance Makers and Charlatans in General'). It should not be surprising that we find themes and characters of the commedia dell'arte so closely intertwined with the practice of playing and singing music in this context. The resulting spectacle, however, remains intangible and scarcely documented, particularly when compared to the well-defined identity of those performers that Tomaso Garzoni called the *istrioni* – the professional actors of the theatre (Garzoni 1996: 1195).

Here, a quick glance at the textual materials appears to show that instrumental and vocal music, as well as dances, were far from frequent on the stages of the commedia dell'arte. This was perhaps due to a concern for avoiding contamination between the status of the professional *comici*, who were continually in search of their own guiding principles, and that of the less privileged street performers.

The iconography of the time often portrays stock characters as playing the lute (see for example the Recueil Fossard, or Dionisio Minaggio's *Feather Book,* now held at McGill University). Typical moments for musical interventions include scenes of courtship, where serenades beneath the balcony of a beloved appear to successfully portray common, everyday habits. In this case, however, connecting the praxis to its 'realistic function' (Pirrotta 1975: 97–144) seems reductive in that the characters who take part in these scenes are rarely the young lovers (who perform without masks), but rather the characters least likely to engage in such actions: Magnifico, Pantalone, the Doctor or the Zanni – all of them base stock characters who should be, by definition, alien to the 'fine art' of music. Music thus takes on the purpose of conveying the inadequacy of the characters that perform it. The theorist Andrea Perrucci confirms this theory, suggesting that the songs in these performances help to create the typical caricatures of comic characters: 'Saranno anche ridicole le canzoni delle parti buffe in Scena, se saranno de' Zanni Bergamaschi, Napolitani' (Songs in the comical parts of a scene will be hilarious if sung by Zanni from Bergamo or Naples) (Perrucci 1961: 252, part II, rule XII).

Comedy and Dance

The *Balli di Sfessania*, a series of etchings in which Jacques Callot carries out a synthesis between the practices of dance and the stock characters of the commedia dell'arte (Posner 1977: 204–5), seem to establish a bond of necessity between dance and professional theatre. However, ballet had by the sixteenth century become a highly specialised art form in its own right, with expert masters and dedicated professional dancers. The danced parts of the *commedia*, once incorporated in a scene, were therefore usually considered to be a category of their own. It seems that whenever a choreographically gifted actor was available, the most common course of action was to exploit this particular talent, but only in the specific settings that were traditionally allowed to include dance numbers, rather than on a larger scale. This was, for example, the case for the pastoral genre (Pontremoli 1995: 34–6). If the famous actress Vittoria Piissimi really was the 'Vittoria comediante a modo di Sirena' (the siren-like Vittoria of the comedies) that the *Prologo* speaks of, and if she really was as gifted a dancer as she was an actress (Castagno 1994: 74; Taviani and Schino 1982: 338–9), it stands to reason that it was she who was chosen to perform in the *Precipitio di Fetonte* staged in Milan in 1594 by the Uniti and their company leader, Francesco Pilastri. However, her opportunities to perform were most likely restricted to the pastorals between acts and the final, allegoric pantomime *Il pastor leggiadro,* which had been choreographed by Cesare Negri, a famous, extremely promising dancer and author of several dance-related treatises (D'Ancona 1891, vol. II: 514; Ferrari Barassi 1984: 214; Pontremoli 2005: 205–10).

This level of professionalism seems to rule out dance from the popular dimensions and manifestations of the commedia dell'arte. And yet, the popular attraction of dance, especially if uninhibited, remains an enduring theme in literature, not least since the character of Belcolore in the *Decameron* (VIII, 2), 'a jolly, buxom country wench' who knew how to 'lead up the haye and the round, when need was, with a fine handkerchief in her hand'. Sweat also drips from the foreheads of Folengo's sixteenth-century peasants as they engage in the same acrobatic dances (Folengo 1997: 217–21; 225–6; 327–9), paving the way for Giacomo Morello's *Ziralda*, a burlesque eulogy written in old Paduan dialect and printed in 1553, which describes the unexpected terpsichorean skills of Ziralda the farmer (La Rocca 1993). Thus, theatre had a fertile ground to draw from, making connections – as has already been mentioned – between the desire to dance and the archetypal vigour of its lowest characters.

However, it is necessary to make a distinction between performed dance and evoked dance. The latter did play an important part in *commedia* performances on stage. What is more, many examples relating to popular dances and their characteristics all fall into the category of evoked dance. Francesco Andreini's descriptions of the dances in which the Capitano – a character he specialised in – took part, stress the exceptional physical prowess of the protagonist rather than giving details of the choreography that is supposedly being performed (Tessari 1981: 171). The character of Proserpina, Queen of the Underworld, also takes part in these evoked dances, and as a result their uncontrolled dynamism acquires a diabolical edge, which Andreini argues is directly borrowed from the sinister physical vigour of the peasants. This, arguably, is the real reason why the practice of evoking dance is so important: Describing the peasants, or *rustici*, in their graceless physicality is comical without necessarily requiring the actors' scenic presence as dancers. In Ruzante's *Betía* (1524–1527), Nale the farmer remembers his prowess as a dancer at the 'feste de Pavana' (celebrations of Pavana) (II, 278), his extremely high leaps (II, 325–8) and his competitiveness with the instrumentalists, without showing any actual proof of them on stage. (II, 336–8; Zorzi and Ruzante 1967: 256–8; see also Padoan 1982: 90–2). And since the discrepancy between words and actions is an effective source of comedy, those recounting their acrobatic dances are often on the verge of paralysis. In Ruzante's *Bilora* (scene IV) the elderly Andronico tries to prove that he is still physically fit enough to seduce Dina, declaring that he would still be able to 'balar quatro tempi del *Zogioso*, e farlo strapassao ancora, e anche la *Rosina*, e farla tuta in fioreti, che non sarave minga puoco!' (dance four measures of the *Gioioso*, and dance them again shuffled, and the *Rosina* too, all in sequences; it would be no small feat!) (Zorzi and Ruzante 1967: 563). Similarly, Andrea Calmo's plurilinguistic comedies that graced the stages of Venice in the mid-sixteenth century contained dance that was sometimes performed and sometimes merely evoked. As an example of the former case we may cite the episode of the *Travaglia* (1556) in which old Collofonio, in love with young Lionora, boasts about his athletic prowess when he was young and ends up being taunted into dancing by his servants, who are farmers (Calmo 1996: II, 13/ 116–26). As an example of the latter category we may consider the *Saltuzza* (1551) and the character of old Melindo – somewhat past his prime – who claims he has in store for the woman he loves the same energies with which he used to dance the Rosina (Calmo 2006: I, 3/ 64–5).

Collofonio and Melindo are both wealthy merchants from Venice, speak Venetian and are thus precursors of the stock character of the Magnifico/Pantalone. Calmo's works were frequently reprinted until the end of the sixteenth century (*Saltuzza* for the last time in 1600 and *Travaglia* in 1601), and his remarkable characterisations of the 'old man' captured the attention of theatre professionals, making it possible to identify them as an important source for the guidelines that professional *comici* would later follow when creating new characters, also with regard to dance. The 'saltetti alla pantalonesca' (small leaps *à la* Pantalone) assigned to the Magnifico in the stage directions of the *Ferinda* (1622: III, 7) are most likely the same ones that were laboriously attempted by those models. And the same tradition is probably the source, albeit only orally evoked, of the weary Dottor Campanaccio's line in the eponymous comedy (1627): 'e' me slungava, e' me sbassava, e' me voltava, e' me storzeva, e' me snodava, e' saltava, e' ballava, e' magnava, e' cagava' (and I stretched, I ducked, I turned around, I twisted, I loosened up, I jumped, I danced, I ate, I shat) (Andreini 1627: 47).

Conclusion

Recent studies of the commedia dell'arte have highlighted a degree of awareness and creative maturity among the professional *comici* that seems incompatible with simple or naive representations of popular archetypes. Although the popular element is undeniably present in the commedia dell'arte, it manifests itself not in passive reproductions of fixed characters and forms, but rather in the careful selection of expressive tools designed to help with the characterisation of scenes and figures. This purpose, pursued by theatre professionals who aimed at creating works which could perfectly resonate with its audiences, has been identified by scholars as the most plausible reason for the assimilation of traditional, popular and folkloric elements and characters within the field of professional theatre. What in the past was interpreted as an unmistakable sign for the direct derivation of the commedia dell'arte from the naive and subversive carnivalesque power of popular protest, now, in the light of recent studies, appears as a deliberate, refined and sophisticated collection of the most suitable elements for an immediate identification of characters, situations and circumstances. From the diabolic connotations of ancient masks the commedia dell'arte retains only those elements which are necessary to remind audiences of the implied association between the malice of demons and the shrewdness of the rustics. Dancing is not absorbed by the commedia dell'arte as a fundamental theatrical device, but rather as a means to define the behaviour and character traits of the protagonists in action. Another element which had long been considered an essential feature of the commedia dell'arte is music. We have argued here, however, that it was not used on stage as frequently as one might expect, as it was associated with generic and lower-level forms of performance such as street performers and acrobats. Music thus frequently had the function of emphasising the characters' grotesque qualities, highlighting their socially inadequate – and thus comic – actions. The use of folkloric elements such as masks, dance and music in the commedia dell'arte should be interpreted not as further proof of an original contact between theatre and the common people, but rather as a clever stratagem used by professional performers in order to attract audiences and maximise the popular impact of their art.

3

Notebooks, Prologues and Scenarios

Stefan Hulfeld

While 'romantic' ideas about the commedia dell'arte emphasised the dichotomy of a freely improvised comedy on the one hand, and a normative literary theatre on the other, research findings of the last decades have corrected such an oversimplifying perspective. Rather than stressing differentiation, this research highlights the high level of mutual influence between amateur and professional theatre, as well as between improvised and erudite comedy. The professional actors and actresses of the early modern age were obviously readers and producers of all sorts of literature; moreover, piracy in the realm of literary culture was their common working technique (Ojeda Calvo 2004). Therefore the crucial question concerns the specific interweaving of corp-/orality and textuality in the production of improvised stage performances in terms of their historical dynamics.

Robert Henke defines 'the structural tension between the linear, well-constructed plot based on a literary model and the centrifugal improvisations of the stand-up performer' as an essential factor for the emerging professional theatre in Italy and discusses the variety of possibilities for coping with this tension (Henke 2002: 1). The various troupes, whether early male ones or those including actresses, as well as troupes playing on the *piazza* during carnival or in the service of ducal impresarios, showed unequal ambitions to be seen as members of the growing humanist republic of letters. The same is true for individual actors and actresses. Tristano Martinelli, for example, defended his autonomy as an improvising actor, while at the same time, as Arlecchino, he became the hero of the burlesque print *Compositions de Rhétorique*, containing woodcuts and begging poems among many blank pages (Gambelli 1993: 421–34). On the other hand, the famous actress Isabella Andreini was a member of the Accademia degli Intenti and the author of well-respected sonnets, madrigals, etc. Others, such as Pier Maria Cecchini, Flaminio Scala or Giovan Battiasta Andreini, proved themselves capable dramaturges and authors of printed comedies and pamphlets, defending their improvised theatre against anti-theatrical prejudices (Ferrone 1993b: 274–308, Fiaschini 2007).

Discussing commedia dell'arte and textuality opens up a broad research field, including not only questions concerning the mutual influence of learned and improvised comedy but also all sorts of intertextual traces in both manifestations of the comic genre and the many initiatives to transform the *improvvisa* into scripted comedy. In the following, therefore, only some aspects and questions can be addressed. First, the notebook of Abagaro Frescobaldi, who was known as Stefanelo Botarga, will be discussed as an example of how an actor of the late sixteenth century used reading and writing as part of his theatre business. The main focus will be on the scenarios and how these more or less detailed performance sketches underwent significant changes in their transition from internal working papers to printed testimonies of a decent and respectable art of comedy in the *Teatro delle favole rappresentative* of Flaminio Scala. Finally, the stage activities and corporeal action called lazzi will be discussed. The structural tension mentioned above by Henke could thus be understood as a tension between independent routines and the increasing obligation to subordinate them to a linear plot according to a literary model.

The Notebook of an Improvising Actor

Frescobaldi toured throughout Spain from 1574 to 1580 as the Magnifico named Stefanelo Botarga of the Zan Ganassa troupe. During these years he kept a working diary to collect excerpts and ideas known as codex II-1586, which is held by the Real Biblioteca of Madrid (Ojeda Calvo 2007). Frescobaldi's notebook contains sonnets, aphorisms, riddles, fragments of stage business, interludes and scenarios, etc., as well as Spanish translations of the beginning sections of Cinzio's tragedy *Orbecche* and Ovid's *Metamorphoses*, to name two features of note (Ojeda Calvo 2007: 57–129).

For their Masks, improvising actors had to build their own repertoire, indicated in Italian with the technical term *robbe generiche* (roughly: stock speeches). Two examples may give a first impression of Frescobaldi's working method. Among the references cited in the edition by Ojeda Calvo are many humanistic encyclopaedias, for example the *Officinae epitome* by Johannes Ravisius Textor or *La Fabrica del mondo* by Francesco Alunno. Ravisius Textor offered his knowledge of classical authors, the Bible and the writings of the Church Fathers to modern authors. For example, the *Officinae epitome* includes lists containing the names and accomplishments of eminent architects alongside the names and deeds of the richest men in history. Obviously Frescobaldi had the two volumes of this book ready to hand when he excerpted 'Architetti: Apolodoro; Nicone; Demorate; Esifone' and 'Rico fu Pifio Bithinio, Scila, Narciso, Marco Crasso' (Ojeda Calvo 2007: 412). With this, Frescobaldi's Magnifico used some famous names whenever he needed them. Actors obviously saw a great comic potential in parodying the habit of academics to 'prove' anything they chose by referring to authorities of ancient times. Yet short excerpts of this kind cannot be considered as *robbe generiche*; more likely they constituted the raw material for more ambitious genres. Another excerpt, this time from Alunno's *La Fabrica del mondo* (a dictionary based on the works of Dante, Petrarch and Boccaccio) served Magnifico as he struggled through Arcadia in a pastoral comedy. Alunno's *Fabrica* was a dictionary principally based on the works of Dante, Petrarch and Boccaccio and was divided into ten books or subject areas. In the fourth volume of the *Fabrica* he listed definitions of things related to the four elements (fire, water, air and earth). First Magnifico describes a garland of flowers made for the individual he is addressing, then he relates what he sees and hears (Ojeda Calvo 2007: 425). The whole speech describes the abundance of Arcadia as a 'locus amoenus', with forty-five special terms associated with it. Frescobaldi thus transformed Alunno's dictionary into a stylistic device, which enabled his Magnifico to build a theatrical space with a scenery of words; further he augmented his *robbe generiche*, transforming a grave cosmography into a comical feature.

To this point, Frescobaldi had benefited from the culture of printed books, compiling from scholarly compilers, and creating something new in the context of stage performances. But his ambitions presumably exceeded this level. In one of his prologues, the lead actor claims to be a poet. Explaining the difference between an acting poet and an erudite author of comedies, he states, 'We intend to be at once poets and performers of our comic poetry' (Ojeda Calvo 2007: 198). Were the prologues themselves an outcome of this ambition? Eight prologues are included in the Codex II-1586, one in Latin, two in Spanish and five in Italian. There are arguments leading one to suppose that Frescobaldi was the inventor and his alter ego Botarga the presenter of at least most of them: references to works of authors that he had excerpted provide strong hints in favour of Frescobaldi's 'authorship'. This means that, at the same time, he referred largely to printed literature in his prologues and did so in 'the rhapsodic and encyclopedic manner of oral culture' (Henke 2002: 49).

Prologues

The prologues follow a similar pattern. First, an orator briefly addresses the audience. Then he establishes his subject matter, usually falling into epideictic oratory. In the most extended part, he then 'argues' by citing an abundance of authorities from ancient times to amass a bizarre body of evidence. In a few sentences he finally links his topic with the upcoming comedy (Ojeda Calvo 2007: 132). This pattern does not correspond with either Plautus or Terence, or with the prologues of Italian Renaissance comedy (Borsellino 1975). But Frescobaldi's prologues are structurally similar to those collected by Domenico Bruni (Marotti/Romei 1991: 344–430). From this, one can conclude that professional actors did indeed establish an autonomous tradition of prologues. And it seems that the theatrical function is responsible for their specific shape.

In the prologue *In laude del ordine*, the orator first assures his audience that he had not been willing to speak the prologue, but that it was his turn – in Italian, 'tocandome l'ordine'. Considering that orderliness the fundamental principle of everything, he proclaims, he therefore had no choice. After this, listing examples from the universe to the human body, he 'proves' that everything is based on the unity of oppositional entities and on hierarchy. Coming to an end, the orator warns his audience that damaging the order causes the decline of republics and families. To illustrate this, he evokes an image of hands wishing to do the work of the feet, and he generally warns people not to usurp the roles of others. Expressing the hope that orderliness will be regarded in the ensuing comedy, he leaves (Ojeda Calvo 2007: 273–6). One can assume that his audience expected to see the Zanni execute handstands or perform other acrobatic skills, as well as using disguises throughout the comedy. These examples of misconduct started to undermine the praise of orderliness and, at the same time, denied any hope of performing an 'orderly' comedy. In many prologues the epideictic mode creates ambivalent messages. If something is praised or blamed, the respective oppositional point of view remains present. Adopting theoretical perspectives on the improvised comedy that emphasise the 'obsession of doubling' (Ferroni 1989: 145) and the duality of theatrical space as a playground for comic acting (Baumbach 2002: 200–45), prologues gain a crucial function. The speaker is a guide for a journey, awaiting his audience on the forestage, ready to lead it into the borderland between perception and imagination. He starts in the everyday reality of the spectators in front of him and ends by alluding to the world behind him, meanwhile training the minds of the spectators in the perception of ambivalence and hidden narratives. Viewed in this light, prologues are a fundamental theatrical tool.

However, it should be mentioned that for one of Frescobaldi's prologues, namely his *apologia* for the improvised comedy in prose, (Ojeda Calvo 2007: 197–200), things look different. The editor gave it the title *Del modo di recitar la commedia*, and this text is connected with literary culture in multiple ways: Botarga refers explicitly to Terence, alludes to Boccaccio's prologue at the beginning of the fourth day of the *Decameron* and places himself in the tradition of authors defending the comedy in vernacular prose. But significant are rather his remarks about the actors' poetic flair, where Botarga points out the special skills of improvising actors. According to him they are able 'to amplify poor stories, to manifest hidden tales and to imitate and demonstrate the secret doctrines of the oddest minds' (Ojeda Calvo 2007: 199). Furthermore, this prologue makes clear that the poetic value of an improvised comedy is independent of any writing-system. Actors, as masters of gestures, gesticulations and attitudes, created visual poetry. These are important clarifications to examine with the so-called scenario, a new type of text.

Reading Scenarios

'It is obvious that these poor writings cannot be considered poetry' (Zorzi 1990: 108). Others described scenarios as 'skeletons' or used similar metaphors denoting lack and imperfection. But why should one expect that the poetic skills of improvising actors would ever manifest themselves in writing? Since from the sixteenth century on Europeans learnt to identify 'theatre' with 'drama' and became accustomed to the 'theatre of the book' (Peters 2000), it seems difficult to read scenarios without incorrect expectations. About eight hundred scenarios have been handed down to us. They differ in length, mode of notation and textual components, which means that they differ in functionality. To avoid misunderstandings, the interpretation of these texts should thus be based on knowledge of the cultural context of the editing processes and collection activities, among other elements. The n° II/43 of the 'Scenari Corsiniani' is entitled *I tre becchi* and can be traced back to the early professional theatre practice. It begins in the following way (Hulfeld 2014: 1303):

Coviello Cintia	They have their scene of reciprocal jealousy. Cintia goes in and leaves Coviello to disclose his passion for Flaminia, the wife of Pantalone; he knocks at her door:
Flaminia	They have their love scene and in the end she tells him about the chest of lemons. Coviello goes in, Flaminia stays; at this:
Pantalone	He is asked to provide her with lemons; he promises to send them in a chest. Flaminia goes in. Pantalone is left to disclose his love for Franceschina, Zanni's wife; he knocks at her door:

As a first step in understanding the basic relationships, the list of the personaggi has to be consulted. In the Corsini scenarios we find it at the very end, usually noted on an individual page together with the props. Horizontal lines demonstrate who lives together. In this case there are three 'houses', in each of which lives a married couple, namely Pantalone with Flaminia, Coviello with Cintia and Zanni with Franceschina. Apart from the couples, a lone Innamorato is listed. The opening scene thus shows a couple involved in jealous lazzi in front of the house. Then Cintia enters, while Coviello remains onstage and reveals that he is in love with Pantalone's wife. He knocks at the door of his beloved; when Flaminia appears, a *scena amorosa* reveals the love to be mutual. The comedy proceeds in this manner as a round dance of adultery. Zanni remains the only devoted husband, while unwittingly helping his mates in their amorous adventures. But because the adulterers brag about their love affairs, he starts to understand what is happening. To catch his wife's lover, Zanni burns down his own house. In the end everyone has something to confess; but afterwards the married couples get back together again and the comedy ends without exhibiting any ambition to restore moral values. The text consists of two major types of indications. The names, written in capital letters and mostly abbreviated in the left column, correspond with stage directions, such as *in casa, resta* or *in questo*. Together with the list of personaggi and horizontal lines between individual scenes in the margin column, this kind of standardised vocabulary reveals all the basic definitions for an improvised comedy. These features are typical of scenarios stemming from practical contexts, which allowed actors to gather the most important information at a glance. A second type of indication concerns topics and attitudes defining relationships and the dynamics of the modular scenes. In this case, a scenario indicates what the actors have to do and tell. The first type of indication schedules the presence of the individual actors onstage, and this is the raison d'être for scenarios in the professional context. In Italian the notion of mandafuora (literally a piece of paper list-ing exits and entrances) described this function of notating stage business (Casella 1975). With the second type of indication, actors knew what they needed to borrow from their repertoire within the framework of a drama-turgy, based on scenes originating from the Masks themselves. This notation technique for improvised comedy is already fully developed in the oldest-known scenarios. Instead of blaming these mandafuora for their poor lan-guage, it should be emphasised that this form of notation fully respects the autonomy of actors in creating theatrical poetry.

But obviously there were many reasons to develop the notation form of scenarios in various directions. Inside the professional troupes, the motiv-ation to extend notation techniques was inspired by pragmatic or idealistic reasons. For example, we know that troupes printed leaflets containing scenarios to invite spectators to representative performances for the town authorities, as was the case in Pavia in 1602 (Hulfeld 2014: 26–30). Another remarkable episode results from Charles Borromeo's Counter-Reformation cultural policy. Obviously the church tried to control professional theatre in Northern Italy by means of censorship. We are fortunate to have a statement from Cardinal Gabriele Paleotti relevant to this attempt, a letter from 1578 to Charles Borromeo:

> One can no longer argue that we should first censor these comedies to cut the evil, as in practice we will not succeed. Because they will always add words or witticisms that are not written down, or – to be precise – they do not write their comedies down at all except as a brief outline or a summary. The rest they achieve by improvisation. To condemn them for these writings has its difficulties. Moreover, they make gesticulations and movements of the most lascivious and dishonourable kind, which cannot be written down. (Taviani 1969: 39–40)

It must be noted that *commedia* troupes occasionally had good reasons for transforming their mandafuora into proper files: to evade the ecclesiastical censorship boards or for advertising purposes. Some intentionally sanitized versions thus have to be expected among the scenarios handed down.

Yet, Flaminio Scala's *Teatro delle favole rappresentative* was an ideal-istic project that exerted the strongest impact on the development of scenarios. Scala's soggetti are remarkable for at least three reasons. The first is a rationalist and realistic attitude in the dramaturgy of the impro-vised comedy; the second is his notation technique, with which he takes over the authorship of the scenarios; and the third is his endeavour to define the improvised comedy through an original story line.

Printed apologies and literary works were weapons employed by actors to fight against hostility towards their profession. In his *La supplica,* Nicolò Barbieri still felt the need to explain that actors were neither magicians nor rainmakers (Marotti/Romei 1991: 634–9). While ordinary people might have been unsure where the enchanting power of travelling actors ended, the Catholic Church was wary of the connection between comedy and 'superstition'. The Church had to combat all rivals pretending to be in possession of transformational power or the knowledge of an 'other world' – and improvised comedy had solid roots in the netherworld. Thus the idea of the 'virtuosic actor' had to be based on a rational legitimation of the profession and the art. The commitment 'to deal with the real' in comedies was at the same time a promise to refrain from magic and the miraculous. The dramaturge Scala had to hide the traces of magical thinking still clinging to such aspects as the Masks. In his first *soggetto,* *Li duo* vecchi *gemelli,* he introduces Pasquella, an old bawd with magical powers, who promises to help Isabella in her love affair. Such a person was no longer tolerable onstage, unless she underwent a learning process (in the third act): 'Pasquella, in a fright, makes up her mind to live as a respectable woman and not to engage any more in witchcraft or procuring, because they are all devilish activities' (Scala/Andrews 2008: 13), a sentence that explicitly shows Scala's commitment to modern comedy.

Another example of the same commitment is his famous piece *La pazzia di Isabella.* A young man is kidnapped by Turks and becomes a slave or prisoner. He meets a young woman, falls in love with her, and together they decide to go back to Italy to get married. The flight turns out to be highly dramatic. They are pursued by the Turks and have to fight them off. Scala narrates that in this combat, Isabella shoots her former husband and her baby boy and then has to convert to Christianity. In the tale as recorded by Giambattista Basile in his *Pentamerone* (1634–1635), it is Rosella's mother, a magician, who follows the couple. The young man, defending Rosella and himself, chops off the mother's arms. As she dies in the sea, the mother casts a spell over her murderer, ordaining that he will completely forget about his bride as soon as his feet touch his native soil. Scala's plot thus was inspired by a popular tale, but he omits the magical explanation for the sudden change in behaviour of the Innamorato. Or, seen positively, he invents another explanation. Of course, as soon as Orazio returns to his hometown, he encounters his first love again. But this is not a sufficient explanation, because Scala depicts his Innamorato as fickle. As Isabella demands he explain himself, he answers that his behaviour is due to his melancholy disposition. Later on she concludes that 'a battle within his breast between love, duty and fidelity' is going on (Scala/ Andrews 2008: 226–30). In this sense, the omission of magical explanations draws attention to the inner motivations and contradictory nature of the male protagonist. It is probably not wrong to regard this as a step towards psychological dramaturgies in the field of improvised comedy.

Scala's notation technique was intended to gain a reading public. Instead of addressing actors, he now had to satisfy even those who were unfamiliar with this form of theatre. That is why his texts allow the reader to comprehend the storyline and why technical terms such as *fare lazzi* are reworked into understandable descriptions of stage actions. Further, he integrated direct speech. Generally speaking, he made himself into the author of a form of text that purported to represent theatrical performances and that served amateur players as a starting point for their stagings.

Scala had further ambitions. He was proud of his capacity to invent original storylines. A comedy such as *I tre becchi* would never have been inserted into his collection, as the piece follows a simple variation and escalation pattern. Mainly the tricks employed to bring a lover into the house of a married woman and to bring him safely out again were of interest. But on the whole, what could be called a plot is much more a pretext to string together favourite routines. In Scala's view such comedies suffered from a lack of dramaturgical composition. The *commedia all'improvviso* he wanted to define required plots and subplots and a somewhat realistic development of relationships, motivations and attitudes. Instead of a chain of spectacular acts, the improvised comedy according to Scala had to be defined by its plot structure. Actors and actresses were increasingly compelled to subordinate themselves to the art of the inventive dramaturges.

The Poetics of Improvising Actors

Botarga's utterances in his prologue about the poetic abilities of actors, and Cardinal Gabriele Paleotti's complaints about improvisation, were both written in the late 1570s. Their points of view are opposed, but one recognises a common awareness of the acting elements that defy the written word. Paleotti refers to 'gesticulations and movements', Botarga to 'hidden tales' and 'secret doctrines'; one can assume that with the reference to 'poor stories', Botarga had exactly 'gesticulations and movements' in mind. If this hypothesis is correct, attention must be drawn to the so-called *pezzi chiusi* (enclosed units or independent routines), to use a term coined by Mario

Apollonio (1968: 165–69). Scenarios and other writings refer to them as *balli* (dances), lazzi (special stage business), *baie* (trickeries), *burle* (trickeries), *scene* (special scenes), *trionfi* (triumphal scenes), *bastonate* (brawls), *inventioni* (make-believe actions), *giochi* (games), etc.

All of these traditional elements of improvised comedy are primarily physical actions functioning in a sphere other than language. That is why theatre historians face a problem in comprehending these slapstick elements. We know that they belong to the genuine heritage of those early actors who stemmed from the realm of jugglers and buffoons and that the adoption of narratives from novellas and comedies led to that structural tension between plot and *pezzi chiusi* (Apollonio 1930: 137–88). Further, we see that with the endeavours of dramaturges such as Scala the *pezzi chiusi* slowly lost their supremacy in improvised comedy. But it remains a challenge to explore the aesthetic dimension of these comic fragments, as can be seen with the research outcomes concerning the lazzi. The only one who drafted a theory of the lazzo was Luigi Riccoboni, in his *Histoire du théâtre italien* (Riccoboni 1728: 64–9), where he showed a major concern for the structural tension mentioned earlier.

4

Between Improvisation and Book

Piermario Vescovo

'If we do Commedie dell'Arte, we are in a nice mess', so ran the *prima donna*'s famous line in *Il teatro comico* (1750) by Carlo Goldoni. He also mentioned it in a footnote to *commedie del mestiere* (lit. 'comedies by those in the trade'). In the eighteenth century, the *commedie dell'arte* (in the plural sense) simply referred to the titles of the popular, widely played repertoire of plays in which masks were present – in other words plays 'whose fundamental characteristic was always Pantalone, the merchant from Venice, the Doctor, a lawyer from Bologna, Brighella and Harlequin, or the valets from Bergamo'. The Commedia dell'arte (singular) would later become to be regarded, in retrospect, as a mythical genre or tradition (Vescovo 1997) – often with the loss of the original meaning of *arte* (which, in Italian, can mean both 'art' and 'professional association'). As a result, a few modern artists have misinterpreted 'professional association' as 'skill' or 'remarkable ability' (Nicoll 1963).

Those *commedie dell'arte comica* took the form of *scenarios*, which could either be original or adaptations of dramas written earlier (all of which has been well documented by seventeenth- and eighteenth-century zibaldoni, replete with annotations such as 'from Plautus', 'from Terence', and so on) (Testaverde 2007). The reduction of dialogue to its *ossatura* or bare bones (another technical term of the time, literally meaning 'framework, skeleton') is therefore a step backwards which ultimately coincides with what every dramatist does – not only in those centuries – namely prepare a framework before writing the dramatic dialogue per se. In this regard see, for example, Lope de Vega's remarks on the *asunto* (topic) and the *sujeto* in his *Arte nuevo de hacer comedias* (1609), or the compositional phases of the dramatic text described by Goldoni and Carlo Gozzi, or Vittorio Alfieri (who evocatively describes three '*respiri*' (breaths): conception, dialogue writing, versification) and many modern dramatists. Eduardo de Filippo stated with regard to text composition that 'dialogue is the final phase of comedy. What you have to do is: first write down the subject – two or three pages – then do the outline and only then compose the dialogue'.

It is not just the Italians and not just the *comici dell'arte* who are characterised by this theatre tradition. It is a tradition in which improvised acting actually means a redistribution of the tasks to be performed: It is not the author who writes for everyone but more the individual actor who writes what he finally performs. The Italian actors 'fanno sopra le parole' (build on top of words, whereby 'words' stand for *soggetto, ossatura, scaletta* (set list) and *scenario*). This is how Francesco Andreini effectively summarises this 'recipe' when introducing Flaminio Scala's *Il teatro delle favole rappresentative* (1611). This is a one-of-a-kind collection of printed *scenari*, normally found in manuscript compilations which were either written by actors as abridgements of their repertoires or by amateur actors who were trying their hands at the trade of theatre. This was the case with all the most important zibaldoni of the seventeenth and eighteenth centuries whose work has survived. They were noblemen, men of law or men of faith – such as Corsiniano and Casamarciano (Vescovo 2010a).

In his *Mémoires* (II, 41), Goldoni offers an extraordinarily sharp observation in describing the ability, acquired over time, to write the dialogue in one go, by skipping the outline and writing on the spur of the moment, just like an actor improvising on stage.

Luigi Riccoboni offered the following definition of lazzo: 'what masked actors do in the middle of a scene that they have interrupted ... and to which it is therefore always necessary to return' (Riccoboni 1728: 65). Notable is the nexus of the definition, which in practice is not related to physical, pantomimic or physical-acrobatic action, but generally finds its place in a dialectic between separation and return to the initial situation. Aside from the clear folk etymology (from *laccio,* noose, the idea of capturing the audience), not even the common reference to *actio*, which is always cited as an agglutinated form of the article (*l'actio,* >*lactio*>lazzo) seems to be well founded. In old Italian and in its northern variant in particular, lazzo means 'addition' in the specific meaning of 'monetary interest': *prendersi aggio, divagare,* but also *avere aggio, guadagnar* (added interest). This metaphor, from the mercantile and banking world, is well suited to commercial theatre: In this case, it indicates something that is added to the framework of the comedy or to the text itself, if the latter is in written form. We can observe a similar procedure with regard to the material metaphors for *generico* or *canovaccio*: On the one hand, there is the old Italian term, *robba generica* (as in the French *robe,* i.e. a garment that can be worn on any occasion); on the other hand, the term *canovaccio*, which came into use later, stems from the Italians who relocated to France (Riccoboni, perhaps first, then Goldoni). They used the term *canevas* when referring to Italian theatre. In French, *canevas* was – and still is – a common, widely used term that indicates any sort of outline of a work (e.g. *canevas* of a parliamentary speech, a novel, etc.), originally denoting the thick hempen canvas used for embroidery.

Hence, a structure of 'fixed roles' and 'changing parts' characterises the specificity of text 'production' in the 'artisanal' system (the *arte* of the *comici* and the *figli d'arte*, literary offspring of actors) of Italian companies between the late sixteenth and eighteenth centuries (Taviani 2006). It is not by chance that the moment in the twentieth century when the myth of the commedia dell'arte was at its zenith – brought about by non-Italians – was marked by the return of a sort of counter-myth, represented above all by Luigi Pirandello. In the famous Volta conference of 1934 in Rome, which attracted the most influential personalities in experimental theatre worldwide, Pirandello took an opposite stance. He had composed a few entirely written texts – the so-called *Trilogia del teatro nel teatro* (*Trilogy of the Theatre in the Theatre*) which appear, but are in fact not, partly or wholly improvised. *Sei personaggi in cerca d'autore* (*Six Characters in Search of an Author*) is, according to the subtitle, '*commedia da fare*' ('A Comedy to Be Made'), in which the actors, shocked by the characters' proposal to improvise, refer directly and scornfully to the commedia dell'arte. The prompter is given the task of 'writing down the script' starting from the characters' improvisations, so that the actors of the company will be able to perform it. Unfortunately, as it turns out, the prompter is unable to write shorthand. Even stronger and more pervasive is the invention, as the title itself says, of *Questa sera si recita a* soggetto (*Tonight We Improvise*). In it, the audience is led to believe they are not watching a drama written by Pirandello, but rather a performance that the company – led by 'Director' Dr Hinkfuss – has created with one of Pirandello's novels as a starting point.

When he used the *Trilogy of the Theatre in the Theatre* as a preface to his last collection of plays, Pirandello certainly remembered that Goldoni had done something similar with his *Il teatro comico*. Goldoni had in fact inserted it at the beginning of every collection of his plays after the first. Another extremely clever concept is Pirandello's idea of *text composition* according to the *comici dell'arte*. This is poles apart from what was circulating in the Italian academic world and also from the myth of the theatre professionals of the contemporary European avant-gardes (Taviani 1980).

He accurately describes the commedia dell'arte as a theatre of authors who either become actors or work alongside actors in order to write their texts in a different way, rather than a theatre of actors who get rid of the authors and act by themselves by reason of their own ignorance and shortcomings. According to Pirandello, Goldoni was *inside* this tradition; in this he was not wrong.

More generally, the twentieth-century concept of 'scenic writing' highlights a switch from a *concertazione delle parti* (agreed arrangement of parts, an eighteenth-century term, also used by Goldoni) to a different, pervasive 'improvisation'. We can find the same inspiration provided by the commedia dell'arte behind the practice of 'collective creation', the term that gained popularity between the 1960s and the 1970s. In truth, the commedia dell'arte in Italy maintains its connection with masks and with the stylisation of a non-naturalistic kind of acting on the basis of the written text. This is confirmed by the great success of mid-century plays such as Giorgio Strehler's *Arlecchino Servitore di Due Padroni* (*Harlequin Servant of Two Masters*) and Giovanni Poli's *La commedia degli Zanni* – the latter inspired by texts, songs and nursery rhymes (for one or more voices) which reflect the performance of the masks in Vito Pandolfi's collection of 1958.

As we can read in the programme of Ariane Mnouchkine's *L'Age d'or* (which introduced modern masks, a wide series of figures, from the *flic* to the capitalist and the North-African immigrant), to draw inspiration from the commedia dell'arte means, for the actors of the Théâtre du Soleil in 1975, 'to write the comedy of our times using their bodies and their voices' (Théâtre du Soleil 1975: 13–14). In short: first, numerous rehearsals, starting from the identification of the characters, then the *canovaccio*. This style obviously had no precedent in the commercial theatre of the Italian *ancien-régime* actors which first appeared with the nineteenth-century legend. The tradition of improvisation – from late nineteenth-century France to early twentieth-century Russia – was in fact cultivated strictly outside of Italy, on the basis of myth. Hence, the idea of improvisation, developed in retrospect, emerges as the characterising element as early as in George and Maurice Sand's convivial experiences in Noailles, in which theatre is practised freely as a game, played before a plot outline is written down (Freixe 2014). Just as Christopher Columbus wanted to reach India, which had already been discovered, and ended up by discovering America instead, so theatre in the twentieth century promisingly invented *improvisation* while trying to recreate the *improvviso*, straying from the *concertato* towards collective creation. In doing so, it invented the commedia dell'arte, or rather, a different kind of commedia dell'arte.

Going back several hundred years, the field of 'Commedia dell'arte litera-ture' acquired in this way, for clear constitutive reasons, a paradoxical status. It is images – or, in any case, images before texts – that nurtured the myth and the act of 'creation' of the nineteenth and twentieth centuries. Jacques Callot's *Balli di Sfessania* – engravings which do not specifically represent theatre but depict masked dancers of *moresche* in Southern Italy – or the earlier *Recueil Fossard*, illustrating the first Italian troupes in France, were vastly more popular than literary records, such as *scenari* preserved in zibaldoni, manuscripts compiled by actors or in Scala's collection or the complete *commedie*, written by professional actors or amateurs who attempted to imitate them.

This tradition was primarily characterised by the non-professional status of its authors and differs essentially from the printed works of great actors and capocomici, in which the distinguishing features of what was retro-spectively defined as commedia dell'arte were either absent or of secondary importance. This is exemplified by Giovan Battista Andreini, for instance, the most important Italian playwright of the seventeenth century, but also by the way a subject is developed in a written text, such as in Flaminio Scala's *Il finto marito* (1618), in which masked characters are eliminated from the 'regular' version. This approach is partly reflected in the publish-ing experience of Carlo Goldoni who, moving from the stage to the printed text, published some of his comedies without masked characters and the stage dialects which characterised them. With the printed version of a work which was to gain immense popularity, *The Servant of Two Masters*, origi-nally conceived as a '*scenario* with gifts' (that is, with the additional 'gift' of written parts) for Antonio Sacchi, Goldoni offered future generations a remarkable model of writing of great significance for the tradition of Italian theatre. He could not have foreseen that *The Servant of Two Masters*, an ur-Commedia dell'arte so to speak, would prompt the revival and development of that tradition into a 'genre', which would spread throughout Europe from as early as the eighteenth century (Mozart considered this comedy perfect for a German opera) up to the era of the great twentieth-century directors, from Max Reinhardt to Giorgio Strehler.

While the zibaldoni were mostly compiled by amateurs or enthusiastic collectors, works of literature by Italian actors, from the sixteenth century onwards, were more numerous in an apologetic or defensive vein than as texts actually to be performed. Only a few of these collections have survived. Some were quite extraordinary, for example Stefanelo Botarga's *Zibaldone*, dating from approximately 1580, or Domenico Biancolelli's *Scenario*, written almost a hundred years later and translated into French by a judge, Thomas Guelette. This *scenario* was exceptional because it was by a single actor and not by a troupe. Most of the works written by *comici* advocate the legitimacy of their profession and of the *'giusto ministerio '* ('honorable ministry') of the trade of theatre. Both were fiercely opposed at the time. Since the very first pages written by the founding fathers, from Pier Maria Cecchini to Niccolò Barbieri and Giambattista Andreini, actors had written to defend themselves and to enhance their social and cultural dignity. However, they did not describe their specialist knowledge, the strategies they used to manage their repertoire or their acting techniques in their works – clearly because they wanted to protect the secrets of their trade. Besides referring to a professional association, the word *arte* in their writings also acquires the meaning of *ars comica*, as *ars poetica* applied to drama and managed by *comici*-writers, with exactly the same connotation as the *arte nuevo de hacer comedias* described by Lope de Vega (whose works Barbieri certainly read). It was through the mostly distorted mirror of the works of detractors and polemicists, especially by clergymen, that the defining characteristics of the *commedia* emerged, after the disappearance of the written dramatic text itself.

In his bizarre encyclopaedia of professions *La piazza universale di tutte le professioni del mondo* (*The Universal Town Square of All the Professions in the World*) (1585), friar Tomaso Garzoni devotes two chapters – using a rigidly dualistic approach – in one case to *formatori di spettacoli* ('performance makers') such as *ceretani, cantimbanchi, ciurmatori* (charlatans and mountebanks) and all *mangiaguadagni* ('money-eaters') of the public square, who spread like weeds and in another to *comici e tragedi, così auttori come recitatori* ('actors and writers of comedies and tragedies'), namely to the superior comici *eccellenti*. These were mostly actresses, or rather divas: Isabella (Andreini), Vincenza (Armani), Vittoria (Piissimi), significantly called only by their first and stage names. These actors and actresses were declared to be above the law: 'Despite bans, [they could] walk in all the squares of the world without any impediments and be received with great honour in places from which their position in society would otherwise have excluded them' (Garzoni 1996). In this context, the word *piazza* acquires a metaphorical meaning, referring to the private audiences of princes and aristocrats.

Europe was therefore the starting point and the centre from which Italian theatre spread, first from France to the northern countries, then from Spain to Russia. Its consolidation was partly due to stable institutions, such as the Comédie Italienne in Paris. The history of this theatre, from its closure to its re-opening, is condensed into two monumental works, the *Recueils* compiled by Evaristo Gherardi and Luigi Riccoboni, at the end of the seventeenth century and in the early eighteenth century. The *Recueils* are collections of plays from the various playwrights involved during the period between the first enterprise and the comedy of Marivaux. The collection shows how Italian theatre nourished and blended with French theatre. A typically Italian imagination and taste are the distinctive features of Italian theatre outside Italy. Fernand Braudel has clearly identified the parallel diffusions of higher and lower forms of Italian culture. In this regard he said that the commedia dell'arte in fact was played by the same companies who put on the *commedia erudite* and travelled from Italy as a sort of double bill with it (Braudel 1991: 146). It is interesting to follow the development of the theatrical taste denoted by the term *all'italiana* (which refers not only to itinerant companies, but also to opera, perspective scenery, the curtain and the theatre space) from a chronological point of view and compare it with the 'international' style of the seventeenth century, namely the European Baroque. It was a fruitful relationship, in which the so-called commedia dell'arte, widely diffused as it was, offered Europe imagination, technique and roots which were deep and in large part beyond theatre. One could say that the 'the commedia dell'arte brought together much of what had developed in the preceding decades and centuries' (ibid.). In this regard, it is relevant to mention the use of masks and the stage life of some masked characters – as exemplified by the case of Harlequin – in the mingling of the classical-style comedy with the folkloristic and carnivalesque roots of Europe.

In the late 1560s, starting from the performances at Trausnitz Castle for the wedding of the Duke of Bavaria and Renata of Lorraine (by cultivated amateurs) and including those at the Ducal Palace of Nevers, in Paris, Madrid and beyond, but without attempting to outline a map of who was where and when (such a map was offered by Ferrone in 2014, retracing the history of Italian actors and actresses in Europe), Braudel focused on an essential element: What was unfolding was not the diffusion of a genre, but rather that 'of a collection of diverse goods generously offered' (ibid.). We might add that in the stereotyped and picturesque image of itinerant *guitti* (mummers), as they are represented in genre painting (which in the following centuries nourished Romantic and fictional imagination, resulting in splendid creations such as *Le capitaine Fracasse* by Théophile Gautier), the commedia dell'arte is placed in public squares, facing a lower-class and partly middle-class audience. This is not that aristocratic audience of princes and nobles which in practice promoted and determined the diffusion of the commedia dell'arte in Europe. Braudel adds that the commedia dell'arte flourished up to the fall of the *ancien régime* which, in an inversion of terms, seemed to 'be made to understand it' and decayed at the same time as the *commedia* when the latter 'was eventually relegated to travelling fairs, and to puppet shows for children' (ibid.).

At this point, Braudel asked himself a crucial question: Was that princely and aristocratic society actually so refined? In France, it had not passed through the Hôtel de Rambouillet and in Baroque and picaresque Europe, the upper classes still felt the need to hobnob with the riff-raff. By looking at the mirror in which the fortune of Italian theatre in Europe was reflected, Braudel concluded that the passage to the modern era happened through theatre: 'The commedia dell'arte has somehow revealed Western theatre to itself', no less (Braudel 1991: 146).

PART II

Commedia dell'Arte and Europe

5

Journeys

Siro Ferrone

Journeys play an important role in the theatre of the *ancien régime* and lie at the heart of performances of the commedia dell'arte in particular. The primary reason for this is that the history of the commedia dell'arte has to be considered as the result of a collective endeavour of actors, rather than of the influence of writers or stage designers. And unlike the latter two, the activities of professional *comici* were decisively characterised by nomadism. It is one of the most significant phenomena in the entire Italian tradition.

Direct and indirect sources from the sixteenth to the eighteenth century allow an interesting view of the network connecting Italian and European court theatres, and also of the urban theatrical system where troupes worked more continuously (Ferrone 1993b: 4–51; Ferrone 2014: 3–51, regarding the changes determined by the seasonal or periodic migrations of professional – and sometimes amateur – actors). Many of the innovations in dramaturgy and acting technique that were introduced during this time resulted from a mobility that connected, and at the same time multiplied, the linguistic and cultural differences between the actors organised in troupes, and the audiences who attended their performances. Certain journeys, short as they may be, can be described as an enzyme triggering the creativity of actors and eliciting unexpected emotional responses from audiences being confronted with actors from various geographical contexts. Some of these actors were amateurs travelling as representatives of civil or religious associations based in territories that were foreign in terms of language and traditions, while others were professional actors whose contractual agreements included trips to culturally and linguistically varied territories.[1] Their performances were met with both approval and scandal, recorded by chroniclers of varying moral or religious persuasions. The overarching effect of this mobility, however, was an acceleration in the pace of theatre history.

In the first half of the sixteenth century, significant migrations of theatrical troupes of different social types and statuses took place. They included the migration, already mentioned, of the *comici* of Siena (the Rozzi), who performed in Rome on the occasion of city festivals or private performances, and the less extensive travel of the itinerant troupe of Ruzante from Padua. The Rozzi were protected by the professional association to which they belonged and by a solid profession, while the Ruzante were funded by a wealthy patron. Whatever the differing civil and social statuses of these troupes, the reasons for the success of their performances was most likely found not only in the quality of the texts they performed, but especially in the fruitful gap between the expectations of local audiences and these 'foreign' actors with their alien linguistic, rhythmic and emotional expressions.

Using gestures, rhythms, words and customs that marked their difference from the spectators – who perceived this first with surprise, then with the satisfaction of someone who experiences a new emotion – was often the starting point for performances by itinerant actors wanting to distinguish themselves from resident actors. Acting thus became a festive occasion, during which the distinctions between actors and spectators diminished as the sense of a temporary community grew. In such contexts, actors were not affected by the same kinds of pressures faced by their professional peers, who had to travel in order to make a profit, and often challenged spectators' expectations with their capacity for innovation.

Throughout most of the sixteenth century, civic organisations such as guilds, *compagnie di piacere* and academies practiced acting and theatrical performance on an amateur level, thus ensuring the continuity of a culture committed to replicating the organisational forms and expressive symbols inherited from the medieval tradition. In order to survive, professional *comici* had to appeal to two sets of audiences: on the one hand the aristocratic patrons, who guaranteed significant profits and protection; on the other, a growing audience alien to court life and indifferent to the themes and symbols of high culture. If the *signorie* wanted the itinerant *comici* to adjust their creativity to courtly conventions, avoiding obscenities and unholy acts, the popular audience rather expected the opposite: carnival and the temporary reversal of civic traditions, conveyed through the festive customs of oral culture.

In the sixteenth century, the differences were marked between colloquial and literary languages and oral and singing traditions of Italy's regions, as well as of the other European countries where the Italian *comici* migrated. Later on, especially at the beginning of the seventeenth century, the intensification and multiplication of the routes of professional troupes, and their sojourns in various cities traditionally associated with the performing arts, led to the development of an increasingly shared theatrical language that consisted of actions, gestures and inventions all derived from the same expressive code. From the first decade of the seventeenth century onwards actors began to publish books, with the purpose of systematically setting down a dramaturgical language of the professional art of theatre. Their models were the treatises of literary and academic intellectuals. The tone of such emulations was sometimes subservient, until near the end of the seventeenth and the beginning of the eighteenth century, when the *comici's* 'dramaturgy in action' crystallised into confident and conventionally accepted forms, if not completely, at least for the most part. This made the dramaturgy more easily exportable while retaining its innate sense of innovation and surprise.

The power of the original commedia dell'arte derived from a pull between opposites – a tense, syncopated language of distances between characters and the physical actions linking them, hinting at hidden forces and objectives. A non-literary and physical language underlying the plot and its literary subjects, it is difficult to recover today. It developed as a consequence of the itinerant nature of the troupes, which were composed of artists of the most varied origins. These actors were accustomed to moving ceaselessly from one city to the other, along the rivers of the Po Valley or the Tyrrhenian and Adriatic coasts, beyond the Alps or the Dolomites, or across the swamps and the dangerous, bandit-infested lands of Central Italy. Somehow 'condemned' to perpetual movement – about which they often complain in their writings (Ferrone 2014: 62–74) – the actors could, however, avoid literary conventions when they were on stage, embellishing their repertoire (which some would define as 'pre-theatrical') with linguistic devices which, being drawn from different languages, could puzzle and surprise, and thus win over a variety of audiences.

Most itinerant troupes were composed – by necessity or choice – of actors from similar geographical areas. Before the theatrical system developed well-established practices and norms (which came into being in the first half of the seventeenth century: See for exemple the descriptive note of the 'ideal' itinerary summarised by the Jesuit Domenico Ottonelli in the treatise *Della Christiana Moderatione del Teatro*), new actors or actresses were usually gradually incorporated into the troupes as they travelled from one important transit city to another. Local talent in search of opportunity could join a newly created troupe or a prestigious, well-established troupe, with the hope of high profits. The coexistence within the troupe of actors and actresses of different linguistic and cultural origins allowed the troupe to deploy on stage a wide range of masks, stock characters and languages, which varied according to the cultural contexts of local audiences. The same characters might be familiar for a specific audience, but exotic for another. Similarly, characters who had carried out the function of foreigners could become familiar thanks to the adoption of a language known to a new audience. By modifying the principles of the linguistic game – and thus the role of the foreigners, too – the troupe could be flexible and rely on a vast, ever-changing repertoire. This was particularly the case because the acting style of the commedia was based on improvisation. While it was not a practice consisting of totally impromptu inventions, it was based on a combinatory exercise within a limited range of possible choices which related to the physical, gestural and vocal features of each actor.

The predominance of stereotypical characters such as the Venetian, the Neapolitan, the Tuscan, and the Spaniard, as well as French, German or Hispanic characters, resulted from the mobile nature of the commedia dell'arte. Each of these stereotypes could be deployed to satisfy the changing tastes of different audiences hungry for parodies of foreigners. Every territory had its own urbanised population – which migrated to the city from the mountains or the country – or had been occupied by a foreign army (French, Spanish or German), whose mores could be compared and contrasted with local traditions. For instance, in the first part of the sixteenth century, the prevailing caricatures recorded were those of the German soldier and, throughout the seventeenth century, satirical descriptions of 'the Spaniard'. Both these theatrical targets were selected because they belonged to the same imperial army responsible for all the wars which raged in Italy during the sixteenth and seventeenth centuries. It is worth noting, however, that some of the most significant caricatures of Germans and Spaniards were invented in France, consistent with the long-term conflict between the Kingdom of Spain and the Empire on one side, and France on the other.

Although statistically less frequent, caricatures of French characters were recorded in the area of Naples, which was ruled for a long time by the Spanish government, at the time particularly tolerant towards characters relating to caricatures of their enemies. Yet it is important to point out that the language and traditions of the commedia dell'arte were never born out of contempt, but only of parody – even when grotesque characters or plots were staged.[2] Everyone was granted the right of comic subversion, which led to a dramaturgy in which all parodic models contributed, in equal measure, to the establishment of the commedia dell'arte.

The multilingualism which characterised the work of professional *comici* fulfilled a need for expressive variants which could satisfy the expectations of spectators from the most diverse linguistic and cultural backgrounds. Travelling from city to city, the most fortunate troupes were the ones which could count on many linguistic tools, thus achieving widespread popularity in as many areas as possible, particularly those open to importing professional theatre. This accounts for the fact that actors from the areas of Veneto, Tuscany and Naples left a distinctive mark on the commedia dell'arte. In these territories there were theatres or courts which played host to theatrical productions continually throughout the *ancien régime*. The consequent addition of Hispanic, German and French linguistic and phonetic competences shaped an often parodic multilingualism that was detached from 'high' literature, which existed in a parallel sphere. The practice of linguistic *pastiche* – at times naive and elementary, at others whimsical, depending on the various areas where the commedia dell'arte was produced – was certainly stimulated by attention to political or military issues. In particular, it was triggered by the desire to tease the audience with light caricatures of the troops fighting in Italy. However, it was also motivated by the intention (and need) to catch the interest and arouse the attention of the various audiences scattered along the routes of their tours.

Evidence of the capacity of repertoires to adapt to local conditions and occasions is provided by the journeys and performances of Alberto Naselli, known as Zan Ganassa, and Barbara Flaminia, who were among the first artists of the commedia dell'arte to emigrate. In the mid-sixteenth century, Naselli and Flaminia performed at the courts of Central Europe together with other *comici* and then moved to Paris and eventually Madrid, where they worked for a longer period. The scenarios attributed to their troupe condense an artistic intermingling of Italian and Spanish sources, collecting traces of their various intercultural experiences (cf. Brunetti 2005: 329–42; Ojeda Calvo 2007; and Simoncini 2011: 106–14). Similarly, two brothers from Mantua – Tristano and Drusiano Martinelli – performed from the mid-1570s onwards and moved first to Flanders, then to England and Spain, and finally spent a significant amount of time in France.

The troupes principally responsible for exporting and spreading the tradition of the commedia dell'arte throughout Europe (particularly in France and the territories of the Empire[3]) were the Accesi of Piermaria Cecchini and the Fedeli of Giovan Battista Andreini. Their tours, commissioned and financed by the French court and patronised by noble families such as the Medici and the Gonzagas, marked the second stage of the transformation of the written and performed repertoire of the commedia dell'arte between the first and second decades of the seventeenth century. Adjusting to the different expectations of the various audiences by developing a vocabulary of gestures and actions that amounted to a 'common living language' of *ancien régime* Italy, the commedia dell'arte was able to satisfy the tastes of spectators from both the cultivated and the popular classes. Independently of literary Italian and resorting to an unconventional multilingualism in which phonemes strategically trespassed semantic communication, the actors created a language which was no less universal than the Latin used by cultivated men of letters. Traces of this can be found in the letters that the artists from the first generations of the acting profession wrote,[4] and aspects of this essentially spoken language can be retrieved from the texts the *comici* had printed, even if heavily corrected by more or less illustrious literary supervisors.[5]

The first documents on the commedia dell'arte date back to the sixteenth century[6] and testify to the contrast between the roles of the Zanni and the Magnifico. The basis of the typical 'duet' between the elderly, aristocratic Magnifico, who speaks Venetian, and the gross but vital, sensual and beastly Zanni is a precise comic measure of distance between the decrepitude of the rich Magnifico and the rough physical strength of the servant who has immigrated to Venice. The archetype of physical and social contrast on stage was destined to become the core of numerous commedie dell'arte, deriving its energy from the journey. The journey is its social and anthropological foundation. The reference here is to the migration of people who were seen as uncouth, ignorant boors descending from the mountains of Bergamo to arrive at the outskirts of the great *signori*'s palaces in Venice. In different forms, this contrast had already been expressed in various dramaturgies which, since the beginning of the sixteenth century, had traditionally opposed peasants to citizens.

The topic of migration, reinterpreted in different linguistic forms and in other contexts, returned later in the same century when the stock character of Harlequin was created and developed by Tristano Martinelli. It is an emblematic example of the importance of the journey in the development of theatre. Having already analysed this key historical aspect in my previous works, I will not discuss it further here (cf. Ferrone 2006 and 2014: 62–83). I will only add that numerous characters inspired by the social figure of the *condottiere* had a similar genesis, often suspended among multiple identities which were all based on the linguistic grotesque and devoted to reminiscing about the character's fantastic journeys. Examples include Francesco Andreini, who was known as Capitano Spavento, and Silvio Fiorillo, known both as Capitan Matamoros and as

Pulcinella. The linguistic repertoire of all these characters gave them an inevitably foreign flavour, and plotlines often transcended the realms of the plausible, logical or rational. Fiorillo, for example, was called to pirouette high up in the air and then plunge to the ground, and Capitano Spavento (played by Francesco Andreini) travelled to the moon, crossing time and space.

Most, if not all, the plots of the commedia dell'arte are based on one or more journeys which precede the action of the play and determine its plot and conclusion through the introduction of characters who were believed to be foreigners because – before the commedia – they had been kept away by their travels and adventures. This dramaturgical element, however, belongs to the literary antecedents of the stage action. The distinctive trait of the material journeys of the *comici* is another matter. It was acted out in the three-dimensional space of the stage before being narrated on the page. In examples such as Harlequin's descent into the underworld, the journey was conveyed by the body and athleticism of the actor. Transcription of such performances in print require a conjectural reconstruction of the material interplay of actions (see the material reading of the literary dramaturgy of Andreini in Ferrone 2001: 233–9).

The plots at the centre of the commedia dell'arte are set in contexts which are alien to the verisimilitude characterising literary drama. The journeys in such scenarios include, for example, quick passages from earth to heaven, or to hell, as found in the adventurous plots reported in *Histoire plaisante des faicts et gestes de Harlequin Comédien Italien*, as well as in related texts (Gambelli 1993, I: 388–416). In many scenarios (and also in the extended versions of commedie derived from the original scenarios by different actors), the characters are protagonists of adventures without limits. Significantly, the basic stage design used by the *comici* enabled them to use a theatrical language free from the restrictions of verisimilitude. Examples of this include the adventure of Francesco Andreini as Capitano Spavento landing on the moon, and Silvio Fiorillo imagining himself to be flying in the sky. In other instances the *comici dell'arte* relied on the familiar topos of heaven and hell, descending into the black depths of hell and then re-emerging or never coming back, as in the famous ending of the scenario by Domenico Biancolelli, which inspired Molière's *Don Juan*.[7]

If we consider the reinterpretation of the extreme journey to the underworld made by the Harlequin Martinelli, as well as his catastrophic return from it,[8] it is evident that the approach he adopted is parodic. The famous short poem *Histoire plaisante des Faicts et Gestes de Harlequin Commedien italien* illustrates the performative strategies used by Martinelli and his fellow actors in the performances in Paris around 1584. They took the trope of the journey to the underworld, regarded as one of the backbones of humanistic dramaturgy (as for example in Angelo Poliziano's *Orfeo*), and filtered it through the point of view of a humble itinerant *comico*, namely Martinelli himself, to comic effect.[9]

Journeys, often seen in the scenarios and commedie of the *comici dell'arte* as mere literary stratagems, are in fact crucial events in their biographies. In order to give a more concrete, less literary, reality to the dramaturgical references to travels and adventures contained in the texts, it may be useful to compare the misadventures of Harlequin and his friends to the real difficulties reported by the *comici* themselves in their letters: crossing flooded rivers with the risk of drowning, navigating rivers so dry as to prevent the passage of the boats meant to take them to their destination, following narrow passes threatened by bandits, snow and rain and other such adventures. These mishaps find a correspondence in the plots and narratives of the characters in the texts which have been passed down to us.

Notes

[1] It is important to remember here the well-known notarial document of 1545 regarding the first emergence of professional actors in a 'fraternal company'. This lay company was different from the system of non-profit – as we would define them today – companies and brotherhoods of medieval origin.

[2] See also the satirical, but never violent, description of the Jews in the *commedia Lo schiavetto* by Giovan Battista Andreini (especially in act 2, scene 9). The play is set in Mantua, where the Jewish community played an important role. As regards the *commedia* cf. the modern edition edited by Falavolti (1982), in particular act 2, scene 11.

[3] Without forgetting the importance of the seasonal migrations of Tristano Martinelli, Flaminio Scala or Piermaria Cecchini – regarding this aspect, see Ferrone 2014. The actor-playwright Andreini was undoubtedly able, like no one else, to reconcile the reasons for professional nomadism with the constant application of Neoplatonic theories as well as with a wide-ranging, profound and long-lasting publishing strategy. For this reason, he deserves to be mentioned among the most important Italian playwrights and theatre scholars. As regards the literary and theatrical theories of Andreini, besides my abovementioned works, see in particular Lombardi 1995: 14–47.

[4] For an interesting sampling of the language used by the comici in their letters – characteristic of oral communication – see Burattelli, Landolfi and Zinanni 1993. The written Italian documented there contains echoes of spoken Italian, partly because many of these letters were dictated to copyists by the comici themselves, as evidenced by the division of the sentences and the syntax.

[5] Again, see Ferrone 1985–1986, II, in which it is possible to read some texts written by the actors, with the related linguistic hypercorrections. The most emblematic example of this hypercorrection is offered by the commedie printed by the highly educated Giovan Battista Andreini.

[6] Here it is relevant to mention 'Il duetto di Magnifico e Zanni alle origini dell'Arte' (Apollonio 1971: 193–220). However, as regards the importance of the contrasting theme in the *commedia dell'arte*, an essential reading is Taviani 1986: 25–75.

[7] For more details on this topic see Ferrone 2014: 78–83. It is worth remembering that these travelling adventures could be performed differently depending on the stage design adopted each time. This is suggested by many surviving scenarios and by some images of the iconographic tradition. In addition to the collection of images contained in the edition by Gambelli, see also the edition with comments by Guardenti (Guardenti 1990, vol. II).

[8] See the various interpretations of the topic of hell by Biancolelli, such as the demonic apparitions in the scenario *Le voyage de Scaramouche et d'Arlequin aux Indes* and in others (cf. Gambelli 1997, vol. II, part one: 340–2 and vol. II, part two: 521 and ff., 527–9 and n. 342). See also S. Ferrone 2014: 14–16.

[9] It is important here to underline the parodic approach that is so characteristic of the *commedia dell' arte*. This interpretation of the traditional repertoire has essentially been overlooked until now, probably due to the fact that parody has always been considered by the scholars of high literature as an inferior literary form. On the contrary, it would be better to consider it as the genre in which high and low, the serious and the comedic can be freely mixed. This mixture, which Andreini attempted to develop, would benefit the Italian dramatic and literary production.

6

France

Virginia Scott

1571–1625

Sandro D'Amico wrote that the Italian theatre in France was a 'colony, characterised by independent evolution' (Gambelli 1993: 196). While this is a neat if somewhat simplistic description of a complex process, it relates only to the last half of the seventeenth century and the eighteenth century. In the sixteenth and early seventeenth centuries, however, Italian performers were not colonisers so much as occasional visitors brought to France to amuse the Italianised courts of the two Medici queens, Catherine and Marie, and their children.

Some documentary evidence exists of Italian entertainers at court and elsewhere in France before 1570, but the first record of an organised troupe playing in Paris is from 1571, when Italians performed for the royal entry of King Charles IX and his new Hapsburg bride, Elisabeth of Austria. This was a troupe led by Alberto Naseli, Zan Ganassa and his wife, Barbara Flaminia, that came not from Italy but from the court of the Emperor Maximilian II. Ganassa was joined by Giovanni Tabarino, Antonio Soldino and other Italian actors and acrobats. When the bride traveled to France, the Italians were in her train. The following February 'Tabarini' received a payment for a performance in Paris and in March Lord Buckhurst, the English ambassador, wrote to Queen Elizabeth I that he had seen a play performed by an Italian company 'that for good mirth and handling thereof deserved singular comendacion' (Baschet 1882: 16). In May 1671 the troupe, now characterised as *Les Galozi* and '*comédiens du roy*', performed at the baptism of a godson of Queen Mother Catherine de Medici.

Henri III, the brother and successor of Charles IX, was on his way from Poland to Paris in 1574 to accept the crown when he saw another troupe also called I Gelosi perform in Venice. He was especially taken with the leading lady, the divine Vittoria Piissimi, and in May 1576, with the Fifth

War of Religion more or less concluded, he invited the Italians to court. After some months of negotiations and an unfortunate kidnapping by a gang of Huguenots, the actors arrived at Blois on 25 January 1577. The chronicler Pierre de L'Estoile took an interest in them – not a friendly interest – and we know from his *Journal* that the actors opened their Paris season on 19 May 1577 in a royal venue in the Palais du Petit-Bourbon, that the public was admitted for four sous each and that the audience was larger than the total of those attracted by the four best preachers in Paris (Baschet 1882: 74). Parlement once again closed down the Italian theatre in spite of the king's *lettres patentes*, declaring that 'all these comedies teach nothing but bawdiness and adulteries and serve only as a school of debauchery to the youth ... of Paris'. This time, however, the king responded with a *lettre de jussion*, meaning 'it is my order', and the actors reopened on 27 July. L'Estoile remarks sourly that 'the corruption of the times is such that the farceurs, the buffoons, the whores and the *mignons* have all the credit with the king' (Baschet 1882: 75–6). Unfortunately, nothing is known for certain about the repertory of this troupe or its composition – although one assumes that it included Vittoria.

The next important visit by Italians came in 1584–1585 when a troupe led by Drusiano Martinelli and his wife Angelica (and including his brother Tristano, who originated the role of Arlequin) played in Paris. The archives yield no letters between Paris and Mantua, the royal accounts no record of payments to the actors. The dates are established by two plays written by *comici* and published in Paris in 1584 and 1585, by a series of pamphlets also published in 1585, weapons in a 'comic war' between Arlequin and an unidentified French actor referred to as Robert Triplupart L'Andouiller, and by a series of visual images collected in the *Recueil Fossard*, now accepted as including depictions of this troupe.

While the scholarship and criticism of this material is vast, conclusions based on solid evidence are rare; even the name of the troupe is in question – I Gelosi? I Confidenti? I Racolti? – and there is no exact indication of when and where they performed. They could once again have occupied a court venue, but court records are silent. The only approved public stage in Paris was the Hôtel de Bourgogne, a purpose-built theatre belonging to the Confrérie de la Passion. The Confrérie had a monopoly on theatrical performances in the city and its suburbs, and visiting troupes were obliged to use the Hôtel or, if proposing to perform elsewhere, to pay a per diem fee to the Confrérie. The pamphlets seem to indicate that Arlequin played at the Hôtel, but Arnold Van Buchel noted in his journal on 4 December 1585 that he had seen an Italian troupe perform in the

Faubourg Saint-Germain and that its 'principal and preferred actor had been Arlequin' (Van Buchel 1900: 150–1). Perhaps the Martinellis chose both options.

In 1599 the increasingly celebrated Arlequin returned to France at the invitation of Henri IV to celebrate His Majesty's marriage to Marie de Medici. After entertaining the king in Lyon, the actors arrived in Paris in late January 1601. The troupe included a number of well-known performers: Martinelli, of course, but also Pier Maria Cecchini, who played Magnifico and first Zanni, and his wife, Flaminia, who played first Amoureuse. Other familiar names included Silvio Fiorillo, Flaminio Scala and Marc'Antonio Romagnesi. Martinelli, who was both opportunistic and greedy, occupied himself while waiting for the king in Lyon with the preparation of a very odd pamphlet which he entitled the *Compositions de Rhetorique de M. Don Arlequin*, an exercise in persuading the king to part with a medal and a gold chain. The actor's chummy approach to the king and queen of France, whom he called his *compère* and *commère*, his buddies, was ultimately successful, since he achieved the medal and chain and remained a court favorite for twenty years.

What changed the French experience of the commedia dell'arte was the visit in 1603–1604 of I Gelosi, starring the diva Isabella Andreini. While Martinelli's Arlequin was to remain popular at the court and especially with Marie de Medici, the Andreinis – Isabella, her husband Francesco, their son Giovanni Battista, and his wife Virginia Ramponi – brought a different repertory and a different approach to court and popular entertainment during the first quarter of the seventeenth century, with visits in 1603–1604, 1613–1614, 1621–1622 and 1624–1625. Luciano Mariti points out that Isabella was the first to use published texts to advertise both her coming to France and her 'singularity as a poet and star' when she published in Paris in 1602 a French edition of her pastoral, *Mirtilla* or *Mirtille* (Mariti 2007: 125). Isabella also published the second volume of her *Rime* in Paris in 1603, lending more support to her self-fashioning as an actress/poet.

Isabella's presence in France made a lasting impression. Although French actors were anathematised and denied the sacraments, the church buried Isabella with full ceremony when she died in Lyon on the way back to Italy, calling her in the *Registre* of the Procureur of Sainte-Croix 'by common report one of the rarest women in the world both for her learning and for her fluency in several languages' (Baschet 1882: 146). A medal was struck in her honor and the French historian Pierre Matthieu, a playwright himself, immortalised her in his record of 'memorable things' in 1604.

Still, lacking as we do much exact knowledge of what Isabella and her companions performed in France and where they performed it, the impact made by the troupe is hard to assess. The visits made later by her son, Giovan Battista, and his troupe, I Fedeli, which have received less attention, were probably more influential.

At least two other Italian troupes were in Paris in the first years of the seventeenth century. Jules Rize and his company leased the Hôtel de Bourgogne in February 1607 and the troupe of Giovanni Paolo Alfieri collaborated with Valleran Le Conte and his troupe at the Hôtel in February and March 1612 (Katritzky 2012). The following year Arlequin finally agreed to return to France, leading a company that included Isabella's son Giovan Battista Andreini and his wife, Virginia Ramponi. This troupe, called the Accesi, arrived at the court in September 1613, and the Queen Mother, delighted to have her favourite back in France, even leased the Hôtel de Bourgogne for him for the carnival season.

In recent years historians and critics have begun to take seriously the work of Giovan Battista, once dismissed as an actor with an eccentric and contradictory history; some now even consider him 'the greatest playwright of the Italian Baroque' (Mariti 2007: 124). He left twenty-one published plays along with two in manuscript; some are based on traditional commedia dell'arte comic scenarios, others are tragedies, pastorals, musical spectacles and even religious dramas. Three of them feature Mary Magdalen; another is a comedy that presents a fully developed lesbian love affair with the central characters played by Andreini himself, his wife and his mistress. Many include elaborate stage directions and instructions for spectacle.

Whatever the repertory of the Fedeli, we can be certain that it was heavily weighted towards music. Andreini's wife, Virginia Ramponi, also known as Florinda, first came to international attention when she saved the day at a Gonzaga wedding in Mantua in May 1608. Rehearsals for the opera *Arianna* with music by Monteverdi were underway in March when the soprano hired for the title role suddenly died. Florinda, there with the Fedeli to perform a series of comedies and pastorals for the festivities, learned the role in six days, or so the anecdote goes, impressed the duchess of Mantua with her audition and performed the role to the absolute approval of all. Between 1606 and 1623, Andreini featured his wife in most of his plays, most of which incorporated music.

After 1624 there were no more Italian actors in Paris for at least fifteen years. The usual reason given for this is the difficult political situation leading up to the war of the Mantuan succession and the 1630 sack of

Mantua. The French court had always negotiated visits from the *comici* via the Mantuan court. Besides this, however, Paris may have pulled in the welcome mat. The king, who clearly liked the Fedeli, whether for its conventional repertory or for Andreini's own contributions, was increasingly under the influence of Cardinal Richelieu, who became his principal minister in 1624 and who had a vision of the arts in France that was both nationalistic and neoclassical. Giovan Battista's fantastic baroque concepts would not have appealed to the cardinal. Finally, the Hôtel de Bourgogne was increasingly occupied by the French *comédiens du roi*, who became the official tenants in 1629.

1644–1659

The first event in the decade involving identifiable commedia dell'arte actors was the spectacular 1645 court production of *La Finta Pazza* (The Feigned Madwoman). With a text by Giulio Strozzi and set to music by Francesco Sacrati, it had opened at the Teatro Novissimo in Venice in 1641. The Paris version differed significantly from the Venice original; it had a new prologue, a significant reduction of classical deities and three comic ballets with bears, ostriches and parrots to amuse the seven-year-old King Louis XIV. The physical production is well documented (Scott 1990: 52–64), however the casting and the contributions of the Italian *comici* are not entirely clear. The *Explication des décorations du théâtre, et les Argumens de la Pièce*, with a dedication by Italian composer and poet Giulio Cesar Bianchi (who may have been responsible for the new prologue) and published by Italian stage designer Giacomo Torelli, indicates that the play was performed by the 'grande Trouppe Royalle des Comediens Italiens entretenus de sa Majesté dans le petit Bourbon'.

This troupe in some configuration remained in Paris until late 1647 or early 1648, when they were driven away by the anti-Mazarin, anti-Italian civil wars of the Fronde. They returned to the Petit-Bourbon in 1653 at the king's invitation and were greeted with delight by the gazetteer Loret. This troupe is often referred to as the troupe of Locatelli, who was indeed entrusted with the task of forming the company, much to the chagrin of Tiberio Fiorillo 'who believed himself to be the holder of that office' (Monaldino 1996: 114).

Nothing is known about the day-to-day repertory of this troupe. However, it produced another spectacle play, *La Rosaura imperatrice di Constantinople*, for the carnival of 1658 (for a detailed account see Scott 1990: 65–70). It was clearly what the French call 'a machine play', designed by

Torelli, with twelve changes of scenery, four ballets, charming music, superb costumes, fire, lightning, thunder, hydras, dragons, seascapes and so forth. Best of all was a scene known as 'the table of Scaramouche' in which the greedy Zanni is prevented from eating by 'many ridiculous accidents' and 'many invisible tricks'. Perhaps the most important feature of this entertainment is the prominence of Scaramouche, who may not have been *capocomico* but who was definitely first in the hearts and minds of the French audience, perhaps because he was a very skillful mime. The only other production known from this period is *Le Festin de pierre* which introduced the iconic Don Juan to Paris in 1658. Notes kept by the Arlequin Domenico Biancolelli for a reprise performed in the next decade give some idea of the probable production (Scott 1990: 71–7).

1662–1697

The Italians disbanded, probably at the Easter recess of 1659. From the previous November they had been obliged to share the stage at the Petit-Bourbon with the troupe of Molière. They came back to France in 1661 and reopened in Paris on 8 January 1662. From that date the Italians continued to perform in Paris, first sharing at the Palais-Royal and the Théâtre Guénégaud and after 1680 in their own theatre at the Hôtel de Bourgogne. By the time they were dismissed in 1697 they had been established in Paris for thirty-five years.

The new troupe included Locatelli, Fiorillo, his wife, Brigida Fedeli, Giovan Andrea Zanotti and Angelo Lolli. To these were added Domenico Biancolelli, known in France as Dominique (Arlequin), Orsola Cortesi (Eularia), who would marry Biancolelli in 1663, Giacinto Bendinelli (Valerio) and Francesco Manzani (Capitan Terremoto: A brilliant bit of historical detective work has uncovered the life of this 'attore perduto' in Lestini 2010). With Locatelli as first Zanni, Biancolelli as second Zanni, and Fiorillo as his own kind of Zanni, the Paris troupe could amplify the comic routines, heavily dependent on physical performance, and minimise the rhetorical elements, the lovers' duets and the tirades.

For the first time, we have significant information about a troupe's everyday repertory in France since Domenico Biancolelli kept a *zibaldone*, or set of actor's notes. Although the Italian original is lost, the manuscript was translated into French in the eighteenth century and is a precious resource in spite of the problems it presents to the scholar (Gambelli 1993: 297–312, for discussions of the manuscript and the problems it presents; Scott 1990: 125–8). It contains descriptions of Arlequin's scenes in seventy-nine plays; the last forty-five, beginning with *Le Régal des dames*, produced in May 1668, appear to be in chronological order.

Most of the entries appear to be part of traditional commedia dell'arte entertainments and eighteen of them correspond in some fashion to scenarios found in other collections. Many have conventional neo-Roman romance plots with Arlequin as a valet, often disguised as someone or something else. A few of the plays are based on Spanish models or are related in some way to *Orlando furioso* or involve magic and magicians, but without any very elaborate scenes or machines. The *zanni* play is very active, filled with beatings and violence. Obscenity is included to the point that the eighteenth-century translator adds: 'Here is a sexual innuendo . . . which is very obscene, and I do not understand how Dominique, who was said to be such a virtuous man, could have dared to use this phrase, either in Italy or in Paris' (Scott 1990: 148).

With *Le Régal de dames* in May 1668, the Comédie Italienne begins its appeal to French taste. The importance of this production is underscored by the gazetteer Robinet, who devoted 122 lines of his weekly *Lettres en vers* to it. It was the first production done by the troupe to be set in France and the first to use the French language, although only in a drinking song. It also had multiple settings and was filled with music and what the gazetteer calls 'little miracles', that is, magic tricks.

The troupe remained relatively stable in the 1670s. Domenico Locatelli died in 1671 and was briefly replaced by an unidentified Briguelle, then by Giovanni Gherardi, aka Flautin. However, the traditional duo of first and second Zanni had been swapped for the couple Arlequin-Scaramouche, and Flautin was valued not as a *fourbe rusé*, a clever rascal, but for his odd ability to imitate the sounds of multiple musical instruments. By the mid-1670s the Italians, now sharing the well-equipped Théâtre Guénégaud with a French troupe, were providing elaborate musical spectacles in addition to their normal fare. *Le Voyage de Scaramouche et d'Arlequin aux Indes* (1676), for example, included music that was 'owing to the genius of M. Oudet'. The production focused on magic and machines, ornaments the actors hoped would attract 'numerous assemblies'. The action took place in Hell, the mountains north of Rome, the Land of Cockaigne, Turkey, the moon, a seashore and Belfégor's house. Machines included a dragon chariot, a fountain spouting wine and fire, two flying dragons and a magic crucible that shrank Scaramouche. The French troupe, to whom the theatre actually belonged, took a 'dim view' of this sort of thing, according to Jan Clarke, and took action in December 1679 to prevent their tenants from 'projects that threatened the destruction of our machines and our stage' (Clarke 2007: 188). This war of the competing spectacles had not been entirely resolved when the issue became moot in August 1680. The French troupe at the Hôtel de Bourgogne was merged with the Guénégaud troupe, and the resulting Comédie Française was granted possession of the latter's theatre. The Italians moved to the old Hôtel de Bourgogne and had their own space for the first time since 1658.

Since the Hôtel was poorly equipped for scenes and machines, the actors needed a new strategy to attract an audience. In 1681 the troupe began to insert full scenes written in French into their improvised plays; by 1685 they were performing nearly complete plays in French. This transform-ation was brought about in part by the addition to the company of the two daughters of Arlequin, Françoise and Catherine Biancolelli, born and raised in France, who played Isabelle and Colombine. The French reper-tory from 1681 is known to us largely from the collections published in 1694 and 1700 by Evaristo Gherardi, the actor who replaced Biancolelli as Arlequin in 1689. It enables us to assert, if not with perfect confidence, that a significant percentage of the troupe was able to play comfortably in French in the 1680s. Eularia speaks only Italian in a few of the early texts, but she is replaced by her daughter after April 1683. Diamantine never appears, nor does the aging Aurelia. Fiorillo appears infrequently, but his character does speak French, as does the Docteur, both Amoureux, and the first Zanni.

In 1688 the troupe lost its main attraction when Domenico Biancolelli died at only fifty-two. Angelo Costantini stepped briefly into the breech, but then a new Arlequin was found: Evaristo Gherardi, son of Flautin, who like the Biancolelli sisters had been raised in France. Gherardi begins his six-volume edition (1700) with scenes and nearly complete plays in French performed before the death of Biancolelli, most of them devised by Monsieur D***, Anne Mauduit, sire de Fatouville, a lawyer from Rouen. Beginning in March 1688, however, French writers of some note began to give plays to the Italians. The first included by Gherardi is *Le Divorce* (1688) by Jean-François Regnard, a leading comic playwright at the turn of the century, who was joined by Charles Dufresny. They wrote, singly or jointly, fifteen of the Gherardi plays. Dufresny also collaborated with the son of Dominique, Louis Biancolelli.

Although these plays occasionally refer to or reflect the traditional Italian repertory, for the most part they are aimed at the Paris audience, which appreciated entertainments that mirrored their own lives. An example of how an Italian mask was converted into a French *emploi* (character type) is the development by Marc'Antonio Romagnesi of a new kind of vecchio, a French *vieillard*, reminiscent of Molière's bourgeois characters and named variously Sotinet, Frequet, Trafiquet, Persillet or Goguet. This character appears especially in the comedies of manners that feature Françoise Biancolelli's Isabelle and Catherine Biancolelli's Colombine (Clarke 2003; Scott 1992). Isabelle, still proclaimed by her name to be an Italian amoureuse, is usually a Parisian bourgeoise, either trapped in an unsatisfactory marriage or about to be. Colombine is sometimes her servant or *suivante*, but can be a bourgeoise herself. In any event, whether mistress or maid, she is a fully developed intriguer, perfectly capable of living by her wits. These two emancipated Parisiennes are often central to the plots of the plays they dominate, and Catherine in particular became one of the stars of the enterprise.

After 1680, the Comédie Italienne like the Comédie Française became a state institution, with continued financial support from the crown along with increasing supervision by court functionaries. The Italians, from their establishment in 1662, always received the largest royal subvention of any Parisian troupe, 16,000 livres a year, and in return were expected to entertain the king and his court in Paris and follow them to the outlying châteaux. After Louis XIV settled at Versailles in 1682, the Italians became part of a regular series shared with the French troupe and the Opéra. The French repertory developed for the Paris audience was almost never requested by the court, which continued to see the traditional scenarios played improvisationally and in Italian. In the last years of the century, however, the Italians lost favor at court. They were not invited to Fontainebleau after 1692, and they played at Versailles only a few times a year. Their declining presence may have contributed to their expulsion from Paris in 1697.

Various scholars have tried to establish the reason or reasons why the actors found themselves barred from their theatre on 14 May 1697 (Brooks 1996; Clarke 1992; Scott 1990). In the increasingly devout climate of the 1690s, they had been warned that they must delete verbal obscenity and suggestive physical behavior from their performances. During their final year, they were subject to daily surveillance (Campardon 1970: I, xxii–iii). Chances are excellent that the actors continued in their profligate and profitable ways, until they finally went too far.

Supposedly they produced or proposed to produce a play satirising Mme de Maintenon. No documentary evidence confirms the production, but two members of the court, the Duke of St.-Simon and the Duchess of Orleans, insist that a play was performed and served as the final straw. In addition, dismissing the Italians saved the empty royal purse at least

16,000 livres a year and perhaps 18,000, according to one source. Finally, the issue of whether the Italians could legitimately perform in French had been raised once again by their competitors, and perhaps the king was tired of hearing about that. In any event, whether for one of the above reasons or some combination of them, the Italians were locked out and the Hôtel de Bourgogne remained empty and silent for nineteen years.

1716–1729

In 1716, after death of Louis XIV, the Duke of Orleans, regent for the young King Louis XV, was eager to lighten the gloom that had settled over Paris in the last years of the old king. He wrote to Parma, requesting his 'cousin' there to choose a troupe of actors who would come to Paris and restore the Comédie Italienne to the Hôtel de Bourgogne. The prince awarded the task of engaging the actors to Luigi Riccoboni, the leader of a troupe that circulated among major cities of Northern Italy from 1706 to 1715. He was a controversial figure, set on introducing a reform repertory of memorised Italian tragedies and erudite comedies, Spanish tragi-comedies, and even translations of Molière, Corneille and Racine to enrich the Italian professional repertory. Although his efforts at reform had met with some success, the failure in early 1716 of his production in Venice of Ariosto's *La Scolastica,* a literary comedy with no Arlequin, may have made him receptive to the idea of moving to Paris where he believed his ideas might be welcomed more enthusiastically (Courville 1967: 259–62). In fact, the Parisians proved even less appreciative than the Venetians of plays that did not feature improvisation and the Zanni.

Although Riccoboni later wrote that there were no good actors in Italy after 1680 or 1690, but only 'ignorant actors without intelligence, talents, or morals' (Riccoboni 1730: 74–5), he nonetheless filled out his troupe with Italians. These actors may have been chosen for their ability to play memorised texts as part of Riccoboni's plan to introduce scripted Italian drama to Paris, but the company seems on the surface to have been an entirely conventional commedia dell'arte troupe with two sets of lovers, two old men, three Zanni and a servant.

The pattern experienced by the seventeenth-century troupe was repeated in the eighteenth, but much more rapidly. Improvised plays in Italian were soon replaced by plays partly or wholly written in French; the audience, its curiosity once satisfied, mostly stayed away from what it could not understand. Beginning in January 1718 entertainments that mixed Italian improvised scenes and scenes written in French increasingly held the stage.

Some were the work of Riccoboni and Biancolelli, while others were refurbished from the Gherardi collection. On 25 April 1718, however, slightly less than two years after it opened in Paris, the Comédie Italienne performed its first French play, *Le Naufrage au Port-à-l'Anglais* by Jacques Autreau. Gradually throughout the next two years the troupe enhanced its ability to perform in its adopted language, with more scenes by Biancolelli, more plays retrieved from the Gherardi repertory, and more scenarios devised by French playwrights. In the 1720–1721 season, the Italians offered a new play by Autreau, *Les Amants ignorants*, with very little Italian, and – on 17 October 1720 – Marivaux's first hit for the Comédie Italienne: *Arlequin poli par l'Amour*.

Marivaux wrote nine plays that were produced by the Comédie Italienne between 1720 and 1729. While *La Nouvelle colonie* (1729) had only one performance, most of the others were reasonably profitable in their initial runs and remained in the repertory. None came close to the great success among the French plays of the 1720s: Delisle de la Drevetière's *Timon le misanthrope*. Not as well known now as his *Arlequin sauvage*, *Timon* had thirty-three performances during its first run, with no need for a parody to prop it up, and could be counted on for decent houses for many years.

1730–1779

While the troupe had lost some old and added some new members in the 1730s, major changes came in the 1740s and with them a renewal of the Italian repertory. Tommaso Visentini died in August 1739 after a long illness, which kept the mask of Arlequin off the stage for several years. Beginning in November 1739, the troupe's search for a new Arlequin restored the improvised comedy to the stage of the Comédie Italienne. The first postulant for the coveted role was Antonio Constantini. Although he could 'sing, dance, play instruments, and do all the acrobatic routines', after a long trial period, he was rejected and a new candidate began a series of debuts on 18 April 1741. This was Carlo Bertinazzi, Carlin, who would play Arlequin until his death in 1783.

Although the Comédie Italienne continued into the 1750s with Italian actors and some Italian plays, the decade was characterised by the increasing importance of the French playwright and producer, Charles-Simon Favart, and his wife Justine, who might be best described as an eighteenth-century musical comedy star. She made her second debut at the Comédie Italienne in 1751 and was received with the share relinquished by Elena

Baletti, Madame Riccoboni. This transition marked in many ways the end of what remained of Luigi Riccoboni's troupe and his idea of the Italian theatre. Unlike the Italian actresses who preceded her, Madame Favart, as she was known, played no specific *emploi*, but could move freely from soubrette to amoureuse to paysanne to naïf to caractère (Campardon 1970, vol. 1, 208).

In 1762, largely due to the negotiations of Favart and his wife, the Comédie Italienne bought the privilege to perform musical theatre from the Opéra and merged with the Opéra Comique, a successful fair troupe. The merger established two separate but supposedly equal troupes, although the Italians were required by the new regulations 'to make themselves useful' as extras in the French troupe's plays. After many retirements only eight Italian actors remained, while the French troupe was twice as large. For eighteen years the Italians soldiered on while matters went from bad to worse.

In 1779, the decision was made to suppress the Italian plays and forcibly retire the remaining Italian actors, except for Carlin, who was spared because his character appeared in French as well as Italian plays. He continued to perform until his death in 1783. The principal cause for the suppression of the Italian troupe and the Italian repertory was financial. The Comédie Italienne, from its inception, had survived from crisis to crisis, saving itself with French scenes, French plays, parodies, ballets, ballet pantomimes and narrative fireworks. In 1760 Denis Papillon de la Ferté, whose job was to supervise the king's court entertainments, was asked to take charge of the Comédie Italienne and oversee its finances. It was so depleted financially, its theatre so in need of repair, that there seemed no way to save it. The merger with the Opéra-Comique was a temporary solution; when the Italian actors were dismissed years later it was largely to save money. If a full and coherent history of this troupe should ever be written, its author should pay a great deal of attention to the relationship among the royal bureaucracy, the actors, the repertory and money.

Finally, it should be said, if only briefly, that what the Italian actors brought to Paris over the course of two hundred years was a style of acting based on improvisation that was more natural, more immediate and more emotionally engaged than typical French acting. According to Luigi Riccoboni, who had much to say about it, 'the actor who plays à l'impromptu is more lively and more natural than the one who plays a memorised role; one feels more and consequently one speaks better. . . . To feel is the actor's greatest art; nothing is believeable unless it is the expression of something truly felt' (Riccoboni 2009: 534–5). Although the troupe's repertory changed radically during the years between 1716 and 1762, the continued performance of the Italian improvised repertory meant that the style of acting remained natural, centered in the 'qui va la,' the sense of immediacy created by improvisation which required the alertness of a sentry on guard.

It was their acting style that kept the troupe alive through all their financial vicissitudes. Even Diderot, who had nothing good to say about the 'insipid dialogue and absurd plots' the Italians offered to mid-century Paris, admitted in 1758 that in the 'Italian plays, our Italian actors played with more freedom than our French actors; they paid less attention to the audience. For hundred of moments they forgot the audience completely. I find in their action something, an 'I don't know what', that is original and effortless. Beyond their silliness, I see lighthearted people who are having fun, and who abandon themselves to their impassioned imaginations; and I prefer this intoxication to the stiff, heavy, and inflexible' (Diderot 1758: 155–6).

7

The Iberian Peninsula

María del Valle Ojeda Calvo

In a letter dated 29 January, 1568, Jacopo Strada, an artist at the court of Vienna, asked Emperor Maximilian II to grant a passport to a company of actors called the *Disiosi* and nicknamed *la compagnia del Ganassa*. They had the reputation of being 'the most excellent who have ever been heard' (Schindler 2005b: 112) and having appeared regularly at the court of the Gonzaga family in Mantua, they now wished to perform at the court of the emperor. It is possible that this request was the start of the international career of one of the most popular theatre companies in Italy in the sixteenth century. We do not know if the request was ever granted but we do know that Zan Ganassa, the stage name of Alberto Naselli, the Ferrara-born director of the company, was at the court of the emperor in Speyer in July and August 1750 (Schindler 2005b: 112–13). The occasion was the departure of Princess Anne to Spain, to become Queen Anne of Habsburg and of her sister Elizabeth to France on 24 October, where she was to marry Charles IX (Schindler 2005b: 113; 115–18). The following year, Ganassa was in France, where he gave both public and private performances at court, as he had been accustomed to do in Mantua (D'Ancona 1891: 445–62). The date of his arrival at the French court is still unknown. The first documented evidence concerning Italian players is a decree issued by Parliament on 15 September 1571, forbidding Italian actors to give public performances. Undoubtedly, parliament was taking advantage of the absence of Charles IX, who had left Paris in July 1571, to ban Ganassa's public performances (Gambelli 1993: 136). In June 1572 the king returned to Paris, where the Italian actors had presumably remained, and in August of that year they performed at the wedding of Margaret of Valois, the king's sister, to Henry of Navarre (Baschet 1882: 42–3). From Paris, Ganassa and his company moved to Madrid. Although it is not known with certainty when they left France,[1] it was probably after May 1574, the month of Charles IX's death. Their presence in Spain was first recorded in October of that year.

After their appearance in Madrid, the company ceased touring internationally but remained on the Iberian Peninsula for the next ten years, moving from Madrid to Seville to Toledo and finally to Valladolid. On 14 March 1584, Ganassa's wife, the actress Barbara Flaminia, withdrew her dowry from Lorenzo Spinola's bank in Madrid to enable them to travel back to Italy (García García 1992–1993: 367–9). Ganassa probably died shortly after his arrival there, a fact hinted at in the *Lament composed by Zan Salcizza and Zan Capella inviting all the philosophers, poets and porters of the valley to weep for the dead Zan Panza di Pegora, alias Simone, the Gelosi actor and seemingly welcoming him to heaven'* (Venice 1585) (Marotti and Romei 1991: 48).

Ganassa and his company of actors probably went to Madrid in the first place because he had been engaged to take part in the festivities at court. In the second half of the sixteenth century it was common for companies of Italian actors to tour abroad, under the protection of influential patrons (Arróniz 1969: 193 and 211). By examining the family connections that existed between the courts of Mantua, Vienna, Paris and Madrid, for example, we can easily retrace the company's movements. The Duke of Nevers was the brother of the Duke of Mantua; Philip II's cousins, Catherine and Eleanor, were married respectively to Francesco and Guglielmo Gonzaga, and the Queen of France was one of the Habsburgs who had already seen the Italian actors perform in Speyer.[2] On this, his first appearance in Madrid and first tour of the Iberian Peninsula, Ganassa was Italy's leading professional actor and was destined to change theatre practice in Spain. In October 1574, he funded the construction of a roof for the *Corral de la Pacheca,* one of the important commercial theatres in Madrid. The following year, in Seville, he sought permission to increase the number of days of the week on which performances could be held. This he had already done in France. In the same year, he requested the municipal authorities of Seville to supply him with the wagons necessary to stage the sacre rappresentazioni, which was performed as part of the Corpus Christi festivities. In the next few years, Ganassa continued to invest in renovating the *corrales* and was granted the right to perform comedies throughout the kingdom on two working days a week, in addition to normal performances on Sundays and feast days.

For Ganassa, modifying the way Spanish *corrales* (theatres) were constructed was a priority. For his plays he needed a stage with a covered roof, from which he could, for example, mount the machinery used for setting up and moving scenery. For his plays staged in Mantua and Speyer, he had used both pastoral and mythological scenery. In addition, he felt that a window was necessary to cast more light onto the stage, to compensate for the darkening effect of the roof construction. These innovations were to have enormous impact, becoming standard elements of the model on which most theatres on the Iberian Peninsula were later built. That the innovations were implemented so extensively is a reflection of the remarkable success enjoyed by Italian actors in Spain at the time. In addition, the actors' high level of professionalism allowed them to participate in the development of the commercial side of the theatre enterprise that was taking shape in those years in Spain.[3]

The extent of the success enjoyed by Ganassa and his players can be gauged by the large audiences they attracted and the profits they made in Madrid (Davis and Varey 1997) and by the rewards they received for their performances at the festivities connected with the Feast of Corpus Christi, starting in 1575 in Seville (Sentaurens 1984: 87–8; 217). Contemporary writers provide further evidence of their successes, stating that Italian *comici* devoted themselves to 'acting and performing comedies and other similar things in our language and in Italian', confirming what the *comici* themselves declared in a contract dated 1580 (García García 1992–1993: 361). Besides performing in the most important Spanish cities, Ganassa's company also gave private performances, both at court, for the *Consejo de Castilla*, and for noble families, for example for the wedding celebrations of the Duke of Infantado in the Palace of Guadalajara. On this last occasion, the duke wanted to have the performance recorded in a painting.[4]

An official document, drafted on the occasion of the creation of the company and registered in Madrid on 13 March 1580, includes the complete list of actors for the 1580–1581 season, confirming that the list had not changed since the preceding season of 1579–1580: Alberto Naselli, known as Ganassa, *capocomico* and first Zanni; Barbara Flaminia, his wife, in the role of his lover Ortensia; Vincenzo Botanelli, manager of the company, known as Curzio Romano (lover); Cesare dei Nobili, who played the female role of Francesca (servant); Abagaro Frescobaldi, whose stage name was Stefanelo Botarga (Magnifico); Giovan Pietro Pasquarello, alias Trastullo (second Zanni), who was responsible, together with the underage Scipione Graselli, for maintaining and looking after the company's props and costumes (in Spanish: *hato*); and finally, Giulio Vigliante and Giacomo Portalupo, who were paid less than the other actors and played the third female role of the lover Isabella (García García 1992–1993: 356–67).

This list of actors remained substantially the same up to March 1581, as evidenced by a document drafted that year and recording that Alberto

Naselli as *capocomico* (chief actor) and Vincenzo Botanelli as manager hired two Spanish musicians, Pedro Salcedo and Antonio Laso. The only significant difference was that Botarga was replaced by Carlo de' Masi. In the 1581–1582 season, Botarga left the company, thus breaking up the popular comic Zanni-Magnifico duo, whose '*Lament of Giovanni Ganassa with his Master Stefanello Bottarga on the Death of a Louse*' (*Lamento di Giovanni Ganassa con Meser Stefanello Bottarga, suo padrone, sopra la morte di un pedocchio*) was praised by many commentators and subsequently published by Cesare Rao (1562). In the same year he and his wife, the actress Luisa de Aranda, formed a company of their own. She was the widow of the famous Spanish *capocomico*, Juan Granado, who had died recently. How did Botarga fare with his Spanish company in the period from 1582 to 1588, after leaving the Ganassa company? A document of that year reports that Botarga was in Seville with other Italian actors (Giovan Maria Antonazone and Paulo Ferraro) and the *Compañía de representaciones de los italianos* (Ojeda Calvo 2007: 89–90).

These documents represent the only evidence we have regarding the composition of the company. Hence, it is not certain whether the troupe was the one that was brought over from France and to what extent its composition remained unvaried throughout their stay in Spain. The only changes we know about are the above-mentioned departure of Botarga and the coming of Carlo de' Massi, the musicians and a Spanish actor, García de Jaraba in 1583. It seems logical to assume that, being composed only of Italian actors, the company was formed before it set off for France and that its members remained together. Away from Italy, it would have been very difficult to find new actors who could adapt to the Italian actors' way of working.

We know that Ganassa's *company* achieved great success right from their first appearance on stage and, as documented by Ricardo de Turia in *El apologético de las comedias españolas in 1616,* 'earned both the applause and the money of people'. What we do not know is what their performances were like. Documents available in Spain do not provide any real answer, in particular because there are no surviving pictures. Not even reports or descriptions of performances have survived. The situation in Italy is different, but scholars of Spanish theatre have only in relatively recent years begun to study the available documents. In 1891, D'Ancona drew attention to the wealth of information contained in the correspondence of members of the court of Mantua. Thanks to detailed notes – such as those sent by Rogna to the Duke of Florence – the repertoires of the companies performing there between 1567 and 1568 are partly known.

One of these companies included Barbara Flaminia, future wife of Ganassa, and another Armani, *primadonna* of his company, until her death in 1568. According to Rogna's descriptions, these companies performed in both public spaces and palaces and had extensive repertoires, including comedies, tragedies, tragicomedies, pastorals and mythological plays. Their titles and contents are also known, one example being a tragedy based on an episode from *Orlando Furioso*. They enriched their performances with music, dances, mythological *intermedi* and, in some cases, with stage machinery. The real attractions for the audience, however, were their rich costumes and the skills of their actresses (D'Ancona 1891).

Further information has been provided by two manuscripts discovered later in Madrid. They have been attributed to Abagaro Frescobaldi, who is better known as Botarga (Ojeda Calvo 2007). The contents of these manuscripts illustrate Botarga's working method and his normal repertoire. He played the role of the Magnifico and had his own way of using the *Letter* by Calmo to create a certain verbal texture for this type of character (Ojeda Calvo 2004). One of these manuscripts (II-1586) reveals part of the repertoire played by Ganassa-Botarga's company in the 1580 season. The main part is taken up with the accounts for the months of April and May, but the last pages of the manuscript include titles of some of the plays they performed (*Cavalier Ingrato, Inocente fanciulo, Bravo falito, Cavallier Costante, Comedia del Intronati, Don Ramiro, La Persiana, Pazoamante, Tarquino, Formenti, Leone* or *Furtinovi*), as well as prose descriptions of some scenarios or plots complete with titles (*Formento, Ramiro, Costante, Leone, Furti, Ambasciatori, Grota, Doi Pazzi* and *Spada mortal*) of comedies, tragedies, tragicomedies and pastorals in their repertoire. Interestingly enough, these plays were mostly the ones also being played in Mantua and described by Rogna, the most obvious example being the tragedy based on *Orlando Furioso* mentioned earlier (Ojeda Calvo 2007). It is also interesting to note that on many occasions, the order in which Botarga's scenarios are sequenced seems to reflect that of the performance. For example, the three acts of any of the comedies were preceded by *intermedi*, or by the acts from a pastoral play or from a tragedy, though the core of the performance remained the *commedia*.

An analysis of these scenarios leads us to believe that the *comici*'s basic intention was to offer a multifaceted treatment of a single topic, for example, women's chastity. This was not, however, confined solely to the commedia dell'arte. The classical comedy *Cofanaria* by Francesco D'Ambra, for instance, was performed at the court of Florence in 1565, with *intermedi* dealing with the psyche and the story of Cupid. As declared in the prologue to the comedy, the purpose was to 'make it seem that what gods did in the fable of *intermedi* – under the spell of a superior power – men would do in the comedy'.

Ganassa was such a popular performer that he remained on the Iberian Peninsula for ten years. In 1584, probably due to illness, he returned to Italy. The other members of the company remained some time longer in Spain. Later, they broke up and tried their luck individually in Portugal, France or Italy. Some of them joined other troupes in Italy – Cesare dei Nobili was taken on by the Desiosi in Genoa in 1586 – while others, like Giovan Pietro Pasquarello, continued their wanderings in Spain. According to Aurelia Leyva (1997: 13) Pasquarello may be identified with 'Juan Pedro italiano andante en la corte' who, at the beginning of June 1587, lent eighteen ducats to Pedro de Plata, *autor* of commedie (this is highly probable because he wrote only 'Joan Pietro' in the two documents of 1580 where his signature appears). Jaime Sánchez Romeralo (1990: 126) reports that in 1586, Pasquarello, together with Giacomo Portalupo, Scipione Graselli and Giulio Vigliante – all highly regarded members of Ganassa's troupe – formed an excellent company with other Italian actors and with the Spanish actress Maria de Baeza. This may be the same troupe which created the *conpania nueba de los ytalianos* performing in Madrid at the Teatro del Principe from February to 5 March – Shrove Tuesday – 1585. This would mean that the actors had already formed the company before Ganassa left for Italy. There are records of performances given by the *Compañía de los Cortesanos* on 7 and 14 July 1585 but it is not known for certain whether this was the new company formed by the Italian actors (Davis and Varey 1997: 324). Vigliante later returned to Italy and was performing with the Gelosi by 1590 (Rasi 1912: 758). Finally, in 1593 Portalupo became *capocomico* in Lisbon, a fact recorded in the account books of the *Hospital Real de Todos os Santos* on 29 December (Bolaños and Reyes Peña 1990: 51).

The popularity and success enjoyed by Ganassa and his company of actors probably encouraged other Italian actors to move to Spain. For example, Massimiano Milamino's *Los italianos nuevos* went to Valladolid and performed there in 1581. However, as can be inferred from the administrative records of the city, they were unable to live up to the expectations generated by their predecessors. The company had a short life. The *capocomico* was killed in a brawl in 1582 and the remaining actors joined other Spanish companies. The same occurred in 1592 when an actor bearing the name Ganassa (Juan Jorge) arrived in Spain. He too was unable to live up to the high expectations generated, in this case, by the name he was appearing under and was soon forced to join a Spanish company.

The *Confidenti*, an Italian theatre company owned and managed by the Martinelli Brothers, including Tristano, the first great Harlequin, in their troupe of performers, fared much better. They arrived in Spain in 1587; it was one of the destinations on their international tour, on which they had already made very successful appearances in Antwerp, Lyon, Paris and London. Significantly, the tour had started from Mantua, which was ruled by the Gonzaga family, a family well established as patrons of the theatre (Ferrone 2006). Their appearances on the Iberian Peninsula were so successful that, as far as is known, they remained there from 18 November 1587 until October of the following year, if not longer. They performed in Madrid and other important Spanish cities.

At one of their performances in the capital, Lope de Vega, still a novice playwright at the time, was in the audience. In October 1588 in Seville, the company fired the musician Juan Bautista Carrillo, accusing him of not knowing *tonadas* (traditional songs) and thus, of not being useful.[5]

The role of the Confidenti company in the history of Spanish theatre has been exaggerated in the past; it was thought that the company was responsible for the introduction of women onto the Spanish stage. It is true that the women of the company did present a petition to the authorities seeking permission to perform on stage. At the time, women were generally banned from appearing on stage in Spain. Their petition was granted on condition that they did not play male roles. However, Italian actresses were not the first to be allowed to perform on Spanish stages. Recent archival research has revealed that Spanish actresses had been acting on a regular basis since the 1570s. Furthermore, a record of litigation against the ban dated 1587 shows that Spanish actresses working in Madrid at the time also presented a petition. They were led by two women, Mariana Vaca and María de la O., who were already established as actresses in the 1570s.

There is no doubt, however, that the performances of Ganassa, Botarga and the Harlequin, Tristano, had a huge impact on Iberian audiences in the sixteenth century. This is confirmed by surviving records from contemporary authors and commentators. Juan de Pineda (1589: 350r), for example, reported that a doctor skimped on food and gave up almost all his day's earnings, simply in order to be able to go with his wife to see a performance by the Italian actors. A character of a *loa* (prologue), possibly in a play by Lope de Vega, commented that even after many years absence, people yearned for Ganassa: 'sisospirava per Ganassa', (Antonucci and Arata 1995: 85). In 1581, Pedro de Saldaña, a Spanish *capocomico*, cancelled his own performance to attend a performance by his Italian rivals. The Portuguese author, Tomé Pinheiro da Veiga mentioned Ganassa and the Harlequin, Tristano in his *Fastiginia* in 1605. Lope de Vega reported that even the austere King Philip II laughed at a joke during a performance by the Italians: Ganassa noticed that Botarga's fly was open and said to him: 'Master, for a dead bird, you opened the cage'. Lope de Vega himself was arrested in 1587 while attending a performance given by the Confidenti in the Corral del Príncipe. In his works he often mentions Italian theatre characters such as Ganassa, Botarga, Trastullo, Franceschina or the Harlequin, Tristano. That these characters were important to him is further emphasised by the fact that he chose the character of Botarga for the play he wrote for the celebrations surrounding the double royal wedding of Philip II with Margaret of Austria and of the Infanta Isabel with the Archduke Albert in 1599 in Valencia.

With the passing of time, and despite their considerable initial success, Italian *comici* went out of fashion. Names like Ganassa, Botarga and the Harlequin, Tristano came to exist only as memories or echoes in the works of authors like Lope de Vega. Spanish theatre companies and actors reconquered the stage on the Iberian Peninsula.[6] In France it was a different story – Italian actors continued to enjoy great popularity there for another century. It was not until the eighteenth century that Italian companies like those led by Bartoli[7] or by *truffaldino*, Antonio Sacchi were successful again in Madrid and Lisbon.[8]

That is another story and another commedia.

Notes

[1] It is worth noting that the account books of the *Espargne*, which offered this information, cannot be found in any archives for the years 1572 to 1574 and for the last years of Charles IX's life (Baschet 1882: 49).

[2] Since there is no historical record of Ganassa's presence in Italy from January 1570, it is possible that his troupe followed Elizabeth of Habsburg in her journey to France. Anne of Habsburg, newly married to her uncle Philip II, left for Spain on 1 July. The festivities continued at court until Elizabeth, married by proxy to Charles of Valois, left for France.

[3] In Portugal this probably happened later, perhaps in the 1580s. The first records of professional companies in Lisbon date back as far as 1582. Perhaps this is why Italian troupes arrived late in Portugal (Bolaños and Reyes Peña 1990: 69–70).

4 In the inventory of the sixth *Duque del Infantado*, Don Juan Hurtado de Mendoza, there is mention of 'seis quadricos de Ganassa de figuras diferentes de ganasa y arlequines en tabla con sus marcos que eran del dicho Duque Don Íñigo que se alló entre los demás vienes que dejó' (Sanz and García García 1995: 484). These paintings have not been found; at least, they are not part of the inheritance of Don Íñigo's heirs.

5 There is documentary evidence that they were in Seville in October 1588 and that they engaged the musicians Juan Baustista Carrillo and Alonso de Briones until Carnival Season in 1589 (Archivo Histórico de Sevilla, Secciónde Protocolos, Oficio XI, Leg. 6799, 21 October 1588, ff. 620v–622v.).

6 In Portugal too, where Spanish troupes performed throughout the seventeenth century, in particular in the years up to 1640. In that year, the Bragança dynasty ascended the throne, deposing the Habsburgs of Spain, who had reigned in Portugal since 1580.

7 In 1702 Francesco Bartoli's troupe arrived in Madrid, following Philip V and his court there and remaining in the capital until 1711 (Doménech Rico 2007).

8 Antonio Sacchi's troupe arrived in Lisbon from Genoa in November 1753 and remained there at least until 1757, though it is probable that they remained until 1759 (Almeida 2007: 177–97).

8

German-Speaking Countries
M A Katritzky

Within a decade of the first definite records of commedia dell'arte performances in Italy itself, and even before Italian troupes transported this
new type of theatre to France, Spain, the Netherlands or England in the
1570s, it had become an established and popular feature of south German
court culture.

The 1568 Munich Wedding

When Crown Prince Wilhelm of Bavaria married Princess Renée of
Lorraine in Munich in February 1568, commedia dell'arte contributed
to the festivities in three contexts. Its stock costumes were popular in
masquerades, and professional Italian actors in the roles of the old Venetian master Pantalone and his rustic young servant Zanni performed short
comic routines together on several occasions as masked entertainers. Addi-
tionally, at least once, on 8 March 1568, a full-length commedia dell'arte
play was performed, albeit not by a visiting professional mixed-gender
Italian troupe, but by male courtiers. The account of this play in the book
on the 1568 wedding festival published by one of its actors, Massimo
Troiano, a Neapolitan tenor then employed as a Munich court musician,
is widely acknowledged to be the earliest comprehensive description of
any commedia dell'arte performance, north or south of the Alps (Katritzky
2006: 44–83).[1]

The central comic master-servant pair of the full-length performance
was played by the internationally renowned Flemish composer and Munich
choir master Orlando di Lasso, as the elderly Venetian Magnifico, and
Troiano as his servant Zanni. That it was, according to Troiano, staged on
a last-minute whim of Prince Wilhelm (presumably using props and
costumes already to hand), suggests that the commedia dell'arte's theatrical tradition in Munich predates February 1568. In January 1569, Prince
Wilhelm called on his Augsburg bankers, the Fuggers, to pay out substantial

sums to 'Jacob of Venice, together with his company', and to the cloth merchant and tailor responsible for costuming them. The four Italian actors played at the Bavarian court at least until 17 February. The continuing popularity of commedia dell'arte performances at the Bavarian court during the 1570s is indicated by Lasso's piecemeal engagement, on Prince Wilhelm's behalf, of what amounted to a small Italian court troupe (Katritzky 2006: 62–3; Trautmann 1887: 222, 244–5). In 1575, bankruptcy forced Wilhelm to sack many court musicians, including all his players. Soon after, he commissioned two major fresco cycles commemorating them at his country seat, Castle Trausnitz. As the commedia dell'arte's most substantial early modern iconographic record, the thirty-two walls of life-size frescoes of the so-called 'Fools' Staircase' linking the castle's six storeys, and sixteen scenes on the ceiling frieze of Wilhelm's adjacent study, represent an unprecedented visual record of sixteenth-century commedia dell'arte costumes and performance practice.[2]

In 1579, the by now deeply religious Wilhelm succeeded his father. As Bavaria's ruling duke, Wilhelm fully supported the Jesuits and their religious drama, and passed elaborate by-laws shielding his sons and subjects from what he increasingly viewed as the deeply negative influence of the Italian players. Commedia dell'arte players were only invited to Wilhelm's court once more, in 1584, when Venturino Casparino of Venice, a core member of his court troupe in the previous decade, received a modest sum for playing with his troupe at the Munich wedding festivities of Georg Ludwig von Leuchtenberg to Maria Salome von Baden (Martino 2010: 17–18; Schindler 2005a: 8; Trautmann 1887: 249–51).

Habsburg and Other German Court Patronage

The 1568 Munich performance marks a significant watershed for the commedia dell'arte in Germany. Prince Wilhelm's younger brother, Ferdinand of Bavaria, brought the Italian fashion for commedia dell'arte performances at court weddings to Germany. Here, it became a prestigious badge of international cultural sophistication within the elite group who could both understand and afford it. During his journey to Florence in 1565 to represent his father at the wedding festivities of his mother's sister, Johanna of Austria to Francesco de' Medici, Ferdinand saw many professional Italian performances, including at least one full-length commedia dell'arte play. He shared his love of commedia dell'arte with his Habsburg uncle Archduke Ferdinand, whom he accompanied with an incognito group of German noblemen to the Venice carnival in 1579, where they watched several private and public performances by the Gelosi troupe. In 1598, Archduke Ferdinand also enjoyed Venetian commedia dell'arte performances on the outdoor stages of St Mark's Square (Katritzky 2006: 59–74, 93–5; Trautmann 1887: 234–5).

The earliest professional Italian players recorded in German cities and courts include 'Italians' who performed for the Habsburgs in Innsbruck (1548); a four-strong Venetian troupe with their interpreter Anthony of Bolzano, who stopped off in Nördlingen and Nuremberg on their way to the imperial court (1549); unnamed Italians in Nuremberg in 1551; the six-strong troupe of Bartholome of Venice (1559) and five-strong troupe of Johann of Mantua (1560) in Nördlingen; Juan of Venice, who entertained Maximilian II (1566–1567); and Sperindi of Venice and Alexander of Polonia, who requested permission to 'perform and demonstrate their skills in acrobatics and comedies' in Strasbourg in 1567 (Trautmann 1887: 225–6.). These pre-1568 tours mostly involved small all-male groups, rather than full-strength mixed-gender Italian troupes of upwards of ten players, performing full-length commedia dell'arte plays, of the type affordable only to the wealthiest German patrons.

Italian was accessible to those who knew Latin, and many German courts' cultural and linguistic links with Italy were strengthened by inter-marriage with Italian nobility. The fashion for commedia dell'arte at such courts, tentatively pioneered in Munich in 1568, was resoundingly endorsed by the imperial festivals for Anna and Elisabeth of Austria in 1570. Alberto Naseli of Ferrara and his wife Barbara Flaminia of Rome played with their troupe at court in Vienna in 1569, before moving on to Prague, where they were joined by Giovanni Tabarino of Venice and his wife Polonia, whose troupe played at the imperial Diets of Linz and Pressburg (Bratislava) in 1568 and 1569. Both troupes performed at the 1570 Prague proxy wedding festivities for Emperor Maximilian II's daughter Anna to Philip II of Spain. They then followed Anna's sister Elisabeth, betrothed to Charles IX, to Paris, performing en route at her proxy wedding festivities at the imperial Diet of 1570 in Speyer. Naseli eventually went on from Paris to Madrid. Tabarino's troupe returned to Vienna for the 1571 wedding festivities of Archduke Karl II to Maria of Bavaria and again in 1574. From 1587, when she was widowed, to her death in 1593, Polonia ran the imperial Viennese tennis court as a theatre (Schindler 2005a: 9; Trautmann 1887: 228–30).

Following the Prague and Speyer weddings, Italian troupes played seasons by invitation of Emperors Maximilian II and then Rudolf II in Linz (1576) and Vienna (1571–1576, 1583); Archduke Ferdinand II in Castle

Ambras, Innsbruck (1589); and other rulers in Graz (1603), Regensburg (1613), Linz and Vienna (1614) and Innsbruck (1614, 1626, 1628) (Martino 2010: 16; Schindler 2010: 92–7; Trautmann 1887: 232–3). Emperor Matthias showed his appreciation of Piermaria Cecchini ('Fritellino') by raising him to the nobility in Linz in 1614. Cecchini's last recorded German season was for the double imperial coronation of Ferdinand III and Eleonora of Mantua in Vienna and Prague in 1627–1628 with the Fedeli troupe, led by Giovanni Battista Andreini ('Lelio'), who left Vienna only in 1629. Tristano Martinelli ('Harlequin') dropped out of this 'all-star' troupe shortly before they departed Italy (Schindler 2010: 107–23; Trautmann 1887: 230–1). Like so many, this tour was facilitated by Habsburg-Italian intermarriage. No further commedia dell'arte troupes visited Vienna until 1660.

Sometimes, troupes stopped off en route to or from imperial engagements. 'Dottore florentinischen *buffone*' received 120 Gulden for playing at the Munich court in 1609, and Giovanni Paolo Agiocohia ('il dottor da Bologna') played there several times between 1603 and 1616 (Trautmann 1887: 250). German courts unable to afford full troupes found other ways of incorporating elements of the commedia dell'arte into their festivals. On 18 June 1585, the ninth entry for a tournament at a Düsseldorf court wedding featured six knights costumed as three pairs of commedia dell'arte masters and servants. 'Stephanello putargo, Il consilier de la singioria de Venetia', the stage name chosen by their thirty-eight-year-old leader, Duke Karl II von Hohenzollern, was first created by Abagaro Francobaldi of Padua, who toured Spain in the late 1570s starring as Stefanelo Botarga to Alberto Naseli's Zan Ganassa in an immensely popular master-servant double act celebrated in diverse texts and images (Graminaeus 1587).[3] Duke Karl's name choice indicates the pan-European interest generated by the commedia dell'arte's international stars. Tournament masquerade groups were typically mounted on thoroughbred horses, led by court musicians. Duke Karl's group, by contrast, perched on donkeys loaded with bales of hay, led by two *buffone* costumed as Pantalone and Zanni. The comic routines with which these unidentified Italian professional actors diverted the tournament spectators included mounting and dismounting a horse, playing tricks with their hats and cloaks, wielding a rustic harrow, singing comic Italian songs to a viola and other acrobatics.

Duke Karl served as a Munich courtier in 1568, during the festivities for Prince Wilhelm of Bavaria's wedding. Deeply impressed by its commedia dell'arte performances, he drew on them again for a festival tournament entry in 1598, when he led a company of ten knights. Their costumes are wrongly identified in Jakob Frischlin's court-sponsored printed festival book. Felix Platter, attending the festival in his capacity as court physician to the bride's brother-in-law, correctly names them as various commedia dell'arte servants (Katritzky 2006: 47, 96–102; Katritzky 2012: 117–26). An Italian master-servant duo was featured at the 1613 Munich wedding festivities for the Catholic convert Pfalzgraf Wolfgang Wilhelm of Neuburg to Princess Magdalene of Bavaria. One of the guests, Augsburg art dealer Philipp Hainhofer, appreciated their version of the '*lazzi* of the hat', already featured in Düsseldorf in 1585: 'two masked Italians performed while we were at the dinner table, one of whom metamorphosised his white felt hat in at least thirty ways'. A month earlier, in the company of Wolfgang Wilhelm's younger brother Pfalzgraf Augustus at the Regensburg Diet, Hainhofer had enjoyed a one-man play performed by an Italian: 'just him alone, so he kept changing his pronunciation and costume' (Martino 2010: 24; Trautmann 1887: 231–2). Official festival books, the formal reports of invited guests and the informal travellers' tales communicated by their socially diverse retinues disseminated such festival commedia dell'arte performances far beyond their German host courts.

1618 to 1770

Raging across central Europe from 1618 to 1648, the Thirty Years' War brutally devastated the German population and its culture. During the half-century preceding 1618, Italian troupes accepted numerous invitations to play at Habsburg courts, and Germany became an attractive, lucrative hub for itinerant foreign performers of every type. During the war decades, musical plays featuring commedia dell'arte stock roles, performed by court singers rather than visiting Italian actors, were staged at the 1622 Diet of Ödenburg (Sopron) and in Vienna in 1624 and 1625, while the 1626 Innsbruck wedding festivities for Archduke Leopold and Claudia de' Medici included a 'balletto italiano' (Schindler 2010: 102–7, 123). One of the few Italians to venture into Germany during the two decades between the Fedeli troupe's Habsburg-sponsored season of 1627–1629 and the end of this war was the Florentine *buffone* Capra, who toured from Munich to Vienna in 1641 (Trautmann 1887: 250). Some of the most detailed early modern descriptions of commedia dell'arte performances on either side of the Alps are by German travellers and students, such as Hippolytus Guarinonius or Thomas Platter the Younger. Such reports, and the numerous colourful depictions of performing quack troupes brought back from Venice in the friendship albums of German noblemen, students and journeymen fuelled a widespread late sixteenth-century fashion for commedia dell'arte in the German-speaking regions (Katritzky 2007: 61–72, 221–30; Katritzky 2012: 215–43). However, unpredictable weather conditions and linguistic barriers lessened the commercial appeal of German market-playing for Italian troupes, and by mid century, German court interest in Italian and English performers had in any case waned in favour of French theatre. Although central Europe attracted significant traffic in commedia dell'arte troupes again after the war years, most relied on public as well as court patronage and many were entirely dependent on eking out their living supporting quacks on market squares.

During the 1650s, the troupes of Pietro Polombara and Francesco Narici ('Trapola') were regularly invited to play at court in Innsbruck. In 1660, Andrea ('Fabricio') and Angela d'Orso brought to Vienna troupe, including the young Domenico Biancolelli ('Arlecchino'), future star of the Parisian *Comédie Italienne*, and his mother Isabella Biancolelli Franchini ('Colombina') (Schindler 2010: 124–31). The twenty-strong mixed-gender troupe of Giovanni Nanini ('il dottore comico'), invited from Venice by Duke Maximilian II Emanuel of Bavaria, stayed in Munich from 1685 to 1686, before touring public and court venues in Augsburg, Nürnberg, Prague and Dresden, where they gained the coveted status of the Elector's official troupe, permitted to style themselves: 'Churfürstlich sächsische italiänische Comoedianten'. From 1697, they played for at least two years in Vienna. Nanini was replaced in Munich by a twenty-two-strong Mantuan court troupe, which returned to Italy in June 1587. Meanwhile the duke, greatly impressed by Francesco Calderoni ('Silvio') and Agata Caterina Vitaliani ('Flaminia') at the 1687 Venetian carnival, invited their troupe to Munich that same year. They took twenty-nine chests of costumes and props back with them to Mantua in 1691, but returned in 1696 to play in Brussels, where Maximilian II Emanuel represented the Spanish Habsburgs from 1692 to 1701, then in Augsburg (1702), before settling for good in Vienna.

Exceptionally, destinations on the lengthy tours of the Venetian Sebastiano di Scio ('Harlekino') included Stockholm and Copenhagen as well as Kiel, Celle, Berlin, Leipzig, Dresden, Prague and Brno. During the years 1687 to 1711, his troupe staged German and Italian language plays, puppet plays, tightrope shows and other acrobatics, in court and market settings. Scio's outdoor street performances showcased the peddling of his own 'orvietan', 'elixir', 'balsamo sympatico' and other patent medicines. In 1710, Scio's troupe played in Vienna with the troupe of Tommaso Ristori, which toured Saxony, Poland and Bohemia from its base at August the

Strong's Dresden court from 1714, playing in Teplice in 1721 and Prague in 1723. From the 1690s, converted tennis courts in Vienna again attracted Italian troupes, including that of Giovanni Tommaso Danese of Piedmont ('Tabarino'). He arrived in 1692 and, like Scio, alternated playing at court with public performances, some accompanied by the sale of medicines (Scherl 2010: 150–3; Schindler 2005a: 14; Schindler 2010: 135–43; Trautmann 1887: 258–63).[4] Records for the numerous small Italian quack troupes touring Northern Europe at this time are sparse. Margaret Cavendish vividly describes the performance practice and medical strategies of one she observed at an Antwerp carnival fair of the 1650s (Katritzky 2007: 1–16).

The commedia dell'arte's continuing impact on German stages, court and visual culture was increasingly mediated by actors of Italian origin who made Paris their permanent base from the 1640s onwards. These *Comédie Italienne* players, banished by Louis XIV in 1696, only returned to Paris in 1716. In 1697, their leader Angelo Constantini, who played Harlequin and created the role of Mezzetin, brought some of them to Dresden as the court players of Friedrich August I, Elector of Saxony ("August the Strong"), to perform at his court festivals and carnivals. August the Strong had already significantly encouraged the German fashion for commedia costumes in court parades, pantomimes, carnival masquerades and porcelain figurines. In 1693, two tournament teams competing at his wedding celebrations were costumed as Truffaldini and Scaramuzzi. The carnival celebrations following his 1694 accession featured a 'Masquerade of the Italian Comedy' of 23 January 1695, with six groups of nine courtiers costumed as Harlequini, Truffaltini, Scaramuzi, Dottori, Pantaloni and Spaciferri. At his grand carnival 'Caroussel-Comique' of 17 February 1722, eight quadrilles of courtiers and nobility in commedia-inspired costume were led by Scaramuzo, Crispino, Harleqvino, Pantalone, Dottore, Brighella, Policinello and Capitano. In Prague in 1718, Claude Rosidor's French company presented the *Comédie Italienne*-inspired comedies *Arlequin enchanteur* and *La fausse coquette*; in 1749 the Munich court engaged the Italian harlequin Giuseppe Falchi to star in their French court troupe, performing the repertoire of the *Comédie Italien*. Andrea Bertoldi's troupe, in Warsaw and Dresden from 1738 to 1756, also played in this French tradition, whose influence shapes the Hall of Masks at the Bohemian Český Krumlov Castle (Czech Republic). Entirely covered with scenes featuring costumed actors and courtiers at a carnival masquerade, the vast walls of this ballroom, painted in 1748 by Josef Lederer, are the first commedia themed decorative scheme in German-speaking Europe of comparable scale to that of Castle Trausnitz (Scherl 2010: 150).

Caroline Neuber, Germany's leading actress, dealt the commedia dell'arte a decisive blow in 1737, when, backed by the playwright Johann Christoph Gottsched, she called for Harlequin to be banished from the German stage. A few Italian troupes, such as Francesco Ferrari's, which toured Brno, Nuremberg and Innsbruck in the 1750s, or that of Giuseppe Franceschini, son of one of Ferrari's actors, which toured around Olomouc, Brno, Ljubljana and Graz into the 1760s, continued to stage commedia plays in the tradition of Goldoni in the German-speaking lands. However, by 1770, the puppet plays, operettas and pantomime of itinerant Italians in Germany contained only pale reflections of the commedia dell'arte, and the commedia dell'arte itself had been thoroughly absorbed into vernacular German performance culture (Trautmann 1887: 266; Katritzky 2007, 261; Scherl 2010: 152–6).[5]

Notes

[1] On this performance and other early modern German records of the commedia dell'arte, see Martino 2010. The fundamental publications on Italian players in pre–1770 Germany are Trautmann 1887, Martino and De Michele 2010 and the essays of Otto Schindler (1943–2008), who had planned to summarise his research into Italian actors in the Habsburg territories in an English monograph co-authored with the present author. On the Italians' German tours within the European context, see Schindler 2005a; Henke 2008.

[2] Illustrated: Katritzky 2006: 364–71. In 1962, fire destroyed the ceiling frieze and badly damaged the staircase frescos.

[3] The ninth tournament entry is described in folios Pi^v-Ri^r. This quote: Qi^r.

[4] On Scio see Dahlberg, whose meticulous archival research emphasises the extreme rarity of pre–1700 Scandinavian tours by Italians (1992: 223–4, 234–8).

[5] On the commedia dell'arte's impact on German culture, see Hansen (1984); Rudin (2000); and essays in Martino and De Michele (2010).

9

Eighteenth-Century Russia

Laurence Senelick

Tsar Peter I's imposition of European manners, science and governance on a closed and conservative Russian society extended to the performing arts. It was during Peter's reign (1685–1725) that such outlandish words as *aktyor* (actor), *amfiteatr* (amphitheatre), *balet* (ballet), *bilet* (ticket), *drama, p'esa* (play) and *teatr* (theatre) were grafted on to the Slavonic tongue from German, occasionally via Polish and Ukrainian.[1] They were needed to express phenomena newly arrived on the Russian scene.

Even before descriptive words existed, European-style drama had been introduced to the Russian court by Peter's father Tsar Aleksey Mikhaylovich, who recruited the Lutheran pastor Johann Gottfried Gregory (1631–1675) to compose and mount a play based on the book of Esther. *Artaxerxes,* interspersed with dance and orchestral music, played on 17 October 1672 for a consecutive ten hours before the seated Tsar and his standing courtiers (with the women behind a grill). Gregory's subsequent 'mysteries' were enlivened by a *shutovskaya persona* or comedian, personified as the outcast figure of the public executioner (Abhorson in *Measure for Measure* is cognate as is Jack Ketch in the traditional Punch-and-Judy saga). In *Artaxerxes* the buffoon appears as Mops, a hangman who dispatches Haman at the end. *Judith* doubled its sanguinary climax with a comic counterpart, for the decapitation of Holofernes was parodied in the mock execution of the soldier Susakim, 'beheaded' by a fox's tail wielded by the servant-maid Abra. *Bajazet and Tamburlaine (Bajazet i Tamerlan,* 1675) introduced the German figure Pickelhäring as a thief of soldiers' food and wine, comic relief evidently copied from various scripts of the *Englische Komödianten,* those players who travelled Central Europe with a simplified repertoire of Elizabethan and Jacobean plays. Pickelhäring had originated as Pickelhering in a play by Richard Reynolds in 1618 (Pesenti 1996: 51–4).

The personal taste of Aleksey's heir Peter I was for *trionfi,* fireworks and jesters which led him to attempt to naturalise the Feast of Fools and

April Fool's Day. In 1702 Johann Christoph Kunst, an 'eminent master of theatrical sciences', was recruited in Danzig to transport a troupe of nine German-speaking actors to Moscow. A Hall of Comedy was built for them on Red Square in three weeks' time. After Kunst's death in 1703, the German goldsmith Otto Fürst took over and operated the theatre until 1707, when continued public apathy led to its closure. Complaints about Fürst cited his ignorance of Russian ways, which is certainly evinced by his repertoire, patched together from German adaptations of foreign operas and comedies, translated into a pidgin Russian by embassy clerks and adapted to the presumably elemental tastes of his audience. Not untypical is the five-act comedy *Prince Pickle-Herring or Jodelet His Own Gaoler* (*Prints Pikel'-Gyaring ili Zhodelet. Samyy svoy tyur'movyy zaklyuchnik*) loosely adapted from a play by Thomas Corneille, *Le Geôlier de soi-même.* This macaronic medley yoked the Anglo-German clown to a French zany, first played in Paris by the farceur Jean Bedeau; in France the character had died with him in 1660.

In 1720, towards the end of his reign, Peter proffered an invitation to actors 'who could speak Slavonic or Czech', but had no takers. Only a foreign circus troupe, headed by the *Starke Mann* Johann Eckenberg, came through Petersburg in 1719 and again in 1723–1724 (Vsevolodskiy-Gerngross 1929: vol. I, 335). It put on German equivalents of harlequinades, this time partnering Pickelherring with Hanswurst: the comic character in many of these interludes was called Gaer, possibly from *Geiger,* violinist. In the *Interlude of Gaer's Wedding,* he introduces himself as a Russian Harlequin ('Garlintin rossiskiy'). *Gaer* became a generic term in Russian for a buffoon and survives in Chekhov's *The Cherry Orchard,* imbedded in the name of the feckless landowner Gaev.

Despite the traces of Jodelet and Arlequin, it was not until 1728–1729, during the reign of Peter II, that a freelance *bande* of French players, Jacques Renaud and his family, played to a mixed audience in Petersburg and Moscow (Berkov 1957: 46–57; Mooser 1948: 31). Little is known of them except that the five schematic comedies they performed included two from the Théâtre Italien of Gherardi. For the most part, however, the same xenophobia that segregated non-Russian diplomats, merchants and artisans into the so-called German suburb confined foreign actors to court circles.

Theatre historians once believed that the first true commedia dell' arte troupe visited Russia sometime between 1733 and 1735; this was deduced from the Russian translation of the scenarios of comedies and interludes played by Italian actors in St Petersburg during those years (Lo Gatto 1954). Thanks to newly discovered documents, it is now known that an Italian ensemble of twenty-two actors arrived in Moscow from the Polish court on 15 February 1731. The original source of this troupe was the dramatic company brought to Dresden by Duke Frederick Augustus I. When the duke was elected King of Poland, he transferred the theatre to Warsaw. Fluctuating political events kept it moving between the two cities. The company's leader was the Arlecchino Antonio Costantini and it reached its maximum size of thirty when, in 1715, he merged it with the troupe of the Coviello Tomasso Ristori.

The performers who came to St Petersburg were headed by Tomasso' s son, the composer Giovanni Alberto Ristori. Tomasso himself led the *commedia* sector of the troupe and, with two assistants, served as machinist and set-designer. The company was an experienced one, including Andrea Bertoldi as Pantalone, Natale Bellotti (just recovered from a fever) as Arlecchino, Carlo Malucelli (1650–1747) as il Dottore, Cafanio as Brighella and Rosalia Fantaria as first Amorosa. Barely a week after their arrival, they played at court on a portable stage before an audience of six hundred a comedy of amorous intrigues, *The Happy Cheat*, and a musical pantomime, *Velasco and Tilla*. Perhaps because few in the audience, including the Empress Anna Ioannovna, understood Italian, the pantomime was applauded more warmly than the comedy, but as the spectators became attuned to the conventions of the genre, the entertainments increased in popularity and complexity (Starikova 2000: 148–9, 152–3).

In August 1731, the next arrivals constituted a company exclusively of Italian singers and musicians, recruited in Germany and headed by conductor Johann Hübner and impresario Giuseppe Avoglio; this company alternated its chamber-music performances with those of the comedians, fostering a taste for Italian music and opening the way for the castrato Johann Dreyer (nicknamed 'il Tedeschino' or the dear little German). However, the *commedia* players' stay was brief: they departed on New Year's Eve, 1731 and disbanded in Dresden. Tomasso Ristori died the following year, 1733.

The vacuum was filled by Persian acrobats, who had already entertained at the Empress's coronation, and the German company of Johann-Peter Hilferding (1710–1769) and Johann-Christoph Siegmund (1705–1747), 'director of German comedy', which performed miniature burlesques. Although its contingent included an Arlecchino named Scolari, otherwise unknown to fame, the Germans were entirely put in the shade by a second

Italian *commedia* troupe, recruited in Venice, which arrived in summer 1733. These seasoned players were to perform in St Petersburg for nearly two years (Ferrazzi 2000; Pagani 2007; Starikova 1989: 80–92). The names of the actors were given in their passports in a Russified form, so that Pyotr Miro stood for Pietro Mira, a fiddler and comic actor, whose playing of Pedrolino won him the nickname Pedrillo or Petrillo at the Russian court, where he was to reside until the Empress's death. Others listed were the singer Alessandra Stabilla and her mother Apollonia; Ferdinando Colombo, an Arlecchino, and his wife, a dancer; Pietro Petrici, a singing comedian; Camillo Gonzaga, and Antonio Fioretti (d. 1761). The most notable visitors were the Sacco family: the actor called great by Carlo Goldoni, Giovanni Antonio Sacco, known as Truffaldino (1708–1788); his sisters and their mother and father Gaetano, another Truffaldino, who was to organise the Italian opera in St Petersburg and die in Moscow in 1735. The company's fourteen Italian comedies and three musical interludes offered a more impressive repertoire than anything previously seen in Russia.

A letter by General Lefort testifies that the Empress Anna Ioannovna 'derived great satisfaction from the comedies and that her satisfaction might be the greater, she hopes that these comedies will be translated into Russian and then played on stage, so that one might better understand the plot and gestures that accompany the dialogue' (Starikova 1995). This hope was in fact a command, leading the academician Stählin to translate the short librettos into German which were in turn translated into Russian by Count Vasiliy Levenvol'd-Trediakovskiy and printed in an edition of a hundred copies by the Academy of Sciences.[2] The stock characters included, along with the standard *commedia* masks, the familiar Italian gambler, the opera impresario in the Canary Islands, and the conventional Molièrean miser and hypochrondriac.

Trediakovskiy's collection of scenarios has led some scholars to surmise that the improvised comedy played by the Italian imports relied not solely on action (slapstick, disguises and mix-ups) but also on speech. There are many references to imitating a character's dialect and, in *Harlequin's Disguises*, speaking like an ox 'in the Czech tongue'. No one mask is prominent as the leading character; rather the ensemble common to the plays is a generic quartet of master, servant, lover and beloved, with the frequent pairing of Arlecchino-Brighella and Arlecchino-Smeraldina. One historian has suggested that the Russian amateur theatre adopted these types as calques for native comic characters (Pesenti 1996: 123).

The repertoire was amplified with another twelve Italian comedies and five musical interludes, aided by the arrival in April or May 1735 of another company of *commedia* players, recruited by Pietro Mira from some of the best performers of the period. The composer and conductor Francesco Araja; Casanova's mother Giovanna (known as Zanetta, c. 1709–1776); the Dresden Arlecchino Antonio Costantini, more an acrobat than an actor; another Arlecchino Carlo Bertinazzi (Carlino, 1710–1783), who would join the Comédie-Italienne in Paris in 1741; five dancers including Giulia Cortesi, the scene designer Bartolomeo Tarsia and the machinist Carlo Gibelli. It became known as the Italian Company and, as a sponsoring body, incorporated other foreigners engaged at court, including Karoline Neuber's German dramatic troupe in 1740. The strength of the ensemble enabled it to stage more elaborate comedies and even a tragedy, as well as the first *opera seria* in Russia, *La Forza dell'amore e dell'odio* (*Sila lyubvi i nenavisti*, 1736), and to introduce such novelties as dance in the intervals between the acts. Its repertoire differed from that of its precursors in mixing characters from chivalric romance with the traditional masks and adding a modicum of psychological shading to the situations.

Few of the leading performers regarded their stay in Russia as anything more than a lucrative tour, and so returned to Europe. By 1737, there were not enough foreign players left in St Petersburg to populate a full production, so native talent had to step into the breach. Anna Ioannovna, constantly in search of fresh diversions and still frustrated by the incomprehensible Italian dialogue, ordered, in the arbitrary manner peculiar to despots, the Archbishop of Novgorod Feofan Prokopovich to write plays. His prolific output, based on religious themes, was performed by students of the Kiev Academy where he was rector and professor of rhetoric. Another initiative resulted in plays staged by the pages of the Cadet Corps, some of them directed by Trediakovskiy: This repertoire included both imitations of Jesuit school drama and such Russian folk-tales as that of the witch Baba Yaga. These amateur efforts, inspired in part by the example of the foreign troupes, were to evolve into the Russian literary drama.[3]

Such experiments were meant as court entertainments, inaccessible to the populace at large. However, the themes and characters portrayed by the foreign troupes would come to influence Russian popular entertainment and circus, both in style and content. This came about not from a need for a foreign model to imitate, but rather from 'cultural seepage' and the tentative efforts of the Italians to assimilate familiar Russian

cultural signifiers to their customary conventions. Russian comic interludes, halfway between folk and professional theatre, were composed of
heterogeneous artistic elements. Fed by foreign novelty, they in turn
became a source of inspiration for both unnamed amateurs and veteran
professionals.[4]

For instance, one of the favourite 'interludes to music' of Avoglio's
company was *The Gambling Husband and the Sanctimonious Wife*, commonly known as *The Gambler at Cards*. Translated, verses and all, into
Russian under the title *Discord between Husband and Wife*, and performed by amateurs, the sung dialogue and customs of this two-hander
became suffused with Russian references (Peretts 1917: 205–15). In
Trediakovskiy's *précis* of another play, a wandering ghost impersonated
by the servant-girl Smeraldina is transmogrified into a *kikimora*, a female
domestic goblin out of Slavonic folklore. In one of her speeches, she
declares that she was born in Moscow, daughter of a doctor of medicine
who practiced in Butchers' Row in St Petersburg; her mother had served
society by brewing beer in Riga. At the end, she performs a Russian dance
for Pantalone. Yet, for all the local colour Smeraldina's other transformations include a 'Roman gentleman' (*rimzhiy dvoryanin*) and 'Neapolitan
women' (*zhenshchiny neapolitanskie*), specifity that would have no meaning
for a Russian spectator.

Masks were, however, a common feature of Russian amusements, worn
at the annual *Koliada* and *Maslenitsa* (Butter-week) holidays. The fairs that
accompanied these Christmas and Shrovetide festivities were, by 1750,
presenting comedies, interludes and farces, the whole spectrum of the
commedia dell'arte. On these occasions, the performers were Russian
amateurs: tradesmen, apprentices and merchants, costumed as jesters and
buffoons. By the mid-eighteenth century, they were sharing space with
foreign clowns, jugglers, wire-walkers and puppeteers. These indigenous
merry-Andreys offered diversions no less ribald and rowdy, if somewhat
less exotic, than the professional European players.

What eased the conflation of the Russian buffoon with the *commedia*
actor for the unsophisticated Russian spectator was a pre-existing manifestation of the fool. Most familiar to the unlettered public were the
skomorokhi, counterparts of the European *Spielmänner* or minstrels,
itinerant entertainers who sang, danced, led bears, juggled and generally
entertained in an improvisatory manner. Since a direct commentary on
everyday life was dangerous, the *skomorokh*'s verbal aggression was chan-
nelled into an oblique critique, the creation of an alternative carnival world,

played out during such holidays as Shrovetide. In 1648, the *skomorokhi* were banned by Tsar Aleksey Mikhaylovich, ostensibly for perpetuating pagan practices and seducing Christians away from church attendance.[5] However, in the aforementioned foreign play of Pickle-Herring and Jodelet, a manuscript note tries to acclimatise this alien genre by noting that 'The Skomorokh is Prince Pickelherring' (Pesenti 1996: 53). In other words, a native professional performer is assimilated to the conventional comic character in an outlandish and unfamiliar scenario.

The ban forced the *skomorokh* into the hinterlands; the traditions survived, but in a clandestine manner. In the absence of the *skomorokh* in urban environments, the influx of foreigners under Peter the Great led this variety of *Volksnarr* to be supplanted by the *Hofnarr*, part of the entourage of a great house. Peter maintained more clowns and jesters than any of his predecessors (over a hundred, with more than seventy dwarves in addition). The practice became traditional with his successors; one professional jester at Anna's court was lodged in a magnificent chamber hung with fifty portraits of his predecessors. Even Catherine the Great, patroness of the Enlightenment, kept as fool the feeble-minded Matryona Danilovna (Farrell 1980: 127–30).[6] With the enforced eclipse of the native entertainer who circulated among the people, the court entertainer, often of foreign origin, replaced him in anecdotage and pictorial imagery.

In the public imagination and that of the court, a clown was a clown, whatever his origin. Stage comedians and court jesters occupied the same function in raising mirth; they might attain a celebrity unavailable to their rustic counterparts, although the fame attached more to the character type than to the human being behind the mask.[7] Kunst's comic character Trazo, an earthy Hanswurst type played by the actor Bendler, was considered the high point of the comedies in which he appeared; his asides often dealt with topical issues. The gamut of the jester repertoire under Anna was wide, ranging from the crudest physical pranks to the refined and theatricalised conceits of comic poets and musicians. Preference was often shown for the former. In the words of the musicologist Aleksandr Famintsyn, 'in the reign of Anna Ioannovna, the debasement of human dignity as personified by the jester reached its supreme limits' (Famintsyn 1889: 112).

One contemporary reports:

> The ways in which this sovereign was amused by these people was passing strange. Sometimes she ordered them all to stand against a wall, except for one who beat them to a pulp and well nigh forced them to fall on the

ground. Often they were made to fight amongst themselves, and they pulled each other's hair and scratched each other till they bled. The sovereign and all her court, entertained by these spectacles, died laughing. Balakirev,[8] who did not care for such sports, once refrained from toppling to the floor, thinking that his apology would be accepted. The poor young man was mistaken and had to endure a beating with rods.

That is an example of the crude prank. One of Pietro Mira's stunts may serve as illustration of a more elaborately staged scenario.

The Duke of Courland [the consort] once called Pedrillo the jester's wife a nanny-goat. Pedrillo replied with the deepest respect that it was true and as soon as his wife was delivered of a child, he dared invite Her Majesty and all her court to visit the mother in hopes of collecting from the guests a sum of money sufficient for the best (appropriate) education for his children. This joke was imparted to the whole Court. On the appointed day they bedded him with a goat beside him. When the curtains parted, everyone saw Pedrillo and his wife in bed. The empress, handing him a gift, personally stipulated the amount each of her courtiers was to give the mother.[9]

As encouragement to similar antics, the Empress founded a special jester's order of St Benedetto, which was awarded to Pedrillo and Jan Lacosta.[10]

Notes

[1] For a full lexicon of European neologisms in Russian during this reign, see Cracraft 2004: 430–70.

[2] The original source of the scripts may have been the French publications, *Le théâtre* italien *de Gherardi* (1701) and *Comédies diverses* (1730s) (Peretts 1923: 144–5, 148).

[3] The possible influence of the Italian comedy on the emerging Russian literary comic drama is discussed in Yawney 1971.

[4] For the embryonic stages of the professionalisation of court theatre see L. M. Starikova 2006 and Pesenti 2006: 12–29.

[5] The standard works in Russian are Famintsyn 1889 and Belkin 1975; in English Zguta 1978.

[6] The practice of tsars keeping jesters goes back at least as far as Ivan the Terrible.

[7] Cf. Muriel Bradbrook's contention in *The Rise of the Common Player* that Richard Tarleton, the Elizabethan comic, might be considered the first 'show business' celebrity.

[8] Ivan Aleksandrovich Balakirev (b. 1699) was a military officer who had been exiled under Peter, but was recalled and promoted by his widow Catherine I. After her death, he remained at court as a kind of semi-official fool. A 'Collection of Anecdotes of Balakirev,' published by K. A. Polevoy in 1830, attributed

to him a wide range of traditional jokes and sayings (Kallinikov and Korneeva 1998: II, 61).

[9] Both anecdotes come from K. G. Manshteyn (Munstein), *Zapiski o Rossii* (Derpt, 1810), quoted in Starikova (1989: 90).

[10] Lacosta, originally D'Acosta, was a Portuguese Jew brought to Russia from Hamburg; master of several languages and well read in Holy Writ, he often debated religion with Peter the Great, who dubbed him 'King of the Samoyeds' and bestowed on him an unpopulated island in the Gulf of Finland (Kallinikov and Korneeva 1998: IX, 217).

10

England

Robert Henke

From the 1570s to the legendary early nineteenth-century performances of Joe Grimaldi and beyond, the commedia dell'arte has exerted a strong pull on the English theatrical imagination. Continually associated, by many Englishmen, with 'lighter' forms of entertainment such as acrobatics, dance, mime and street performance, and scandalously foregrounding female performers during the Shakespearean period of the presumably 'all-male stage', the influence of the commedia dell'arte on the English theatre has generated controversy and debate, from Stephen Gosson's fulminations against English playwrights for 'ransacking' Italian plays to eighteenth-century laments over the theatre's perceived descent into pantomime from the heights of Elizabethan/Jacobean and Restoration greatness (O'Brien 2004). Although it is certainly possible to overestimate the influence of the commedia dell'arte on Shakespeare and other foundational English dramatists – and it is important to recognise when other forms such as ancient New Comedy may be playing an equal or more important role – the *arte* certainly left its mark on English theatre from Hamlet to Garrick to Grimaldi.

If one regards the totality of documented contacts between the English and the commedia dell'arte in the sixteenth, seventeenth and eighteenth centuries, a pattern emerges that France, only a channel apart, mediated between England and a theatre whose home was based beyond the Alps. The sudden flurry of visits by Italian actors to England between 1573 and 1578 was probably prompted by the attendance of English ambassadors at several commedia dell'arte performances in France in 1571 and 1572. On 4 March 1571, Lord Burkhurst, while in Paris as an English ambassador to the wedding of Charles IX and Elizabeth of Austria, viewed a 'comedie of Italians' produced for him by Luigi Gonzaga (Duke of Nevers), the brother of the Duke of Mantua, where the commedia dell'arte really gained its footing in the 1560s and 1570s (Baschet 1882: 13–6). Then, before the English ambassador Lord Lincoln on 8 June 1572, at the

Louvre, Italian actors also performed (Baschet 1882: 40–2). Although certainly Englishmen such as Thomas Coryate, George Whetsone and Fynes Moryson traveled to Italy where they recorded viewing *arte* perform-ances, Robert Dallington and several other Englishmen also saw Italian actors perform in France (Lea 1934: vol. II, 342–50). Thomas Kyd, in *The Spanish Tragedy* (Mulryne 2009: 4.1.164–6) and Thomas Middleton and William Rowley, in *The Spanish Gypsy* (Middleton and Rowley 1653: 4.1) both associate extempore acting not only with Italian, but also with French players, probably referring to French *farceur* actors imitating the Italian improvisatory style, or possibly to Italian actors who had installed them-selves in Paris. One of the most likely places for English traveling actors and itinerant *commedia* troupes to have met each other would have been Paris, where in 1598 the Confrères de la Passion leased to English players the Hôtel de Bourgogne, where we know that Italian actors were perform-ing at about the same time. As a three-year-old boy, Louis XIII was said to have watched English actors perform at Fontainebleau in September 1604 – very close to the time when the Gelosi were in Paris (Chambers 1923: vol. II, 292–4).

To be sure, besides the visits and reports of travelers to Italy such as Coryate, there were certainly direct exchanges either in England or Italy. In *An Almond for a Parrat*, Shakespeare's friend Thomas Nashe seems to recount an actual trip to Italy and a conversation he had with the 'famous Francatrip Harlicken', who asks him whether he knows Will Kemp (McKerrow 1958: vol. III, 342). For his part, Kemp is recorded as traveling to German and then Italy in 1601 and is represented in John Day's *Travailes of the Three English Brothers* as performing a scene with an Italian Harlequin before Sir Anthony Shirley in Venice (Lea 1934: vol. II, 381–2). Upon reentry into the London theatre scene after this trip, surely Kemp would have shared his knowledge of the commedia dell'arte with his fellow English actors. Possibly prompted, as we have suggested, by French-mediated reports to the English court of the new theatrical form, the Italian players began a flurry of visits to England in 1573, including a group of actors who performed pastoral drama before Queen Elizabeth during her progress through Windsor and Reading; a company of actors and acrobats who performed before the Privy Council at Durham Place in April 1577; and, most intriguingly, a troupe led by Drusiano Martenelli, who was granted permission to perform within the city and the Liberties in January 1578 (for records of Italian actors in England between 1573 and 1577, see Chambers 1923: vol. II, 261–5). (Might Martinelli's troupe possibly have performed in James Burbage's recently constructed theatre in the Shoreditch Liberties?) When George Gascoigne, in 1576, refers to 'These Enterludes, these newe Italian sportes', he registers the novel effect of this innovative new Italian form in an era when there was generally great excitement (and equally strong apprehension) in England about emerging Italian cultural forms (Lea 1934: vol II, 355–6). Only ten years before, Gascoigne himself had capitalised on this excitement by translating and helping to stage his translation of Ariosto's play *I suppositi* at Gray's Inn.

As would be true for the important commedia dell'arte presence in eighteenth-century England, acrobatics and acting came together and sometimes must have been indistinguishable. Italian entertainers who 'dawnsyd antycks and played dyvrse other feets' performed in Norwich in 1546/7, an Italian acrobat performed before Elizabeth at the famous Kennilworth entertainments in 1575 and Italian 'tumblers' were recorded in the Chambers accounts of 1577/78 (Lea 1934: vol II, 352–5). Italian women were especially expert in acrobatics, which Thomas Morton seemed to find sexually suggestive, denouncing the 'unchaste, shameless, and unnatural tomblinge of the Italian women' (Lea 1934: vol. II, 354). A 1591 letter to Francis Bacon reports of Italian spies in England disguised as acrobats, suggesting their continued presence (Lea 1934: vol. II, 357).

Possibly because Norton was not the only Englishman who objected to female performers, there are no subsequent documents of Italian players in England until much later. Still, there appears to be renewed English interest in the *arte*, and of a distinctly professional kind, in the late 1580s and early 1590s: the time when Kyd mentions the Italian players' capacity, with but 'one hour's meditation', to 'perform anything in action'. Among the papers of Edward Alleyn in Dulwich College, discussed by Andrew Grewar in an important article (Grewar 1993) are stage 'plottes' or 'platts' that bear some similarities to commedia dell'arte scenarios: they consist of stage directions mostly referring to entrances and exits, with some minimal instructions for action, and were set on pasteboard with a hole bored through the top so that it could be hung backstage as an aid to actors during performance. One of these 'plottes' contains the name of several actors who would join the Lord Chamberlain's men with Shakespeare in 1594, and another one, 'The Dead Man's Fortune', contains one of the first references in English to the *commedia* character Pantaloon.

The list of early modern English playwrights who explicitly refer to the acting style or the characters of the commedia dell'arte is long and diverse, suggesting that the English interest in avant-garde Italian cultural forms continued unabated through the turn of the century. George Whetstone, Thomas Nashe, John Marston, Shakespeare, Thomas Dekker,

Ben Jonson, Thomas Heywood, George Wilkins, Thomas Kyd, Thomas Middleton and William Rowley, Philip Massinger and John Day all refer to the *arte*, and often in quite performance-specific ways that reveal some real acquaintance with Italian professional theatre. To the character Alvarez, who prepares to play a father in a play within a play from Middleton and Rowley's *The Spanish Gypsy*, Ferdinando advises him to 'Play him up high: not like a Pantaloone' (Middleton and Rowley 1653: 2.4) – suggesting theatre-specific familiarity with Pantalone's low center of gravity. In Thomas Heywood's *If You Know Not Me You Know Nobody, Part 2*, a character describes his apprentices who 'peepe like Italian Pantelownes behind an arras' – nicely matching *commedia* staging as represented in the Recueil Fossard and other visual documents (Heywood 1606).

The commedia dell'arte's 'influence' on Shakespeare should be differentiated from traditional, source-to-target linear influence and should be seen in a more systemic and modular way, since actors' and playwrights' sources are mediated as often through oral, performative means as through written texts. Also, as demonstrated by a play such as *The Taming of the Shrew*, the purchase of the *commedia* on Shakespeare should not be separated from that of scripted Italian comedy: the subplot of *The Taming of the Shrew* is based on Ariosto's *I suppositi* and also contains explicit references to Pantaloon and other *commedia* characters. Shakespeare and other early modern English dramatists appear to have considered 'Italian comedy', whether scripted or improvised, as one system.

Still, one can roughly distinguish between three different kinds of relationships of the commedia dell'arte to Shakespeare's work. During the 1590s, when the Italian professional theatre appears to have been 'in the air' of London theatre as an exciting novelty, Shakespeare deploys the *commedia explicitly*, in the Pantaloon Gremio and other characters in *Shrew*, with the Capitano Don Armado and the Dottore Holofernes in *Love's Labour's Lost* and (if given more British coloring) in the braggart Caius and the pedant Evans in *The Merry Wives of Windsor*. Second, we can observe the more *marginalised and vestigial* presence of the *arte*, such as the fleeting reference to the stingy master-starving servant dyad in the backstory of Launcelot Gobbo and Shylock: the former complaining that he has become 'famished in his service' (*Merchant of Venice* 2.2.106) and the latter accusing Gobbo of being a lazy, gourmandising drone (2.5.3–5) (Shakespeare references are to the second edition of the Riverside Shakespeare 1997). Third, and after the 'novelty effect' had worn off, a *transformational* use of the commedia dell'arte might be noted, especially in tragedy. As Frances Barasch has argued, the Polonius family in *Hamlet* strikingly recapitulates the *commedia* family of blocking vecchio, absent mother and male and female children/*innamorati* (Barasch 2011). *Othello* is replete with a Moorish Capitano; a Brighella (Iago) who has paid his dues, understands his worth and knows how to play hardball; a near-perfect Venetian Pantalone in Brabantio, a comically desperate innamorato in Roderigo and a tragically doomed *innamorata* in Desdemona. That Emilia's counterpoint of an earthy, sexually experienced Franceschina to Desdemona's more perfect lover can also be located in scripted Italian comedy, as Louise George Clubb has shown, demonstrates yet again how closely related were the two kinds of theatre (Clubb 1989: 24–5). In *The Tempest*, Shakespeare returns to more explicit commedia dell'arte charac-terisation and comic plotting: as several scholars have demonstrated, a group of commedia dell'arte scenarios from the period constitute a form of 'magical pastoral' remarkably cognate with *The Tempest*, with an iras-cible magician ruling an island populated by local spirits and suddenly hosting a group of shipwrecked travelers from Italy, who perform buffoon-ish antics very similar to those of Shakespeare's Stephano and Trinculo (Andrews 2004; Henke 2007; Lea 1934: 443–53, 610–74; Neri 1913). Deftly absorbed into the complex fabrics of the plays, the commedia dell'arte provided a generative and evocative theatrical language in *The Tempest* and, indeed, throughout Shakespeare's works.

Although we cannot rule out the possibility of professional Italian actors performing in London after the 1570s and before the closing of the theatres, the lack of documentation is indeed striking and suggests that England was not a desirable site of *commedia* travel because of its antipathy to actresses, the difficulty of the Channel crossing and the absence of anything like the Medicean and Habsburg dynastic networks that both prompted and facilitated *commedia* travel to France, Spain, the German-speaking regions and the Czech lands (Henke 2008). Direct contact between English actors or travelers and Italian players during this time, as we have suggested, was much more likely in France, as well as at the Habsburg courts, and we also cannot dismiss the possibility of undocu-mented Italian actors, acrobats and mountebanks in English fairgrounds and streets, such as we know prospered after the Restoration. Demonstrat-ing the close connection between all three of these activities, in 1630 a certain F. Nicolini received a license 'to dance on the ropes, to use interludes and masques and to sell his powders and balsams' (Lea 1934: vol. II, 361). After having twice viewed a play performed by the Affezionati troupe in Venice in 1632, Sir Aston Cokayne wrote an English version entitled *Trappolin, creduto principe, or Trappolin Suppos'd a Prince* (printed

1658) on his circuitous way home to England (Lea 1928). The play, for which Kathleen Lea has identified a 'scenario family' of nine different Italian versions, relies upon supernatural magic much like the group of scenarios related to *The Tempest*, and was remounted by Nahum Tate as *A Duke and No Duke* in 1684.

One supposes that the exiled Charles II had ample occasion to view Italian actors in Paris. In 1660 the restored king signed a patent for Giulio Gentileschi to build a theatre for 'opere musicali, con machine mutationi di scene et alter apparenze' (musical works, with machines for changing scenes and other mechanisms) (Fletcher 1954: 86). No evidence exists confirming whether or not the project, which appears to refer to operatic work but might also indicate theatrical performance, was realised. Surprisingly, we find the king going out of his way in 1672 to support the Italian fair and booth performer Antonio Devoto, suggesting that Devoto might have performed at court as well as in Charing Cross and Bartholomew Fair booths, where we have records of his appearances from 1667 to 1677. By far the most important visit of an Italian troupe to England during the Restoration – and indeed for the entire seventeenth century – is that of the renowned Scaramouche, Tiberio Fiorillo, and his troupe to England in 1673 and 1675. Although the famed 'maestro' of Molière would have been sixty-five years old at the time, his Scaramouche impressed Charles II enough so that he awarded Fiorillo, as well as the actor playing Harlequin, a medal and chain of gold. In 1675, it is particularly the practice of charging 'his Majesty's poorer subjects' money at Whitehall that attracts the attention – and disapproval – of Andrew Marvell (Fletcher 1954: 88). Physically vigorous into his eighties, Fiorillo must have still been adapt at musical instrumentation, singing, dancing and physically based acting in ways that would have appealed to a foreign crowd, as he evidently had learned to do in Paris.

The apparent failure of the troupe sent by the Duke of Modena to England in 1678–1679 – they were said to have performed only six times in three months and to have received but 'little applause' – probably reflects political circumstances rather than the English taste for the commedia dell'arte, which by all other measures appears to be growing in the period (Bader 1935: 368). Sent by the Duke of Modena to entertain his sister the Duchess of York (Maria d'Este), the actors had the misfortune to arrive at the very moment when Titus Oates was fanning anti-Catholic paranoia worthy of the communist witch-hunts of the 1950s. In late 1678, anything connected with the Catholic Duchess and Duke of York (the latter the brother of Charles II) would have been a cause for suspicion, not least the importing of a troupe of Italian Catholic actors; warned by his brother, in March 1679 the duke and duchess fled England for Brussels. That the Fiorillo residency marked the real turning point in the English appropriation of the commedia dell'arte during the Restoration period, rather than the anomalous visit by the Duke of Modena's troupe, is registered by the fact that in 1677 there began a significant wave, sustained to the end of the century, of scripted English plays fundamentally structured by commedia dell'arte characters, plots and gags. Far from merely literary demonstrations, these plays were animated by two great actors who were significantly influenced by *commedia*-style physical acting and developed the two major *maschere* that Fiorillo's troupe had played to the English court: the famous Scaramouche Joseph Hayns, who traveled to both Italy and France, and the renowned Harlequin Thomas Jevon. In 1677 Hayns played Scaramouche in a performance of Edward Ravenscroft's *Scaramouch a Philosopher, Harlequin a School-Boy, Bravo, Merchant, and Magician* – a play probably unthinkable without Fiorillo's recent visit while also borrowing from Molière's *Les fourberies de Scapin*, *Le marriage forcé* and *Le bourgeois gentilhomme*. (As with England's first encounter with the commedia dell'arte, and as for later eighteenth-century engagements, the Italian and French strains are coincident and difficult to disentangle.) In 1685, Jevon performed at the Dorset Garden Theatre the role of Harlequin in Mountfort's *The Life and Death of Dr. Faustus, with the Humours of Harlequin and Scaramouch*. Hayns and Jevon then joined forces, as Scaramouche and Harlequin respectively, in Aphra Behn's *Emperor of the Moon*, performed in 1687 at the Dorset Garden Theatre. Behn's play again demonstrates the Italian-French connections, for it is based on the great Harlequin Domenico Biancolelli's *Arlequin Empereur dans le Monde de la Lune* (1684) and features a famous routine of Biancolelli that Jevon inherited: the love-lorn Harlequin's 'scene of despair' in which he rejects hanging by suicide, then cannot kill himself by auto-suffocation because of involuntary flatulence and finally resolves to tickle himself to death.

In the eighteenth century, actors, managers and actor-managers developed a form that was both distinctly English but also certainly inflected by the commedia dell'arte. In the early eighteenth century, the dramatic and scripted presence of Harlequin had significantly diminished related to the age of Aphra Behn. By 1715, as the pages of publications such as the *Daily Courant* attest, *commedia* characters such as Harlequin, Scaramouche and Pulchinella had become relegated to dancing entertainments either performed at intermission or at the end of the play (Beaumont 1926: 88–9).

Although he did not invent the form of the English pantomime, it was the actor-manager John Rich who established the form both aesthetically and economically. From his first pantomime *Harlequin Executed* in 1717 to his death in 1761, Rich achieved such extraordinary success at Lincoln Inn's Fields and Covent Garden that he obliged rivals such as Colley Cibber and David Garrick to add pantomime to their own repertoires. Rich's felicitous innovation was to alternate a 'serious' story from classical mythology, embellished with operatic songs, with a comic and grotesque 'Harlequin-ade', featuring Harlequin's use of stage trickery and magical transformation to win Columbine from her *vecchio* father or her husband (O'Brien 2004: 3–4). Rich's own version of Harlequin – the renowned 'Lun' – was highly acclaimed in his day, drawing Garrick's tribute that he 'gave the pow'r of speech to every limb' (O'Brien 2004: 226). An actor of great agility, athleticism and mimic skill, Rich became famous for routines such as that of Harlequin as primal man, being hatched from an egg by the rays of the sun. While, like Cibber, complaining of the triumph of Harlequin, Garrick (who had actually played the role himself as a young actor) reconciled himself and countered Rich in 1759 with *Harlequin's invasion*, which represents Harlequin as a French interloper who must be driven from the English shores. Despite being, as a riposte to Rich, a sort of 'antipantomime', Garrick's play owes much to the form, and he began regularly ballasting the Shakespeare and Jonson that he produced with pantomimes featuring the virtuosic actor Henry Woodward as Harlequin.

Despite an unbroken succession of Harlequin-based pantomimes through the end of the eighteenth century and beyond, by 1800 many perceived a decline from the days of John Rich. The famous clown Joe Grimaldi (1778–1837), whose grandfather Giovanni had worked the French *foires* and whose father Giuseppe had played the role of Pantaloon for Garrick's pantomimes, certainly carried forward the Italo-Franco tradition of his family, as he acted in pantomimes as a boy in tandem with his father. But as the form was declining, and during the Napoleonic period of 1793–1813 when cultural contact between France and England sharply abated, Joe Grimaldi invented the unforgettable and powerful Clown persona of 'Joey', replete with the white face paint, red mouth, and thick eye brows that soon came to signify the heart of the English Clown. Still, as Jackson Cope has argued, the birth of Joey did not signify a national break with the continental tradition, but a return to the 'daemonic', subversive power of the *zanni* and the Italian Arlecchino.

Northern Europe

Bent Holm

Charlatans and Comedians

In Danish playwright Ludvig Holberg's satirical 1722 comedy *Witchcraft or False Alarm*, the main character, the actor Leander, evokes Mephistopheles while rehearsing the company's next spectacular performance which should save the troupe from a threatening bankrupcy. Leander however is believed really to conjure the devil. Upset, the authorities set out to arrest the presumed magician, but are scared away by a 'Doctor-Machine' from the 'Italian comedy . . . about doctor Baloardo', a mechanical construction which can extend the actor to a terrifying height, topped by a horrifying mask; little by little the simple-minded citizens of the narrow-minded provincial town steal out to frequent Leander as a presumed magician and healer, confiding to him their dreams, secrets, aspirations and infirmities. Leander involuntarily has become a charlatan, a doctor in spite of himself. Being able to improvise, he manages to exploit the situation commercially, so he can save the company; he transfers his consultation to an inn, where, it is said, 'a Harlequin is painted on the wall in the corridor' (Holberg 1970: 326, 352). In the end Leander is proven to be merely a simple actor, not a healer or magician.

Up to 1722 professional theatre in the Northern European countries had been performed by foreign strolling players. In that very year a professional theatre in the national language was established in Copenhagen. Academic and ecclesiastical authorities reacted rather drastically to the new cultural phenomenon, referring to the theological argument that the stage was the church of the devil. Holberg's comedy is an implicit exposure of the ludicrousness of such an attitude in a modern context.

The actor in the play and in real life as well was related to obscure forces; that combination of witchcraft and stagecraft is furthermore accentuated in the comedy by references to the commedia dell'arte: the 'magic' doctor-machine, the image of Harlequin. Those circumstances raise the question of what the Italian masked comedy stood for in that era in a northern European context. The iconic Harlequin figure points both backwards in history, to buffoons and charlatans, and forwards, towards drama and theatre in a modern sense. The attempt shall be made here to suggest some kinds of interaction between historical-cultural circumstances and masked comedy, as it progressed through three centuries from a courtly to a popular phenomenon, from an exotic to a familiar one.

The association of the actor with the magic healer refers to the motif of the charlatan, the quack or mountebank. As a matter of fact, that is exactly how the commedia dell'arte was introduced in practice in Northern European countries in the late seventeenth and early eighteenth centuries. The northern countries in that era meant Denmark and Sweden. Denmark was a double monarchy that included Norway, and Sweden also included Finland in its territory, apart from both countries' possessions in Northern Germany. In the second half of the seventeenth century Sweden grew into a great power that furthermore conquered substantial territories from Denmark, its neighbouring country. That was the age of the touring companies. Being a strong power Sweden was an attractive area for the troupes, primarily Dutch and German companies, who gradually also included Harlequinades in their repertoires.

However, before Harlequin made his physical entry onto the Nordic stage the masks had been depicted in art and engravings and appeared in small amateur shows. The very first traces of commedia dell'arte in Northern Europe are iconographic images. In Christian IV's collection of pictorial art at the Castle of Rosenborg Castle in Copenhagen there is a painting of Venetian masked comedians from around 1605 (Holm 2013; Katritzky 2006: 136, 436). And in a pyrotechnical manual by Carl Christmann from around 1650, at the Royal Library of Copenhagen, four fire-breathing *zanni* appear, modelled after Jacques Callot's *Balli di Sfessania*, three decades after the original engravings. Real masks perform for the first time during the *Triumphus Nuptialis Danicus*, the crown prince's gigantic wedding festivities in 1634, when four Pantalones worked as stage hands in a theatrical show. In Sweden a performance by noble amateurs of Racine's *Iphigénie* in 1684 was augmented by a scene with Harlequin and Scaramouche, played by two young high-born boys.

The first professional Italian Harlequin appears in 1688 in Stockholm, in the shape of Sebastiano di Scio, the Venetian theatre manager and charlatan. In the years 1687–1711, di Scio was capable of delivering drugs, walking tightropes and executing puppetry, ballet and comedy, from Vienna to Stockholm. In 1690 Di Scio was employed at court in Celle in Northern Germany in a troupe of Italian and *Théâtre Italien* players, but was also allowed to tour Europe with his own troupe. During visits to Stockholm he signed himself 'Arlechino Comoediant Italiano' (Baumbach 2002: 100ff; Hansen 1984: 59f; Heed 2007: 144; Nyström 1918: 56). In Denmark he signed himself 'Sebastiano di Scio deto Harlekino' and was highly esteemed at the royal court, where he obtained a concession as court distiller and was even nominated court comedian. Di Scio toured Denmark with an entourage of twenty-four persons and several horses. He is the prototype of the charlatan-comedian.

Ballet and Satire

The Northern War in the first decades of the eighteenth century meant the decline of Sweden's great-power status and of the era of the strolling troupes. For Denmark the post-war period comprised a cultural flowering including, in 1722, the founding already mentioned of a national theatre which took important inspiration from the commedia dell'arte as a point of departure for the development of a contemporary stage. The genre comedy was now accessible also to the middle class, not only to the francophone upper classes.

In 1703, during wartime, the French court troupe in Stockholm had presented Charles Dufresny and Louis Biancolelli's *Pasquin et Marforio*, although it was not the moment for comedy. After the conclusion of the peace, however, the Swedish court hired ballet master Jean-Baptiste Landé, previously in the service of Auguste the Strong. Landé engaged a French troupe in 1723 and presented Italian plays after serious performances; soon after Landé came to play a role in the history of the commedia dell'arte in Copenhagen, as well.

The artistic leader of the new Danish stage, the French actor René Magnon de Montaigu, was the former head of a royal French troupe that had been dismissed in 1721; in his Majesty Frederik IV's service he had visited Paris four times to update his knowledge of for instance *Théâtre Italien*, whose influence is traceable in his productions. The second founding father, the playwright Ludvig Holberg, was an early reformer in line with Luigi Riccoboni and Carlo Goldoni. His dramaturgical point of departure was the work of Molière and the commedia dell'arte, and his gallery of types in many ways corresponds to that of Riccoboni in his *Nouveau Théâtre Italien*, a number of stock characters (*tipi fissi*), however not as masks but as 'real', individualized figures.

Holberg's attitude toward Italian comedy reflects his philosophy in general (Holm 2012: 143ff.), concerning the necessity of a 'foolish' and irrational component to adjust and counterbalance the illusion of rationality in social life, all kinds of sentimental or affected performance – the mask being thus an instrument of unmasking a fundamental chaos of human existence. For that reason he found a mental resonance in the 'old' Italian theatre.

Holberg wrote two harlequinades. The first, *Ulysses von Ithacia or A German comedy*, is a parody of a rival company, and was written in the period when German theatre was represented by *Haupt- und Staats-Aktionen*, spectacular, heroic plays full of heroes, dragons and virgins, and by the Hamburg opera company which the king had installed in the royal castle instead of the rejected French troupe. For his majesty's birthday in 1722 the Hamburg singers presented a pompous work entitled *Ulysses*.

An example of official theatricality, Holberg's 'German' comedy is a grotesque in the manner of *Théâtre Italien*'s burlesque exposures of mythical heroes and lofty manners centred on Harlequin Domenico Biancolelli. At the same time it is a masterpiece of sublime nonsense, in the absurd tradition from Aristophanes to Alfred Jarry, a satire of wars in general and of generals in war. The plot presents an absolutely anti-heroic version of the Trojan War, mixed up with the *Aeneid*, the Old Testament and all kinds of fabulous reading. It was even an implicit parody of the regime's fundamental imagery; the absolute prince was mirrored in classical-mythological figures, and could appear in performative and pictorial connections dressed in 'Roman' garb similar to the heroic stage characters' pompous costumes. So, by caricaturing conventional theatrical heroes, Holberg in a single stroke exposed the baroque-ritual staging of power as empty and outdated, in a manoeuvre that in a broader context refers to the *querelle entre les anciens et les modernes*. The orbital axis in the comedy's surreal universe is noble Ulysses' simple and sarcastic servant, Chilian, whose name happens to be just a Low German version of Harlequin. He stands for modernity in this context.

Holberg's affinity to the Italian comedy is furthermore reflected in the fact that when in 1725 he tried to break through internationally as a playwright he went to the head of the *Théâtre Italien* in Paris, Luigi Riccoboni – not to the French stage – and suggested to him a couple of his comedies, which Riccoboni rejected: it would have meant a 'translation' to the masked equivalent figures in Riccoboni's troupe. To put it mildly the new harlequinades Holberg saw in Paris were not to his taste, and he went home furious about Riccoboni's betrayal of the true Italian theatre – not to mention outraged at having been rejected. To Holberg the real thing was the old *Théâtre Italien*, the theatre of Biancolelli and

Gherardi, ruled by unsentimental, carnivalesque comedy; not the refined, sentimental *marivaudage*. Harlequin was the embodiment of coarse satire, not an ingenious fellow, *poli par l'amour*.

Holberg's second harlequinade, *The Invisible Lovers*, was created in 1726 after his failure in Paris and encounter with the new sentimentality. In the play Harlequin is infected with his noble master's refined ways of courting a mysterious masked ('invisible') lady. Inspired by this aristocratic coquetry, Harlequin begins to despise Colombine's sound and direct erotic approach. As a didactic revenge Colombine dresses old Magdalone up as an 'invisible' lady, and predictably Harlequin immediately falls madly in love and gives himself up to pathetic romantic bizarreries. After the 'invisible' lady has been persuaded to marry him, she reveals her ugly old face. In the end poor Harlequin is forced to accept Colombine's harsh and humiliating conditions for their marriage. In other words, the moment Harlequin betrays his clownish nature and moves into a zone of staged coquetry he loses his sense of prosaic stolidity, and reality will strike back and take its revenge. The conclusion is: Harlequin should be faithful to his mask.

In 1726 Jean Baptiste Landé set out for Paris to hire actors for his troupe of French court actors in Stockholm. However, on his way to France he was engaged by Montaigu. In Copenhagen Landé presented divertissements with Harlequin and Scaramouche and probably even trained Danish actors for *Théâtre Italien* performances. Landé came back to Copenhagen a second time in 1728 as part of a plan to transform the Danish stage to a kind of French-speaking *Théâtre Italien*. The Danish actors replied to the challenge by billing a couple of *Théâtre Italien* comedies, among which was *La fille de bon sens* including the 'Doctor Machine' which appeared in Holberg's *Witchcraft or False alarm*; although references to Paris and Venice in the translation were replaced by Copenhagen and Hamburg, the main characters remained Harlequin, Scaramouche and so on, and appeared in their traditional Italian outfits. When the – semi-professional – Swedish-speaking stage opened in 1737 a similar combination of local and Romance references was practiced; in Delisle's *Arlequin sauvage* Marseille had thus been replaced by Gothenburg. However, in both the Swedish and the Danish version of that comedy Pantalone is described as wearing the traditional long black coat, dagger in his belt, red garb and long pointed beard.

From 1728 the Danish stage remained closed for almost two decades for religious reasons. When, after the death of the pietistic ruler, public entertainments were relaunched in 1747, a French, a German and a Danish stage were opened in the capital. All of them included harlequinades in their repertoires. The Danish theatre had now become an officially recognised institution – a 'royal' theatre; it was still ruled by a Holbergian dramaturgy, staging middle-class characters. Plays from *Le Théâtre de la Foire* and *Le Nouveau Théâtre Italien* formed a specific niche, meeting the popular taste for light comedy. A surprisingly extensive use of masks, including those of Harlequin and Pantalone, can be derived from the theatre's inventory (Krogh 1931: 48f.).

The influence of masked comedy coloured works by national authors; and conversely the masked comedy was localised. In addition, those two levels of impact merged. When for instance Goldoni's *Servant of Two Masters* was premiered in Copenhagen it was named after Ludvig Holberg's comic main character – his 'Harlequin' – and was called *Henrik Who Serves Two Masters!*

In the wider perspective commedia dell'arte became a decisive factor in the development of theatre as an art form in the Northern countries, especially in Denmark, and thereby even in the process of developing identity in a period when a bourgeois class was growing stronger as an actual pillar of society; the cultural and mental impact of for instance Holberg's works and world view should not be underestimated.

Pantomimes and Clowning

By the 1770s the harlequinade genre appeared outdated and was dying out. Moralism and patriotism displaced frank comedy. In 1772 the first Danish theatre critic Peder Rosenstand-Goiske excused his use of a hideous metaphor – a 'Harlequin's costume' (Krogh 1931: 97) – to refer to certain incoherent comedies. Harlequin recalled too much the fairground booths from which the stage as a cultural institution had to distance itself. But of course Harlequin could not die. For in the meantime another version of the commedia dell'arte had grown up: the pantomimic harlequinade. *Io rinasco* [I am reborn] was the proud motto of Harlequin in Paris. Apparently it is true.

Already in 1754 'a pantomime-comedy with Harlequin, Pantalone and other masks' had been presented as an *intermezzo* of Metastasio's *Ciro riconosciuto* in Copenhagen. The *intermezzo*-pantomime *Harlequin Desperate for His Beloved* by Angelo Pompeati – who incidentally was married to Theresa Imer, daughter of Goldoni's impresario – dates from the same period and contains the basic structure of the pantomimic harlequinade as it was developed in London and Paris. The main characters are Pantalon;

Piro, his servant; Colombina, his daughter; Harlequin, her lover and Mago, a magician. Harlequin has now become an *amoroso*, whereas the *zanni* function is performed by Pierrot and Colombina, the maid, has been upgraded to il vecchio's daughter. In his desperation for love in the play Harlequin turns to the Mago who strokes Harlequin's bat with his magic wand, thus bestowing magic power on him. Now Harlequin appears in a number of disguises and plays all kinds of tricks that give occasion for several mechanical and acrobatic effects. The crucial point, however, lies in the ending; after the magician has forced Pantalone to give his paternal consent to Harlequin and Colombina, he knocks on the ground with his wand, and the stage is transformed to a beautiful castle where the couple is united in a kind of *grande finale* which was later on further developed into a real apotheosis in Bengal light. The original 'witchcraft' had become a 'magic' effect.

In the 1770s another Venetian, Antonio Brambilla, toured with a troupe of comedians and acrobats who performed equilibristic acts and pantomimes at such venues as the Royal Theatre of Copenhagen, until a commission declared it improper. From then on time was up in general for the masked comedy as an official genre. It was banished to popular environments.

In the year 1800 Pasquale Casorti came to Denmark with his troupe of twenty-four pantomimists, equilibrists and acrobats. They were allowed to perform at a fairground near Copenhagen. The pantomimes were centred on Pantalone, Pierrot, Colombina and Harlequin – master and servant, daughter and lover. Another troupe, the English Price family, who had toured Sweden earlier, began to present pantomimes in competition with the Casortis. Soon after, the two rival families merged. It became somehow romantic to attend pantomimes; Danish ballet's great master August Bournonville and other leading artists admired the artists. The Price family delivered dancers and actors to the 'real' (royal) stage for generations. Outside the season some pantomime artists toured the provinces in Scandinavia, as troupes of mountebanks and equilibrists had for decades. Circuses might also include Harlequinesque pantomimes in their shows. Comedy became clowning.

The decisive year, however, was 1843 with the founding of the amusement park Tivoli and its pantomime theatre, first in the Turkish, then in the Chinese style. Denmark was hard up, after the Napoleonic Wars and the loss of Norway. A development of points of orientation – in opposition to the norms of the old ruling classes – which involved Norse, exotic and Romantic references should be seen in a context of the 'people' as the upcoming social agent. Tivoli may be seen as a manifestation of a 'different' culture. In the increasing urbanisation Tivoli even played a role as a first literal opening of the capital hitherto locked up behind ramparts and town gates, as the garden included an area outside the ramparts. The so-called Casortian pantomime is still alive in Tivoli, in uninterrupted tradition, as a kind of living museum, and nowadays, as it frequently goes with popular traditional forms, mostly performed for children and tourists. Exotic-Italian Harlequin has become totally Danish, part of Danish national identity, ending up with both successful integration and complete harmlessness.

What we see is an Italian art form starting its Nordic life as exotic entertainment for crowned heads and common audiences alike, and later on appealing only to the masses; the baroque theatre machinery became spectacular popular magic, just as the genre of fashionable *carrousels*, which were royal choreographed shows on horseback, became carousel, the merry-go-round with wooden horses of the fairgrounds.

Commedia dell'arte has been like an infection in the Northern European countries. It appeared in pictorial and performed practice, on amateur, professional, foreign or national premises, in dramatic, balletic, pantomimic or charlatan contexts, for the courts, for the middle class and for the broad public. On the one hand, it meant vitalisation, bringing an immense source of energy to the artistic life of the region. On the other hand, it implied something to be fought, to be rolled back in order to advance theatre as a cultural institution. In any case, it has been integrated as an inspiration in especially Danish drama from the very beginning.

PART III

Social and Cultural Conflicts

Commedia dell'Arte and the Church

Bernadette Majorana

The open war that raged between theologians and moralists, on the one side, and professional Italian actors, on the other, for more than thirty years after 1545 is well documented. It can be retraced by examining a series of texts that emerged in the latter part of the century, when this new type of theatre had developed and consolidated its formal characteristics and had become integrated in urban social life.

There was no lack of restrictive provisions issued by consecutive popes to regulate the masked, improvised and commercial theatre that was to become known as commedia dell'arte. Among those responsible were Gregory XIII and Sixtus V (Ciancarelli 2008: 43–55, 57–8), not to mention bishops such as Charles Borromeo and Gabriele Paleotti (Taviani 1969: lxxvi–viii, 5–24, 37–40; Taviani and Schino 1982: 379–89). Though authoritative, these and other, later interventions nonetheless remained contingent and temporary. The one prohibition that remained firmly in place was the ban on performing comedies and public entertainments in consecrated places or during periods of contemplation such as Advent and Lent. This rule may have even worked to the advantage of professional performers, who were thus able to leave the performing of sacred plays in the context of holy days to amateurs and instead take legitimate possession of the working days, touring the network of cities and towns that formed their theatrical itineraries.

These disputes took place not on stage but primarily through public debate and rhetorical, or prescriptive, discourse. The church – in both its religious and its lay components – condemned the professional *comici* and their way of working and acting. In order to do this it made use for the most part of written and printed texts, but also of preaching – which became, during this period, a plentiful source for further publications. The tone of these surviving speeches is indeed vehement: far from sounding conciliatory, they evoke the persuasive tone of voice one would normally expect to hear from a pulpit during an intense exhortatory speech.

The wider availability and distribution of printed texts in this era caused the subjects of debate to multiply, as those who wanted to express their opinions about Christian codes of behaviour were given a way to do so. In print, their arguments found new vigour and at the same time gained an air of permanence. By the same means, however, these authors became targets for criticism by the more cultured of the *comici*, who were eager to root their trade in the *civitas christiana* and did not fail to take advantage of the opportunity that the publication of printed treatises offered them. Possibly due to a miscalculation on the part of their detractors, the *comici* found themselves in the spotlight concerning a number of matters which were essential for the church after the Council of Trent. The effects of the texts written by these actors thus greatly outlasted the effects of the performances themselves. By the act of writing, the *comici* put themselves in the hands of the press – some by reflecting on the value of writing and performing techniques, some by examining the social implications of commedia dell'arte and some, including for instance Giovan Battista Andreini, the most prolific writer of them all, by pursuing the possibility of walking the Christian path of perfection as actors.

The written works that allowed the *comici dell'arte* to take part in high-level public debate were accompanied by a number of other, similarly significant works, designed to help elevate the status of ever-discredited professional actors. These included long theatrical treatises, letters, prologues and short texts, all with high literary ambitions. In the process, the art form – based, as it was originally, on improvisation – became less and less improvisatory, developing instead into a more regular, accessible form of dramaturgy (Ferrone 1985: 21–2).

Meanwhile the clowns, charlatans and little known comedic troupes who were not as inclined towards the written form lacked an effective means of standing up for themselves publicly, despite the fact that they were being targeted in the same way as their more literary colleagues. Sharing the cultural values of the church and drawing from these values the motivation to improve their social status, the *comici* were not above using the distinction between themselves and the clowns as a core strategy of defence.

Church arguments drew on a long-established Christian anti-theatrical tradition, which associated *histriones*, mime actors, jesters and wandering performers with paganism and condemned their connivance with Satan, their masks, their verbal and gestural obscenity, the public commercialisation of their bodies (which were offered to the avid gaze of the spectators) and their nomadism. In doing so, however, the opponents of actors also recognised a number of specific elements pointing towards the recent professionalisation of the acting profession, thus showing a renewed ability to observe and analyse the mechanisms of theatrical performance. It is important to note that the texts criticising comedic performances were usually the result of direct knowledge, that is, of an analysis of the scenes of 'modern' comedies as experienced by the critic. Aiming to clarify the relationship between regulations and conscience, they highlighted, without finally justifying, the underlying systems motivating the *comici*'s actions and the audience's behaviour.

The debates on theatrical performance were enriched by contributions from didactic literature, a genre that had become very extensive and was intended to support daily behaviour and the upbringing of children (written variously for fathers, mothers, daughters, sons, families, princes, priests, confessors and farmers). In this context, the activities of the *comici* were simply part of a broader moral framework, reflected upon by religious figures and by philosophers or scholars of law and medical science (Majorana 1996a). The wide dissemination of such ideas, however, is proof of the great interest generated by the commedia dell'arte within the Christian community.

The controversial, thorny and frequently recurring dispute between church and acting companies is 'a story of words rather than one of facts' (Taviani 1969: xliii). This dispute did not result in actual prohibitions and sanctions, although it did produce clear-cut normative boundaries that, in practice, seemed to allow room for interpretation. Evidence of the conflict abounds throughout the sixteenth century and well into the seventeenth, indicating spectators' enduring interest in comedies. As time went on, however, actors would almost completely cease to respond to either preached or printed attacks. This happened before the middle of the seventeenth century, with the final text published with the intent to address 'those who write about *comici*' being the republication of *La supplica* (The plea) by Nicolò Barbieri, in 1636 (Barbieri 1971). Actors had by this time switched strategies, devoting themselves to communicating their opinions and the value of their art form directly from the stage to their audiences.

Just as the phenomenon of the commedia dell'arte was new, the concept of theatre developed within the church during the Reformation and Counter-Reformation was also new.

The first document of Italian professional theatre known to us – a contract, signed in the presence of a notary – dates back to 1545, when a number of *comici* who wanted to share and regulate the means and purposes of their profession decided to form a group. The year 1545 was also the year of publication – in Paris – of one of the most representative documents of the humanist Renaissance: the *Secondo libro di perspettiva* by Sebastiano Serlio, which contained a discussion of scenes for theatres and reflections on theatrical genres and dramaturgical units. On the part of the church, 1545 fell within the Reformation and was also the opening year of the Council of Trent (ended in 1563). During this time professional theatre companies had begun to implement a radical transformation of their organisational structure. Not only did they introduce areas of specialisation (such as masks and improvisation), but they adopted a commercial approach that included itinerant weekday activities, a business model of playing to undifferentiated audiences and, most importantly, the casting of women in all female roles, as certified by a notarial act of the same year, 1564. It was an unprecedented move, in Italy or anywhere else in Europe. These developments form the basis of the conflict between theatre and church and testify to the *commedia*'s distinctively modern nature.

The Council of Trent did not address theatre per se as – unlike the figurative arts – the Council was not directly involved in doctrinal and cultural matters. However, the overall post-Council orientation and a few crucial decisions made during the assembly (about faith, preaching, images, piety and devotion) did concern all those processes which, through live performance, contributed to define, strengthen or rectify the 'true' Christian. The aspects of traditional popular theatre – both religious and secular – that were detrimental to the reform of liturgy and piety were either prohibited or restrained, and this course of action became a background to the performances of newly professionalised actors and to the experiences of their audiences. The stage was primarily considered in the context of morality, since it belonged to the sphere of social action.

However, it is important to also consider the role of theatrical performance within religious and liturgical practice. The fact that the church itself employed a variety of intensely performative and theatrical strategies, while at the same time condemning secular theatrical performance, complicates the idea of church and theatre as two opposing factions or 'enemies'. Christian rituals and celebrations were designed to be understood and enjoyed universally, from scholar to illiterate peasant, and to this end utilised the most advanced technical and artistic resources a community had to offer. This was true for every city and inhabited place, even in the most remote corners of the Catholic world. In the wake of such festivities new theatre groups were born that embodied what might be called the 'pastoral' tendency of religious theatre: to be steadfast and far-reaching, intending to guide, discipline and delight the lives of the faithful. The stage thus accommodated people who were, on the one hand, supporters and advocates of a Christian theatre, but who, on the other hand, displayed the deepest contempt for the *comici* and their audiences. There is a strange paradox in the fact that they would condemn stage action in general for its effectiveness, while at the same time appropriating the instruments of theatre so as to make the Christian cultural and educational model more vivid, persuasive and affective.

The new orientation of the church was capable of tipping the balance of anti-theatrical arguments passed down by the patristic and later traditions in its favour. Until the first occurrences of humanistic ideas during the Renaissance – which were born out of the culture of rhetoric, and during the great era of scholastic pedagogy in the Protestant and subsequently in the Catholic areas (Majorana, 2000: 1043–52) – the church had only addressed the topic of theatrical performance in order to deny theatre professionals their dignity as Christians. Exceptions must however be made for the moderate positions of Thomas Aquinas and of Scholasticism, to which, in fact, the modern *comici* tended to turn in search of support for their theories (Fiaschini 2011). But even here, approval was limited. Given the frailty of the boundary between sacred and profane and the acknowledgement of reciprocal influences (Bernardi, 2000: 1024–6), the church had only legitimised the actor by virtue of his temporary, uncertain and perhaps even servile identity. In short, his role was one of mere support, of physical and verbal representation of the memory of figures and events from the scriptures and gospel and from hagiography. Actors were only useful to the faithful within the dimension of festivity and ritual of the community – from which occasional actors, anonymous delegates, would detach themselves temporarily, only to re-enter it immediately after the performance (Allegri 1990).

The modern age, on the other hand, was marked by the foundation of a Christian theatre in the strictest sense of the word: actors who played on a stage the characters of a text written in advance, a text that represented their vicissitudes as a plot of actions, in front of spectators gathered for this specific reason, aware that they were subscribing to a fictional pact. Many of those who practised theatre as non-professionals intended to comply with the ethical and spiritual programme of the Catholic Church precisely through acting. Religious orders, schools, academies and congregations of the faithful became the agents of a theatre offered to the community as virtuous exercise and pious entertainment. This theatre was linked to a written kind of dramaturgy, which was also printed for its readers and designed for extra-ordinary times and spaces, with complex stage structures prepared in theatrical venues linked to the company that produced the plays, and it could be freely accessed by a varied audience. This kind of theatre was free of commercial implications. Performances were rare, even though preparations were extensive. The plays were always performed by male amateur actors, who underwent intense training to refine their oratorical acting for ethical and practical purposes, thus giving the weight of responsibility to words and gestures (Filippi 2010; Gros de Gasquet 2007; Majorana, 2000: 1052–9; Vicentini 2004).

The social implications of such an edifying kind of theatre were soon recognised, and theatre was thus integrated into the most advanced concepts of Christian life. Silvio Antoniano for example, a future cardinal, refined humanist and friend of Borromeo, devoted an entire chapter of his highly acclaimed 1584 treatise on education to this kind of theatrical representation. He took as his model the activities of the colleges of the Society of Jesus, the most influential and widespread religious educational institution of the early modern age and the most significant with regard to the theatrical practices of schoolchildren (Chiabò and Doglio 1995; Filippi 2001; Fumaroli 1990; Zanlonghi 2002).

On the one hand, Antoniano repeatedly warned fathers about taking their children to the theatre to watch comedies – vain performances that inadvertently administered a poison that would slowly kill the soul. On the other hand, he extolled the value of 'useful and delightful . . . recreation' of edifying scenes involving 'serious and fruitful . . . matters, such as the lives of saints and other such, so that they can give the example and instruction of true virtue' to young actors. The latter, he added, would attain an advantage through the exercise of 'memory, pronunciation and action', as well as a manly attitude and the 'ease' and 'readiness' of the orator.

Almost a hundred years later, Giovanni Battista De Luca – one of the most talented Italian jurists and canonists – confirmed with similar authority in his work *Il vescovo pratico* the necessity for seminarians to practise 'spiritual representations' in 'a fair way and in proportion' to priestly formation.

With this new kind of religious theatre, which could be encountered in schools, monasteries and convents (Cascetta 1995), as well as in academies, plays with scriptural, hagiographic and heroic subject matters increased in number. Their purpose was to galvanise viewers into emulating the noblest Christian role models. They were also informed by historical philology, to which the church had turned during the Reformation in order to reconstruct and strengthen both its roots – as represented in the stories of the martyrs – and its modern perspectives on holiness (De Maio 1973: 253–74). The contrast between the theatrical knowledge of amateur actors on the one hand, and the everyday behaviour of secular players and spectators on the other, produces a gap that exemplifies the relationship between church and *commedia*.

The extent of edifying works of theatre being created was revealed in the bibliographical catalogue *Drammaturgia*, compiled by the erudite theologian and keeper of the Vatican Library, Monsignor Leone Allacci (1666). The dramatic repertoire of this emerging genre featured a pantheon of heroic characters and admirable virtues, already evident in the titles of the collected texts, most of which were staged at least once. A vast array of 'actions', 'representations', 'fairy tales', 'dramas', 'tragedies' and 'tragicomedies' were all described with adjectives such as 'spiritual', 'sacred' or 'moral'.

Martino La Farina (1633), scholar and bibliophile of prestige who would later become a bishop, and a close friend of Allacci, stated that, out of the 'two kinds of actors', the 'mercenaries', i.e. those who 'practised the toughest profession ... in order to live from it, rather than for other more honourable purposes', were not suited for tragedies. Instead they should only perform plays which were performed 'almost every day', without 'much expense', collecting revenue from spectators 'who do not seek spiritual profit' but 'mere diversion'. Moreover, he added, the *comici* had better be careful not to represent 'obscene things, if they do not want to sully their conscience with mortal sin. They should just pursue what is ridiculous but also honest'. The question of obscenity was a fundamental and recurrent topic in this debate, addressed by, among others, the Jesuit Giovan Domenico Ottonelli, who would write a weighty attempt at mediation (Taviani 1969: 315–20).

According to La Farina, 'the actors of tragedy must be serious men, who are not interested in profit, and only represent tragedies out of the desire to benefit others. Not more than ... once or twice a year, in order to hold high their reputation as well as that of the poem they represent, and to keep the audience always interested, and not saturate them with their acting'. They will also 'avoid every impropriety in the representation'. Female parts 'may be played by good-natured young men, knowledgeable in belles-lettres and devoted to honourable studies', all the better if they are members of an 'honoured academy, whose purpose is the study of belles-lettres and the prestige of the city in which it is founded'.

The implication of this was that acting in edifying tragedies was not only a privilege, but also a duty for virtuous citizens. They would transfer their own judiciousness and representativeness to their characters, passing these virtues on to the spectators in a Christian and civic way. As stated by

the Turin canonist Guglielmo Baldesano, these were essential conditions
for Christian tragedy, since, if played by 'people with a vain ... and
versatile mind, of perverse ... habits, licentious life', tragedies would be
no different from the 'wicked comedies' of the itinerant *comici*. As part of
the overall process of regulation that was occurring in the confessional age
(Di Bella 2012; Prodi 1994) and for the first time in its history, the
Catholic Church thus acknowledged that theatre could have a legitimate –
or indeed essential – function in public life. The seductive powers of
theatrical ambiguity were too evident for the church not to want to use
them to its own advantage. Theatre was in the first instance to support the
positions of the church, which would then finally be able to address the
phenomenon of professional comic practice. This had, in a parallel development, been growing in influence, rapidly gaining the attention of the
same audience that the church was reaching and progressively becoming
integrated among the guilds of the city.

To sum up we can say that not only was theatre accepted by the church
as an art form at this point, but that the church actively promoted and
regulated it. By performing works of fiction based on religious teaching,
Christian actors assumed a social function, promoting values such as
holiness and virtue.

This kind of religious theatre, then, established itself alongside the other
new form of theatre, the commedia dell'arte. Although the two were pro-
foundly different, they began to compete: While the *comici* had no part in
the church's free and festive amateur performances, they did erode the
Christian ideal of how audiences were supposed to behave. The fact that
comedies were performed on weekdays undermined aspirations of an
everyday life led in holiness. The church further accused the *comici* of
introducing customs inspired by sensual pleasures, perverting the enjoyment of virtue and exemplarity and the responsible use of emotions and
imagination. Commedia dell'arte, in short, was seen to lead to the neglect
of Christian behaviour and thoughts.

But what about the audience? For the most part they did not, as Cesare
Franciotti, member of the Clerics Regular of the Mother of God of Lucca
feared, succumb to the 'authority' exercised 'over them by force' of the
comedies. Instead of being driven to mortal sin, they became 'voluntary
victims', 'new worshippers' of the Devil 'in the big rooms' – those of the
commedia – where, with 'maximum joy' and freedom, 'considering it an
innocent occupation', they drank the 'extremely sweet' poison that gradually led them to spiritual death.

The Jesuit Paolo Segneri, admired across Europe as one of the most influential missionaries and preachers of his time, described this guilty and irredeemable light-heartedness and its consequences in his work *In detestazione delle commedie scorrette*. Regarded at the time as one of the most insightful books written on the matter, Segneri's work contained a formidable image designed to expose what he saw as *commedia* spectators' misuse of the powers of the soul. It was through memory, will and intellect that Christians should process what their senses show to them, not through direct enjoyment as in the *commedia*:

> You leave the theatre. Immediately, another action starts in your memory, and the more intimate it is, the worse it becomes for you. *Quae spectasti ad memoriam redeunt*. The impure sayings you heard, the jokes, the formulas, the audacious gestures come back to your mind; and you become a portable theatre to yourself, the actor, the stage, and the spectator and the subject and anything you like . . . this is what the Devil does. He lets you out of the theatre enclosure where he hurts you, well aware of the inauspicious consequences of the bad thought he has implanted through your eyes, your ears and your imagination, in the shape of a pointed dart driven to the depths of your guts. (Segneri 1687: 301)

Even though he relies on the authority of St John Chrysostom, Segneri here demonstrates in an exemplary way how Christian thinkers' reflections on the commedia dell'arte were influenced by the valorisation of intentional, measurable psychophysical procedures in which senses, body and mind were constantly disciplined. His argument was substantiated by references to various graduated ascetic experiences used by Christians and believers of a wide range of other religions for self-perfection or for the purpose of radical conversion.

Consistent with the Christian view of theatre, there is an assumed ability to anticipate the inner changes in the spectator's soul based on the actor as either a good or a bad role model. Segneri's description of the effects of watching a comedy is striking because he relates them to the instrumentalisation of direct experience as practised by the Jesuits – in many ways polar opposites to the artists of the commedia dell'arte. And yet, he interprets the 'inner world' of spectators remaining alone with themselves after a play in the same way as he might analyse the mind and soul of someone practising the spiritual exercises proposed by Ignatius of Loyola (founder of the Society of Jesus in 1540). Loyola's exercises aim to create an experience in which mnemonic, imaginative and meditative processes always lead the subject to be the protagonist of the mental scene he has created in his inner self, just like the spectator who becomes a 'portable theatre'. The idea of the 'portable theatre' thus refers to the similarly meditative, often overwhelming, religious experience of the Eucharist, known by the liturgical expression of 'portable altar'. For Segneri it stands in irreducible opposition to the 'excommunicated' world, the world 'with a crazy will and a foolish intellect', capable of judging things only 'by appearance' and intent on taking revenge on God through the 'actions of the comici', with their 'sacrilegious enchantments' (Segneri 1687: 298).

Segneri saw the comici as engaged in ritual courtship with Satan, along with a host of other enemies of Catholic faith and virtue: magicians, enchanters, witches and wizards (whose Italian name, stregoni, carries strong connotations with istrioni [histriones]), as well as prostitutes, gypsies, idolaters, Jews and heretics. All were accused of superstitious credulity and obstinate paganism, most of all the actresses whose enchanting art attested to their nature as favourite 'disciples' of that 'race of devils' presiding over lasciviousness. In the theatres, Segneri wrote, spectators 'succumbed to' an 'enchanted hibernation' which made them fall into a 'sleep' which was also a 'dream'. Even though Jesus Christ had been sent into the world to 'show them what is true and what is false', they 'could not see reality, like anyone who sleeps. Likewise, they could see what is not real, like someone who dreams in his sleep'. They were therefore 'cursed in their soul' and 'possessed . . . in their spirit' (Segneri 1687: 295, 297–8, 303).

The devil was a ubiquitous figure in these anti-theatrical writings – a weaver of illusions, who preyed on the fickleness of spectators and their inability to distinguish good from evil among the deceptions of the stage. There seemed to have been a concern that what the theatre needed was a form of priestly competence, a crucial concept during the Counter-Reformation. It required priests to resort to the doctrine of discretio spirituum (the discernment of the spirit) in order to assess the actual origin, be it divine or diabolical, of prodigious signs, prophetic gifts, mortifications or ecstasy. Women were regarded as being particularly vulnerable to such states and therefore were the devil's favoured instruments. Only by exposing and rooting out witchcraft, the possessed and those simulating holiness, could those who really aspired to a life of perfection be identified and promoted (Di Simplicio 2010; Zarri 2008).

The discourse against actors was therefore intended to warn spectators who found themselves in the grip of the devil or in a state where 'the spirits proper to a Christian mind' were inactive (Segneri 1687: 303), and to instruct them in how to cultivate doubt in the face of the deceptions of comedy. The aim was to make viewers suspicious of the seductive excesses and immoderate extremes characteristic of theatrical performance as pure entertainment, as opposed to the more temperate and reflective enjoyment of edifying, religious theatre.

It was understood that in Catholic doctrine the salvation of souls was entrusted to the care of the religious authorities, who were tasked with the job of mediating between the people and God. This idea had been rejected by Protestants during the Reformation, but had subsequently been reaffirmed by the Council of Trent. Its implication was that salvation depended directly on the faithful, on individual behaviour and the desire to make progress in Christian practice. In contrast with the Lutheran thesis of justification by faith alone, the Council debate had defined the doctrine of *salus animarum* through faith as not separate from conduct: It stated that men and women had to cooperate with God through their own deeds: Their choices and actions were crucial. For theatre this meant that the act of attending or performing in works of edifying theatre was meritorious, demonstrating faith and virtue. Conceived as a transformative and imitative process, it was seen as being capable of transforming the habitus of actors and spectators. It also strengthened priestly control, as Catholic playwrights were often clergymen or members of religious orders (Valentin 1978: 14–15).

By contrast, comedy was seen neither as the expression of an imitable Christian model nor as a plausible representation of the created world. *Commedia* created a world in itself – a world that was as separate from reality as it was from the idealised worldview of Christian mythology. The church's concern was that spectators of such plays would not only be unable to recognise what is good, but that they would also be unable to see past mere appearances, becoming confused by masks, language, actions, postures, relationships, conflicts and plots that would not allow for positive imitation. Comparing the *comici* on stage with the performers of religious tragedy, La Farina wrote that, 'much is about the usual attitudes of such people, whose ridiculous gestures would not ... suit' a 'modest and well-behaved man'. It was, in short, pure fantastic theatre, where actions were not necessarily linked to formal or informal forms of everyday behaviour nor designed to emulate the steadfast demeanour of good Christian citizens. The commedia dell'arte could only follow a divergent path: *divertere* (to diverge) as opposed to *convertere* (to converge) (Arcangeli 2004; Majorana 1994a: 478–87).

The fluctuations in the debate under discussion here underscore the essential contrast between pious theatrical amateurs and comedic theatre professionals. The anti-theatrical tradition and arguments used against professional actors derived their suggestive power from centuries of authoritative Christian writing and from the fear of stigmatisation, rather than from the arguments themselves, which were not in fact capable of reflecting the issue at hand or unravelling its knots. The preacher and ordained priest Carlo Borromeo, for example, wrote of the 'certain damage' that could be done to the professional theatre by the alternative religious theatre, specifically by performances on topics endorsed by the Church Fathers. By recalling them all, he wrote, it will be possible to 'root out such corruption' (Taviani 1969: 13).

At the same time, those among the *comici* who were able to respond to such attacks in a literary fashion presented an idealised vision of the *commedia* and its performers that was equally combative. The arguments from both sides were first of all addressed to the audience, that is to say, to the faithful, as the entire population was generally understood to be. It was, however, an essentially silent audience, the enduring object of the greatest concerns. The wide ranging project of the Counter-Reformation necessitated an investigation into the pastoral needs of the community and its individuals, specifically into their moral and spiritual lives. The church's competition with the *comici* was for the possession of souls.

If this was the reason for the disagreement, it was crucially important for the church. Not even the professional actors, who were turning against old church doctrines in the name of modernity and humanism, could afford to be insensitive to its importance. This is why Giovan Battista Andreini firmly stated that the *comici* of his rank belonged, without a doubt, to contemporary Christian society. He wrote: 'The comedy of which I write is modern, and it was born in a time in which everything was renovated in a similar way, so that any censorship or scrutiny by the most cultured Christians would be unexpected' (Andreini 1625: 2). In contrast, in 1621 Francesco Maria Del Monaco, an eminent theologian from Chieti, confessor to Cardinal Mazarin and preacher to the Italian community in Paris, bemoaned as 'unfortunate' the century in which the commedia dell'arte established itself. (Del Monaco 1969: 222).

The one novelty of commercial theatre which especially concerned polemicists was the presence of women, who had never held a similarly significant place in the European pagan or Christian traditions. Now they were no longer just acrobats, singers or dancers, as they had been until then – on the stages of the commedia dell'arte, women were eloquent (Taviani and Schino 1982: 331–44; Nicholson, 1991: 306–7). They sounded like self-confident teachers, made possible precisely by public speech, from which they had been banned by St Paul himself (1 Tim 2;

Majorana 1996a: 124–5). By performing with men, they showed scenes of seduction to be powerful and authentic. Without women, Andreini wrote, performances would lose their 'plausibility' as well as 'all grace . . . and affection' (Andreini 1991: 510). An opposing argument was proposed by the Dominican monk Domenico Gori, who said that all that 'is done' in comedies 'is in preparation for lasciviousness: the music . . . the plots, the gestures', so that, 'when the performing female enters, one has become so weak that it is morally impossible to resist' (in Taviani 1969: 136).

Lowered eyes and bowed head were the two defining gestures of monastic habit, the *forma cleri* marking Christian perfection. One of the projects of the Counter-Reformation was to attempt to extend this habit as widely as possible, ideally to all the people of God, including the laity, men, women and children. According to the polemicists, actresses transgressed against the Christian ideal of the *forma foemine*. Their conscious use of their bodies, eyes, faces (the *innamorati* performed without masks), voices and words meant that all these parts were exhibited, valued and eroticised. The relationships that actresses entered into with their fellow actors, on and off stage, were also evident (Taviani 1969: 85–6), so that they were likened to adulteresses and prostitutes (Del Monaco 1969: 211; Segneri 1687: 300–3), only with a wider audience and superior technical means. Giovanni Domenico Ottonelli wrote that the 'defeat of the army of Christian perfection' comes from the '*comica* by profession – expert in the arts, familiar with the stage, curvaceous by nature, specious by artifice and adorned with pomp and vain diligence'. Thus, 'a single glance is enough . . . to kidnap the heart and affection of a spectator' (Ottonelli 1648: 131–2).

Theatre was characterised as a living power able to overwhelm all the senses. It could not therefore be compared to any other kind of representation such as paintings or books, poetic words, secular songs or even dancing. These art forms were all subject to repeated criticisms, but none was criticised as much as the lascivious art of comedy as symbolised by the figure of the actress. In it, words were 'supported by the movements of the person, the looks, the sighs and the disdain . . . the embraces, and more', all 'highly studied, with histrionic artifice' (Franciotti 1969: 178).

The presence of women on stage was thus at the heart of the controversy between the church and the commedia dell'arte (Majorana 1996a; Majorana 1996b). Depicted as the incarnation of the *commedia*'s most fearsomely immoral qualities, the actress became a crucial point of intersection between stage and reality, taking the 'principle of consonance' between the inner and outer worlds (Pozzi 1986: 170–1) to a conclusion that proved unacceptable to the church's theorists. Their assumption was that anything depicted onstage would instantly become a moral reality for those performing or watching it. Christians were therefore advised to only expose themselves to edifying religious theatre and to avoid the morally ambiguous commedia dell'arte.

The *comici*, however, rejected this principle of correspondence between stage and reality. Unlike traditional clowns, whose theatrical acts were at one with their off-stage personas, they regarded themselves as modern professionals. Nicolò Barbieri, who played Beltrame in the commedia dell'arte, first as a member of the Confidenti, then of the Fedeli troupes, argued that any 'pretence' was entirely in the service of the character. It was the very structure and surface of the representation and it belonged to the realm of technique. He wrote, 'the *comici* are other people when they are off stage, are called by other names, they change their clothes and practise other habits' (Barbieri 1971: 24). For the most experienced *comici*, the distinction between person and character was both substantive and formal. It defined their profession and self-discipline and informed their behaviour in the public sphere. The civil role they aspired to was that of the modern Christian, embodying a particular combination of honour and conscience that could, according to Pier Maria Cecchini (Frittellino), *comico Acceso* and *capocomico* for the Duke of Mantua, only be recognised by a 'cultured' audience. It is evident from this that these *comici* regarded themselves as part of the most educated sphere of society.

Spectators expected to be able to recognise and appreciate the distinction between person and character. They should not confuse reality with stage appearances, but rather notice the 'excellence of language, voice and gesture' (Cecchini [1608] 1991: 70) that defines theatre. Andreini highlighted the moral integrity and seriousness of the actress, who must combine her functions as a wife and a mother with the preparation of her performances (Andreini 1991: 505–7). As regards the difference between *comici* and clowns, Barbieri stated: 'The same action should be judged differently depending on the subject who performs it, and the merits of performing it may vary depending on the intention' (Barbieri 1971: 24).

The *comici* thus maintained that their performances were independent works of art, with no moral or transformative functions. As regards the recreational and benevolent value of comedies and the technical prowess of actors, they argued that such aspects did not contradict the idea of a Christian experience of theatre, nor indeed that of a Christian comedian. Recalling his companion Girolamo Garavini who – unbeknownst to all – wore 'a large and sharp cilice of stinging iron plates' (Andreini 1991: 507) on stage under his *Capitan Rinoceronte* costume, Nicolò Barbieri wrote:

'It really seems a marked contrast: haircloth and comedy, punishment and amusement, mortification and cheerfulness. However, it does not appear strange to everyone, because many people know very well that men can be cheerful even while atoning for their sins. There are some who have played the fool out of mortification, or danced out of spiritual bliss. Many things are not what they seem to be' (Barbieri 1971: 27–8).

For the *comici*, skill and technical prowess represented not moral failings but, on the contrary, demonstrations of human qualities and social competence. Skill referred to virtue, in the double meaning of moral and technical virtue: It was a new way of conceiving roles – on stage, socially and personally – without escaping the human condition of the actor, but by means of it (Majorana 1992). Giovan Battista Andreini, son of the great actors Francesco and Isabella, who became a member of the Fedeli troupe and worked as a *capocomico* and playwright, was a perfect example of this. He attributed to the theatre of the commedia dell'arte a quality of revelation, believing that it could offer glimpses of the divine. The quest of the actor towards perfection mirrored and depended on the Christian subject's path towards truth and awareness. Andreini developed this vision throughout his life, writing a series of poems, essays and treatises in defence of the commedia dell'arte. Numerous long dramas, which he wrote and performed together with the other members of the Fedeli, marked his strong commitment to the opportunities offered by an established professional theatre with a regular schedule of performances – exactly the kind of environment that he himself worked in all his life. Significantly, he never doubted that his work would also be suitable to be performed on academic stages. In many of his plays, sometimes obliquely and sometimes explicitly, Andreini reflected on the status and responsibilities of the Christian actor and on the possibility of theatre having a regenerative function (Ferrone, 1993b: 223–73; Majorana 1992). He was seventy-six when he performed in the last of his published works in Milan, *La Maddalena lasciva e penitente* (1652). It was the fifth time that he had written about this particular saintly figure.

As the commedia dell'arte developed as an art form, it became increasingly involved in the pastoral care of its audiences, concerning itself with questions such as for example the guidance of souls. The *zelus animarum* motivated not only the supporters of religious, edifying theatre, but also parts of the professional, commercial *commedia*. As the earlier discussions have shown, the quality of theatre, its morality and its support of – or opposition to – the Catholic project, depended as much on the intentions of the individual who conceived and staged it as it did on the external circumstances of the performance, the nature of the audience's perceptual experience and the internal reorganisation and practice of what was performed. The stage was seen to be ambivalent, providing benefit as well as harm.

Although the originators of the conflict between church and *commedia dell'arte* in Italy were intent on making a strong stand on both sides, there would finally be neither winners nor losers. It was not the same everywhere: In the Germanic and Catholic areas of Europe, battling as they were with Protestantism, the improvised buffoon comedy imported by the Italians was no more than a passing fashion, soon replaced, through a political-religious operation, by a particularly Jesuit form of edifying theatre (Vianello 2009). Across the Italian states and principalities, professional theatre and pious amateur theatre continued to coexist side by side. The *comici* of the commedia dell'arte continued to perform well into the eighteenth century, when the *commedia* slowly disappeared and the debates around the function of theatre moved from pastoral and moral questions towards ideas of cultural and civic representation.

Commedia dell'Arte and Dominant Culture

Raimondo Guarino

Organisation and Creation

Benedetto Croce's philosophy and way of thinking have provided the groundwork for the manner in which contemporary historiography depicts the commedia dell'arte, a manner that is characterised by a recognition of the centrality of the relationship between organisation and the act of creation. Croce imposed an economic and cultural perspective, linking the phenomenon of Italian comedy to a 'professional or industrial' concept: a process of 'industrialisation of theatre', an 'itinerant practice of this industry from one city to another' that led to a 'lasting institutionalisation' of the theatrical profession (Croce 1933: 503–4).

Based on these assumptions, any investigation of and reflection on the identity and condition of Italian actors and companies involve two primary issues: on the one hand, the relationship with the performance culture of court theatre and, on the other, the search for those specifically Italian traits which reveal a more transcultural diffusion in comparison to the professional theatre found in other European countries. Italian companies developed their artistic and organisational identity by elaborating, transforming and otherwise influencing the business conditions, performance techniques and symbolic repertoires of Renaissance court theatre. Professional theatre had always been a part of the entertainment business. The adoption of the idea of a 'theatre for money' was a constitutive feature of the new phenomenon (Taviani 1982: 376–8) and involved transposing the main features of court theatre into the context of a broad-spectrum audience and touring theatre companies. This development runs parallel to the general shift from patronage to the invention of a business and is just one aspect of the development of spaces and customs in urban culture in early modern Europe.

As a result, the training and activities of theatre companies bred more general changes and transformations. The paths taken and the resources utilised by the Italian *comici* are very frequently and superficially mentioned in historical anthropology and cultural studies. They were considered significant and fascinating examples of a dialogue between different 'levels of culture' and of the spread of knowledge, all of which served to bridge the gap existing between humanistic models and commercial entertainment: the Italian *commedia* appeared as the most readily comprehensible synthesis of high culture and the populist – or 'mass entertainment' – tendency of Renaissance theatre (Burke 1997).

In order to define the relationship of the companies to their material, ideological and institutional contexts, it is necessary to start with a general look at the period in which they existed. The dynamic elements of their endeavours, their serial production and their appeal to various types of audiences must be seen in a context which was characterised by restrictive economic, political and religious factors. Society was becoming feudal again and there was talk of the 'betrayal of the bourgeoisie' (Braudel 1991: 222). This coincided with the establishment of financial institutions and the social control systems of the modern state. Freedom of conscience depended on the outcome of religious wars and conflicting factions within a divided Christianity. The confrontation of Italian theatre companies with the 'dominant cultures', which had an impact on their organisational and expressive experiment, played out in the context of a normalisation which included the reduction of the circulation and consumption of tangible and intangible goods and the establishment of new rules and regulations. Carlo Dionisotti summarises the change of mood around 1560, linking the language and dramaturgy of the commedia dell'arte and, in a sense, the influence of its protagonists, to the fact that the values and rules of literary production were becoming stricter:

> Open rifts were being created, exclusive definitions and classifications were being established ... Among the examples which can be put forward with reference to this general process, I will mention the one which appears to be the least relevant, yet is both characteristic and fundamental: in the recent years, the decline and precipitate shift in perception of the *commedia dell'arte* from militant literature to commercial theatre, a change which is irresponsible in literary terms, but which was for the commedia essential, although uneasy and disturbing, because of the dramatic and satirical unrest pertaining to this kind of literature. (Dionisotti 1967: 248)

Although this diagnosis needs to be corrected with respect to their supposed 'irresponsibility' towards literary implications, it identifies the ideological constraints and the new intellectual profiles which, together with economic factors, shaped the developments and conditions in which the companies' founders and artists were making their decisions.

The social innovations introduced by theatre companies were only possible because the context of reception and the network of available spaces had stabilised. The emerging material context of the *stanze delle commedie*, indoor performance spaces, marked a significant shift in the topography of symbolic practices and, at the same time, pointed to their hybridisation. The passage from solemn celebration to commercial theatre is related to the way places of performance developed in reaction to the ever-changing history of cities. The theatre of *stanze*, in which performances were for sale, emerged in Venice as a result of patronage from young groups belonging to the oligarchy (Guarino 1995). In the 1540s in Rome, during the papacy of Paul III, commercial theatre was first staged in spaces located near the Palazzo Farnese, the residence of the Pope's family and the heart of Rome's public life (Boiteux 1981; Cruciani 1983). It is very well known that for many decades, starting from the 1580s at the latest, the Teatro della Dogana, alias Teatro di Baldracca, in Florence was an intermediate station for several theatre companies. Managed by the customs officer, the *stanza* was adjacent to the grand duke's residence, next to the Uffizi. The link between court and popular entertainment developed 'in all the major cities in the north and centre of Italy at the end of the 1570s' (Monaldini 2005: 375). Only in the metropolises of Venice and Naples was it possible to observe a process of contraction and consolidation in the variety of theatre on offer. In Venice – as a result of the constant struggle between oligarchy and government – public theatres were closed by order of the state. Organised by noble families, they were active up to their closure for the five years between 1580 and 1585, only to re-emerge in the first decades of the seventeenth century. In Naples, a dialogue between theatre managers and companies commenced in the same period. Coinciding with the dynastic and diplomatic crises of the Italian courts in the 1620s 'Venice and Naples replaced the courts creating a new bipolar division' (Ferrone 1993b: 305). Yet patronage from the courts and the oligarchies continued. At the same time, the number of locations for popular performances increased. The two forms of organisation continued to coexist. The carnivals of Rome, the perspective stages of Mantua and Florence and the closely knit texture of the *commedia* seasons in the Po Valley were still crucial destinations for the touring *comici*.

The origins of the spread of the Italian theatre phenomenon throughout Europe are quite complex. In 1576, Drusiano and Tristano Martinelli were able to perform in different cities such as Antwerp, Lyon and Paris, thanks to a combination of the *comici*'s initiative, the support of the merchant-bankers from Lucca, the Gonzagas' military and diplomatic connections and the relationship between the French monarchy and 'the transnational settlement of the Italian colony' (Ferrone 2006: 28).

The considerable magnitude of this 'lasting' phenomenon, the distances covered by touring companies and the diversity of spectators attracted all implied specific forms of leadership, a mingling of personal relationships, successful recruitment and the formation of groups which could collaborate for many a long year, as the *comici* did, but also split up and reform again. The most significant result of the studies of the last few decades on the material culture at the root of economic processes and cultural exchanges is the notion of the universe of companies as a microculture, a microsociety characterised by internal features and external relationships. In this regard, the troupes of Italian actors are considered a prototype (Meldolesi 1984; Taviani 1982). They were 'free in a society of subjects' (Ferrone 1993b: 287), but their freedom was unstable and suspect. They were subject to the protection and patronage of small Italian courts and of other European courts and gave daily performances in the major cities of Western Europe. Companies combined high and low traditions, genres and repertoires, putting on a performance as a daily celebration. Used as living coin of the nobles' ostentation, the *comici* of the major companies were the aristocracy of a difficult but recognised art. They endeavoured to defend and regulate the opportunities and shortcomings of their profession while maintaining a visible distance towards the theatre scene of the day – still, however, intending to occupy a dominant role in that scene.

Imitation and Transformation

The actors created an autonomous and approved way of life, which was separate from normal society in regard to material conditions but was, at the same time, dependent on it as far as economic dynamics and the development of values were concerned. The business model of the companies relied on a combination of princely patronage and paying city audiences. The 'encompassing' and 'dominant' culture which allowed the companies to be tolerated and to survive was characterised by opacity and contradictions. Submission to princely patronage guaranteed protection and the privilege of free movement. The establishment of the daily performance as a product to sell generated an active but remote social group, whose role in the functioning of city life was indispensable but unstable, oscillating between what was prohibited by the Christian city and inoffensive to the developing institutions of the modern city.

Between the mid-sixteenth and the mid-seventeenth centuries, there emerged several episodes of negotiation between the most prominent representatives of the theatre profession and of the old and new systems of control. The resulting solutions were characterised as being personal and intuitive in nature. Rather than go through a macroscopic analysis or an analysis centred on institutions, it is possible to outline the process of self-definition of the *comici* and their companies by starting from their personal strategies of survival, adaptation and metamorphosis. Borrowing the apt expression coined by a scholar of the English Renaissance (Greenblatt: 1980), biographies and writings of the *comici* provide various examples of 'self-fashioning', of self-definition by social actors who, in the case of theatre professionals, were overexposed. The expression 'self-fashioning' is related to the state of uncertainty and mobility which characterised the early modern age and offers an interesting methodological key to theatre studies. Self-definition in the age when feudalism was returning, religious wars were being fought and the Counter-Reformation was at its dramatic zenith – all this demanded a continuous effort of adaptation and initiative – in order to be able to claim and defend one's rights. These processes shaped the relationship between status and skill and modelled personal realities in the microsociety of actors.

Theatre studies cover a central aspect of the actors' relationship with the multifaceted reality in which they lived and worked. According to Taviani, the outer layer or visible side of their individual and collective identities was always based on an imitation of the behaviour of figures characteristic of the encompassing society. Actors sought out 'models on which to base their public personas ... Hence the need to choose some figures of the encompassing society and to imitate them in actors' circles'. This need arose from 'the serious necessity to bury differences'(Taviani 1984: 42–5). In the *comici*'s world material conditions were different from those of the society around them. The distance between the two was corrected and reduced – by desire or need – by adopting values similar to those of the spectators' community. In some cases, this attitude of social imitation led to the adoption of extreme examples of the dominant values. It also accounted for an element of ambiguity in social objectives and coloured family memories and legacies as described in biographies and monographs. Adopting such values was in line with the claim of the excellence of theatre practice and was inseparable from the desire of the major companies to bestow a certain distinction on the lower ranks of their profession, associating it with moral superiority. The resultant tension between difference and similarity emerged in the style and topics of apologetic literature and in the minute moralising practised by letter writers.

Siro Ferrone interpreted the letters which the *comici* exchanged with their princes as well as with their masters of ceremonies, their festival planners and company recruiters as 'the symptom of a need for moral conformism . . . Through their letters to the nobles, the *comici* negotiated their loss of freedom' (Ferrone 1993a: 21). These texts illustrate the tension that they felt towards the security offered by patronage and thus define the relationship between identity and power. Here follow some brief excerpts illustrating basic concepts, then current, of a personal definition of art. In a side note to one of his literary works, Giovan Battista Andreini discussed the convergence of writing skills and the cult of 'virtue and honour', describing this convergence as a goal of his personal and artistic search. In his dedication of the comedy *Lo schiavetto* (1612), he wrote: 'Those *comici* who wove and disentangled such fables were people who endeavoured to learn the art of making dramas and to understand that the men who pursue virtue and honour are far superior to the others' (Ferrone 1993b: 212).

'Distinction in the profession': In a letter written in Piacenza in 1620 and addressed to Ercole Marliani, a gentleman by the name of Pier Maria Cecchini who was in the service of the Gonzagas and dabbled in playwriting, organising the Duke's companies, evaluated the performances of minor *comici* acting in small towns between Mantua and Bologna. Cecchini cast his expert eye on the quality of the actors, dividing them into either *comici* or charlatans and postulating a classification which included categories for the extremely good, the moderately good and those in between. 'It will be a test to see whether, as a consequence of the fact that many charlatans were successful, those who are between the *comici* and the charlatans could also be included' (Burattelli, Landolfi and Zinanni 1993: 291). The group portrait offered by these letters points to a certain degree of professional free will, consisting essentially in the possibility of choosing between the unity of the company and acceptance of the patron's wishes. In March 1620, Don Giovanni de' Medici – illegitimate son of Grand Duke Cosimo I, the protector and organiser of theatre groups – wrote to Marliani explaining the reasons why Flaminio Scala's Confidenti should remain together as opposed to accepting offers which threatened to break up the troupe. In the letter he asked to 'let the poor Confidenti enjoy that liberty which the good Lord concedes to all those who were not born to be subjects' (Ferrone 1993b: 337).

In literature favourably oriented towards them, the *comici* were seen, in the most elaborate cases, as having developed a specific moral code, in which deference was transformed into an attitude of emphatic pride and into a particular demonstration of the relationship between morals and the exercise of power. In his work, *La supplica*, published in 1634, dedicated to Louis XIII of France and addressed to those 'who speak about *comici*, neglecting the merits of virtuous actions', Nicolò Barbieri, known as Beltrame, propagated a pragmatic view of the *commedia* as suitable for the entertainment of princes and not offending the mores of the city. Methodically exorcising all anti-theatrical superstitions, Barbieri repeatedly described episodes which demonstrated that the honesty of the theatre profession was compatible with Christian ethics and argued that the flaws of theatre were irrelevant in comparison to what was wrong with the world in general. Recalling the sensation caused by the discovery of a hair shirt in the deathbed of Capitan Rinoceronte (Girolamo Garavini da Ferrara, who died in Paris in 1624), Beltrame extolled the quiet piety of knights and ladies and contrasted it with the false devotion of the authorities, as well as with the eagerness of those who quixotically wanted to 'correct the faults of centuries, by starting with the *comici*', although 'the *comici* are such a small and insignificant part of the world' (Barbieri 1971: 27–9). Opposing the tolerance of the *Ius de' Superiori* to the gossip of the falsely pious, Barbieri argued the case that the *comici* were morally similar to saints and knights, revealing a conscious aspect of the social imitation that was being enacted by moralist actors. It was a declaration of the superiority of those who cultivated honour and piety, making it possible to balance appearance and substance in public and private life. Threats of censorship and general criticism appeared more a matter of values than a conflict with the powers that be. This issue was raised when – torn between old inhibitions and new freedoms – civil government and spiritual authorities subjected actors to discriminating restrictions.

Another side of the actors' mirroring of society was their making common cause with groups of intellectuals who experienced similar conditions of subjection in different circumstances and in neighbouring territories. The feelings of similarity with and attraction to academies were the result of their imitation and admiration of figures and groups belonging to 'high' culture, rather than to classes and circles from the dominant culture. Retracing the career of the Gelosi troupe in the 1570s and 1580s, Apollonio declared that 'the Gelosi troupe ... claimed to be resolutely academic and refined. ... Their performances were aimed at forging the most numerous and conspicuous bonds with contemporary culture'

(1930: 99–100). This mirror game played with the associations and classifications of intellectuals regarding the intertwining of various traditions of discourse and gesture and involved influences which determined the creation of stock characters. The aspiration to a refined style for the roles of the lovers and for actresses 'also concerned the style of comic roles, as in the case of Magnifico Giulio Pasquati da Padova, actor of tragedies and pastorals, who praised the Gelosi before Henry III' (Apollonio 1930: 103). In light of their constant involvement with genres and literatures for feast days and special occasions, it is possible to explain certain episodes and hypotheses, such as the participation of the Gelosi in the first performance of Tasso's *Aminta* in Ferrara in 1573 and their presence at the celebrations for the visit of Henry III to Venice in 1574, in which some of the actors of the troupe sang in the cantata by Frangipani (Taviani and Schino 1982: 365). Some eulogising chroniclers testify to the success of Vittoria Piissimi in the role of Silvia and in the following years, of Isabella Andreini as Aminta in Tasso's pastoral drama. The remarkable presence of the pastoral genre throughout the commedia dell'arte repertoire, the mythology and the actresses' literary production emphasised 'the Petrarchan elements which the productive system based on personal repertoires intertwines with serious and buffoonish elements' (Cruciani 1985: 186–7). The incorporation and removal of the buffoon heritage were associated with excellence in literary improvisation and familiarity with classical drama. As claimed in the oration by Adriano Valerini, Vincenza Armani was the first to adopt the pastoral genre. Reasonable importance was also given in the available studies to the presence of Isabella Andreini and the Gelosi in the interludes performed in Florence in 1589. The performance of the *Pazzia d'Isabella* (*Isabella's Madness*) was described as having a value of inversion, or of original resonance, in comparison with the cosmologic vision attributed to the interludes written by Bernardo Buontalenti on the occasion of the Medici wedding.

Recent studies have emphasised an affinity between the experiments of large actor troupes and the expressive and ideological dissensions of academies. In Milan in 1583, the Gelosi of Francesco and Isabella Andreini also performed in the 'small and minor rooms' of individuals, probably belonging to Jews (Taviani 1984: 20). In those surroundings, discussions between academics, booksellers and painters laid the groundwork for encounters with the community of the Accademia dei Facchini della Val di Blenio, known for its extravagance of language. In the works of academics, the *comici* personified the singularity of multilingualism and other aesthetic values related to the grotesque and the realistic, which had always been

connected to the mirroring of subordinated cultures by cultivated observers. On the other hand, troupes of actors were inherently unstable social
groups in which interpersonal problems were dealt with in an ad hoc
manner. They adopted models and symbols which for intellectual elites
were long-established and stable.

Furthermore, for people with an intellectual bent of mind, writing
comedies was an activity which transformed them into special spectators,
who were sensitive and acute observers of the *comici*'s performances. The
attraction of troupes of actors and groups of intellectuals and artists for
each other has been investigated in several locally based and general
studies, which have identified in this exchange the value of a convergence
of points of view as representing an alternative to 'open rifts' and the
exclusive classifications of the Counter-reformation culture (Tamburini
2010). The real influence one group had on the other is independent of
speculation regarding the formation of these groups. Apollonio believed
that the group of Ruzante and his followers from Padua had transmitted
not only the 'organic autonomy' but also the 'spirit of artisanal cooperation' to the 'fraternal company' which signed the contract in Padua in
1545. This contract is a relic showing when and where the company was
founded (Apollonio 1981: 550, 556). Research on the situations in Padua
and Venice and on the cooperation between the actor-playwrights surrounding Andrea Calmo reveals subtler elements in the motivation determining the relationship between the oligarchy of Venice and the local
nobility. This relationship was aimed more at reinventing and perfecting
ceremonies and festivities at court and bringing fame and glory to the local
men of letters, rather than shaping the development of everyday theatre
(Guarino 1995; Vescovo 1996). The most prominent representatives of
comic art aspired quite early to acceptance in elite circles and to honours
from the academies, endeavouring to emancipate themselves from previous
compromising relationships. As professional theatre absorbed literary and
artistic trends, the expert voice of the *comici* rekindled and sustained
exceptions to an otherwise inevitable linguistic uniformity.

Interpretations of Fame and Honour

The theatre profession – even within the confines of the limited number of
comic troupes – produced a massive body of behavioural studies covering
such aspects as self-definition, social imitation, moral exception and expressive extravagance. The theatre experience – a place of struggle – became the
context where personalities were visibly transformed (Taviani 1984: 58).

The actor's familiarity with the collective memory and what the public were interested in resulted in unusual interpretations as to what constituted fame, while activating processes of interaction in detail between individuals and knowledge. The letters exchanged in 1601 and 1602 between Isabella Andreini and Erycius Puteanus – then a student of Giusto Lipsio and author of the epigraph to the first edition of Isabella's *Rime* – explore with a wealth of metaphors the new ideas on immortality which had been brought to the notice of European humanists by Italian actors. Similar considerations have been prompted by studies on the relationship of Isabella with Torquato Tasso and other men of letters. Contacts with professional writers offered opportunities for actors to develop personally, improve their social position and emancipate themselves from their previous backgrounds. These contacts between *comici* and intellectuals opened up new possibilities for cultural development. In this regard, it is worth mentioning a letter which Maria Malloni, also known as Celia – an outstandingly talented actress, according to Barbieri, 'a young lady of letters and famous *comica*' (1971: 19) and first lover of Flaminio Scala's Confidenti – sent to Don Giovanni de' Medici in November 1618. Replying to criticism of her 'conversations' with intellectuals, she explained to de' Medici that she had compensated for the shortcomings in her education by becoming acquainted with intellectuals: 'Gentlemen and academics, scholars and literary figures have come from this and other cities to visit me. I declare and confess I have learnt from them, not having other ways to pursue the path of knowledge and study' (Fantappiè 2009: 224–5).

Crucial to the lives of the *comici* were the issues of imitation and emancipation. How this played out in the sphere of personal honour is described as what are called the 'sinister accidents' (Barbieri 1971: 124) in biographies. These incidents were experienced as self-assertion, avenging or making amends for some foregoing act. They were characterised by being in marked contrast to the norm for virtuous behaviour. In August 1609, for example, Pier Maria Cecchini, while in Turin for a series of performances, attacked and injured Benedetto Ricci, son of the *pantalone* Federico. Some days later, Cecchini killed Carlo De Vecchi, an expert *comico* and well-known troublemaker, who played roles of female servant (Franceschina). Ricci and De Vecchi were both actors of his troupe, the Accesi, and probably the two episodes are linked to slanderous remarks made against Orsola Posmoni (whose stage name was Flaminia), Cecchini's wife. A horoscope handwritten by Cecchini attributed the fact to *uxoris causa*. In his dedication to the *Lettere facete e morali*, published in 1622, Pier Maria hints at 'honourable reasons' (Ferrone 2006: 161; Taviani 1979).

These blows to personal honour fuelled hostilities. Informed of Cecchini's crimes and of the quarrel between rivals within the Accesi, Giovan Battista Andreini, leader of the Fedeli, wrote to Vincenzo Gonzaga, saying Gonzaga's intervention was justified as 'shepherd of this flock' and imploring him 'to preserve and cast out the infected sheep' (Burattelli et al. 1993: 91). Imprisoned with his wife and her alleged lover, Jacopo Antonio Fidenzi (Cinzio), Cecchini was pardoned after one month and returned to lead troupes of *comici*. The task of restoring honour fell upon the descendants. At the Carnival of 1645, Cecchini's son, Francesco died in Florence, stabbed by a young Venetian who was following the troupe, attracted by the seductive performances of Angela Nelli, a comica from Siena (Monaldini 2002). After the murder, as had happened to the Accesi of Pier Maria, Angela Nelli and Francesco's fellow actors were briefly arrested. Stefano Boncompagno Trevisan, the young murderer of Francesco Cecchini, was hanged. Before the law, actors were often granted immunity because they were regarded as being bound by a different moral code. Sexual promiscuity, however, was punished. Cecchini père killed a fellow actor and his own son was killed by an obsessed spectator. The cause of both murders was an offence against and a defence of the actresses' honour. These violent events were the symptom of a crucial problem: respect for women of the theatre. On the same page on which he argued for a professional foundation for the Italian *commedia*, Croce recognised the power of the sexual impulse. The presence of women in theatre opened up possibilities of an 'erotic-theatrical life'. The philosopher deduced that 'eroticism too has its contingent causes, in other words its history' (Croce 1933: 505).

Energy and Meaning: Nurturing the Rift

Studies on Italian acting troupes induce us to reconsider the terms under which cultural conflicts arise and the tensions they generate. The small world of theatre companies absorbed and distorted the values and practices of the ambient encompassing culture. In their moralistic, apologetic writings, the *comici* defended, in the name of theatre and *commedia*, their theatre as a field of virtue which corresponded to the morals of their audience, but was at the same time incongruous or extreme. They did this because of their specific need to live from theatre. Fascination and eroticism, protection and expiation refer to the body and to physical expression on the stage which were also key aspects of the daily confrontation with hostile authorities as well as being important instruments with which the *comici* achieved their limited but endangered sovereignty and their relative liberty. Italians had opened new ways, beyond their literary and musical skills, towards acquiring a presence in European theatre by sharpening the basic instruments of posture and gesture. Moreover, they created a repertoire of plots and figures where appearances and acts of being men and women, servants and masters, the astute and the fool, were produced and distributed among statutes, figures and passions of the present. The social imitation emerging from the *comici*'s writings was combined on stage with a form of abstract realism (so evident as to be inaccessible to us) resulting from mastery of the action. The *comici*'s expressive repertoire could be seen as indicative of 'realism' and 'social protest' (Braudel 1991: 141, 145); at the same time this repertoire could increase the timeless store of theatrical resources as it was based on the ability to absorb conventions and patterns starting from the principles of physical action. Apollonio perceived the essence of nature being recreated in the daily performances, when he wrote about the versatility and profound equilibrium between patterns and improvisation in the actors of large companies: 'They seemed always ready to adopt a habit and always ready to change it' (Apollonio 1981: 575).

The connections between power and truth and between the sense of belonging to a locality and yet having transcultural horizons emerge in the text *Frutti delle moderne commedie* by Pier Maria Cecchini (Marotti and Romei 1991: 77–97), which discusses the quality and the decline of the Neapolitan *comici*'s style:

> In our area of Lombardy, several Neapolitan-style characters have become popular. They are not really from Naples and they do not have the qualities or characteristics truly innate only to those who were born there. Their renderings of the Neapolitan accent, manners and sayings can only be described as murderous. The only thing Neapolitan about them are the names they use, Coviello, Cola, Pasquariello, or others. This seasoning seems to them a distortion of life, disgusting dancing and disgraceful gestures. (Cecchini in Marotti and Romei 1991: 88–9. This extract was also quoted by Croce in 1898, with reference to the origins of Pulcinella)

This comparison between ethnic background – a condition necessary for the purpose of endowing theatrical presence – and its imitation marks the decline of that theatre form. In his pamphlet, dedicated to Ferdinando II de' Medici, Cecchini claims to be not only a comico with the stage name of Frittellino, but also a nobleman from Ferrara (Matthew of Hapsburg had bestowed the title of 'gentleman' upon him during a visit to Bohemia in 1613). Writing about Neapolitan *comici*, Cecchini-Frittellino discusses the conflict between Lombards and Neapolitans as it influenced the origins and directions of the commedia dell'arte community. Cecchini arrived in Naples during Lent 1616 to recruit fellow actors. He remained there until October for a series of performances and returned later to experiment with the local theatre management systems. He talks about Neapolitan *comici* because he had seen them and wanted to record their names and various talents. By contrast, he says nothing about the skills and respective merits of Lombard *comici*, cautious of inciting rivalries between troupes. Nor does he mention female roles, in order to avoid conflict arising from a round of criticism. The excellence of Neapolitan *comici* is recognised in two characters immediately associated with two actors: the Coviello, played by Ambrogio Bonomo, and the Dottore, performed by Bartolomeo Zito. Cecchini describes the erudition of Zito as follows: 'a great scholar of history, he has a smattering of poetry, and a considerable knowledge of popular literature'. A member of the Accademia dei Risoluti, he commented in 1628 on the posthumous edition of the burlesque poem in dialect, *La Vaiasseide* by Giulio Cesare Cortese, praising the expressive and semantic richness of the Neapolitan dialect and contrasting it with the purism of other literary forms (Domenica Landolfi in Burattelli et al. 1993: 334). According to Zito, dialect as a mode of expression had to be cultivated 'for the great energy and meaning it conveys'. Zito personified all the most characteristic qualities defining how the educated actor thought and acted: his authenticity in action, his energy of dialect and his participation in disputes between academies. In the energy put into his actions and in the language of the doctor, it is possible to read the genetic code of the profession of the Italian actor, including how destiny made him different from actors in other countries and cultures. Cecchini's pamphlet closes with a final invitation: 'Let's turn to the lesson of Father Master Egidio Gottardi and we will improve'. Gottardi was a celebrated preacher from Rimini and translator of the sermons and spiritual exercises of the Augustinian friar, Pedro de Valderrama. These texts were of crucial importance in the dissemination and preaching of Jesuit meditation. Perhaps Cecchini mentions him to refer to other means of persuasion, other demands on the imagination and the importance of the well-chosen word. The imitation of social behaviour served as a counterbalance to the primary mimetic requirement, i.e. the ability to trace the roots of behaviour and to frame the contemporary ethos in suitable formats. This resulted in a game of roles. A stubborn ability to adapt coexisted with the preservation of differences.

Aside from sermons and pleading, pointless censorship and violent reprisals, there was a crucial conflict: on the one hand, well-ordered communities shielded themselves from the 'wind' generated by theatre by means of rules, prohibitions and limitations; on the other, the leaders of the art of the *commedia* were the first to articulate opposition to the mores of the Christian city and later to the more rational ideals of the modern city.

By the middle of the seventeenth century, the custom of theatre-going together with tolerance towards the art of the *comici* enabled the troupe to exist as a separate body. In 1646 appeared the first volumes of *La cristiana moderatione del theatro*, by the Jesuit Giovanni Domenico Ottonelli. This text testifies to the neutralisation of theatre. Theatre can be tolerated if it becomes more moderate and constantly corrects any moral deficiency in relation to the ordinary world. We are on the threshold of the Enlightenment. The Italian *commedia* created a custom and accepted a norm – but at the same time produced dissident and critical material pitting society against theatre and theatre against society. At the time of the Reformation when the commerce of theatre was regulated and when the neutralisation of non-conformance was being planned – the *commedia* survived and found the necessary resources for the internal regeneration of theatre families.

When arguing that the treatises and notes of the *comici* formulate postulations as to how civil life should function – one of which being the revival of the dignity of theatre – studies on the subject should not undervalue the deviations, accidents and inconsistencies which were the essence of the internal workings of theatre microculture; nor should they overlook the specific perspective of the theatre profession in relation to institutions of state. The city which the *comici* had in mind when they joined the public debate should be conceived as a multifaceted city. Their breeding ground was not established customs or norms. The city of the *comici* met – and sometimes merged with – that of reformers and authorities. The point of contact was the more or less regulated 'market' of patrons and managers. This point of contact was always evolving – beyond the calendar of normal events and the topography of established functions. For the encompassing and determining culture, the *teatro delle stanze* incorporated the possibility of daily leisure; for the troupes who provided this possibility, it was the platform on which to play out the rifts between the individual and established order, the inconsistencies between public and private life and those between habit and heresy. The breeding ground of the theatre profession is to be found in the clash of ideas determining diverse possible cities and in the area of 'open rifts'.

According to Braudel, 'the commedia dell'arte served to reveal Western theatre to itself' (1991: 147). From the early modern age onwards, theatre – a seductive and alluring concept for cultivated people – with its hybrid and sparse performances, became an established custom. Up to the twentieth century – through bodies, disjointed traditions and illusion – the ethnic and technical difference of the Italian diaspora fostered the trauma, provocation and energy of rifts.

PART IV

Opera, Music, Dance, Circus and Iconography

14

Commedia dell'Arte in Opera and Music 1550–1750

Anne MacNeil

Long before the advent of opera in late sixteenth-century Italy, music and the commedia dell'arte were intimately intertwined. Earlier reports of commedia dell'arte troupes indicate that comedians regularly included music in their entertainments and iconographic evidence highlights the importance of music in comedians' repertories. Some musicians, too, were known for their involvement in commedia dell'arte productions. An early description of a *commedia*-inspired performance at Trausnitz Castle in Munich in 1568 tells of an improvised comedy by Massimo Troiano, which featured the composer Orlando di Lasso playing the role of Pantalone (Troiano, 1569). Later musical works, including those by Orazio Vecchi and Adriano Banchieri, comprise stylised, semi-dramatic compositions that allude to commedia dell'arte characters and situations; these are known as madrigal comedies.[1] And some seventeenth-century operas, such as Virgilio Mazzocchi's *Chi soffre speri*, on a libretto by Cardinal Rospigliosi, include *zanni* characters among the interlocutors.

Descriptions of comedians' performances in the sixteenth century suggest that laments, mad-scenes and competitions were staples of the commedia dell'arte repertory, thereby implying that virtuosic musical display was an important aspect of a comedian's craft. Two commedia dell'arte troupes, led by Flaminia Romana and Vincenza Armani, competed in Mantua during the Inquisition in 1568 and impressed their audiences with tragic representations of noble tales from the epics of Virgil and Ariosto. Isabella Andreini's composed pastoral play, *La Mirtilla*, published in 1588, features a Virgilian singing contest between Mirtilla and her rival Ardelia, adjudicated by the goatherd Opico. And at the Florentine wedding of Ferdinando de' Medici and Christine of Lorraine in 1589, Andreini and Vittoria Piisimi vied for their audiences' approval in *intermedii* performed between the acts of Girolamo Bargagli's comedy *La pellegrina*. Piisimi was the more experienced actress, but just as Flaminia was favored in Mantua in 1568 with her lament of Dido, Andreini won in

Florence in 1589 with her mad-scene, which included French songs that delighted the bride. The nymphs in *Mirtilla* were judged to be equal in song and in love.

Musical settings for these scenes do not survive, but scholars have suggested that popular songs of all kinds formed comedians' repertories. Thus, manuscripts and publications of such genres as the *canzonetta, canzone alla francese, ciaccona, canario, villanella, villanesca, giustiniana, grechescha,* madrigal, scherzo, *strambotto,* and *frottole* of all kinds offer a treasure trove of potential musical artifacts from the commedia dell'arte. Indeed, some music alludes directly to commedia dell'arte performers. Instrumental versions of monodic songs, for example, bearing titles like 'Aria della Signora Livia', 'Aria della Signora Fiord'Amore', 'Aria della Marchetta Schiavonetta' and 'Aria di Scapino' are named for commedia dell'arte characters (Pirrotta, 1984). And Remigio Romano's five-volume collection of *canzoni* and *canzonette* published in the 1620s includes numerous songs known to have been sung by comici dell'arte.

A number of comedians were known especially for their musical talents. In 1574, Vittoria Piisimi performed in Cornelio Frangipani's *Tragedia* in Venice for the new French King Henri III, the description of which is replete with music-making:

> All the performers sang in the softest harmonies, sometimes singing alone, sometimes together; and at the end, the chorus of Mercury was of instrumentalists, who had the most various instruments that were ever played. The trumpets heralded the entrance of the gods on stage, which was done with a tragic machine that was impossible to regulate because of the great tumult of people who were there. Neither was it possible to imitate antiquity in the musical works, which were composed by Sig. Claudio Merulo, of such quality that the ancients could never aspire to it. (Nolhac and Solerti, 1890)

Piisimi had learned the role of Pallas Athena in Frangipani's tragedy in less than a week's time, which has led scholars to wonder if comedians performed music from composed scores (in this case, by Claudio Merulo) or if they improvised their songs on the spot. Virginia Ramponi Andreini was said to have learned the role of Arianna in a similarly brief time span for the Gonzaga wedding festivities in 1608. The famous *Lamento d'Arianna,* composed by Claudio Monteverdi to a libretto written by Ottaviano Rinuccini, became a centerpiece of Andreini's repertory for the rest of her life (she died in 1631; Buratelli, Landolfi and Zinanni, 1993). Whether comedians learned or improvised their music, the examples of Pallas

Athena and Arianna cast into stark relief the relationships between composers and performers in these repertories.

The Bolognese *zanni* Francesco Gabrielli, *in arte* Scapino, specialised in dancing athletically, singing rude songs and playing exotic instruments. He had a notorious reputation for composing and singing *tagliacanzoni* and *villanelle* and his extensive musical instrumentarium was one of the wonders of the commedia dell'arte stage, memorialised in both Dionisio Minaggio's *Feather book* (1618) and an engraving by the Milanese artist Carlo Biffi (1633).[2] In 1634, the composer Claudio Monteverdi wrote to a Roman correspondent believed to have been Giovan Battista Doni:

> You asked me to engage the services of Scapino in order that I may send Your Worship drawings of the many extraordinary instruments that he plays ... I have never seen them myself [!], but from the little information I am sending, it seems to me that they are new as regards shape but not in sound, since all fit in with the sounds of the instruments that we use.

The only composed music known to be associated with Scapino was printed in his *Infermità, testamento, e morte di Francesco Gabrielli* in 1638. These two pieces, printed with *alfabeto* notation for the Spanish guitar, are a *ciaccona* (a lively, repetitive dance based on a short harmonic progression that supports ornamented variations) and the so-called Aria di Scapino, 'I più rigidi cori'. In this twenty-eight stanza aria, Scapino leaves his various musical instruments to the cities of Italy: his violin goes to Cremona, his bass to Piacenza, his viola to Milan; Venice inherits his guitar and Naples his harp; Rome receives his bonacordo, the trombones go to Genoa and the mandola to Perugia; to his home town of Bologna, Scapino leaves his theorbo and to Ferrara, his lute; Florence inherits all that remain.

Virginia Ramponi Andreini (wife of Isabella Andreini's son Giovan Battista) was a gifted singer and instrumentalist, her roles in her husband's composed plays often calling for songs she herself accompanied on the lute or Spanish guitar. In her role as the slave in Giovan Battista's comedy *Lo schiavetto* (1612), Andreini sang the aria 'Tu c'hai le penne Amore', written by the Florentine composer Giulio Caccini and later published in his *Le nuove musiche e nuova maniera di scrivirle* (1614). She and her husband had sung and danced for the rulers of Mantua in 1608 at the wedding of Francesco Gonzaga and Margherita of Savoy in the *Ballo delle Ingrate*, in the *intermedii* performed between the acts of Battista Guarini's comedy *L'idropica*, in a second ballo *Il sacrificio d'Ifigenia* and in Rinuccini's tragedy *L'Arianna*, set to music by Claudio Monteverdi.

With these performances, together with Caccini's *canzonetta*, we have the first direct evidence of comedians' musical abilities in the surviving scores written by Monteverdi for the final lament in the *Ballo delle Ingrate* and the *Lamento d'Arianna*, both sung by Andreini. The *ingrata* sings a strophic aria with instrumental accompaniment and a choral refrain, about the sorrows of having lived a life without love. Arianna, in contrast, sings an extended recitative-soliloquy with orchestral accompaniment in which she curses her erstwhile lover Teseo for abandoning her on the island of Dia (Naxos). Taken together, these two laments show what narrow straights women had to navigate in sixteenth-century Italy on the way to marriage.

Giovan Battista Andreini is perhaps best remembered as an author of composed comedies, although he performed lifelong in the role of the innamorato Lelio and danced in *Il sacrificio d'Ifigenia* in Mantua. Among his composed plays, the one that shows the greatest involvement with music is the sacred drama *La Maddalena lasciva et penitente* (1617), set to music by a quartet of composers associated with the court of Mantua: Claudio Monteverdi, Muzio Effrem, Salomone Rossi and Alessandro Ghivizzani. In the preface to his comedy *La Ferinda* (1622), Andreini declared the influence of opera on his own compositions:

> It has been my good fortune in Florence and in Mantua to be a spectator of '*opere recitative e musicali* '; I have seen *Orfeo, Arianna, Silla, Dafne, Cerere* and *Psiche* – truly marvelous things, not only for the excellence of those fortunate swans who sang their glories, but also for the rarity of the musicians who realized them in harmonious and angelic song. (Andreini, 1622)

Ferretting out the cross-influences of opera and commedia dell'arte can be a rigorous exercise and few scholars, to date, have undertaken it. Examination of scene-types offers a fruitful entrée into analyzing their similarities. Some scene-types are familiar, for example, lament-soliloquies, mad-scenes and scenes of the hunt, but others – such as sleep scenes or prophecies – are less apparent until one looks at a broad spectrum of theatrical activity.

Laments and mad-scenes form the core of solo virtuosic displays that became arias in early opera. Venetian operas especially, such as those written by Francesco Cavalli, include at least one lament; some of his operas have as many as four. Invariably, these laments are in triple meter and a minor mode, and many make use of what Ellen Rosand has called an emblem of lament, the descending tetrachord (Rosand, 1979). This descending four-note phrase was sometimes used as a melodic motive, but often appeared as an ostinato in the lowest instruments of the orchestra. When used as a bass progression, the descending tetrachord offered a repeating harmonic foundation that grounded the singer's flights of emotional extremity and distress. Monteverdi's *Lamento della ninfa* and Endimion's lament 'Lucidissima face' from Cavalli's opera *La Calisto* are good examples of this.

Like lament-soliloquies, mad-scenes offer the performer an opportunity to express passionate excess. Whether spoken or sung, mad-scenes tend to make use of a multiplicity of emotions, ranging from sorrow and self-doubt to anger and revenge. Many comedians had in their repertories mad-scenes stylised to their characters and named after them. Giovan Battista Andreini, for example, specialised in the *Pazzia di Lelio*, and his mother in the *Pazzia d'Isabella*; Francesco Gabrielli, of course, reveled in his *Pazzia di Scapino* (a version of *La pazzia d'Isabella* may be found in Flaminio Scala). Operas are similarly rife with madness. The music historian Paolo Fabbri credits the Venetian poet Giulio Strozzi with transferring the comic mad-scene to the opera stage with *Licori finta pazza inamorata d'Aminta*, offered to Monteverdi in 1627 for musical setting but never realised, and with *La finta pazza* (1641), set to music by Francesco Sacrati. In the latter half of the seventeenth century, the operatic mad-scene became a tour de force for singers to demonstrate their virtuosic prowess and talents for ornamentation as they raged and fumed onstage. Iarba, for example, goes mad for love of Dido in Cavalli's and Busenello's opera *La Didone*, rending his garments and bursting into an angry harangue of poetic *sdruccioli* (trisyllabic rhymes). Just as the descending tetrachord is emblematic of lament, poetic *sdruccioli* are characteristic of mad-scenes. In its expression of anger and resulting musical virtuosity, the mad-scene also spawned an operatic cousin, the rage aria. Often sung by castrati, as was the role of Tolomeo in Handel's *Giulio Cesare*, rage arias highlight the unique characteristics of the castrato voice and its capacity for extended phrases, wide vocal ranges and agile embellishment.

One of the most substantive points of interaction between the commedia dell'arte and opera is the scenario. This is also the area that is most open to new scholarship. Materials in this area encompass not only recent discoveries of manuscript collections of commedia dell'arte scenarios, but also a wide variety of textual sources, from the classical writings of Homer, Virgil and Ovid, to operas by such composers as Claudio Monteverdi, Francesco Cavalli, Henry Purcell, George Frideric Handel and Wolfgang Amadeus Mozart. It also engages with written descriptions of commedia dell'arte performances, censors' records and complaints against comedic performances.

Cross-disciplinary analysis of scenarios and opera libretti falls into three general categories or tale-types: lessons in the foundation of empire (the Dido and Aeneas tale-type), lessons in the continuation of empire (the Ulysses and Penelope tale-type) and lessons in the dissolution of empire (the Emperor Nero tale-type). Not all presentations of a given tale-type fall into the same category. Sometimes, Penelope is dead when Ulysses finally reaches Ithaca, and sometimes the Emperor Nero tale-type is concerned with the continuation of empire rather than its dissolution. Thus, a study of the Dido and Aeneas tale-type – by far the largest and most significant corpus – encompasses diverse versions of the story as presented in Virgil's *Aeneid*, various commedia dell'arte scenarios (including the description of Flaminia Romana's performance in Mantua in 1568), Francesco Cavalli's Venetian opera *La Didone*, Henry Purcell's *Dido and Aeneas* and Pietro Metastasio's libretto *Didone abbandonata* and its more than sixty musical settings by such composers as Albinoni, Porpora, Hasse, Jomelli, Paisiello, Mercadante and others.

As an example of the multivalent interactions between commedia dell'arte scenarios and opera libretti, together with their associations with ancient Greek and Roman narratives, I would like to focus briefly on the Emperor Nero tale-type. Materials under analysis are the pseudo-Senecan drama entitled *Octavia*, Claudio Monteverdi's opera *L'incoronazione di Poppea*, the early eighteenth-century commedia dell'arte scenario 'Nero imperadore' from the Casamarciano collection in Naples and George Frideric Handel's opera *Agrippina*. Even this simple listing of titles indicates that these works concentrate on different characters within the tale-type and that their lines of action and even their plots are bound to be quite different.

The pseudo-Senecan drama *Octavia* is the sole extant *fabula praetexta* in the classical Latin literature. Its dramatis personae include Octavia and her nurse, Poppea and her nurse, Nero, his mother Agrippina, his tutor Seneca, a messenger, a prefect and a chorus of Romans. The argument concentrates on Octavia's marriage to Nero, his turn of affections to Poppea, his banishment of Octavia and the Roman people's support of the fallen empress.

The tragedy opens with a lament-soliloquy by Octavia, in which she bemoans the fact that she did not die alongside her mother Messalina and that now, Agrippina has poisoned her father, the emperor Claudius. Octavia's laments for her cruel destiny and the severity of her misfortunes, and her focus on the dynasty of the Julio-Claudian household, mark the central plot of the drama as one concerned with the Roman imperial succession and its dissolution due to broken bloodlines and marital infidelity. While we may recognise similarities between this soliloquy and Octavia's recitative-lament 'Disprezzata regina' in Monteverdi's opera *L'incoronazione di Poppea*, structurally it forms a closer pairing with Penelope's opening lament in another of Monteverdi's operas, *Il ritorno d'Ulisse in patria*, which similarly cues a plotline concerning the continuation of imperial hereditary lines. In contrast, Monteverdi's opening of *L'incoronazione di Poppea* with a love song from Otho to his wife Poppea sets the plotline of that opera as one concerned with the personal, human trajectory of Otho's and Poppea's passions.

Returning to the pseudo-Senecan tragedy *Octavia*, act 2 begins with an extended soliloquy from Seneca, who praises the stoic simplicity of his former life and bemoans the fact that contemporary society is in a state of decline. The act continues with a debate between Seneca and Nero about the virtues of stoicism versus imperial excess and passion. The debate ends with Nero's announcement that he will wed Poppea with twenty-four hours. This is strikingly similar to the act 1 duet between Seneca and Nero in Monteverdi's *L'incoronazione di Poppea* and both scenes carry the function of demonstrating that Nero's marriage to Poppea embodies his repudiation of stoic reasoning. This dynamic opposing passion and reason forms the foundation of nearly all operas from the seventeenth to the nineteenth centuries. What follows each of these scenes in their respective works is crucial. Monteverdi's opera turns immediately to Poppea, her seduction of Nero and the power that Cupid wields through her. In pseudo-Seneca's *Octavia*, the debate is followed immediately by the appearance of the Ghost of Agrippina, who arises from the underworld carrying Stygian torches to the wedding of Nero and Poppea and prophesying Nero's death in retribution for his having disgraced his ancestors. The subsequent action (act 4) shows Poppea startled from sleep and narrating her dream of impending doom to her nurse. Again, this is a scene that has a rough parallel in Monteverdi's opera but there, rather than use Poppea's sleep as a portal to prophecy from the underworld, Monteverdi uses Poppea's sleep as an opportunity to show Otho's increasing inner turmoil of passion for his wife. At every turn, we see Monteverdi emphasise the comedic aspects of the tale-type and its potential for passion on a human scale. In contrast, pseudo-Seneca emphasises the tragedic elements of the tale-type and its implications for dynastic continuity. Both works contain scenes where Poppea's beauty is extolled – in Monteverdi's opera, this is the scene between Nero and Lucano; in pseudo-Seneca's *Octavia*, the chorus marvels at Poppea's beauty even while the Roman populace takes up arms in support of Octavia. The final act of the *fabula* shows Nero, boiling over with rage, announcing Octavia's banishment. The chorus bewails the end of the Cesarean dynasty and Octavia sings her farewell to Rome. This end of the imperial succession marks the end of the tragedy, whereas Monteverdi's opera must move past the tragedy of Octavia's banishment to offer personal satisfaction in love relationships for both Otho and Poppea. It's a weird Venetian twist to this plot that they do not find love with each other.

The commedia dell'arte scenario 'Nero imperadore,' included in the Casamarciano collection conserved in the Biblioteca Nazionale in Naples, bears little resemblance to the works described thus far, although several stereotypical scenes demonstrate the works' similarities (Cotticelli and Heck, 2001). It opens with Nero talking about the burning of Rome and saying that the city should be rebuilt within the month. He talks about disposing of his mother Agrippina and having himself crowned emperor. At the end of the scene, a messenger appears with a letter and Nero orders Otho to set sail for Portugal to become its governor. It isn't until act 1, scene 3 that Octavia opens the scene with her lament-soliloquy. As is true of Monteverdi's opera, this placement of Octavia's lament after the initial action of the drama displaces the tragedic focus of the plot. In the scenario, attention is drawn to the pre-existing destruction of Rome, the subsequent destruction of its enemies, the reinstatement of the Julio-Claudian hereditary line and its hope for rebuilding the empire.

Later in act 1, Agrippina and Octavia conspire together to murder Poppea, demonstrating a desire in both women to maintain the imperial dynasty. This is the only source in which these two women conspire, but it is important to note that both Agrippina and Octavia – in all sources where they appear, whether together or individually – stand for the continuation of the Caesarean dynasty. Act 1, scene 5 opens with Seneca bemoaning his pupil's tyranny and Rome's decadence, as he does in every other source in which he appears. When Nero enters, they have the stereotypical debate contrasting stoicism and passion. The act ends with Nero ordering his henchmen, the *zanni* Coviello and Pulcinella, to kill Agrippina, which they do by stabbing her to death on stage. Note that, here, it is the death of Agrippina that embodies Nero's repudiation of Seneca and stoic reasoning, rather than his wedding to Poppea. Octavia opens act 2 with a lament over Agrippina's death and Nero holds a mock trial in order to repudiate his wife as an adulteress. In the following scene, 'Octavia [enters] alone, [laments] of her sorrow at leaving, and departs'. This is an exact synopsis of her aria 'Addio, Roma' in Monteverdi's opera and of Octavia's final lament in pseudo-Seneca's *fabula*. As in Monteverdi's opera, the placement of this lament in the middle of an act displaces the significance of the lament with regard to the central plotline.

Act 3 of 'Nero imperadore' is a whirlwind powerhouse of action. It begins with Seneca, who slits his veins, laments and dies. Nero, meanwhile, falls asleep on his throne. The allegorical figure of Justice appears to him, threatens him and departs. Note that, while Nero has taken the place of Poppea in the sleep sequence, there is an otherworldly apparition who prophesies doom for Nero, and sleep functions as a portal to the next world. As he awakens, Poppea enters, warning Nero to flee because Octavia and Servius Galba have incited the Army of Rome to seize power and are outside the gates with the army. Nero becomes angry, kicks Poppea and leaves. She makes a speech and dies. This is the sole theatrical source in which this unhappy ending to Nero's and Poppea's love occurs. Then, in a fit of remarkable bad taste, the *zanni* Coviello and Pulcinella enter and, believing Poppea to be drunk, perform rude lazzi with the corpse. They finally realise that she is dead and leave. Act 3 concludes with a great tumult, during which Nero kills himself with a dagger and Octavia is entrusted with the reins of government – yet a third mighty ending to this tale-type, in as many of its presentations.

Just as Monteverdi's opera has no role for Agrippina, Handel's opera has no role for Octavia. As a result, it is bereft of those glorious laments that otherwise perform a central function within the tale-type. Indeed, Handel's telling of the story seems to be a kind of 'prequel' to the other versions of the Emperor Nero tale-type: Claudius is emperor, Nero is a child, Poppea is not yet married to Otho and Seneca seems not to exist at all. Still, several important structural elements of the tale-type persist in Handel's opera. Most notably, Poppea sleeps – or pretends to – and while she sleeps, the end of her story is foretold by the appearance of Otho. In her dream, Otho reveals his love for Poppea in the course of a lament, 'Vaghi fonti'. Otho does not prophesy doom from the opposite bank of the River Styx, and sleep is not utilised here as a portal to the underworld, but Handel's sleep sequence does fulfill the similar function of allowing Poppea to see into the future. The opera ends with Claudius announcing Nero's succession to the throne and Otho and Poppea's marriage.

Handel's *Agrippina* has often been derided for presenting an unhistorical, fantasy-laden version of the history of the emperor Nero, and scholars working with Monteverdi's *L'incoronazione di Poppea* often grapple with its non-conformity to historical sources. Historians of the commedia dell'arte never vex themselves with questions of this kind. In the case of the Emperor Nero tale-type, variations on the central historical theme all involve a healthy dose of fantasy and delight, as each source uses

the tale-type to forward a particular ending, one usually grounded in the
dichotomy between individual passions and the stoic reasoning required
to rule. As more scholars take up the work of comparing opera libretti to
commedia dell'arte scenarios, analyses of this kind will yield more subtle
readings of their shared tale-types and stereotypical elements.

Notes

[1] The most prominent among these are Vecchi's *L'Amfiparnaso* and *Veglie di
Siena*; Banchieri's contributions include *La pazzia senile*, *Il metamorfosi musicale*, *La saviezza giovanile* and *Il festino del giovedì grasso*.

[2] Digitised reproductions of the images in the *Feather book* are available online
at http://digital.library.mcgill.ca/featherbook/. For a reproduction of Biffi's
engraving and other images of Scapino, see MacNeil 2003.

15

From Mozart to Henze

Andrea Fabiano

The Exemplary Case of Da Ponte and Mozart's Opera *Don Giovanni*

Don Giovanni (1787) offers us the opportunity to examine the peculiarities and intertextual playfulness of the *dramma giocoso* (comic opera) and in the process to demonstrate how deeply runs the comici dell'arte's evident knowledge of drama. Wolfgang Amadeus Mozart's acquaintance with Italian culture was based, for the most part, on his study of comic opera librettos, specifically the comedies of Carlo Goldoni and the dramas of Pietro Metastasio. Reading such works – which was necessary for his development as a composer – Mozart learned the Italian language and gradually achieved mastery of it. Initially guided by his father, he was later helped by the soprano Giovanni Manzoli – with whom he had studied singing in London in 1764 – and finally by Father Martini, his teacher of music theory in Bologna in 1770. As he became more and more fluent in the language, however, he increasingly distanced himself from making use of it in his professional life, preferring instead to use it as a secret, playful, comical and sometimes vulgar means of communication, particularly in his letters (Folena 1983).

Mozart did not stop at a superficial reading of the *drammi giocosi*. Through the prism of his 'own' Italian language, he identified their essence, their fundamental core, as being a cathartic release of comicality. He believed that the disarticulated dramatic framework of the libretto had its own raison d'être, since it allowed the creation of a farcical comicality quite unlike any other dramatic genre. Looking at it this way, he seems to have intuitively grasped the very origins of this specifically Italian comic tradition, which ranges from the reformed comedies of Goldoni to the comedy of stock characters and, finally, to fully improvised comedy. Together, these three manifestations of comedy make up the paradigm of the comici dell'arte's theatrical knowledge, forming the basis of their unrivalled expression and the naturalness of their improvised comic performances.

In eighteenth-century Vienna, the first steps on the path towards the development of an indigenous theatre were taken by the Volkskomödie and the Kärntnerthortheater, specifically by their beloved actor, playwright and librettist, Joseph Felix von Kurz, creator of the comic character Bernardon. Later, in Mozart's time, this 'heretical' dramaturgical path was rediscovered by Emanuel Schikaneder. In doing so he took on several roles: actor, playwright and librettist – initially with his itinerant troupe, later at the Kärntnerthortheater in 1784 and finally, from 1789 onwards, at the Freihaus-Theater auf der Wieden (Honolka 1984).

Mozart, who was a friend of Schikaneder, followed the same ambiguous path, navigating the faultlines between classical drama and the newly revived comic routines of popular theatre. Motivated by a strong desire to write one of his works in German – as a gesture of national affirmation – Mozart was nonetheless attracted to the theatrical works of Goldoni as a literary source.

Goldoni, a dramatist of rationalist comedy, was regarded by his contemporaries in theatrical circles as having been expelled from the sphere of eighteenth-century cultural enlightenment. Yet today he is seen as the playwright who developed stock character comedy to its highest level of expression. Mozart was very impressed by Goldoni's *Il Servitore di Due Padroni* (The Servant of Two Masters), a *canovaccio* comedy which had been written as a vehicle for one of the most famous Truffaldinos in the history of the commedia dell'arte, Antonio Sacchi. Some years later, when the play was being translated, Goldoni's Arlecchino was replaced by Schikaneder's Papageno.

With *Don Giovanni*, Lorenzo Da Ponte and Mozart made use of a figure highly representative of the Italian theatrical tradition in general and of the *commedia* in particular. Their choice contributed to the popular and financial success of the opera and created a persistent set of expectations among audiences for this type of comedy. By having Don Giovanni talk to a statue and by having the statue move, Mozart was introducing something into his opera which had in fact been dismissed by eighteenth-century Enlightenment theory of theatre as an outmoded symbol of the older theatre of improvisation. Its actors – the comici dell'arte – were regarded as undisciplined and vulgar. Da Ponte and Mozart however were searching for a more flexible concept of theatre and went so far in adopting an open dramaturgical logic that what they finally composed was really an *opera* buffa which makes constant reference, both at the macro- and microstructural levels, to the commedia dell'arte, the genre from which it originated (Fabiano 2007). The classical unities of time and place which applied to most libretti of the time were not followed in any plausible or credible way. The number of characters was reduced but Da Ponte also added new episodes and places (such as the tragicomic finale of the first act) to the structure of the already compressed libretto written by Giovanni Bertati for the opera *Don Giovanni or The Stone Guest* in 1787. The music for this work was composed by Giuseppe Gazzaniga and can be considered Mozart's main source of inspiration. The fluidity of Mozart and Da Ponte's libretto makes the insistence with which it explicitly states the observance of the Aristotelian unity of time appear unlikely and parodic. This insistence reaches its peak when Don Giovanni pulls out his watch to announce the exact Aristotelian time to the audience, in the simple recitative at the beginning of act 2, scene 11, which takes place in the cemetery and represents a challenge to the authority of the Father, the Commendatore (Vescovo 2002). This mockery of the theatrical *auctoritas* overlaps, in the same scene, with the blasphemous invitation addressed to the statue of the Commendatore, a mocking challenge to moral and religious authority.

At a microstructural level, the recurrence of a number of lazzi that are typical of improvised comedy is remarkable; also remarkable is the fact that the *lazzi* fall into three categories, a fact which is characteristic of the commedia dell'arte. The categories are:

1. Lazzi of a verbal nature:
   - The ironical comments of the servant to the audience, while a 'serious' character is speaking (Leporello on Donna Elvira and her master, 1.5).
   - Serialisation, perfectly exemplified by Leporello's characteristic catalogue (1.5). In the *Stone Guest,* staged by Italian actors in 1658 in Paris, Domenico Biancolelli as *Arlecchino* read the catalogue at the front of the stage, mockingly unrolling a long scroll on the heads of members of the audience below and asking them whether their wives' names were in Don Giovanni's list of conquests (Biancolelli, n.d.).
   - Nonsensical expressions, indicating *Arlecchino*'s madness or stupidity, often encountered in Leporello (1.5).
   - Lewd double entendres, often musically highlighted by Mozart, for example at the end of the catalogue aria (1.5), in Zerlina's aria (2.6) or in 1.8.

- Counterfeiting, i.e. the imitation of voice and expression, doubled by the subtle game of imitation in Mozart's musical compositions. Don Giovanni, for example, imitates Leporello's voice as he is trapped by Masetto and the farmers (2.4) and Leporello imitates Don Giovanni's voice when he is sent to talk to Donna Elvira (2.3).
- Parodic references to mythological comic characters (2, last).

2. Topical lazzi of a gestural nature (mime):
   - The beatings risked by Leporello (1.2; 2.8, at Donna Anna's house) and by Don Giovanni (2.4), the beating Don Giovanni gives to Masetto (2.5) and the beating dreamed of by Zerlina, in an aria in which violence – transfigured by mime – takes on an erotic value, emphasised by the sweetness and mystification expressed by Mozart's music (1.16). In the same category, it is especially worth mentioning the incident at the end of act 1, in which three aristocrats, including two women, in headlong pursuit break down the wrong door. The scene follows the typical *modus operandi* of the commedia dell'arte, which had already been strongly criticised by Andrea Perrucci in his treatise, *Dell'Arte rappresentativa premeditate e dall'improvviso* (1699) as being a mere collection of routines (Perrucci 1961: 251).
   - The characters touching each other's bodies on stage, with a more or less lustful, sensual or comic intent: Leporello and the female farmers (1.8), Don Giovanni and Zerlina (1.9; 1.18) and Zerlina and Masetto (1.16); in parallel, Don Giovanni and Zerlina as well as Leporello and the other female farmers (1.20), again, Leporello holding Masetto tightly while they dance to the triplet rhythms of a popular *Deutscher Tanz* (1.20), Leporello kissing Donna Elvira while imitating Don Giovanni (2.3) and Don Giovanni recounting the caresses he gave and received during his meeting with Leporello's friend (2.11).
   - Leporello dressing up as Don Giovanni and vice versa, which creates new ambiguities (2.1).
   - Leporello's mimed lazzi of terror at the cemetery and at Don Giovanni's house – shivering, panicking, stammering and hiding under the table – are typical of Arlecchino (2.11; 2.14).

3. Topical lazzi of a thematic nature:
   - The opening aria – in which Leporello complains about his own condition and expresses his desire to live like a 'lord' – is modelled

on a *cliché* found in Arlecchino's monologues about his master's selfishness, avarice and wealth which he is unwilling to share with anybody. Cf. *The Servant of Two Masters* (1.6).

• The servant mocking his master (1.15).
• Don Giovanni's huge mouthfuls and Leporello's eating in secret are part of the comic repertoire of the servant in the commedia dell'arte (2.13).
• The talking and moving statue (2.11; 2.15) becomes comic, because the audience perceives it as unlikely – and thus funny – rather than something able to induce terror.

In this 'game of references', the most symbolic reference to the tradition of the commedia dell'arte is the use of the somersault, the acrobatic leap used mostly by Arlecchino in order to escape very difficult or dangerous situations and which highlights his acrobatic skills. As an example, Thomas-Simon, author of Gueullette's transcription of the *canovaccio* of *The Stone Guest*, wrote, in a note that has been saved for posterity, that he was very impressed by the performance of the Arlecchino, Tommaso 'Thomassin' Visentini, a member of Luigi Riccoboni's troupe, during which he did a somersault while bringing a glass of wine to the statue of the Commendatore, without spilling a single drop of the wine (Biancolelli, n.d.: 209). In Da Ponte's libretto, we should also interpret Leporello's amazing and far-fetched escape – despite being surrounded by Masetto, Don Ottavio, Zerlina and Donna Elvira – as a harlequin-like somersault, both cathartic and liberating (2.9–10).

The comic elements we have highlighted so far are indeed part of the dramaturgical framework of eighteenth-century *dramma giocoso*, since the genre itself stemmed from the commedia dell'arte. However, in *Don Giovanni* the frequency with which they appear and most of all their role in the dramaturgical framework – as well as the wealth of quotations inspired by the commedia dell'arte – allow us to say that Da Ponte and Mozart really intended to compose an *opera buffa*, in an effort to preserve this Italian comic tradition in a cultural and historical context in which it was slowly disappearing from the stages of Italy and Europe in general.

From Rossini's Farces to Verdi and Boito's *Falstaff*

In the cultural framework of nineteenth-century opera, the comic component seems to find new life in the short, condensed dramaturgy of the farces set to music by Gioachino Rossini. It is obvious that these works, through the tight dynamics of the plot and the choice of characters, owe much to the dramaturgy of the commedia dell'arte, by then seen as a repository of a spectrum of dramaturgical traditions.

We can assume that by having direct access to the theatrical knowledge of Italian comedians, Mozart, Da Ponte and the musicians and librettists of their generation were able to consider the commedia dell'arte as a genre with its own specific characteristics and identity. Librettists and composers after them – as they progressively lost direct knowledge and experience of the dramaturgy of the commedia dell'arte – must have started inventing or reconstructing mythic interpretations *à la* Maurice Sand (Sand 1860), in which they imagined the commedia dell'arte as a *modus operandi* rather than a genre. The result was to allow the return of a dramaturgy that had been eclipsed and forgotten. In their search for surviving traces of the commedia dell'arte – a search which often became almost archaeological in nature – librettists and composers were frequently led to explore the comedies of Goldoni's Parisian period, which was perceived as being closest to the world of the *commedia*. This is precisely what Rossini did in *La Gazzetta* (1816), which was inspired by Goldoni's comedy *Il matrimonio per concorso* (1763). Another example of this is Pietro Raimondi's *Il Ventaglio* (1831), named after Goldoni's comedy of the same name.

From this point of view, the one true example of interpretative uniqueness and of original reinvention – maybe not of the *genre*, because that would be impossible, but at least of the dramaturgical intentions of the commedia dell'arte – is Arrigo Boito and Giuseppe Verdi's 1893 opera *Falstaff.* The character fuses the medieval and renaissance novella – in which the practical joke is a central theme – with a dramaturgical framework that gives new life to the interpretative medieval frenzy of the commedia dell'arte. The work also reinvents Shakespeare's character through Goldoni's multifaceted way of looking at things. Goldoni, like most playwrights of the nineteenth century, regarded Falstaff as nothing but the synthesis of all the symbols of the commedia dell'arte, and Boito and Verdi did, in fact, read and reread Goldoni for the occasion, as their letters show. Finally, it is a work in which the servant, a Mozartesque Leporello-Arlecchino, finally fulfils his wish of becoming a 'lord' by casting himself in the role of Sir John Falstaff to imitate – somewhat roughly – the deeds of his old master, Don Giovanni the seducer.

The frantic climax of the finale of act 2, in which three dramaturgical elements are simultaneously brought into play around two banal, everyday situations – a screen behind which the naïve, dim-witted lovers Nannetta and Fenton are hiding, and the large basket in which Falstaff is gasping for breath amid dirty socks and underwear – is without a doubt the most impressive example of the resurgence of the spirit of the commedia dell'arte in opera in the nineteenth century.

The polymetric verbal lazzi of Boito's libretto, the dialogues exploding in a firework of insulting metaphors, the disguises and the beatings, the counterfeit voices and the obscene puns, the pathetic and the comic, as well as the many references to food, together present Verdi's creative genius with an opportunity to express in this his last work an immense outburst of hilarity. The result was a work that, after so much tragic grandeur, sounds like the final, harlequinesque joke of the eighty-year-old composer.

Richard Wagner, by contrast, removes all elements related to the commedia dell'arte in his Hoffmannesque revision of Carlo Gozzi's *La Donna Serpente* (The Snake Woman) for the libretto *Die Feen* (1888). The implication is that he was searching for an essential, mythical foundation on which to build the spirit of his own operatic dramaturgy. Gozzi should therefore be considered a playwright dealing with ancient myths rather than someone who gave the dramaturgy of the commedia dell'arte a new life.

The Return of the Forgotten: Reviving the Commedia dell'Arte in Twentieth-Century Opera between Modernism and Archaeologism

In twentieth-century opera, the symbolic object commedia dell'arte became the instrument used to express opposition to late Romantic and veristic opera in its anti-naturalistic form. In the typical manner in which the return of the forgotten was perceived, the *comici*'s theatrical knowledge was accessed through two sources – the rival 'brothers' Gozzi and Goldoni. Gozzi was often seen as the precursor of the creative freedom of early Romanticism, as opposed to Goldoni, who is usually presented as the creator of modern realistic and naturalistic dramaturgy.

In *L'amore delle tre melarance* (The Love of Three Oranges) (1921), Serge Prokofiev incorporates into his anti-conformist dramaturgy the anti-rationalistic and symbolist approach adopted by Meyerhold in his adaptation of Gozzi's first fable (1913). The result is an opera which brilliantly parodies melodrama, retaining the element of lively theatre criticism which characterises Gozzi's work generally. Starting from the prologue, the opera combines the deconstructive strategy of the commedia dell'arte with a metatheatrical approach and a desire to break away from the 'fourth wall' of rationalistic theatre by drawing spectators, tragic and comic actors and lyric poets onto the stage and into the action, creating a *mise en abîme* effect.

In Ferruccio Busoni's *Arlecchino* (1917) and *Turandot* (1917), singing alternates with spoken dialogue, following the eighteenth-century *Singspiele* model and thus leaving space for comic acting by the commedia dell'arte stock characters. These were perceived as *Übermarionetten*, in line with Busoni's aesthetic intention to create a sort of poetics of entertainment within an anti-realistic perspective. The fact that in Busoni's opera Harlequin does not sing, but only speaks, is significant. The strategy Busoni adopted to compose his operas was based on irony, alienation and parody – elements which he considered to be the foundation of the dramaturgy of the commedia dell'arte, as derived from Gozzi's works. As the choice of an opera with set arias suggests, Busoni's *Arlecchino* and *Turandot* are part of the revival of classic opera tradition, infused with the illusionary dimension of the commedia dell'arte.

La Donna Serpente (The Snake Woman) (1932), composed by Alfredo Casella to a libretto by Cesare Ludovici, consistently follows this burlesque interpretation of the opera as a free stream of entertainment and fantasy – unhampered by claims of rationalism or realism – with references to eighteenth-century musical styles and to Rossini, all in a whirlwind of free association.

Ermanno Wolf Ferrari composed operas adapted from Goldoni's tetralogy – *Le donne curiose* (1903), *I Quattro rusteghi* (1907), *La vedova scaltra* (1931) and *Il campiello* (1936) – as well as from *L'amore medico* (1913), titled after Moliere's *L'amour médecin*. In doing so, he adopted an even more archeological method. His objective was to bring back the Italian dramaturgy of the eighteenth century, both in the musical and in the theatrical field, using the stylistic devices of *opera buffa*. This method – almost a counter-trend to the musical modernism of that time – had already, in fact, been adopted by Pietro Mascagni in his failed experiment, *Le Maschere* (1901). Here, the libretto was written by Luigi Illica and references to Italian comic dramaturgy were presented through a metatheatrical play whose protagonists were the stock characters of the commedia dell'arte.

In contrast, Gian Francesco Malipiero, in *Le tre commedie goldoniane* (The Three Goldonian Comedies) (*Le baruffe chiozzotte, La bottega del caffè* e *Sior Todaro Brontolon*, 1926) uses eighteenth-century Venetian urban comedy in a very manipulative way, transforming it to create an impressionistic, nostalgic, ghostly vision of Venice, now transformed by the changing everyday life and routines of its citizens. Malipiero does not try to follow the tracks of the commedia dell'arte, but instead searches for remaining memories of a long-gone Venice. Here, the search for the traits and comic characteristics of the eighteenth-century *opera buffa* is not passive or archeological, but focuses on an artificial but dynamic contrast between two worlds and two eras which are inevitably far apart.

It is also noticeable that in the second half of the twentieth century, a re-appropriation of elements of the dramaturgy of the commedia dell'arte became evident in the manner in which the works of the two rival 'brothers', Gozzi and Goldoni were adapted. In *Re Cervo* (*König Hirsch*, The Stag King) (1956), based on Gozzi's fable of the same title and with a libretto written by Heinz von Cramer, Hans Werner Henze formalises his criticism of the *doxa* of Darmstadt's serialism by reintroducing a musical approach that combines the traditions of nineteenth-century Italian opera and that of street singing. In *Mirandolina* (1959), based on Goldoni's *La locandiera*, Bohuslav Martinů uses the plot dynamism of Italian comedy in order to legitimise his own vision of theatrical work. He utilises scenic episodes rather than the psychological development of the characters to build this dynamism, thus adopting a modern strategy in order to construct references to eighteenth-century opera.

As regards the dramaturgy of modern and contemporary opera, the *fil rouge*, for example, maintains a – more or less coherent – relationship to the commedia dell'arte. It uses anti-conformist poetry and finds in the dramaturgy of the Italian comedians the freedom of expression needed to build the dramatic subject, while coexisting at the same time – in a condition of artistically fertile tension – with an established theatrical format. The purpose here is not to regain absolute creative freedom, but rather to achieve the capacity of moving within a rigid structure in a flexible manner.

16

Commedia dell'Arte in Dance

Stefano Tomassini

There exist at present no comprehensive studies on the relationship between the commedia dell'arte and the history of the art of dance. Such a study would, first and foremost, have to retrace an historical timeline of all performances since the sixteenth century and would have to be based on the literary records dealing with the influences which shaped both the commedia dell'arte and dance theatre (Bragaglia 1953). These influences, however, should be considered separate from each other, because further reflection on dance as a skill as used by the comici dell'arte in comedies or *canovaccio*s has already been undertaken. Nor is there any lack of convincing hypotheses that the two might originally have had nothing to do with one another. What really needs to be further researched is how the world of dance theatre has, over time, incorporated a style of move-ment within the terms of a tradition and how this cultural appropriation is the consequence of an attempt to increase the artistic autonomy and aesthetic legitimacy of dance theatre – more specifically, choreography – as regards its conventional relationship with the written word, as well as, from Jean-Georges Noverre onwards, with visual texts. This chapter can only be considered a limited, incomplete point of departure for this research project.

According to Charles Mazouer's authoritative analysis of court ballet – a branch of ballet in which the text still governed the actions of the dancers within the performance – the presence of the Italian stock characters is on one hand due to the presence of the Italian *comici* in Paris, but on the other hand, 'is effaced and tends to disappear in the versions created by the ballets' (Mazouer 1986: 325). However, if in Molière's comedy-ballets the presence of the stock characters of the commedia dell'arte was generally associated with joy and a sign that the finale was imminent, as early as in *Les Fâcheux* (1661) their entrance during act 3, alongside 'noisemakers and drums' ('des crin crins et des tambours de Basques') filling up the entire stage, turned the dance interlude into a piece of dramatic action, 'displacing the conventional expectation of dance and music' (Franko 1994: 117). In doing so, they overturned the dance-text paradigm, extending the exploration of dramatic interruption to its extremity. This insertion of a theatrical tradition – that of Italian stock characters – should be understood in this case as an attempt to 'break the limit', that is, a victory of ornamentation in the same fictive space as the comedy (Mazouer 2006: 107). The conventional performance by stock characters represented a parody of the nobility 'without the mitigating effect of impersonation' (Smith 2005: 32).

The matter of expression and its central place in the aesthetic system of dance theatre at a professional level was first dealt with in Gregorio Lambranzi's treatise of 1716 (Lambranzi 1928), a fully fledged textualised vocabulary of the comic gesture materialised in correspondence relating to the *Ballo Nobile,* although with various controversial points. Further examples of this include John Weaver's English ballet-pantomime and *Harlequin Turned Judge* (1717), John Thursmond's double *Harlequin Doctor Faustus* (1724, Drury Lane), John Rich's *The Necromancer, or Harlequin Doctor Faustus* (1724, Lincoln's Inn Fields), as well as Gennaro Magri's and Onorato Viganò's grotesque dance. The two Italians performed respectively in *Pantomimo tra Pulcinella, Arlecchino e Coviello* at the San Carlo in Naples in 1767 and *Il Re pastore, o sia Pulcinella re in sogno* at the Teatro di Torre Argentina in Rome in 1786. Paolo Franchi also created the pantomimic dance *Pulcinella cavaliere d'industria* (1784) for the La Scala Theatre, in Milan, and Domenico Lefèvre created, again for the San Carlo Theatre in Naples, *Le astuzie amorose: Ballo Comico* (1787), in which the stock characters almost evolved into characters able to become part of the environment and the plot. The ephemeral characteristics of a tradition thus became a historical phenomenon, in a protracted attempt to update the repertoire of the *comici* and the performances of the Italian stock characters – which 'raise with particular urgency the issue of absence' (Franko and Richards 2000: 1). In this process, according to Marian Hannah Winter, one figure in particular attracts our attention: James Byrne, English dancer and choreographer, ballet-master at Sadler's Wells and later at Covent Garden in London. Byrne, who went to Philadelphia in 1796, made his debut there at a charity event on the evening of 4 May 1798, performing *The Origin of Harlequin.* In it, according to Grimaldi's *Memoir* as edited by Boz (Charles Dickens), Byrne made epochal changes in the character of Harlequin and his costume, starting with a new mobility, with particular innovations as regards *attitudes* and jumps. Before this, during the first season of 1792, the John Street Theatre in New York City witnessed a performance of the pantomime *Harlequin Protected by Cupid, or The Enchanted Nosegay.* However, the most genuine coming together of Italian stock characters and patriotic, Native American themes probably occurred in 1810 with the pantomime *Harlequin Panattaha, or Genii of the Algonquins,* performed at the Park Theatre in New York City.

The magic of the stock character of Arlecchino enjoyed lasting success in Stockholm, up to the point when ballerinas and Romantic ballet as a feminine form of the art of dance became predominant. In 1793 Jean-Rémy Marcadet, the French dancer and choreographer who worked mostly at the Kungliga Teatern in Stockholm, staged *Arlequin magicien par amour,* to music by E. Du Puy. Later, in 1796, Federico Nadi Terrade created *La mort d'Arlequin, ballet pantomime,* while Louis Joseph Marie Deland, a Swedish dancer and choreographer who had been Pierre Gardel's student in Paris, staged *Arlequin magician, comic ballet.* One year later, Deland appeared once again with *The Two Harlequins, divertissements-pantomime.* In 1798 Terrade produced *Arlequin fausse momie, pantomime ballet.* In 1799 Deland was active again with a staging of *The shipwreck or Harlequin aviator, pantomime.* This performance marks the final triumph of the French style as well as the further development of an alternative perception of the comic dancer's masculinity, more in the sense of brusque and bawdy. It is a perception which has yet to be fully analysed. In 1824, Duberval's Swedish student in Paris, Charles-Louis Didelot, also choreo-graphed a performance of the *Scène comique d'Arlequin* with music by Turik. However, it was a woman choreographer – Elise Juliette Christiane Price, Bournonville's student and later prima ballerina, who retired as a performer as early as 1865 – who would, in 1884, most likely in Vienna, stage *Arlequin électricien* to music by J. Hellmesberger and include the traditional stock characters of the commedia dell'arte. In doing so, she created one of the legends of emerging modernity.

Meanwhile in Paris, in 1823, the rivalry between the private theatres of the Boulevards and those financed by the Maison du Roi (Opéra) was played out precisely on the issue of the role of the stock character of Pulcinella. On the one hand, Charles-François Mazurier performed Polichinel vampire, Ballet-pantomime et Divertissemens burlesques en un Acte et à Spectacle – created and choreographed by Frédéric-Auguste Blache with music by Alexandre Piccini (Théâtre de la Porte Saint-Martin) – for his Parisian debut. On the other hand, Jules Pierrot performed Polichinelle avalé par le baleine by François-Charlemagne Lefèvre (music by Hostié) at the Théatre de la Gaîté. But the competition between the theatres seeking commercial success and between the dancers seeking increased prestige, is the rationalisation of an historical problem which is far more difficult to set aside: the regulation of desire within the boundaries of comic performance, waiting for the comic performance to be recreated and transformed into its nobler form which is typical of the *demi-caractère* genre.

In his memoirs, Marius Petipa mentions, from the list of his greatest successes in Moscow, *Les Millions d'Arlequin,* a ballet in two acts set to music by Riccardo Drigo (Hermitage Theatre, St Petersburg, 1900). Thanks to the written and visual memoirs of Alexander Shiryaev, who played the role of Cassandra in the revival of 1902–1903 (originally created by Petipa for Enrico Cecchetti) (Shiryaev 2009: 31) and partly thanks to Pyotr Gusev's (re)construction for the Maly/Mikhailovsky Theatre Ballet filmed by BBC in 1978 (most likely closer to Fyodor Lopukhov's version of 1933), it becomes especially evident in regard to choreography that pantomime allows ballet to remain connected to the narrative framework, although the medium of this process is a dancing body whose technique is disciplined and marketable and whose aim is to conceal every effort and objectify every form of physicality.

After completing *Bal Poudré,* which its creator had defined as 'a ballet in the style of a harlequinade of the seventeenth century' and *charity ball* which was performed only once in St Petersburg before 1909 (Fokine 1961: 121), the Russian choreographer Mikhail Fokine staged his *Le Carnaval* in 1910 and thereby inaugurated a long-lasting revival of the figures and themes of the commedia dell'arte within European theatrical dance (Rudnitsky 1988). Fokine and Sergej Legat had already played the parts of the two Pierrots in 1903 for Nikolaj Legat's *The Fairy Doll* (Gavrilovich 2013: 56–57). However, what really demonstrated the radical potential of a dramaturgical inclusion of the commedia dell'arte in modern dance was Kassian Goleïzovski's tragic interpretation of the Italian stock characters in the form of a parody on ballet and its 'regime of truth' in the ballet, *Harlequinade* (1919, music by Cécile Chaminade) and *Tombeau de Columbine* (1920, music by Boris Beer). These are the political roots and the social implications of modernist individualism which favour danced monologue as a form of expression. They appear evident – although in different ways – in Max Terpis's *Der Letzte Pierrot* (1927, music by Karol Rathaus) or the moving *Pierrot in the Dead City* (1935, choreography by Ted Shawn for Barton Mumaw and music by Erich Wolfgang Korngold). Many further cases could be cited, for example, Martha Graham's initial solo venture, *Harlequinade* (1930, music by Ernst Toch). It consisted of two satirical, thematically opposite dances (*a.* Pessimist; *b.* Optimist); in her solo, Graham 'was humorously woeful and joyful by turns' with a comical effect which was immediately recognised as devastating (Martin 1930).

From Diaghilev's extensive musical library and his notes on Italian publications by Benedetto Croce (*Saggi sulla letteratura italiana del Seicento*, 1911) and Michele Scherillo (*L'opera buffa napoletana*, 1916), the Russian impresario got the idea to invite Igor Stravinsky to orchestrate a few melodies attributed to Giambattista Pergolesi for a production of *Pulcinella*. Léonide Massine did the choreography and it was performed by the Ballet Russes in 1920 at the Théâtre Nationale de l'Opéra in Paris. The costumes and sets were designed by Pablo Picasso. The libretto, written by Massine, was inspired explicitly by an episode of the commedia dell'arte (*Les quatres Polichinelles semblables*, 1700) which he found in, and selected from, a manuscript bought in a vintage book shop in Naples. It also draws on material he was able to gather during his trip to Italy in 1917, among which was a mask which belonged to the Neapolitan actor Antonio Petito (1822–1876), the renowned Pulcinella of the San Carlino theatre in Naples. To Massine, the history and role of the mask and its inclusion in the plot were opportunities he used to create, within a crippled yet very flexible body, scenes of disguises and amorous jousting including 'a grotesque ritual dance during which Pulcinella came back to life', ultimately merged in a happy ending 'in a multitude of imaginary, folkloristic steps reminiscent of a *saltarello*' (Massine 1995: 173–4). This was an example of the survival of popular elements from the past in the modernist imagination during the first few years after World War I and provided the liveliest reasons for a new, future-oriented manifesto. In the same way Fedor Lopoukhov's 'Sovietised' version (*Pulcinella*, Leningrad, GATOB, 16 May 1926) revealed the influence of Meyerhold's antiliterary experiments, as well as something of Evgeny Vakhtangov's 'fantastic realism' and Alexander Tairov's 'synthetic' or total theatre.

Significantly, the commedia dell'arte returned to the Opéra in Paris in 1980 with Douglas Dunn's Stravinsky-inspired production of *Pulcinella*. The author, a postmodernist American dancer and choreographer, a former member of Grand Union who was in contact with the dancers of French theatre, attempted to accomplish the difficult task of decentralising the presence of the dancing body by building the rhythm of the action on the use of scenic space rather than on the vocabulary of steps. In 1984, *Arlequin magicien par amour* was staged at the Opéra, as well as the revival of Fokine's *Carnaval,* as part of an *All commedia dell'arte Program* curated by Ivon Cramér. It was an eighteenth-century pantomime ballet, originally made for the Court Theatre at Drottingholm, with music by Édouard du Puy and arranged by Charles Farncombe. The idea of a programmatic union between tradition and modernity, brought about by the practice of reconstruction – which is, in itself, far from neutral and often compromised by excessively rational considerations – has important implications for the critical relationship of postmodernity with history as well as with museum imagination. The Prague-born choreographer Jiri Kylián also drew on Lambranzi's treatise in order to create *Tanzschule* (music by Mauricio Kagel) for the Nederland Dans Theater. It was staged again in 1989 by the company of the Opéra for the reopening of the Palais Garnier which had undergone major restoration work. However, in this case the ballet revolves mainly around a grotesque reflection on how studying the past has a coercive and inevitable influence on schools of ballet and on the authoritarian figure of the *maître de ballet.*

In 1985, the American master choreographer Merce Cunningham, reflecting on, from a choreographic standpoint, the speed of movement as witnessed through a video camera, drawing inspiration from the improvisational method of the *comici* of the eighteenth-century Italian commedia dell'arte as illustrated in a few printed *canovaccio* collections (most likely Lambranzi's), and in collaboration with Elliot Caplan, created *Deli* Commedia – a choreography explicitly intended for visual media (Gruen 1986: 88). The images were accompanied by background piano music reminiscent of silent films; the music itself was arranged and performed by Pat Richter. Here, the roles of dancers were equivalent to those of masks to be exchanged rather than of characters to be interpreted, because the plurality of action was considered more important than the uniqueness of the character. In a series of hilarious variations, the scenic space and the elements employed are dominated by inventiveness, gags and continual transformation, with regard even to objects, all of which strongly hints at the scenic compositional characteristics of the commedia dell'arte. Furthermore, by employing visual media, a meta-visual effect was achieved. This corresponded to the typical metaphor of baroque theatre and was one of the most important acting practices used by the commedia dell'arte.

In Italy in 1990, at the Teatro Ponchielli in Cremona, Virgilio Sieni staged a *Pulcinella* based on Stravinsky's *canovaccio* with costumes by the Italian stylist Miuccia Prada, in the spirit of being a real 'escape from the past'. The purpose here was to free, remove and subtract from the modernist tradition – from which both the music and the ballet stemmed – each and every theatrical stereotype, including those related to the commedia dell'arte, thus introducing new points of emphasis. In his more recent *De Anima* (Biennale Danza Venezia 2012, Piccolo Arsenale theatre) Sieni worked on almost exclusively visual sources, among which were those that accompanied Jean Starobinski's essay *Portrait de l'artiste en saltimbanque* as well as the paintings of Longhi, Tiepolo, Watteau, Picasso's comic figures in his blue and rose periods and many more. Sieni, with the help of the stock characters of the commedia dell'arte which, in this case, were often accompanied by their shadow, launched a metalinguistic process of reflection on the body of the dancer and on the matter of the soul, in accordance with an idea of spectacular acrobatics that only refers to the body itself, to its grace, vigor and erotic appeal. The stock characters of the *commedia*, on the other hand, are presented as scapegoats for the suffering of the world and in *Imitatio Christi*, as archetypes of the sacrificed savior.

A great misunderstanding still needs to be clarified, which probably stems from the success of the commedia dell'arte with regard to the art of dancing: the alleged contrast between ballet and modern dance which was, for example, recorded by Adrian Stokes in his 1935 book *To-Night the Ballet*. Here, the expressive repertoire of the commedia dell'arte introduced by Fokine is seen as being capable of renewing the academic technique rather than helping to overcome it altogether. For this reason, Columbine *sur les pointes* is able to look more emancipated than a heavy, barefoot expressionist dancer:

> And yet it is in this delicious mode that the woman's earthiness, her closeness to earth, is suggested, and far more succinctly suggested than by the heavy, barefoot or sandaled dancer, the expressionist dancer, who slowly enacts a kind of dream, whose movements infer that the stage is but a poor substitute for meadows and woods. (Stokes 1935: 38–9)

Here, the emancipation of women, represented by the new role of Columbine, can only be realised through the academically trained grace of a body rigorously standing *sur les pointes*. Literally, and not surprisingly, a little earlier Stokes quoted Theophile Gautier's words regarding the *temps de pointe* of Sofia Fuoco, the stage name of the Italian dancer Maria Brambilla, who was also Blasis's student.

A possible answer, perhaps not exhaustively but only partly formulated, of a harmonious convergence between modernist ballet and new dance, in the spirit of the commedia dell'arte as a tradition of movement alternative to that provided by the academies, was offered by Bronislava Nijinska. In 1932, at the Théâtre National de l'Opéra-Comique in Paris, Nijinska staged the ballet *Les Comédiens Jaloux* (music by Alfredo Casella da Domenico Scarlatti, for the Théâtre de la Danse Nijinska company). The libretto, written by Nijinska herself, tells the story of a troupe of *comici dell'arte* who, upon their arrival, are immediately commissioned to perform. Nancy Van Norman Baer points out that, despite its humorous theme and inspiration, the ballet is permeated by a powerful atmosphere of social satire, probably resulting from a reflection on the consequences of the Great Depression (Van Norman Baer 1987: 63). The grotesque farce accompanying the preparations for the performance features several typical stock characters of the commedia dell'arte: Harlequin, Pantaloon, Columbine, the servant, Captain Crocodillo. For the male role of Pedrollino, Nijinska adopted certain characteristics of Charlie Chaplin, 'a modern-day Pierrot, a Chaplinesque clown who was also a tragic figure' (Van Norman Baer 1987: 63).

The logic behind this conversion, though restrained by the conventions of the conservative and the bawdy, also influenced the libretto for the Faustian Pulcinella choreographed by George Balanchine and Jerome Robbins for the Stravinsky Festival in 1972. From the letters exchanged between George Balanchine and Eugene Berman (1899–1972), the painter and stage designer for the production, which was performed at the New York Public Library for the Performing Arts, a discussion emerges about the design of the masks of the commedia dell'arte. Two possibilities are compared, Giovanni Domenico Tiepolo's and Picasso's. A firm decision is made not to conform to the aesthetic values of Massine's original version promoted by Diaghilev:

> I have seen series of drawings by Tiepolo depicting 'Pulcinella', which I think would be excellent, rather than the type of Picasso decor that Diaghilev used. Of course it would not be at all like the Diaghilev production. (Berman 1971–1972: folder 1)

Furthermore, Balanchine's choice of a structure based on 'contrasting interludes' highlights how the constant juxtaposition of the comic and the popular with the noble register (Columbine dances *sur les pointes*) characterises his digressions into continuous variation. This contrastive use of the past serves to harness anxieties concerning the present. From the letters, we learn that, at the level of the plot for example, 'homosexual acts of the Devil' were discussed, which in the ballet were to evolve into a disconcerting predatory act of pedophilia. Pulcinella (Edward Villella) has sold his soul to the devil (John Clifford) who, at the moment of taking it, is 'distracted' by an adolescent who has intentionally been placed in the centre of the stage by his Girl (Carol Summer). In addition, in one of the first scenes, Pulcinella, who has just been rescued from certain death, is seduced by two prostitutes who turn out to be transvestite males. This scene was partially censored out of the version produced for the German television and transmitted the following year (filmed in Berlin for television, by Hugo Niebeling, R. M. Productions – Munich, 1973). In conclusion, this Pulcinella, misogynist and hyper-virile, rapacious and bawdy, who drags everyone and everything into his deformed, tragicomic world, typical of the commedia dell'arte, seems to correspond perfectly with the transformation of the Fool into Knave ('what Stendhal called *le coquin fieffé*, "unmitigated scoundrel"'). This transformation was used by Jacques Lacan to distinguish between two types of contemporary intellectuals, identifying the Knave with a dangerous, reactionary form of collective stupidity for which no one, in the end, would pay the price (Lacan 1992: 182–3).

The Circus and the Artist as Saltimbanco

Sandra Pietrini

If they are so different, how can commedia dell'arte and circus intertwine, to the point of overlapping, in our figurative and literary imaginations? Why, in the commonly accepted idea of performance, are harlequins and clowns members of the same great family of artists? First of all, because the characters of the commedia dell'arte achieved legendary status soon after they first appeared, taking on a life of their own outside of their original context. Like every character of this status, they changed their characteristics and functions, interacting with each other in a fertile contagion of gestures. It was not by chance that, starting in the fifteenth century, they left the stage and started to establish a parallel existence in the figurative arts. Thanks to the publication of almanacs and other forms of promotional material, their art was widely disseminated. Iconography is not only a very powerful way to propagate images, but is also a forge in which poetic myths are created and implanted in the collective imagination. In the interaction between the two genres, iconography played a decisive part.

Specifically in twentieth-century painting, the stock characters of the commedia dell'arte were absorbed by the sparkling phantasmagoria of the circus, which is a spacious container, a fertile space of contradictions, in which splendour and misery coexist. As the name itself implies, it is also all-around performance, circularity and absolute visibility, in which everything becomes pure performance. In his work *Portrait de l'acteur en saltimbanque* (Portrait of the Actor as an Acrobat) (1970), Jean Starobinski expressed his thoughts on the metaphorical dimension of circus artists between the end of the nineteenth and the beginning of the twentieth century, analysing the figure of the acrobat as an archetypal image which finds its fullest form of expression in the circus. It is not by chance that the rise in popularity of the circus began in the Romantic period, when several poets had recourse to the image of the acrobat as a metaphor for their own artistic condition. Therefore, the circus and its itinerant artists became exemplary images of an idea of performance which is very close to that of the *comici dell'arte* or, more precisely, to their image.

In certain respects, we might indeed think of the long history of the *comici dell'arte* as a kind of parable. In the phase in which their popularity was increasing, the *comici* switched from improvised performances on the streets, side by side with acrobats and charlatans, to more structured forms of drama, which enabled them to avoid any association with the most vulgar kinds of entertainers. On the other hand, when the fortunes of the commedia dell'arte were waning, the stock characters regained their absolute, characterising dimension outside of the framework of drama (from which they had nevertheless taken up many impulses) and became part of our collective imagination in both the literary and figurative arts. As we know, they first demonstrated their overflowing vitality in Paris, in the theatres of the fairs of Saint-Germain and Saint-Laurent. Principally by extending into other forms of art, they were able to perpetuate their popularity as well as react against the decline in the performing arts. Popular culture was obviously ready to reabsorb them, their accentuated characterisations on one hand and their symbolic value on the other hand. A vital medium in this process was carnival folklore, in which the stock characters of the commedia dell'arte have actually been present from the very beginning (it has been suggested that this may have been their true origin). By merging into circus, the stock characters regained their original, gesturally vivacious, acrobatic expressiveness. The *commedia* – a frontier area in which different ways of communicating mix – was influenced by other forms of art, transforming and regenerating itself in the process.

The question that now arises is: what were the key developments and events that led a few stock characters to become part of the standard circus repertoire? Historically speaking, pantomime was the common ground shared by the commedia dell'arte and the circus, having been part of the circus performance repertoire from the very beginning. Not by chance, both phenomena are rooted in a popular culture that, for the most part, builds its own legends through the figurative arts. We know that the circus as a distinct form of entertainment emerged from the horse shows performed in London in the second half of the eighteenth century. Soon afterwards, the circus came to include performances by clowns, trained animals and jugglers – that is, forms of performance typically used by jesters. As early as 1770, Philip Astley began enrolling Italian acrobats in order to enrich his own equestrian and acrobatic shows. When he introduced the figure of the clown, Astley accomplished a synthesis between theatre and circus that would reap considerable success in later times and also transform stock characters into irresistible attractions in their own right.

In France, with the founding of the Cirque Olympique by the Franconi Brothers in Paris in 1807, circus became the form, par excellence, of popular, performance entertainment, attracting large and varied numbers of spectators. In England too, following the Theatre Regulation Act of 1843, which granted *legitimate theatres* the right to perform spoken drama, music halls concentrated their efforts on the visual aspects of their productions, giving life to a new wave of remarkably visual forms of entertainment. In the second half of the nineteenth century, acrobats and jugglers actually came to be regarded as respectable, even renowned professionals (Serena 2008: 30) and not belonging to the bustling, debauched world of street performers. In the collective imagination, however, circus artists retained an aura of abnormality and eccentricity, which made them perfect representatives of the way of life of the *bohémiens* but excluded from stable, bourgeois society.

It was not by chance then, that the first element common to performers of both the commedia dell'arte and the circus was their nomadic lifestyle. It has an existential dimension with a tendency to acquire a metaphoric significance, linked to the fact that neither group belong to any well-defined social class. The nomadic way of life of medieval entertainers was, at the time, regarded as reprehensible and dangerous. In the case of the *comici dell'arte*, it took on an almost legendary dimension, considered intrinsic to the profession itself. Just like the companies of the commedia dell'arte and the gypsies, circus artists were seen as being unstable and stateless, yet among themselves very cohesive, like a large family that traverses different countries and cultures with its caravan. In literature, a positive – almost idyllic – example of this is to be found in Charles Dickens's *Hard Times* (1854) and a more detailed example in Edmond de Goncourt's *Les Frères Zemganno* (1879), in which the generosity of some characters is portrayed alongside the envy and rancour of others.

The other essential element that comici dell'arte and circus artists have in common is obviously their comic sense. The figure of the clown is rooted in Elizabethan theatre, but is also influenced by the stock characters of the commedia dell'arte. This influence manifests itself firstly in the choice of themes and styles borrowed for, what would now be called, marketing reasons. Circus needs to arouse curiosity and interest through advertising, which in turn favours the introduction of attractive images, easily able to captivate the attention of an audience. In addition to displaying female bodies in all their nimble agility and '*mirabilia*', monstrous-looking human beings and ferocious-looking wild beasts, circus should exude a direct, universally understood comicality. For this reason, circus resurrected the sixteenth-century image of the clown, but transformed the essence of that image. Let us remember that in Elizabethan culture the 'clown' was a well-defined and universally known comical figure, associated with the image of the man from the country living in the city and personified by the actor, Richard Tarlton, who became the first clown to build a double career, accepted by the nobility and running one of the new professional companies (Wiles 1987: 11–22). This clown was, however, overshadowed by the shrewder and many-sided 'fool' which had such an essential function in much of Elizabethan and Shakespearean drama and later in the birth and development of stock characters. As a result, the generic figure of the clown which re-emerged was confined to the pure comicality of circus. In doing so, it ended by taking on a symbolic meaning – exactly like the one that characterised for centuries the stereotyped image of the buffoon. In the process of defining this figure, the role of iconography proved to be crucial; it reinvented the typical repertoire of the clown by drawing on various sources, such as the mimes of antiquity and bifurcated Janus figures. The clown's two-sided mask, laughing and weeping at the same time, is an obvious reference to the ambivalence of the two-headed Janus. However, the figure of the clown was still dependent on a repertoire which was strongly influenced by the pervasive presence of the stock characters of the *commedia,* among them Pierrot, the precursor of the refined white clown.

If the origin of the commedia dell'arte can be traced back to the duet between Pantalone and the *zanni,* it is also true that these stock characters evolved in different ways. It has been rightly observed that Pantalone, being more clearly defined, was also more sterile and unable to produce the creative variations of the more generic *zanni*: Arlecchino, Brighella, Mezzettino, Pulcinella, Pierrot and so on. What is certain is that the characters most frequently adopted for the circus repertoire were, predominately, eighteenth-century variations of the *zanni,* such as Pierrot, Pulcinella and Arlecchino – all of which had become graceful, elegant dancers. All of this happened through the reworking of the literary and figurative repertoires, within a complex framework of reciprocating influences. From the figurative arts, that fertile breeding ground for pervasive imaginations, scenes typical of the eighteenth century in which the comici dell'arte are either associated or coupled with more marginalised figures such as gypsies and acrobats, were adapted so as to become part of that specific, spectacular container which is circus. The ideal vehicle for this transformation was circus pantomimes, which from the early nineteenth century started to include the stock characters of the commedia dell'arte, Arlecchino and Pierrot in particular, among their cast of protagonists.

Antonio Franconi's Cirque Olympique moved to Paris at the beginning of the nineteenth century. It was a time when the *opéra-bouffon*, that last, ephemeral trace of the heritage of a commedia dell'arte, was looking to the past and destined to merge into entirely different forms of performance, such as opera. From the start, Franconi reintroduced the main stock characters of the commedia dell'arte, for example, the *Arlequin statue*, *Pierrots mannequins*, *Les deux Polichinelle*, as he wanted to stage equestrian pieces that were short and comical (Pretini 1988: 87, 88, 91). In general, the stock characters became part of the circus anyway, as icons taken out of their original context, but even so, they were able to influence other figures such as acrobats and horsemen. In a colour picture showing the Franconi family's equestrian performances, Pierrot appears in two out of the nine scenes depicting equestrian fun and games. In the first, entitled *Les farces de Pierrot*, he rides a horse backwards while grasping its tail, in a gesture which is reminiscent of the medieval 'festivals of the madmen'. In the second, entitled *Le cheval mort*, he stands by the trainer's side, raising his arms in a gesture of desperation. In each of the two illustrations, Pierrot's costume is different: In the first he wears a hat and red trousers while in the second he is seen in the typical white costume, complete with collar. Philip Astley's circus evolved in much the same way. The first clowns hired by him were traditional acrobats and tightrope dancers. Soon enough, other kinds of ideas made their way into his performances. In fact, from a contemporary leaflet we learn that he had some of his riders dressed like Pierrot (De Ritis 2008: 108). Usually, what theatre impresarios did was to rework successful pantomimes emphasising their visually spectacular side and at times combining them with equestrian numbers. For a performance in 1800, Astley himself reworked and adapted a pantomime which he had previously staged at London's Covent Garden in 1791. It was called *Blue Beard, or The Flight of Harlequin* and William Barrymore played the part of Pierrot (Kotar and Gessler 2011: 83–4).

Thus, circus established a dialogue with theatre from the very beginning, sometimes even with the same actors. This is what happened, for example, with the English mime Laurent who, after working alongside Deburau in the Funambules, switched to the Cirque Olympique. But above all, what gave circus its aura of being spectacular were the individual stock characters. It was more than the bare survival of comic, harlequin-esque scenes with a minimum of plot behind them; the characters tended to become symbolic, absolute figures. Transformed into immediately recognisable icons, they were used for advertising purposes, to attract and captivate an audience – on the basis of their popularity rather than for the unique characteristics or functions of the various characters. Furthermore, whenever the circus employed one of the more popular stock characters in some dramatic-narrative dimension – such as in pantomime – the plots were always reworked according to the demands of the performance.

It is also true that pantomime reached one of its highest points with the great Jean-Gaspard Deburau, who had become extremely popular at the Théâtre des Funambules at the beginning of the nineteenth century. The lunar melancholy piece of his portrayal of Baptiste-Pierrot greatly influenced the figure of the white clown. In contrast to this, in the giggly, clumsy Augusto, with his red nose and his ridiculous costume, we find the heritage of medieval jesters and to a lesser extent, the expressive, vital Harlequin of the original commedia dell'arte. This has led to fundamentally different developments. In England and Germany, from the eighteenth century onwards, the interaction between the stock characters of the commedia dell'arte and characters of local folklore – such as *Hanswurst* – has taken on mostly comical connotations. On the other hand, in France and Italy there emerged a melancholic, almost tragic vein that has been the basis of future reinterpretations. It would be safe to say that the character that played the central role in the reinterpretation is Pierrot. In the evolution of this particular stock character, the figurative reinterpretations of the eighteenth century were especially important, along with Antoine Watteau's paintings – in which a melancholy Gilles appears in his characteristic white tunic. If it is true – as has been said – that Deburau did not draw inspiration directly from Watteau's Gilles and that a direct relationship between the two figures was established only after the great success of Deburau's pantomime (Jones 1984: 21), then the undeniable similarity of the two characters' hints at the continuous transformation of a collective imagination which is simultaneously pervasive and receptive. After all, Pierrot – together with Pulcinella – has always been one of the stock characters more subject to change because of their strong literary and figurative mythicisation. The idealistic reinterpretation of the stock characters of the commedia dell'arte, however, began with the dreaming Pierrots and the gallant Harlequins of the end of the eighteenth century. They seemed to try to lure the spectator into a refined, yet futile worldly game, in which the ephemeral, fleeting nature of passion acquires a melancholic shade. The commedia dell'arte was by that time part of an idealised, spiritual dream, taken away from the brutal physicality of the body and made abstract, almost disincarnate. The melancholy Gilles, whose gaze is always lost in an ecstatic reverie, is the perfect symbol of this. Watteau, who is seemingly poles apart from the acrobatic frenzy of circus, does however anticipate the melancholy of the sad clown.

After the nostalgic reinterpretation of the eighteenth century came the romantic era, characterised by a mythicised point of view in which the world of comedy identifies with free aesthetic creation and with the genius of extempore creation. The literary peak of this tendency was reached in the nineteenth century by Maurice Sand and Théophile Gautier. In a study of the legend of the commedia dell'arte in nineteenth-century France, a number of essential stages of this process have been retraced, resulting in the identification of four essential periods: the first marks the passage from theatre to theatres and the scattering of the *comici* among the stages of the Parisian *foires*; the second follows the path of literary reinterpretation and ends with the staging of Maurice Sand's *Masques et bouffons* (1860); the third is characterised by a process of worn-out, decadent symbolisation; in the fourth, figurative artists and directors at the beginning of the twentieth century give new life to the legend of the commedia dell'arte. The key passage of this transfiguration into legend has been identified with the movement 'from theatre to literature', in the period immediately preceding the destruction of the boulevard theatres in 1862 (including the theatre of the Funambules, where Deburau's Pierrot had triumphed; Cuppone 1999: 28). It was, indeed, a fundamental turning point in the evolution of the image of the commedia dell'arte. Nevertheless, literature had been decisively influenced by the figurative repertoire of theatre from the very beginning, in a fertile, reciprocal exchange of impulses. The refinement of the stock character of Arlecchino and the invention of Pierrot himself did not really take place long before their literary and theatrical adaptation. Watteau's dream of the commedia dell'arte is a clear example of this. Certainly, the figurative arts played a crucial role in the redefinition of a repertoire which had already been elevated to legendary status. It is worth recalling, among other things, that Grimaldi – commonly regarded as the first of modern clowns – also used to play the role of Harlequin and drew on several comical traditions in order to invent the character that made him famous.

Theatre, the visual arts and literature are thus intertwined, in a continual game of references and implied citations. Hence, the great invention of Jean-Gaspard Deburau – the melancholic Pierrot in love with the moon – recalls the stock characters of Watteau and Nicolas Lancret and acts as a prelude to the tragic fate of this new character, created in the collective imagination rather than on stage. After Deburau's first performances at the Théâtre des Funambules in Paris in 1819, Pierrot became the symbol of pantomime and as such, was later copied by circus performers. The proximity between the two forms of entertainment finds confirmation in the variety of performances offered by *boulevard* theatres. In Marcel Carné's film, *Les enfants du paradis* (1945), the first scenes showing the Boulevard du Temple begin with a series of performances that are reminiscent of Parisian fairs and of the tradition of circus: feats of strength and dexterity, numbers with trained monkeys and various *parades* – and of course Pierrot, with his sad mask. He is prominent and important in the advertising *parade*, first as a motionless statue – as if it were the emblem of an anti-spectacular kind of ineptitude – then in the pantomime created by Baptiste/Deburau, in order to recount the episode of the robbery which he has just witnessed.

Certainly, Carné's film contributed significantly to the establishment of the image of Pierrot in its sentimental sense on a visual level. This character then had a stimulating effect on the collective imagination of the commedia dell'arte. In fact, Pierrot's spirituality and extreme sensitivity ended up by influencing Arlecchino, the stock character whose physicality was closest to the human body. This became evident in the nineteenth century, when the stock characters underwent a literary transformation that often involved reference to grotesque dreams, as in E. T. A. Hoffmann's long short story, *Prinzessin Brambilla* (1821). The transformation of the original comicality of the stock characters dates back to the collective imagination of the nineteenth century, during which they took two divergent paths: on one hand, the representation of the purely comic and acrobatic part, on the other the discovery of tragedy. This second path, which is obviously far removed from the circus, found its highest form of expression in literature. In his short story, *Le vieux Saltimbanque* (1869), Charles Baudelaire reinterprets the myth of the misunderstood artist as the tragic metaphor for being abandoned and condemned to solitude. Similarly, in Paul Verlaine's poem *Pierrot* (1885), the stock character becomes a spectral figure; his ability to experience joy has faded like the flame of a candle in a draught and he has become a pale, tormented, thin shadow of his former self; in the wind, his tunic looks like a shroud. The decadent, symbolist culture prevalent at the end of the nineteenth century brought out the tragic side of the romantic Pierrot in the figurative arts too, as shown in Aubrey Beardsley's drawing, *The Death of Pierrot* (1896). This aspect had a long-term influence on the other stock characters as well.

From the end of the nineteenth century, even Pulcinella – poor, miserable and always famished – would acquire, from time to time, a tragic aspect. Not even Arlecchino, in the twentieth-century reinterpretations he was subjected to, would be spared by the new, existentially tragic dimension that artists in this era wanted to see in comic characters.

Circus, apparently far removed from any temptation to turn melancholic, did on the other hand contribute to the renewal of the collective imagination in several ways. First and foremost, by propagating a powerfully effective and widespread penchant to spectacularism – the success of the commedia dell'arte in the iconography of the twentieth century as well as its influence on the circus are, in fact, mainly linked to the figurative arts. Moreover, there is the legend of the Artist, which was analysed by Starobinski among others. The stock characters of the commedia dell'arte reappear in the iconography of the twentieth century in a generic context which recalls the widely held idea of performance in which itinerant artists become the symbol of an existential condition characterised by marginalisation and precariousness. In descriptions of the twentieth century, the circus does not usually appear as a realistically defined environment but rather as a generic context that recalls a certain idea of performance. Thus, when searching for the poetry of performance, the attention of the figurative arts was generally far from the superficial, sparkling splendour of circus attractions, tending to linger on the elegiac melancholy of impoverished acrobats and outcast artists, whose existential condition corresponded to their professional situation. In other words, the difference between the individual and the character disappeared as the latter completely absorbed and swallowed up the personality of the former. Behind Henri de Toulouse-Lautrec's 'clownesses' we can still see the tormented existences of disillusioned, perhaps alcohol-abusing female artists. The human being in Picasso's Harlequins and Pierrots exists merely as a stock character; his function ends with his role, and his role becomes the inescapable existential dimension.

Nevertheless, the artistic movements of the first decades of the twentieth century played an essential role in the process of the interaction of the circus with the commedia dell'arte. If the stock characters had already inspired such artists as Jean Renoir and Paul Cézanne, the new century witnessed a renewed interest in the commedia dell'arte on the part of every single avant-garde movement, from Russian ballet to Italian futurism, from the great Russian directors to figurative artists. After all, one of the objectives of avant-garde movements is to break down the barriers between different kinds of art. Thus, theatre was called on to engage with the circus and, starting from an aesthetic point of view founded on the assembling of attractions, restored the stock characters, making them in the process, for fictional purposes, vaguer. The Russian directors, Aleksandr Tairov, Yevgeny Vakhtangov and Vsevolod Meyerhold in particular, used the joyful multicoloured stock character of Harlequin repeatedly in order to restore creativity to their scenic action. Meyerhold played Pierrot several times, while the Russian ballet contributed substantially to the commedia dell'arte, giving it much new life. In addition, poets and figurative artists frequently drew inspiration from it, in the process creating analogies that would later enrich the legendary dimension of this kind of performance. Even the spectators were drawn, time after time, into this sphere of transgressive vitality. Guillaume Apollinaire wrote in 1913, in a note to Jacques Copeau: 'Marinetti wishes to open a variety theatre where there would only be acrobats, clowns and dancers, while the spectators would fight and shout there, each playing his improvised role like in the commedia dell'arte' (Décaudin and Apollinaire 1965–1966: 881).

In this fertile blending of the arts, the stock characters represent an impressive dynamism, a breeding ground of ideas and an escape route towards the free creativity of improvisation. A roguish, rebellious spirit merges with the glittering attractions of the circus, which in turn welcomes the stock characters of the commedia dell'arte as symbolic and by now, legendary figures. Their attractiveness reached a climax with the artists who gravitated towards Paris, from Apollinaire to Picasso, from Gino Severini to André Derain. The fascinating shows of the Cirque Médrano inspired an aesthetic reinterpretation of the stock characters as plastic bodies, which could be transformed into a cubist artwork or perhaps remain just a fantastic shape. By identifying with the stock characters, the artist's identity dissolves, while the carnival and the circus act as generic contexts of reference, almost as escape routes towards nonconformity and otherness. In other words, the artist tends to identify with the eccentric, transitory condition of the stock characters.

Thanks to Picasso's paintings, the fertile exchange between commedia dell'arte and the circus became, in turn, the inspiration for new aesthetic paths which have been retraced and reworked up to our own times. It is known that Picasso intensified his interest in the commedia dell'arte by spending time in the theatrical environment and by collaborating with Sergei Diaghilev for his Russian ballet performances. For the curtain designed for the ballet *Parade*, Harlequin is depicted from behind, playing cards in the middle of a group of figures that recall the otherness and exoticism of somewhat bohemian artists. It is worth noting that the subject of the picture was the parade of the performers promoting the ballet. Clearly, the power of attraction of the stock characters of the commedia dell'arte was so great as to justify the inclusion of a character that was not amongst the fictional characters of the ballet. Three years later, Picasso designed the sets and costumes for the ballet *Pulcinella* (Cooper 2005: 409–46), reluctantly abandoning the temptation to make use of cubism and abstract art in order to keep the stock character readily identifiable as an icon.

Picasso loved theatre outside theatre, i.e. performance outside its scenic framework. He also loved clowns and used to spend hours chatting with them at the bar of the Circus Médrano. His self-absorbed, thoughtful clowns were influenced by the iconographic tradition of the jesters, while his Pierrots and Pulcinellas seemed to be drawn into a sphere of dreamlike, visionary fantasy. This was Watteau's vision too, but Picasso's was enriched by impulses from the circus. His Harlequins, whether completely stylised or employed in a context that hints at the nomadic existence of small family companies, initially call to mind an existential dimension rather than a professional one. The gouache, *La mort d'Arlequin* (1906) is the perfect example of how the legend of Harlequin can be removed from its original context. The character is reduced to a pale, emaciated figure, starved to the point of inducing compassion and recalling a sort of painful, artistic asceticism. This grim condition should not prompt us to think, as some have hypothesised (Clair 2004: 21–2), that the origin of the name, Harlequin (Hell-quin) comes from a possible relationship with the realm of the dead. In general, Picasso's Harlequins do not seem to try to exorcise death with their acrobatic leaps. Rather they are static and still, in a way that recalls absence and a particular kind of melancholy which comes from a feeling of perpetual exile rather than from thoughts about an afterlife.

This nebulous extension of the collective imagination of the commedia dell'arte is precisely what suggests an analogy with the world of itinerant circus artists, who are also drawn into the idealising sphere of a diversity which – time after time – takes on a melancholic, dream-inducing or elegaic connotation. Picasso's acrobats hint at a broader idea of perform-ance which shrouds the characters in a seemingly abstract state of suspension and in which their existential and professional circumstances coincide. This is not very different from the concept of circus artists as aesthetes searching for an absolute, almost metaphysical dimension that is impossible to reach. This idea reaches its climax in Franz Kafka's short story *Erstes Leid* (1921) in which life and art merge into a grotesque perspective. The trapeze artist, who spends most of his life literally walking

on the tool of his trade, represents the inevitable overlapping of performance and everyday life which was an essential element in the way of life of
the stock characters of the commedia dell'arte (and even more so when
their way of life was idealised into legend). However, he develops the
concept to such an extreme that it is transformed into a paradox. The
artist, in fact, is ill at ease whenever he feels observed by onlookers and
exposed to their distracted looks – during the time which he regards as
belonging to his private, everyday life. Always being a subject of performance can also be a terrible condemnation. In particular, Picasso's acrobats
seem to be condemned to play the part of themselves, never being able to
transcend a form of existence defined solely by their professional status.
Among other things, his acrobats always exude signs pointing to a condition of marginalisation and poverty within society. This is part of a certain
mythicisation of the circus that can be found – albeit with different
characteristics – in Charlie Chaplin's film *The Circus* (1928).

However, the stock characters of the commedia dell'arte which Picasso
evoked, also recall the world of medieval professionalism. In the painting
Acrobat et Jeune Harlequin, the comparison between commedia dell'arte
and circus is clearly embellished by allusions to the world of entertainers,
in particular by the jester-like costume of the acrobat. The essence of this
comparison – in which Starobinski detects a reference to the condition of
the artist in bourgeois society – is above all a broad idea of performance.
However, this also implies a distortion of the historical notion of commedia dell'arte. Jesters, clowns, acrobats, jugglers and various other kinds of
performers were influenced by the corresponding stock characters, which
are in turn drawn into in the nebulous sphere of a gleefully transgressive
professionalism which borders on legend. The main difference between the
comici – who play dramatic parts – and simple performers is thus removed
from and then reabsorbed into the collective imagination, which is strong
enough to be able to forget the historical data. After all, legends are mostly
fostered by separating facts from their contexts and by plain lying.

In the twentieth century, after becoming symbols of the idea that art
should be reused in the most diverse of contexts, an idea strengthened by
interaction with circus in the collective imagination, the stock characters
underwent, at times, a process of abstraction. This was characterised by an
extreme stylisation of their elements, sometimes leading to the loss of their
distinctive traits. In a sort of symbolic simplification, they can nevertheless
reach solemnity by becoming enigmatic figures, taking on possible allegoric values or acquiring the form of a surreal caprice. From icons bearing a
number of characteristic traits, they became abstract symbols of an idea of

performance in which the circus may be evoked in various ways, representing variously imagination, movement, precariousness, skill, comicality, otherness or a symbiosis of life and art. The long-lasting existence of the comici dell'arte in the collective imagination of figurative and performing arts continues – made possible by a process of transformation – which on each occasion reinvents its characteristics by exchanging elements with other genres and thus revives the global idea of the theatre in which the legend of a creative, nomadic artist prevails.

18

Iconography of the Commedia dell'Arte

Renzo Guardenti

The agglomeration of images which go to make up the iconography of the commedia dell'arte may appear nebulous to us; it has, however, never stopped expanding, slowly at first but steadily and relentlessly over time. In fact, even today, almost five centuries after the emergence of the first companies, it is not uncommon, in the world of theatre iconography, to come across images inspired by the activities of the *comici* in the seventeenth and eighteenth centuries. The birth of the iconography of the commedia dell'arte coincided exactly with the first appearances of the *comici* as professional theatre companies and became known in Europe as early as the first tours there of Italian companies. The images were created in a variety of artistic techniques (drawings, paintings, etchings, frescoes, statues, porcelains, marquetry and tapestries) and for a variety of purposes (promotional, illustrative, documentary or decorative). They portray subjects which are directly or indirectly linked to the commedia dell'arte and include scenes from comedies, performances by actors, acrobats and charlatans, stories about stock characters, carnevalesque scenes, portraits of actors and stock characters and aspects of theatrical life. In other cases, the performative physicality of the actors of the commedia dell'arte seems to have been captured in images which are not directly related to theatre. This can be observed in some paintings by Domenico Fetti who, it has been hypothesised, may have used Virginia Ramponi Andreini as a model (Ferrone 1993b: 243–7). Taken together, this mass of images covers most of the constituent elements of the commedia dell'arte, documenting the actors' characteristics, the influences they exerted or suffered under, the aesthetic and cultural repercussions of their activities, the material condition of their lives, the legendary aura emanating from the actors and the way images were filtered and distorted by the visions of the artists. What is more, a regular trade in these images developed in several European countries, mirroring a parallel development in commercial theatre. The pictorial reproductions of these images, real or fictitious, contributed to perpetuating the memory of the *commedia* and found their way into the most popular environments. The *comici* themselves were sometimes active in promoting these reproductions. It is safe to assume that the images thus reproduced effectively constituted a visual record of the legend of the commedia dell'arte and played a fundamental part in its diffusion as a theatrical phenomenon and in its continued survival.

We are unable to determine which image reproductions of the commedia dell'arte were the first to appear. What is certain, however, is that as early as the end of the sixteenth century, images illustrating characters, scenes and perhaps even actors of what was a new theatrical phenomenon began to become available throughout Italy and Europe. The range of artistic techniques employed and the variety of contexts in which images were reproduced testify to the increasing vitality of this new form of spectacle, which could be performed for different kinds of audiences – from the heterogeneous ones in public squares and *stanzoni delle commedie* (lit. 'comedy rooms') to the noble spectators of Italian and European courts. The images also documented contact situations between tumblers, acrobats and *comici* and were circulated in the alba amicorum – the notebooks of travelling students of the late sixteenth and early seventeenth centuries – and in Giacomo Franco's famous engravings. They were also to be found in unusual galleries of characters, such as Dionisio Menaggio's codex, a colourful collage of bird feathers.[1] The images definitely did reach a bourgeois audience. They may also have reached a popular audience, thanks to woodcuts (such as the Fossard Collection of Stockholm, which refers to a performance of Italian *comici* that took place in Paris) and copperplate engravings. Reproduced images such as the painting *Comici alla Corte di Carlo IX*, kept in Bayeux,[2] documented and immortalised encounters between *comici* and members of foreign courts. The images found their place in series of frescoes such as those of the *Narrentreppe* (Fools' Staircase) of Trausnitz castle[3] or in handwritten drama notebooks, such as the watercolour paintings of the *Scenari Corsiniani.*

Image Reproductions: Some Paradigmatic Examples:

A few significant aspects appear at the start of the iconographic parabola, and therefore possess paradigmatic value. Consider Ambrogio Brambilla's etching, *Che diavolo è questo* (What the Devil Is This),[4] made up of nine illustrations, each representing a sketch with Zanni and the Magnifico, and occasionally the innamorata (female lover), the *fantesca* (maid) and the

Captain. The sketches are brief, with minimal scenes characterised by a physically performative dimension: the fight between the Zanni, the Magnifico being slapped and mocked, the dance, Zanni's hideout, the grooming and inoculation of the Magnifico, the Magnifico as dentist, the drunk Captain. Based on the crude dynamics of encounters between a limited number of characters, these nine images can be considered the visual counterpart to one of the scenes which formed part of the dramaturgical core of the early commedia dell'arte: the well-known duet *Dialogo de un Magnifico con Zani bergamasco* (Dialogue between the Magnifico and a Zanni from Bergamo).

In contrast to the above, the painting *Comedians at Charles IX's Court* portrays court dignitaries and characters of the commedia dell'arte caught in their typical poses, against the background of a pavilion and an Italian garden.[5] The image has been the subject of various interpretations. According to some (Sand 1860), it represents a court ballet in the year 1572 with the members of the French court disguised as stock characters of the *commedia* – the Duke of Guise (Scaramuccia), the Duke of Anjou (Harlequin), the Cardinal of Lorraine (Pantalone), Catherine de' Medici (Columbine), King Charles IX (Brighella). Others claim to be able to identify eleven characters in the painting (including the alleged author, Frans Pourbus the Elder), on the basis of an inscription on a wooden panel attached to the bottom of the picture, mentioning the troupe of Zan Ganassa, Alberto Naselli (Duchartre 1924). Still others believe that the picture has no documentary value and reject its attribution to Pourbus (Sterling 1943), but agree with Duchartre in considering the image to be the oldest depiction of a scene from the commedia dell'arte. Finally, there are those who identify the adolescent in a multicoloured patch costume, standing behind the Magnifico, as being Tristano Martinelli, the inventor of the stock character of Harlequin. They also identify the man wrapped in a cloak on the left of the picture and portraying a comedian as his brother Drusiano (Ferrone 2008).

But beyond these different interpretations, what the painting proves above all else is that the *comici dell'arte* had acquired such a high status as performers that they were easily accepted at the most elite European courts. Further proof of this appears evident in the contemporary frescoes of the *Narrentreppe* in Trausnitz, painted by Alessandro Scalzi, also known as Paduano. The frescoes run the length of a spiral staircase and contain scenes with characters of the commedia dell'arte (serenades, slapstick lazzi, greedy Zanni, scenes with Pantalones, Ruffianas, Innamoratas, and so on), separated by allegorical figures.[6] The characters were portrayed in a picture showing Orlando di Lasso and Massimo Troiano's *Comedia all'improvviso alla italiana* (Italian-style improvised comedy) for the wedding of William V of Bavaria and Renata of Lorraine but not in a manner in any way connected to specific performances.

A different case is that of the woodcuts belonging to the Fossard Collection of Stockholm, a broad, representative selection created in the second half of the seventeenth century by François Fossard, Louis XIV's *Intendant Ordinaire de la Musique*. It is made up of drawings and prints illustrating everyday celebrations, royal celebrations, performances and funerals. The collection was split up after the musician's death in 1702. Part of it was held at the Kongelige Bibliotek in Copenhagen (Holm 1992) while a second, more interesting part found its way to the Nationalmuseum in Stockholm. In 1783 the Swedish Ambassador in Paris, Carl Gustav Tessin, brought the eighty, then anonymous prints of the series together in a single volume. The book was later found by Agne Beijer, in the second decade of the twentieth century in a non-catalogued section of the Nationalmuseum. In 1928, together with Pierre-Louis Duchartre, Beijer published forty-four prints of the series under the title *Recueil de plusieurs des premières fragments comédies italiennes*. These woodcuts were made in Paris in 1584–1585; according to some, they may have been created in a *peintres en bois* workshop in the Rue Montorgueil, not far from the theatre of the Hôtel de Bourgogne (Guardenti 1990). What they were intended for, however, is uncertain. As each print is provided with double captions – one in the upper margin, with the names of the characters and another in the lower margin, describing the scene depicted – it has been speculated that the series had a function similar to that of an opera libretto, using pictures and captions to facilitate the Parisian public's understanding of the performance. The series, in fact, may well portray the performance of a play by a theatre company of the commedia dell'arte, during a tour there in the 1580s. This hypothesis is based on an analysis and sequencing of eighteen prints of the collection which allows a reconstruction of the plot of the play, suggesting it may revolve around Harlequin's amorous misfortunes. But beyond the hypotheses made by Mastropasqua and Katritzky, the Fossard collection is of significant documentary value from the performative point of view. These images illustrate credible scenic practices, fully compatible with the technical possibilities available to the first generation of the comici dell'arte. They evoke the element of music and singing, which recurs in the iconography of the time, the acrobatic episodes or again those episodes in which explicit situations manifest the erotic dimension.[7] They are all perfectly compatible with the accounts which a shocked Pierre De l'Estoile wrote on the Parisian shows of the *Compagnia dei Gelosi* in 1577.

In those years, a few paintings appeared which testify to the vitality of the commedia dell'arte. One such case is the painting attributed to François Bunel the Younger which offers an effective visual representation of the manner in which the commedia dell'arte was structured. The company of *comici* was traditionally divided up into *vecchi* (old people), *innamorati* (lovers) and *zanni*; the painting illustrates visually the fundamental dramatic core of the animosity between *vecchi* and *innamorati*, with the inevitable addition of jokes and lazzi. Also worth mentioning in this regard is a painting at the Musée Carnavalet in Paris[8] which illustrates the play of dramaturgic opposites between the characters. Its relationship with the Fossard collection has been highlighted. Thus, the commedia dell'arte also becomes a pictorial genre, with many *improvvisa*-related images never seen before, housed in various galleries and ideally grouping together, both on paper and on canvas, actors from different generations.

These images illustrate typical, conventional scenes as well as promotional ones (Sterling 1943). The *comici* themselves noticed the power of images and quickly, over the course of the seventeenth century, started to use them for promotional purposes. This is the case of the Harlequin Tristano Martinelli, who published the *Compositions de Rhétorique de Mr Don Arlequin* between the end of 1600 and the beginning of 1601 in Lyon, on the occasion of the marriage of Henry IV to Maria de' Medici. In doing so, he followed the typical pattern of clownish practices. The book is a strange one, consisting of around seventy blank pages, a letter in verse dedicated to the King and Queen of France – a true *captatio benevolentiae* of the solitary buffoon – and seven woodcuts, five of which represent Harlequin, one Pantalone and another the Captain, and fit perfectly into the framework of the editorial strategies adopted by the *comici*, as an original source of exceptional importance. Not only does it testify to a duality of word and image in Martinelli's self-promotional project but it also establishes a few basic postures of the character which would subsequently be adopted by many actors in later generations all of whom would answer to a sort of 'energetic acting' code (Taviani 1986): the head tucked between the shoulders, the hands resting on the belt worn low on the hips, the footwork – one leg extended, the other bent – that hints at Harlequin's distinctive gait.[9]

The *Balli di Sfessania*, twenty-four etchings by the engraver Jacques Callot, who returned to France after a long stay in Florence, appeared around 1622. These images compete with those of the Fossard collection for the honour of being the most famous series of engravings dedicated to the commedia dell'arte. Each of the etchings features a pair of figures in the foreground, depicted in characteristic postures and identified by an inscription with their names, some with connections to the commedia dell'arte (Riciulina, Metzetin, Pulliciniello, Scaramuccia, Francischina, Gian Farina, the lovers – Signora Lucia, Lucrezia, Lavinia, Lucrezia, the various Captains – Bonbardon, Spessa Monti, etc.) and others invented (Cucorongna, Pernovalla etc.). These characters move *en plein air*, against a background of varied urban settings. The figures in the background are either engaged in various kinds of activities – such as feats of strength, acrobatics, musical performances, slapstick lazzi, dances or comical duels – or are performing on a makeshift stage. But what is especially interesting is the posture of certain characters in the foreground. They are depicted in contorted poses while flexing the muscles of their arms and legs, frozen in almost spasmodic, sometimes blatantly obscene movements: Captains using their swords as phalluses and Zanni-like characters nonchalantly putting their back-sides on offer.[10] These images have become symbolic of a commedia dell'arte which was completely focused on a physical and performative dimension, on postural and acrobatic lazzi, on contortionism and on the triumph of the body. At the other extreme, there are those (Posner 1977) who rule out the possibility that these images could represent the performative practices of the commedia dell'arte, suggesting that the etchings illustrate a Moorish dance called, in fact, *Sfessania* and most likely of Turkish origin. It was performed in and around Naples in the seventeenth century; the *Balli* company presented it in a popular country setting. In truth, however, a connection with the theatre of the Italian *comici* cannot be completely ruled out. The *Balli* company maintained their relationship and affinity to the commedia dell'arte not only by their manner of placing a few characters in the foreground, but also by their use of figures in the background. These sometimes seemed to be imitating what was happening in the foreground, but they are also situations depicted which, in Callot's time, had become true scenic *topoi*: slapstick *lazzi*, burlesque duels between Zanni and Captains, back-to-front horseback riding, acrobatic walking handstands and donkeys pushed by being hit on the rump with a bellows. This scenic *topoi* did indeed persist through many eras and countries to become established stage practice and claim its place in the records. In the *Balli* company these *topoi* were re-enacted in the light of the eclectic temperament of the artist from Nancy, who was able to reinterpret – transfiguring them with a significant input of fantasy – the images of what was one of the most important forms of spectacle of his time and which he must have known during his Italian travels.

The Great Iconography of the Commedia dell'Arte between Documentation and Transfiguration

What can be regarded as the great iconography of the commedia dell'arte only developed in France in the second half of the seventeenth century, when the Ancien Théâtre Italien was established (1660) (Guardenti 1990). Clear traces of this process were already detectable in a few early seventeenth-century prints depicting Italian characters (Harlequin, Scaramuccia, the Doctor, Brighella and Trivellino, Pulcinella and Panta-lone) and created by prominent artists of the time (Jérémias Falck, Grégoire Huret, Gilles Rousselet, Charles Le Brun, Jean I Le Blond and François Joullain). Some of these images were used as models by the Italian painter Verio for the composition of his painting, *Farceurs Français et Italiens* (1670), which was kept at the *Comédie-Française*.[11] The most representative characters of the commedia dell'arte are easily identifiable as the Italian actors who were active in Paris at the time: Harlequin (Domenico Giuseppe Biancolelli), the Doctor (Angelo Agostino Lolli), Pulcinella (Michelangelo Fracanzani), Pantalone (G. B. Turi), Scaramuccia (Tiberio Fiorilli) and Brighella and Trivellino (Domenico Locatelli). Standing beside them are members of the French Comic theatre (Molière, Jodelet, Turlupin, Captain Matamoros, Guillot Gorju, Gros Guillaume, Gautier Garguille and Philippin). To paint these figures Verio probably used earlier pictorial material, such as Pierre Mariette's etching dedicated to the *Farceurs* of the *Hôtel de Bourgogne*, or those by Falck, Rousselet and Jean Le Blond. By bringing together on the stage of Molière the characters of the commedia dell'arte and the actors of French farce, the *Farceurs Français et Italiens* became a symbol of the great Parisian comic theatre of the *Grand Siècle*, in which the Italian comedians were an integral part.

The establishment of the Italian company in Paris was accompanied by a parallel increase in the production, and the *comici* themselves were undoubtedly customers for such material from time to time. This was certainly so in the case of three almanacs, published between 1685 and 1688 by Nicolas and Jean-Baptiste Bonnart – printers and engravers on the Rue Saint-Jacques – and a series of drawings by Bernard Picart (between 1694 and 1697). The almanacs document comedies performed at the Hôtel de Bourgogne – *Arlequin Protée* e *Arlequin Jason* by Nolant de Fatouville[12] and the anonymous *Arlequin Grand Visir*[13] – which are an exceptionally important source of information because they describe, by means of various illustrations, the most important moments of the three comedies and include contributions on actor performances, stage motifs and the use of stage props and scenery that cannot be inferred simply by reading the comedies themselves. The Bonnart almanacs allow us to understand how varied and complex the quality of spectacularity of the Ancien Théâtre Italien was, having been founded on a union or synthesis of the performing techniques of the commedia dell'arte and the scenic and stagecraft techniques of the great baroque theatre.

Bernard Picart's drawings – which were later printed by Jean Mariette, perhaps at the request of the *comici* themselves – are of particular interest too. The collection consists of eleven small pieces, each of which depicts an actor of the Comédie Italienne on stage, shown in costume before a painted backdrop. Not only do these drawings allow us to reconstruct the overall image of the Italian company, but above all, they possess a direct documentary value, as they depict the stock characters of the commedia dell'arte in Paris, in poses taken from successful comedies. Take for example the drawing that portrays Giuseppe Tortoriti (Scaramuccia) in Charles-Rivière Dufresny's *Le Départ des Comédiens* (1694), a comedy that, oddly enough, predicts the disbandment of the Italian company in 1697:[14] with a rural scene as background, Scaramuccia walks with guitar in hand, then turns and looks back, perhaps in a gesture of regret. What leads us to consider Picart's drawings as being a direct reflection of a scenic practice of the commedia dell'arte is the fact that his drawings of Harlequin and Scaramuccia appeared later on the title pages of the comedies *La Fontaine de Sapience* and *Le Départ des comédiens*.

These publications were part of the collection, *Le Théâtre Italien*, brought out by Evaristo Gherardi in 1700 and containing fifty-five comedies performed by the first Comédie Italienne between 1680 and 1697. This is an extremely rich repertoire and gives evidence of the ability of the Italian actors in Paris to perform comedies which tackled – often through the distorting lens of parody and satire – fantastic, mythological and exotic subjects, reformulated according to a scenic practice that combined acting, music, dance and stagecraft. Each comedy in the collection was accompanied by an etching, which dealt with some aspect or aspects of the piece – sometimes describing scenes or individual episodes, or providing an overall image of the comedy, often by means of an illustration of the main theme, or alternatively, depicting different moments of the same play in one picture. But the real value of these illustrations on the title pages of the *Théâtre Italien* was the resulting emphasis that they focussed on the spectacular dimension in the plays – not only in its implications for scenography and stagecraft, but also from a performative, musical and choreographic perspective. Dance is seen on these title pages as both choreography and acrobatic performance. This appears evident in exotic *pièces* such as *Les Chinois* by Jean-François Regnard and Charles-Rivière Dufresny[15] or the usual dance numbers of the stock characters in Gherardi's *Le retour de la Foire de Bezons*. This attention to the spectacular dimension did not come about purely by chance. It is more probably the result of the curator's interventions with the authors of these title pages. Given the attention to detail brought to bear on the individual prints and setting aside the occasional use of earlier pictorial sources, the composition of the images of the *Théâtre Italien* seems to have been guided directly by Gherardi. It was a 'visual direction' of sorts, which brought out a number of elements that were not easily inferred simply by reading the plays and was surely influenced by the memory of the Ancien Théâtre Italien's last Harlequin.

At the end of the seventeenth century, during the period in which the Ancien Théâtre Italien was being disbanded (1697), there began a unique process of transfiguration of the pictorial representation of the commedia dell'arte. It involved a gradual move away from the concreteness of the stage towards a more allegorical mindset and found in Jean-Antoine Watteau its greatest exponent. A pioneer of this phenomenon was Claude Gillot, assiduous frequenter and interpreter – at times visionary – of the Italian actors' performances. He was the 'director' of the bi-dimensional performance which Watteau saw when he began his apprenticeship in Gillot's workshop. In the eyes of the painter from Valenciennes, Gillot's 'comedies', which intertwined memory and amnesia, sometimes exhibited an almost metaphysical quality with his use of oil on canvas and sometimes a vibrant and phantasmal quality with his quick strokes of ink and sponge strokes of bistre on paper, but generally veered towards the nostalgic. Paintings such as *Arlequin soldat gourmand*[16] exerted a profound influence on the student who would later develop a very unique, personal style. Watteau worked with Gillot from 1705 to 1708. In those years, the legacy of the Ancien Théâtre Italien was embraced by the small theatres at the fairs of Saint-Germain and Saint-Laurent, which subsequently adopted both the repertoire and the characters of the Italian company (Guardenti 1995). In 1716 the Parisian theatre scene was to be enriched once again by the arrival of Luigi Riccoboni's second Comédie Italienne. This is the context in which Watteau operated; the artist's rarefied settings place the stock characters of the commedia dell'arte in a situation removed from the immediate: Gillot's influences, the *forain* (fairground) little theatres and perhaps the performances of Riccoboni's company itself steer the artist towards creating nostalgic panoramas, steeped in dreams and memories. Although animated by an undeniable theatricality, they inexorably suggest distance from the goings-on on the wooden boards of the stage. In Watteau's paintings, the stock characters of the commedia dell'arte are placed in rural settings among female figures: wrapped in their innamorata costumes, they appear unvaried from painting to painting, sometimes languid or indifferent guitar players, sometimes still, as if taking a break in the game of love. Watteau's *innamorati* do not express any passion and delegate the manifestation of their sensuality to their complexion, to the softness of a gesture or to subtle games of glances – pictorial expression of a budding *marivaudage* (Tomlinson, 1981). Even when the action seems to become more pressing, as in *Voulez-vous triompher de belles* from the Wallace Collection in London, the female protagonists in Watteau's paintings remain imperturbable, like ladies at the *fêtes galantes*, confining themselves to expressions typical of the spirit of the Regency. Not even paintings such as *L'amour au Théâtre Italien* or *Comédiens Italiens*[17] allow us to forget the veil of suspended indeterminacy in Watteau's compositions. The former may portray Luigi Riccoboni's entire company, because the Italian troupe arrived in Paris around 1718, the probable date of the painting (Dacier and Vuaflart 1929: I, 66–7). However, this hypothesis may be brought into question by several inconsistencies related to the way in which the characters are represented. *Comédiens Italiens* appears even more 'theatrical' due to the positioning of the characters. They are seemingly gathered together as if to take their leave of the public at the end of a show; above them an architectural cornice delineates the scenic space – all this seems to be inspired by an engraving by Abraham Bosse, which portrays the theatre of the Hôtel de Bourgogne around 1630 (Tomlinson 1981). Indeed, the game of similarities and differences between the paintings and their possible sources of inspiration – including the influence of the artist's own points of reference – does point in the direction of Watteau's method of composition. The artist, as related by the Count of Caylus in his work, *Vie de Watteau* (1748), made sketches and drawings on pages in a notebook, which formed the repertoire he habitually drew on to compose his paintings, placing the characters on the canvas as he himself saw fit, often using a predetermined background. Caylus's argument is doubly interesting, first and foremost because it seems to confirm that Watteau's interest in theatre was not sustained by specific familiarity with stage practice. Secondly and most importantly, however, because it emphasises how the artist created his works on the basis of a true dramaturgical system, using a compositional procedure akin to that of the Comici dell'Arte, in which the spatial setting drawn on the canvas corresponds to the connective tissue of the scenario, while the collection of sketches can be compared to the heterogeneous materials at the disposal of utility actors and zibaldoni. Watteau, then, seems to consider the Italian stock characters as simple pretexts to evoke distant worlds where time is suspended and where everything, every gesture, every little daily event – a serenade, a walk in a park, an amorous encounter – becomes a spectacle and an unreal and abstract one at that. In Watteau, theatre invades life: the characters of the Comédie Italienne enter and exit a broader and less defined scene, which is made to appear spectacular by the dreamlike, sometimes hallucinatory interpretation of the artist. A good example of this is the painting *Le rêve de l'artiste*,[18] which is very characteristic of his entire artistic production.

Watteau's work influenced several artists, crystallising in genre-specific compositions which reflected the melancholic lightness of their master: Nicolas Lancret, Jean-Baptiste Pater and Jean-Baptiste Oudry placing the Italian stock characters in an anecdotal, everyday setting. In works such as Lancret's *An Italian Comedy Scene*,[19] the overall atmosphere has lost that sense of suspended time and that feeling of amorous expectation which are typical of Watteau's representations. Instead they focus on the vividness of the single episode, with hints veering towards a material, carnal eroticism: girls who shun or even repel Harlequin's or Pierrot's daring *avances*, only to accept the doubly insistent attentions of others – as in Pater's *Actors of the Comédie Italienne in a Park*.[20] These paintings reiterate, in the wake of Watteau, the distance that had developed between the figures related to the commedia dell'arte and actual stage praxis, placing the characters in a parallel universe: the camera obscura of a little paper theatre. Yet sometimes, these masked figures seem to recover, under the eye and the expert hand of the painter, their original distinctiveness, as in Jean-Baptiste Oudry's *Italian Actors in a Park*.[21] Here the mechanisms of seduction reveal themselves not through the inducement of suspense and apprehensive waiting, nor through the explicit tendering of attentions, but rather, with the spectacular still in mind, take the form of timid dance steps.

Outside of Theatre: The Life of the Stock Characters between Painting and Porcelain

As early as the beginning of the eighteenth century, a trend in painting and illustration called 'the life of the stock characters' appeared in Europe. In it, the stock characters – freed of the constraints of stage practices and of specific dramatic scenarios – lived a life of their own, motivated solely by the imagination of the painters and captured on the canvas in ways that are reminiscent of contemporary comics. An example of this is the series of engravings, *Het Italiaans Toneel* created by Gérard Joseph Xavery and Pieter Schenk (Amsterdam 1710), which light-handedly and vividly develops the themes of the pregnancy, birth and 'motherhood' of Harlequin, rediscovering a long-term dramatic and figurative *topos* in doing so. Another similar case is that of Johann Jacob Schübler and Johann Balthasar Probst's prints that illustrate the abduction of Isabella, Pantalone's daughter. The same trend also developed in Italy where Giovanni Domenico Ferretti authored numerous works inspired by episodes from Harlequin's life, including two series of *Travestimenti di Arlecchino* (Harlequin's disguises), each consisting of sixteen pieces. The first series is preserved in Florida at the John and Mable Ringling Museum in Sarasota but was once owned by the German director Max Reinhardt in Schloss Leopoldskron (Salzburg); the second series, identical to the one held in Sarasota in all but one of the sixteen subjects, is characterised by a higher-quality execution and is part of the collection of the Cassa di Risparmio di Firenze. Recent studies have revised both the dating of the two series and their commissioners (Sottili 2008 and 2011). Contrary to Ferretti's traditional historiography (Maser 1968) – which dated the paintings in the years between 1742 and 1760, linking their creation to the Compagnia del Vangelista, of which the painter was a member – the series was actually created between 1746 and 1749 and was commissioned by Orazio and Giovanni Sansedoni, both members of an important Sienese family. The Florentine series was created to beautify the Gabbinetto detto degl'Arlicchini (Room of the Harlequins) in Orazio Sansedoni's palace in Florence, situated near the Ponte Vecchio, which – in addition to hosting Ferretti's paintings – was decorated with tapestries showing typical Harlequin costumes. The other series was commissioned by Giovanni Sansedoni for his villa near Siena. Here Ferretti depicts Harlequin in the most diverse situations: as robber, painter,[22] veteran, embroiderer, doctor, dance teacher, farmer, cook, scholar, glutton, rejected lover and attacked lover. Regardless of any possible connections to the performances organised by the Florentine *Compagnia del Vangelista* or to archival documents which might testify to Ferretti's interest in a Harlequin who was active in Florence around 1746, it appears evident that these paintings, while still depicting typically Harlequinesque situations, do in fact live a life of their own, free of any references to specific scenes.

Perhaps it was not Harlequin, but rather Pulcinella who became the most important figure in the eighteenth-century iconography of the commedia dell'arte (Stefani 2009). As we have seen above, in Giuseppe Bonito's paintings, Pulcinella and other stock characters are portrayed in genre-specific situations which are furthermore the result of a careful composition, as in the famous *Mascherata* (Masquerade).[23] In the works of Pier Leone Ghezzi – who was active between the late seventeenth century and the mid-eighteenth century – it was important for the artist to have the character dressed in white. Perfectly in line with the trend of liberating illustrations of the stock characters from the need to deal with happenings on stage, on the one hand, Pulcinella is immortalised in fundamental moments of his life (the wedding of his son, the fire at his house and the will[24]); on the other, especially in the drawings, his humanity is revealed through small feats such as holding his son's hand, lying on the ground drunk or playing with a kitten. In contrast, the daily life of the stock character takes on a grotesque, dramatic connotation in the works of the Genoese painter Alessandro Magnasco. Placed in the middle of bleak settings, hallways, basements and ruins, Pulcinella's body appears deformed, swollen, as if it were about to decompose. The actions depicted – the seduction of Colombina, Pulcinella singing with the children, Pulcinella's midday meal[25] – still find their place in the poetry of ordinary, everyday life; however, they also gain a surreal, disturbing connotation and give the character an almost macabre dimension.

A characteristic element in the iconography relating to Pulcinella is the multiple appearance of the character within the same illustration, in one part, in the company of his countless children, in another with other Pulcinellas. Pulcinella is not a single character, but a *multitude*: this feature is the significant trait of the work of Giambattista and Giandomenico Tiepolo. Giambattista's hunchbacked Pulcinellas are placed in outdoor settings, often busy observing, with metaphysical amazement, very ordinary, everyday activities such as cooking gnocchi in a pot, feeding others like them or bizarre and inappropriate behaviour like defecating in the open air. Giandomenico's illustrations, in contrast, develop the serial dimension to almost distressing levels, as can be seen in the frescoes of Ca' Rezzonico in Venice[26] and especially in the series, *Divertimento per li regazzi* (ca. 1797–1804), a sort of visual biography of the character, which covers the basic episodes of his existence.[27]

In the eighteenth century, the figurative representation of the commedia dell'arte found an outlet in other contexts too. Examples include the frescoes of the Castle of Český Krumlov[28] (Noe 2011) and Castle

Eggenberg in Graz (Neuhuber 2011) as well as in the ceramic production of several European manufacturers, including those in Meissen and Nymphenburg (Chilton 2001, Jansen 2001). These companies produced objects for everyday use – dishes, snuff boxes, powder boxes and clocks, as well as ornamental pieces, such as statuettes – dedicated to a variety of subjects. These pieces of porcelain, by master modellers such as Johann Jacob Kändler, Franz Anton Bustelli, Johann Wilhelm Lanz and Peter Reinicke, testify to the fortune of the Italian stock characters in the eighteenth century in Germany, showing that their fame was due more to the images in circulation than to the theatrical activity of the companies themselves. Many of the characters appearing on the porcelain – sometimes inspired by the works of painters such as Gillot, Watteau and Pater – were subjected to significant changes in their costumes, both by the introduction of different colours and by the inclusion of motifs created independently by the decorator. In addition, if we consider the most famous set of porcelain ever dedicated to the commedia dell'arte, the one crafted by Franz Anton Bustelli (ca. 1760), it is noticeable that the original traits of the Italian stock characters have been diluted by the exquisitely Rococo quality of the figures. This trend was widespread; not even masked stock characters such as Harlequin and the Doctor were spared. Like many of the porcelain pieces manufactured in Meissen and Nymphenburg, those crafted by Bustelli were also inspired by iconographic motifs taken from prints circulating in Germany and other parts of Europe.

After the Commedia dell'Arte

The last years of the eighteenth century saw the end of the *ancien régime* but also the end of the commedia dell'arte. The ideological and productive contexts which had allowed it to develop and thrive on the European scene for over two hundred years had, by this time, disappeared. However, the essence of the commedia dell'arte did survive in latent form, thanks to its iconography, which had accrued over the long centuries of its history and was rediscovered in the nineteenth century, an era sensitised by the retrospective gaze of Romanticism. Among the protagonists of this renaissance, animated by the desire to keep the legend of the commedia dell'arte alive as the very idea of theatre, was Maurice Sand, son of the legendary George Sand. In 1860, he was responsible for the printing of *Masques et Bouffons* – the first modern study on the theatre of professional *comici*. It brought together, in the form of colour prints,[29] some of the many drawings he had dedicated to the Italian characters, often reinventing or

reinterpreting earlier figurative sources. These images have enjoyed enormous success and been reproduced up to the present day, often ending up
on the shelves of second-hand book dealers and in *bric-à-brac* flea markets.
Somewhat kitschy, suitable for the living room of an elderly person, they
are, for this very reason, the tangible sign of an enduring legend, which has
become an integral part of the European collective imagination, to the
point of diffusely seeping into various areas of everyday, civic and political
life (Foglia 2013). For example, Harlequin and his companions did
become a means of entertainment for nineteenth-century bourgeois
children. Sometimes these children would cut out the limbs from paper
representations of the stock characters, only to reassemble the small
puppets again;[30] at other times they might build small paper theatres for
their favourite characters. Again, in the early twentieth century, Italian
children would read with delight the comic strip relating the adventures of
the stock characters. It appeared regularly on the pages of the *Corriere dei
Piccoli*, the illustrated supplement of the *Corriere della Sera*. During the
nineteenth and early twentieth centuries, the stock characters of the
commedia dell'arte took satirical newspapers by storm – in particular those
openly aspiring to political satire, such as the Italian *L'asino* (The Donkey),
which mocked the Italian colonialist aims in Libya. Also, it was certainly
not by coincidence that the English magazine *Punch* took on the name of
the popular character Pulcinella.

The characters of the commedia dell'arte have also become an effective
advertising medium: if Pulcinella is destined to advertise for a macaroni
manufacturer,[31] then Pierrot must endorse a French liqueur, while the
kaleidoscopic costumes of the stock characters embellish the pages of a
promotional calendar for textile dyes (Foglia 2013). It should also be
remembered that at the end of the nineteenth and the beginning of the
twentieth centuries, the stock characters kept stimulating the imaginations
of illustrators and artists and became a true obsession that often took on
nuances that transcended the simple, grotesque element physiologically
inherent in the original Italian characters. Who does not know Pablo
Picasso's Harlequins or the series depicted by artists such as Toulouse-
Lautrec, Ensor, Rouault, Seurat, Severini, Gris, Dérain, Miró and Gual, to
name only the most popular among them? The presence of the characters
of the commedia dell'arte is a tangible sign of the crisis affecting the role of
the artist in European society at the turn of the century, a crisis highlighted
by Jean Starobinski in his *Portrait de l'artiste en saltimbanque* (1970).
Suspended in a rarefied, nostalgic, clownish and circus-like atmosphere,
the world of the stock characters took on different forms becoming one of

the leitmotifs of early twentieth-century visual arts, almost replacing the more common themes from classical mythology (Cowling and Mundy 1990). Picasso is the most representative artist of this trend, no doubt by virtue of his close relationship with theatre. One only has to think of the Russian ballets of Sergei Diaghilev and Léonide Massine, with whom he collaborated in creating sets and costumes for *Parade* (1917)[32] and *Pulcinella* (1920). The character of Harlequin, which recurs insistently in Picasso's paintings, might even be considered as a metaphor of his entire work. The constantly shifting presence associated with this figure manifests itself in the classical form of the portrait, with the features of his little son Paulo[33] which was later reduced to geometric chromatic stains, in accordance with the Cubist cannon regarding the dissolution of forms. At other times, the idea of commedia dell'arte withdraws from the world of circus. Picasso's paintings are then populated by diaphanous and ectoplasmic Harlequins, appearing alone or in family groups, or again as adolescents, often with acrobats at their side, as in *Acrobate et jeune arlequin*.[34] Both of the characters are projected into the stillness of a metaphysical desert and thus collaborate in creating a figurative constellation in which Derain's Pierrots and Harlequins both find their places.[35] This is also the case in Gino Severini's works – which sometimes resonate with echoes of Callot, as happens with the Montefugoni Castle frescoes (Alberti 2011) and sometimes reproduce Pulcinella's epic feats,[36] with a series of images comparable to that of the Tiepolos.

On other occasions, the Italian masks take on a horrific appearance, as in a drawing by Gustave Courbet, *The Black Arm*:[37] a murky landscape at night in which Pierrot, having lost his left arm, gazes in terror at a black arm emerging from the ground. In *Paillasse*,[38] a caricature by Honoré Daumier, the screaming Pierrot leads a parade accompanied by a drummer, in a terrifyingly apocalyptic posture, with his limbs in a state of decomposition, calling to mind Magnasco's Pulcinellas. This tendency reaches its highest level of expression in the macabre works of James Ensor. His parades of masks, which appear almost like walking corpses, suggest a morbid, hallucinatory relationship with death[39] and transform the stock characters of the commedia dell'arte into symbols of the tragic, ephemeral condition of mankind.

After this period, which was dominated by avant-garde artists, the commedia dell'arte continued to be featured in various twentieth-century visual art forms, giving rise to suggestive reinterpretations of eighteenth-century figurative legends. One example is Joseph Cornell's *A Dressing Room for Gille* which reformulates the famous *Gilles* by Jean-Antoine Watteau. Another is Domenico Purificato's paintings representing Pulcinella, which rediscover the themes and atmosphere of the eighteenth-century iconography of the Neapolitan character. Yet another is Robert Metzkes's terracottas or, finally, the tragic solitude of Robert Longo's *Pierrot in a Vest*.

However, the legend of the commedia dell'arte underwent variations due to the influence of the ideals and the practices of theatre professionals and was definitely stimulated by the repertoire of illustrations which began to become available in the early twentieth century, thanks to, among other things, the nascent but explicit historiography of the actors of the *improvvisa*. These images constitute the foundation on which the visions of many theatre professionals were based, a fact which gave rise to the unique phenomenon of 'rebound': the iconographic source generates ideas of theatre which, through the interpretation of the original phenomenon, end up becoming part of, or even determining the planning and implementation of individual performances. Finally, it is necessary to mention that this rediscovery of the commedia dell'arte is largely due to the extraordinary contribution made by the Russian and Soviet theatre of the early twentieth century. We may think of Vsevolod Meyerhold's most famous productions, such as *Balangànčik* (The Tumblers' Hut) (1906), *Colombina's Scarf* (1910), *Masquerade* (1917) or of Yevgeny Vakhtangov's *Princess Turandot* (1922) which started a pattern that continued throughout the century, until the appearance, in more recent times, of people such as Giorgio Strehler, Ariane Mnouchkine, Dario Fo, Marco Martinelli and Leo De Berardinis. At the beginning of the third millennium, especially in areas on the threshold between artistic languages, the commedia dell'arte continues to inspire contemporary artists.

Notes

1 http://digital.library.mcgill.ca/featherbook/images/tavola110.JPG
2 http://amati.fupress.net/media//immagini/TristanoMartinelli_ico001.jpg
3 www.burg-trausnitz.de/deutsch/burg/narren.htm
4 For a reproduction, see Katritzky (2015: 287), fig. 30.2.
5 http://amati.fupress.net/media//immagini/TristanoMartinelli_ico001.jpg
6 www.burg-trausnitz.de/deutsch/burg/narren.htm
7 http://amati.fupress.net/media//immagini/TristanoMartinelli_ico011.jpg
8 www.scalarchives.it/web/dettaglio_immagine.asp?idImmagine=WH13651& posizione=6&inCarrello=False&numImmagini=297&
9 http://amati.fupress.net/media//immagini/TristanoMartinelli_ico033.jpg
10 www.culture.gouv.fr/Wave/image/joconde/0686/m021102_0002392_p.jpg
11 www.scalarchives.it/web/dettaglio_immagine.asp?idImmagine=WH03826& posizione=1&inCarrello=False&numImmagini=2&. There also exists another version of the painting preserved at the Comédie-Française, entitled *Les délices*

du genre humain. Les délices differ from the *Farceurs* in the background, which represents a large pavilion, and by the absence of Philippin's character.

[12] http://gallica.bnf.fr/ark:/12148/btv1b6945494z

[13] http://gallica.bnf.fr/ark:/12148/btv1b69455252

[14] www.culture.gouv.fr/Wave/image/joconde/0310/m503501_d0209678-000_p.jpg

[15] http://utpictura18.univ-montp3.fr/GenerateurNotice.php?numnotice=B0389&tab=B0349-B0359-B0362-B0364-B0375-B0382-B0389-B0392-B0396-B0398

[16] http://utpictura18.univ-montp3.fr/GenerateurNotice.php?numnotice=B0406

[17] www.nga.gov/content/ngaweb/Collection/art-object-page.32687.html

[18] http://utpictura18.univ-montp3.fr/GenerateurNotice.php?numnotice=A2648&tab=A8379-A8380-A0931-A1187-A2642-A2643-A2644-A2646-A2648-A8377

[19] http://wallacelive.wallacecollection.org/eMuseumPlus?service=direct/1/Result DetailView/result.inline.detail.t1.collection_detailInline.$TspImage.link&sp= 13&sp=Sartist&sp=SfieldValue&sp=0&sp=0&sp=1&sp=SdetailView&sp=0 &sp=Sdetail&sp=1&sp=T&sp=0&sp=SdetailView&sp=2

[20] http://cartelfr.louvre.fr/cartelfr/visite?srv=obj_view_obj&objet=cartel_10682_ 13080_p0005902.001.jpg_obj.html&flag=true

[21] www.culture.gouv.fr/Wave/image/joconde/0498/m006504_0008783_p.jpg

[22] http://catalogo.fondazionezeri.unibo.it/foto/160000/125200/125113.jpg

[23] www.museocapodimonte.beniculturali.it/wp-content/uploads/2016/02/Bonito-mascherata.jpg

[24] http://media.gettyimages.com/photos/pulcinella-making-his-will-watercolour-lithograph-by-pietro-leone-a-picture-id466291373?s=612x612

[25] http://ncartmuseum.org/art/detail/the_supper_of_pulcinella_and_colombina

[26] http://images.alinari.it/img/480/PAA/PAA-F-004269-0000.jpg

[27] https://s-media-cache-ak0.pinimg.com/236x/6c/bc/08/6cbc08e2e38570ae1e1 d075e91193650–giovanni-metropolitan-museum.jpg

[28] www.castle.ckrumlov.cz/img.php?img=1041&LANG=en

[29] https://s-media-cache-ak0.pinimg.com/236x/14/54/0e/14540e6ce47c8ea1078 9594d8543386b–george-sand-dell-arte.jpg

[30] https://fr.pinterest.com/pin/519532506994535357/

[31] https://s-media-cache-ak0.pinimg.com/originals/5f/bb/b7/5fbbb71edef872ed d764890321474e5e.jpg

[32] http://chatelet-theatre.com/www/tdc/media/image/2015–2016/divers/Parade-620.jpg

[33] www.scalarchives.it/web/dettaglio_immagine_adv.asp?idImmagine=0030353& posizione=3&numImmagini=8&SC_Titolo=arlecchino&SC_Artista=picasso& prmset=on&SC_PROV=RA&SC_Lang=ita&Sort=9

[34] www.barnesfoundation.org/collections/art-collection/object/5878/acrobat-and-young-harlequin-acrobate-et-jeune-arlequin?searchTxt=picasso&submit= submit&rNo=11

[35] www.scalarchives.it/web/dettaglio_immagine_adv.asp?idImmagine=0146301 &posizione=13&numImmagini=98&SC_Artista=derain&prmset=on&SC_ PROV=RA&SC_Lang=ita&Sort=9

[36] www.artribune.com/wp-content/uploads/2014/12/3_Gino-Severini-Lequilibrista-o-Maschere-e-rovine-1928.jpg

[37] https://s-media-cache-ak0.pinimg.com/originals/f9/ca/04/f9ca041641c02a64278f5a38d0d6cd52.jpg

[38] http://images.metmuseum.org/CRDImages/dp/web-large/DP810311.jpg

[39] www.scalarchives.it/web/dettaglio_immagine_adv.asp?idImmagine=0131074&posizione=1&numImmagini=91&SC_Artista=ensor&prmset=on&SC_PROV=RA&SC_Lang=ita&Sort=9

PART V

Commedia dell'Arte from the Avant-Garde to Contemporary Theatre

19

Stanislavsky and Meyerhold

Franco Ruffini

Meyerhold

'How long will it be before the following law becomes part of universal theatre canon: words in the theatre are only embellishments on the design of movement?' (Meyerhold 1969: 124). This is what Vsevolod Meyerhold wrote in his book, *Meyerhold on Theatre*. He did not make distinctions. Actors have to create a solid 'design of movement' suitable to express words, whether the text is written or improvised. Without this law, both actors and theatre would lose their autonomy. If words are deprived of the body, theatre is fated to become a podium for writers.

Meyerhold loved slogans. They were an essential part of his predilection for open, direct confrontation. 'Design of movement' was not his first slogan, nor his last. He used it to introduce the commedia dell'arte, which was the banner under which he pursued the idea of theatre autonomy and at the same time his laboratory, or workshop. The actors of the future must claim their descent from the *commedia*, but not in the name of an abstract genealogical right. As successors of the *comici* of old, they have the professional – and ethical – duty to remodel their technical skill appropriately. Commedia dell'arte could not but become a slogan for Meyerhold, and a very durable one at that. He used it explicitly for the first time during his period of work at his Studio on Borodinskaia Street, between 1913 and 1917, then more covertly. However, there had been echoes of it in his work long before that. In the beginning, the 'theatre of the straight line' was opposed to the 'triangle theatre'. The battle cry was adjusted to the enemy of the moment, although the goal of the confrontation was always to confirm categorically the supremacy of the actor. Words were weapons, but the final confirmation had to be found in the work for the stage. This is also what occurred with the words 'commedia dell'arte'.

In 1906, following a failed attempt at collaboration with Konstantin Stanislavsky in the Studio on Borodinskaia Street (1905), Meyerhold's enemy became naturalistic or literary theatre. He asserted the primacy of convention, based on technique and rejected the imitation of reality – or worse, the illusion of re-enacting it by hypnotic suggestion. This is how he referred to Stanislavsky's process of re-experiencing (*perezhivanie*): When you take aim with your weapon in battle, the actual body wearing the uniform hardly matters. According to Meyerhold, the protagonists of theatre are the author, the actor and the director. In the 'triangle-theatre', the director blends the contributions of the author and the actors into a work which he or she offers to the audience. In the 'theatre of the straight line', it is the actor who presents the director's interpretation of the author's text to the audience. The actor's flexibility turns from a handicap to a strength. Theatre, then, reveals its most profound essence: the here and now of the actor's living presence.

Meyerhold wrote *On the Theatre* in 1912. Although he never explicitly mentions the commedia dell'arte in the book, he hints at it by referring to historical sources and methodological foundations in order to prove his law of the 'design of movement'. From the celebration of the historian – thanks to whom 'true theatre was created' – to the rehabilitation of the *jongleur* and the *cabotin*, Meyerhold hopes that writing pantomimes could be an exercise 'to make a dramatist out of a story-teller who writes for the stage' (Meyerhold 1969: 124). He concludes by saying that 'should the dramatist wish to help the actor in this, his role might seem at first to amount to very little – but he will quickly find that he is faced with the intricate task of composing scenarios and writing prologues containing a schematic exposition of what actors are about to perform. Dramatists will not, I trust, feel degraded by this role' (Meyerhold 1969: 127). Rather more than a project, or a hypothesis, the work of the dramatist thus becomes an adventure.

In 1909, a group of scholars at the Department of German and Romance Philology of the University of St Petersburg gave a series of courses on the history of theatre. One of the students attending these courses was Vladimir Solovyov and he, together with some colleagues, organised a night called 'Harlequin in the Library'. His dream was to bring the commedia dell'arte back to life. Two years later Solovyov – no longer a student – wrote a scenario titled *Arlecchino Paraninfo* and presented it to Meyerhold, who accepted and staged three different versions of it in rapid succession. The last and definitive version was performed in the summer of 1912 in the small theatre of Terioki, a holiday resort near St Petersburg, where an association of artists led by Doctor Dapertutto (Meyerhold's pseudonym) was active. The prologue was read to the audience by the author himself, who, sitting on the edge of the stage, introduced the actors and their roles as described in 'Doctor Dapertutto 1908–1917' (Meyerhold 1969), but even more so, Solovyov certainly did not feel 'degraded by this role' (this episode is described in detail in Raskina 2010: 51–5).

In addition to what he wrote, Meyerhold's actual work on the commedia dell'arte was done for the stage. All activity at the Studio, inaugurated in September 1913, was also dedicated to this purpose. In contrast to the enthusiasm of his collaborators for literary texts, who were also eager to discover new theoretical laws of staging and verbal improvisation, Meyerhold continued to explore the design of movement and silent pantomime.

Besides Meyerhold and Solovyov, there were other hybrid figures involved in the Studio, suspended between literature and the stage: Konstantin Miklashevsky, the first real historian of the commedia dell'arte, Konstantin Vogel, and Mikhail Gnessin, under the aegis of the two gurus, Carlo Gozzi and E. T. A. Hoffmann. From Hoffmann, Meyerhold derived the name Doctor Dapertutto, almost as if he were his direct descendant.

Beyond personal mythologies, this connection was supported from a historical-critical point of view by Sergei Ignatov, a renowned theatre scholar, specialising in the period in which Antonio Sacco's troupe was performing in Russia. As a friend and admirer, Meyerhold invited Ignatov to the inauguration of the Studio, asking him to give a lecture on a subject discussed in his book, a monograph on Hoffmann Ignatov had worked on since 1912, but which was not published until 1914. In it, Ignatov demonstrated that Meyerhold was, in a theatrical sense, a blood relative of Hoffmann's. Thus, assuming the name of Doctor Dapertutto was a duty to historical truth.

Meyerhold certainly could not expect that a scholar like Ignatov, with such a background, would want to collaborate with someone like Stanislavsky. Yet this is exactly what happened. In September 1912, Ignatov told Meyerhold that he had written a stage adaptation of the novel *Princess Brambilla* and that he wanted an amateur troupe to perform it. Meyerhold answered, expressing his enthusiasm for the project. However, he did not agree that the artistic cabaret calling itself The Bat should perform it. His objection did not matter because the idea came to nothing (Raskina 2010: 68–71).

The project was revived one year later, this time with the participation of Stanislavsky. On 24 October 1913 – when the Studio had just opened – Ignatov wrote to Meyerhold saying that he had offered his scenario to the First Studio. 'I think that it can accomplish my projects' he stated 'as his

[Stanislavsky's] Studio is prepared for the commedia dell'arte'. On 7 November, surprised and outraged, Meyerhold replied: 'Not only is Stanislavsky's Studio not prepared for the *commedia dell'arte*, but I strongly believe that it never will be. I'm closely following Konstantin Sergeievich's work, and I know everything that happens there. Consider this: he is going to stage Goldoni's *The Mistress of the Inn'* (Mollica 1989: 170, which omits the conclusion of Goldoni's comedy, conveniently mentioned in Raskina 2010: 71). In Meyerhold's view, staging Carlo Goldoni meant betraying the commedia dell'arte. This was enough for Meyerhold to dismiss Ignatov's idea as nonsensical and almost against nature. Ignatov, however, had developed it, being, as he was, a professor and a recognised expert on the subject. Stanislavsky's First Studio could be seen as being 'prepared for the commedia dell'arte'.

The First Studio

1906: the 'cliff in Finland'.[1] After his repeated successes in the role of Doctor Stockmann in Ibsen's *An Enemy of the People*, Stanislavsky realised that his 'muscular memory' had completely replaced his 'affective memory'. He began, then, to develop his system of actor training.

However, for a long time he approached the issue of experience from a pragmatic point of view. He analysed the role of the actor, distinguishing three separate levels. First, the stagecraft or profession, based on the use of pre-established clichés: the nobleman is performed in this way, the soldier in that way and so on. Then, the 'art of representation', based on experiencing a role only to establish the model. Finally, the 'art of experiencing', in which actors relive the feelings of characters every time they play them on the stage. This was the subject of a text now known as 'On Various Trends in Theatrical Art'. Stanislavsky abandoned the text in 1922, although he rewrote most of it in *An Actor Prepares* (Benedetti 1990: 197). He had worked on it since the beginning of the twentieth century, when the accepted dramaturgical points of reference were personified by Anton Chekhov and Maxim Gorky.

For Stanislavsky, the military in Chekhov were not soldierly enough and the nobles insufficiently aristocratic to be performed through clichés. The only solution was to 'experience' them. In contrast, Gorky's works offered an ideal ground for the theatrical profession. Dominated by ideology, his characters tended to be stereotypes. The problem was that this did not work on stage. Stanislavsky first had doubts, when he was playing Doctor Stockmann and Gorky's *The Lower Depths* confirmed them. He wrote that 'the work itself led me to the conclusion that in plays with a social and political content, you have to live the thoughts and feelings of the role and then the politics of the play will be conveyed by themselves. A more direct approach to transmitting a political message ends in mere staginess' (Stanislavsky 2008: 225).

Before the 'cliff in Finland', at the inception of the system, Gorky's influence was strongest, even stronger than Chekhov's. While with Chekhov the process of re-experiencing (*perezhivanie*) was obligatory, with Gorky it was merely preferable. Chekhov's more intimate approach required *perezhivanie*. Gorky's more 'social' works could also be performed by adopting a more mechanical style of acting. Stanislavsky tested both of these approaches and, basing his decision on the factual evidence, opted for *perezhivanie*. To be able to choose on the basis of facts is far more instructive than being forced to do so.

It is no surprise then that it was Gorky who opened the way for the commedia dell'arte. Towards the end of 1910, Gorky wrote to Stanislavsky, inviting him to his house in Capri: 'I want to see you, you great rebel. I want to talk to you, I want to communicate certain ideas to you – add some fuel your blazing heart, the flames of which I have always admired and shall continue to admire whatever you may be doing, my dear sir' (Magarshack 1975: 320).[2] At that time, Stanislavsky was ill. Leopold Antonovich Sulerzhitsky, known as Suler – Stanislavsky's faithful soulmate and colleague – accepted the invitation for him. It could not have been made at a more appropriate time, as Stanislavsky was eager to show Gorky his first draft of a 'grammar of dramatic arts', on which he had worked for a long time. He was referring to 'On Various Trends', which at the time must have been almost completed after the crucial experience of staging Ivan Turgenev's *A Month in the Country*, in 1909. Considering the role that Gorky had had in it, it is no surprise that Stanislavsky, although still convalescent, took it upon himself to make the journey.

The beginning of their encounter was exhausting. It seems they talked for two days about the art of acting.[3] Finally they took a break. Stanislavsky's daughter Kira reported: 'Together with Gorky, we set out for Naples. . . . In the evening Gorky and my father went to the performance of a group of itinerant artists. These street artists aimed at bringing the commedia dell'arte back to life. K. S. watched the show with great interest. It is important to notice that the text, invented by the actors themselves, was not written, but improvised on the stage, in front of the audience. Dad was so intrigued that he said he wanted to watch it again' (Alekseeva, n.d.).

Stanislavsky's enthusiasm was not generated by the improvised text – which he could hardly appreciate, not knowing the language – but by the pantomime skills of the actors, which allowed the audience to follow the story regardless of the words spoken. It is well known that Stanislavsky's interest in pantomime, or mime with music, was of long standing. In March 1911, Gorky sent him a pantomime, or mime drama in Moscow (Mollica 1989: 123–5). After the performance in Naples, Stanislavsky's interest veered off in the direction of the commedia dell'arte.

Looking back, Gorky wrote in 1930: 'Twenty years ago, I suggested to Stanislavsky that he should organise a studio in which young actors, in addition to studying theatrical art, could create shows collectively' (Magarshack 1975: 320–1). Not an impromptu suggestion, this certainly had an impact on Stanislavsky. When he returned to Moscow, he talked about it with his friend Nikolaj Efros, a critic, discussing the possibility that actors could contribute to the text of the author with improvised passages of their own (Benedetti 1990: 200). It was not the collective show which Gorky dreamt of, but it was a first, immediate step in that direction.

The encounter between Gorky and Stanislavsky is not just an interesting anecdote. It marked the beginning of something deserving its own lasting place in history. A fable became the legend of the foundation of something important. The Studio suggested by Gorky was inaugurated shortly afterwards, on 1 September 1912, under the name of First Studio. Suler was appointed director. As Gorky had hoped, young actors were offered the opportunity to 'study dramatic art', but also to experiment with the practices of the commedia dell'arte.

During a meeting, Stanislavsky – according to a report by Sulerzhitsky – explained the goal he wanted to achieve by founding the Studio: 'The Studio ... is concerned with the problems of the actors' creative process (system), the educational formation of the artist, providing him with a set of practices, help through exercises ... It provides new experiments on the creative process common to authors, actors and directors in the making of plays (Gorky's method)'(Benedetti 1990: 209–10).

In a letter dated 12 October 1912, Gorky explained his method in detail. The playwright had to write a general scenario and create the characters. Starting from this, actors had to work independently on their roles. As he pointed out, this 'will make characters more alive and real and would suggest how every character should behave towards the others and what his attitudes hould be towards the subject-matter of the play, for the presence of firmly sketched characters must inevitably lead to some kind of dramatic collision between them' (Magarshack 1975: 321). The text would emerge gradually and, eventually, once the actors had reached an agreement, the playwright would intervene for possible final adjustments.

In September, a few weeks beforehand, he had sent, as requested, some dramatic material which could be used for improvisations. With the help of Yevgeny Vakhtangov – who, with his *Turandot* of 1922, was to become the bard of the commedia dell'arte – Suler worked enthusiastically on the method, reporting the results directly to Gorky. In a letter of 9 March 1913, Suler wrote: 'Last year I already started to do some exercises with the students' text . . . I chose the subject according to the purpose I wanted to pursue: concentration, exterior attitude, capacity of communicating with the other actors on the stage, and of influencing them etc. When imagination failed me, I used some short stories or extracts from stories, and students improvised on a given topic inventing the words themselves' (Mollica 1989: 168; Sulerzhitsky, n.d.).

Gorky and his method were not a marginal or clandestine presence in the First Studio. 'The experience of the Studio', as Stanislavsky pointed out, 'stemmed from Gorky's idea of creating a collective play'. Then he added:

> The essence of these experiments could be illustrated only in a schematic, superficial way. The author gives a first impulse, he plants a seed – as it were – in the actors' imagination. According to their own experience of life, their feelings and their talents, the actors let the initial idea grow. The author works on the actors' suggestions and give them back to the troupe in a dramatic form. This method of work is a new variation on the ancient Italian tradition of the commedia dell'arte (Mollica 1989: 175; Stanislavsky 1954–1961: vol. 8, 326).

These words mirrored Gorky's method word for word. In a letter to Meyerhold dated 24 October 1913, Ignatov gave his approval: The Studio was 'prepared for the commedia dell'arte'.

Gorky's Method and Stanislavsky's System

Although Stanislavsky recognised the key role played by Gorky and the commedia dell'arte in the creation of the Studio, he did not intend to sacrifice his system to them. Almost as a reaction to Ignatov, Stanislavsky pointed out that the Studio did not aim so much 'at bringing the commedia dell'arte back to life, as at working on emotional [*pereživanie*] processes in improvisation' (Mollica 1989: 175). He was very clear about this point. Gorky's method and Stanislavsky's system, verbal improvisation and experiencing, had to work together and reinforce each other.

In his letter to Gorky about his work on the method, Suler also
described in detail the 'improvisation of the wardrobe'. In his opinion,
this form of improvisation was closer than any other to the idea of actor-as-
author developed during the encounter with Stanislavsky on Capri.

> Where am I? I am in the First Studio, and I am first of all myself. I am free,
> calm, and ready to improvise.
> Where does the improvisation take place? In the wardrobe.
> Who am I talking to? To the old tailor who has sewn and cut cloth all
> his life.
> Who else is there? There's the wardrobe mistress or master, the tailor
> assistant and the girl who is learning the trade, etc.
> All the people in the wardrobe start to work. This is the beginning of
> improvisation. There is no need for real objects. Everything is done with
> imaginary objects. Ironing with an imaginary iron. (How heavy is it? How
> hot is it? What do you do if you burn your finger? If you are sewing, how do
> you thread an imaginary needle? How do you eat an imaginary apple or
> drink from an imaginary glass? etc.). (Sulerzhitsky, n.d.)

The interplay of Gorky's method with Stanislavsky's system, combining
in-depth research into given circumstances, physical actions with imaginary objects and improvisation on the text, could not be clearer. It is in this
mediation – in this subtle coexistence of opposites – that Stanislavsky's
'preparation' for the commedia dell'arte, within the Studio experience,
must be sought.

Stanislavsky's work on Molière's *The Imaginary Invalid* began in
September 1912. His relationship with Vladimir Nemirovich-Danchenko,
the literary director responsible for the financial aspects of the Moscow
Arts Theatre, had deteriorated. After the experience of *A Month in the
Country* and after having written most of 'On Various Trends', Stanislavsky was determined to exploit each performance as an opportunity to
test his system. Rehearsals turned increasingly into experiments and this,
according to Nemirovich, jeopardised the preparation of the performance
itself. Feeling restrained, and in order to be able to work freely, Stanislavsky obtained permission to rehearse *The Imaginary Invalid* in the First
Studio. Completely at ease there, Stanislavsky turned the rehearsals into a
workshop which was also open to actors not actually part of the cast. It was
his most direct and his most significant contribution to the pedagogy of
the First Studio.

After a visit there, Alexander Blok wrote: 'Actors – especially young
actors – are given a scenario, a subject, a plot, in which everything is
"concentrated". The person who wrote down the plot (for example the

author) knows in detail how the story develops, but the actors provide the words'. With regard to Stanislavsky, he added: 'In the same way they rehearsed Molière (!), but without Molière's words. Knowing the characters and the situations, the actors have to fill in the silence with their own words. According to Stanislavsky, they are getting closer to Molière's text' (Malcovati 1988: xix).

Stanislavsky explained:

> Currently (1912–1913), I divide the work into *large bits* and clarify the nature of each bit separately. Then, immediately, in my own words, I play each bit, taking note of all the movements involved. Then I go through the experiences of each bit ten times or so with the movements involved (not in any fixed or consistent way). Then I go through each bit in the order laid down in the book. Finally, I make the transition, imperceptibly, to the experiences as expressed in the actual words of the part. (Benedetti 1990: 212)

Experience is meant here as an 'emotional process' which Stanislavsky considered to be closely related to verbal improvisation. Using their own words assisted actors in their process of experiencing. If they had to perform a given text, actors had to 'take possession of' the author's words – gradually. For instance, Scaramuccia – master of 'absolute improvisation' – did improvise, but he improvised on Molière.

'However great Scaramuccia was, Molière surpassed him', said Charles Dullin when he first fell in love with the commedia dell'arte (Dullin 2005: 164). Stanislavsky's strategy resolved the conflict, fostering collaboration between Scaramuccia and Molière – each of them doing their part, focused on the only objective which really mattered: the truth – life in the fiction of the stage.

However, there was still a problem. Who is the Scaramuccia who improvises in the commedia dell'arte? The answer is not the actor. The actor – and even more 'the actor according to Stanislavsky' – was quite different from the 'actor of the commedia dell'arte'. It was not a theoretical problem; Stanislavsky had to experience it in his own body.

Count Aleksey Nikolayevich Tolstoy – a distant relative of the great author – was an original intellectual, man of letters, socialite and expert in political games. On Gorky's recommendation, Stanislavsky asked him for scenarios which could be used by actors. Tolstoy accepted, but pointed out that, 'although immersed in a Russian context and in the circumstances of contemporary life', the characters would have to be of 'limited number', as for example Colombina or Pierrot, 'exactly as in the commedia dell'arte' (Mollica 1989: 168). Tolstoy, who could speak Italian, knew very well that a character in a commedia dell'arte scenario, besides being a real person, had to be a stage persona. Besides being an actor, she/he had to be a 'role'. The actor in the commedia dell' arte does not get into a part directly but uses the role as an intermediary. That is an important point. Rejecting the role because of the clichés associated with it, the 'actor according to Stanislavsky' would also reject the stage character which it represented, without which – whether a role or any other 'persona' with the same mediating function – improvised words and the related process of experiencing would just dangle in the air.

This is what happened to Stanislavsky while working on Argan in *The Imaginary Invalid*. After preparing the 'psychological aspect' of the character, he waited for the inner impulse to create – through its own force – the physical form he would finally perfect, becoming the 'external image'. At the time, Stanislavsky's conviction was that his faith rested on the 'soul that believes' which prompts 'the body to live'. In this case he waited in vain. His body refused to jump spontaneously into action. He attempted to act on impulses from outside, in retrospect, trying to stimulate the body through the process of experiencing; it did not work. If it had not been for a fortuitous event – as he confessed with some embarrassment – he would have been forced to adopt a model from an external advisor specialising in French characters (Benedetti 1990: 213).

It was time to take stock of his work on Gorky's method. On the one hand, he had found that, by using their own words, actors could take possession of the author's words. This technique would become a permanent feature of Stanislavsky's formal tools. On the other, there was a question which remained unanswered and which could not even be expressed clearly as a question. Verbal improvisation could not exist without a persona predisposed to embody it. Meyerhold talked about the 'design of movements'. How did Stanislavsky see it?

The Commedia dell'Arte and its Legacy

The text on *The Government Inspector*, written in 1936–1937, is considered to be the best exposition of Stanislavsky's theory of the 'method of physical actions'. However, the word 'theory' is misleading when referring to Stanislavsky. Before postulating bold hypotheses, the main question about a 'theoretical' text by Stanislavsky concerns which episode or stage of his artistic development it may refer to.[4]

In this matter clues are certainly not lacking. Stanislavsky begins by describing the usual commencement of rehearsals with a reading of the text. The acting teacher Torzov asks his student, Nazvanov to act the scene of Chlestakov's entry in act 2. Nazvanov complains that he does not remember the text. Torzov reassures him, saying that he just has to perform the 'small physical actions' of the scene, regardless of the author's words. Seeing Nazvanov's difficulties, Torzov reproaches him, reminding him that they have been working on 'physical actions without objects' for '*nearly one year*'. The 'first experiment, *one year ago* [. . .of the] 'counting of money', was in the exercise of the 'burnt money' (Stanislavsky 2010: 52, 54, italics added).

Physical actions without props – even the strong emphasis on the 'burnt money' – are clearly dated as occurring in 1917. In that year, in order to achieve 'tragic immobility' in Knut Hamsun's *The Drama of Life* and Leonid Andreev's *The Life of Man*, Stanislavsky introduced the practice of 'physical actions with nothing', which boosted concentration.

In 1908 Stanislavsky staged *The Government Inspector*. It achieved both critical and public acclaim and, even more significantly, was also a great success for Nemirovič-Dančenko. It came to be regarded as Stanislavsky's 'obsession' and was officially included in the work of the Moscow Arts Theatre (1936–1937). Undoubtedly, this later, 'theoretical' production of the *Inspector* resulted from reflections on the earlier *Inspector*, recorded in the 'life in art' of 1908. Stanislavsky simply described how he would work on that fundamental performance, on the basis of the experience he had gained after 1908; that is, after further developing the method of physical actions and that of verbal improvisation, based on the gradual introduction of extracts from the author's text. This is clearly stated in the 'theoretical' text of 1936–1937.

After tracing the origin of the method of physical actions back to his own biography, Stanislavsky, with the equal precision, did the same for verbal improvisation. In order to overcome the resistance of the actors – who were used to starting from the words of the text – Stanislavsky stated that it was possible 'to act out a play that has not yet been written', creating the text on the basis of improvisation. He added jokingly that, at the end, playwright and actors would 'share the royalties equally' (Stanislavsky 2010: 46). The reference to 'Gorky's method' could not have been more explicit.

In the periods 1907–1908 and 1912–1913, in both Hamsun's and Andreev's plays and in the work on *The Imaginary Invalid* at the First Studio, the method of combining physical action and verbal improvisation with the progressive incorporation of the author's words was employed. The biographical basis of the 1936–1937 text is enclosed between these two coordinates. Rather than illustrating a theory, the famous 'twenty-four stages' of the new production of *The Government Inspector* point in the direction which Stanislavsky's research was taking, starting from these two coordinates defining time and method.

Physical actions, which had previously been used as a technique to strengthen presence, were now aimed at building the 'physical line of the role'. Verbal improvisations were no longer performed to bring the character's 'psychological aspect' to light through experiencing, thus postponing the construction of the 'physical aspect'. Now, verbal improvisations and physical actions, psychological and physical aspects all went hand in hand.

If the goal of the work on *The Imaginary Invalid* was the 'I believe', the purpose of the twenty-four-stage work on *The Government Inspector* was the 'I am'. It was only after the fourteenth stage – more than halfway through the journey – that the actor began to incorporate the author's words into his/her own, so that she/he became a complete 'persona': a soul that believes and a body that lives. This persona was not Scaramuccia – because a stage persona had to be predisposed to each single part; neither could it be an actor like Tiberio Fiorilli.

On 25 February 1545, a group of *comici* signed a contract in the presence a notary committing themselves to founding a 'fraternal company'. This is rightly regarded as the founding act of what was to be 'theatre on sale'. For its twentieth-century descendants, things went differently. Charles Dullin's enthusiasm was aroused by the improvised performance of Levinson and his fellow soldiers at the front; Copeau's enthusiasm was already considerable and Louis Jouvet soon shared it. They wrote to each other, dreaming of bringing old-time *farceurs* back to life. It was not a matter of signing papers, but of falling in love. What did Solovyov, his fellow students and his professors at the University of Saint Petersburg feel, if not love? It was the same atmosphere of burning enthusiasm which pervaded the encounter in Capri between Gorky and Stanislavsky.

Once they left the notary's office, the sixteenth-century group of *comici* entered the 'battlefield' of the marketplace; their supposed twentieth-century heirs entered the safe environment of schools and workshops. Rather than being just different, it was actually an alternative to an environment devoted to commerce. Finally, the winning answer to the market from the original *comici* was the 'performance without book', which the audience – not knowing or caring about the books which might be behind the performance – saw as the miracle of a performance without a text.[5] There is no trace of this in their twentieth century descendants. Echoing Dullin, for example, Jouvet declared that 'absolute improvisation' was not only impossible, but also pointless (Copeau 2009: 164); as regards Copeau, he stuck to the playwrights he had designated as masters of tradition. Meyerhold was simply uninterested in any improvisation of the text. In contrast, Stanislavsky, master of long-range strategies, believed that the words invented by the actor were intended to be at the service of the book containing the text.

The revival of the commedia dell'arte is just a cursory formula: Copeau, Meyerhold and Stanislavsky did not want to revive the commedia dell'arte. Nevertheless, each of them looked on that ancient form of theatre as an underground mine, from which they could unearth a treasure of theatrical knowledge. Since they were opposed to an organic relationship with the market and indifferent to the lure of the 'performance without book', the question at stake is: what aspects of the work they based on the commedia dell'arte can be identified as belonging to the legacy of the commedia dell'arte?

Between supply and demand and improvised text, the *comici* had built a complex system of transmission, in which the role was a fundamental part. It was on the theme of the role that their twentieth-century heirs focused their research. This has been proved objectively on the basis of the factual evidence available. Leaving aside the market and 'absolute improvisation', what has remained is a persona – in all its facets – created by the actor capable of getting into the part. Originally, it was the part which adjusted to the persona, rather than the other way round; after the revival of the commedia, it was the persona which adjusted to the part, as the part was no longer available to the actor. Originally, the role had been the persona for many parts; after the revival it was the persona for only one part.

There are many differences, all equally important. Is it still possible to talk about the 'role'? Evidently not. And yet . . . Stanislavsky preferred to use simple expressions, even at the expense of accuracy. He trusted the actors' pragmatic intelligence. For instance, he used the term, 'physical actions' instead of 'psycho-physical actions', which would have been more correct, because no actor could think that the physical aspect of the action was separate from its corresponding psychological aspect. This is mentioned by Vasili Toporkov at the end of his reference book on the method of physical actions (Toporkov 1979: 211).

Likewise, Stanislavsky simply defined the line created to get into the part as the 'physical line', because no actor could think that this line referred to the body only. He said that there is no line without the 'logic and sequence' of the actions of which it was composed and that where there are 'logic and sequence' there is the 'I am' (Stanislavsky 2010: 62). Finally, where there is the 'I am', there is the persona of the actor – imbued with the persona which is not yet the character, but which will become the character through the part. Although it is difficult to express all this in words, it is in fact easy to carry out in practice.

Stage persona, design of movements, the psycho-physical line of the part and the role: there are differences between these various concepts, but also a certain familiarity. It is better not to get entangled in words – Stanislavsky would have said. Why complicate the actor's work in the name of accuracy?

Notes

[1] 1906 is a significant date in Stanislavsky's biography. After a successful tour in Germany in 1906, Stanislavsky took a holiday in Finland. As he wrote in his autobiography, while he was sitting on a cliff overlooking the sea, he began to lay out his System.

[2] As regards Gorky's invitation to Stanislavsky, scholars report different dates: autumn 1910 according to Magarshack and December 1910 according to Benedetti.

[3] Scholars disagree on the dates. According to Benedetti the encounter in Capri took place in December 1910; Margarshack and Mollica report February 1911. In Benedetti's opinion the two days of conversation were 18 and 19 December.

[4] Not by chance, the whole of *An Actor prepares* mirrors – year by year, episode by episode – without exception, *My Life in Art* (cf. Ruffini 2005).

[5] This essential distinction between 'performance without book' and 'performance without text' was made by Ferdinando Taviani (cf. Taviani and Schino 2007).

20

Copeau and the Work of the Actor

Marco Consolini

Jacques Copeau (1879–1949) counts among the most eminent representatives of European theatre in the first half of the twentieth century, alongside Edward Gordon Craig, Vsevolod Meyerhold, Aleksandr Tairov and a few others. By rediscovering and investigating the lost tradition of the commedia dell'arte, Copeau aimed to renew contemporary theatrical practice and strengthen the role of the actor. In France, Copeau is regarded as a true pioneer in this field. His theoretical and practical initiative launched several new theatrical practices in France that in different ways all relate to a somewhat idealised model of the Italian *comici dell'arte*: a focus on improvisation, stock characters as the basis of the actors' work, the creation and use of masks and extensive training in expressive and acrobatic bodily techniques. Milestones in Copeau's artistic development include the foundation of his Théâtre du Vieux-Colombier in Paris (1913) and his move to New York (1917–1919), on which occasion he developed a theoretical model and first expressed his intention of implementing it. Then, during his years at the École du Vieux Colombier (1920–1924), this intention took a pedagogical turn and finally, in the years of the Copiaus (1924–1929), his young troupe of improvisers in Burgundy, it resulted in an actual theatrical production:

> Starting from the end of 1915, Copeau's idea of improvisation shifted from literature (the plot determines the action) to pedagogy, which is centred on the body of the actor (the body and the action determine the plot). Of course, this radical change of perspective did not take place in one day, but was rather a gradual, demanding process determined by the discoveries made by Copeau and his collaborators, between 1915 and 1922, regarding the role of play, the nature of the actor's body and the actor's training in silent and spoken performances.
>
> Unfortunately, this aspect has not always been perfectly understood, especially in France, where the commedia dell'arte is still interpreted on the basis of a system of literary values. Gignoux, for instance, defined the

Comédie Nouvelle as a 'chimera', deeming those early attempts 'pathetically vain'; he did not consider that, despite all their limitations, those attempts constituted a sort of necessary intermediate stage to reach a *new understanding of the relationship with the dramatic text*. Gignoux judged these experiments quite severely, as all he could see in them was 'their rather old-fashioned style, reminiscent of a 19th-century Parisian feuilleton, the cheap nicknames, the flaws, the looseness, the conventions of the contemporary social context'. He was even astonished that 'a man like him [Copeau], with World War I in full progress, in an age of profound historical changes, could have believed for a moment in such cheap creations. Unfortunately, Gignoux was doubly wrong, both as regards the paradoxical survival strategies deployed by artists in war time, considering the harsh discipline under which they had to live, and the intrinsic value of these speculations, although we can – at least partially – agree on their naivety. (Aliverti 2009: 35; quotations from Gignoux 1984: 71–9)

The crucial issue identified here is that Copeau, a man of letters who started to devote himself to theatre when he was thirty-four years old with hardly any prior practical experience in this field and motivated purely by literary reasons, was in fact the first intellectual in French theatre who transformed the commedia dell'arte from a legendary object of mere literary admiration (as in the case of Georges Sand) into an instrument of theatrical inventiveness which could be exploited to create a new theatrical language. This theatrical language was destined to lead to 'a new understanding of the relationship with the dramatic text' and thus to a new generation of dramatic poets. When Copeau referred to this new generation of poets, he clearly considered himself to be one of them. This awareness was particularly strong in the early years of his career, between 1911 and 1913; then it weakened progressively, first at the beginning of the 1920s, when the École du Vieux-Colombier was established, and then in the second half of the 1920s, when the Copiaus were more active; but it never completely disappeared.

In the aftermath of World War II Gignoux stood out as a successful creator of French popular theatre, practicing a highly traditional form of text-based theatre. At the same time he was also a student of Léon Chancerel and, through him, came to see Copeau as a legend. Copeau seemed to perfectly embody the struggle faced by text-centric theatre intellectuals who endeavoured to radically change their perspective and consider the actor as the real source of dramaturgy, but felt their conversion to be somehow forced. It must be said, however, that this view of Copeau originates in the persisting erroneous belief within French culture that Copeau was an advocate of dramatic poetry, the prophet of the sacralisation of the text. This interpretation is as unjustified as its opposite, the description of Copeau as an advocate of theatre centred on the moving body and nothing else. Although Copeau opened the way for Decroux and Lecoq, he cannot be regarded as the 'father' of modern mime; likewise, despite preparing the ground for the post-war decentralisation of theatre promulgated by Jean Dasté, Michel Saint-Denis and Hubert Gignoux, he cannot be considered a 'decentraliser' himself. Copeau's charm lies precisely in the sum of his unresolved contradictions. Particularly considering the legend of the commedia dell'arte, the relations between stage and text, body and action – admirably explained by Aliverti – remain unresolved, and thus extremely fertile.

'The commedia dell'arte was not the ultimate goal for Copeau as a tradition to imitate. Copeau resorted to improvisation not to revive a lost theatrical form, but because he identified it with a still living principle of a 'natural origin' of theatre' (Aliverti 2009: 40). One of Copeau's important ideas was the *tradition de la naissance*:

> There is no question of making historical reconstructions, or of exhuming the old scenarios of the Italian farce or the French medieval mansions in the name of historical curiosity. We shall study the commedia dell'arte and the fairground theatre. We shall learn the history and development of improvisation, the manners, the methods and peculiarities of the actors who practiced it. But our goal is to create new improvised comedy using contemporary types and subjects. (Copeau 1990: 153)

He adds:

> At first there is discovery, not learning. We are not in the same situation *vis-à-vis* the old Franco-Italian France, nor even *vis-à-vis* Molière, as the one in which Molière found himself *vis-à-vis* the ancient farceurs. The tradition has been interrupted. The only way we can rediscover it is inside us, by responding to a need, to an inner aspiration. For Molière this passage was natural, spontaneous. We have to stimulate a natural renewal and mistrust all that is artificial and scholastic, and all forms of bookishness, etc. (Copeau 2009: 160–1)

Copeau's approach to the commedia dell'arte was thus not animated by a philological interest, but rather by a spirit of reinvention. In this aspect, he falls into the same category as other founding fathers of twentieth-century theatre, such as Craig and Meyerhold. Craig is particularly important here, because it was after a 1915 encounter in Florence with this man of the theatre that the man of letters, Copeau, discovered the commedia dell'arte. These facts are not irrelevant and need to be taken into proper consideration. Copeau resisted the broadsides fired by the iconoclast

Craig against the dramatic text, as well as the charm of past and present Italian actors championed by Craig himself. For instance, Copeau went to see a performance featuring Petrolini (whom, interestingly enough, he called 'Petrolino', believing that this was a stage name inspired by Pedrolino – quite a revealing misunderstanding) and concluded: 'I hate virtuosos – however good they may be' (Copeau 2009: 135). Even by resisting such forces, he was deeply and definitely influenced by them. As a result, as soon as he returned home, he started to dream of a *confrerie de farceurs* working towards a *comédie improvisée*.

Copeau's approach to the commedia dell'arte was not mediated by Carlo Gozzi, E. T. A. Hoffmann or Georges Sand, who did not greatly appeal to the *Nouvelle Revue Française*, the austere literary circle to which Copeau belonged; nor by books or illustrations, although Craig's journal, *The Mask*, contributed to arouse his interest in this genre. The decisive factor was the controversial encounter with a fully theatrical perspective – both from a theoretical point of view (Craig) and a practical one (the Italian actors). Another significant element which drove Copeau was his interest in children's games. Almost with the eyes of an anthropologist, he had carefully monitored the games played by his three children for many years. This close observation, together with his interest in the pedagogy of Emile Jaques-Dalcroze (whom he had met in Geneva, where he went immediately after leaving Florence and where he also met Adolphe Appia, in 1915) led him to the belief that playing games and, through them, cultivating the imagination was 'the key to a new form of theatrical training, which could produce surprising results thanks to the emergence of a new category of actors, creators and improvisers' (Aliverti 2009: 27). This initial focus was subsequently broadened to include other elements such as the music hall and the circus (the clowns Fratellini of Cirque Medrano, for whom Copeau coined the definition 'artisans of a living tradition'). Further inspirations were Charlie Chaplin, the observations and experiments carried out during the war by Charles Dullin on his fellow soldiers and Copeau's exchange of reading material and letters on theoretical issues with Jouvet, who was at the front as well. Copeau's interest in the commedia dell'arte, however, was sparked by Craig in Italy and by improvisation as a theatrical equivalent of children's play.

In a special notebook devoted to the improvised comedy which he wrote in 1916 and which also contained the letters he exchanged with Dullin and Jouvet, Copeau's agenda seems clear:

It is an art which I don't know about, and I want to study its history. But I see, feel and understand that it is necessary to renew this art, revive it and keep it alive. Only this art will restore a living theatre: a comedy and actors. Leaving the boundaries of literature. . . .

To create a brotherhood of actors. I had really felt from the outset that this was the problem. People living together, working together, playing together; but I had forgotten that other phrase, the one which inevitably remained: creating together, inventing games together, extracting their games from within themselves and from one another. (Copeau 2009: 145)

How would this brotherhood work?

At first, I play the role of the poet in front of these jesters. This new thing springs from me. I know its origin and its early development. In order for them to retain all their freshness, I forbid research by the actors. The lessons of the past, and the contributions of tradition filter down to them through me, as much as I feel necessary and salutary to provide. I propose the characters and then the scenarios. First the characters, one by one, then the scenarios. . . . Soon, the characters develop entirely without me; they escape from me completely. The scenarios are created one after the other from within themselves. My only role in relation to them is that of critic. (Copeau 1990: 154)

However, putting his theories into practice was not exactly smooth sailing. It is an apt expression, evoking the actual voyage Copeau's *farceurs* undertook when they sailed the oceans to rebuild the Vieux-Colombier brotherhood in America between 1917 and 1919. It also effectively underlines how difficult it was for Copeau to abandon his aspiration to be 'the poet' to these farceurs, and that only intermittently did he actually let the 'characters develop entirely without me'. Incapable of relinquishing any form of control, he chose to be poet and actor at the same time.

The *Comédie nouvelle* sketched by Copeau between 1915 and 1916 was never fully developed, crushed by the pressures of managing the brotherhood in New York and of theatrical activity itself. Nevertheless, Copeau continued to work on its theoretical outline during a period of inactivity in 1919, which preceded the reopening of the Vieux-Colombier. Having lost Jouvet and Dullin as his main interlocutors, Copeau now discussed his ideas with another man of letters, Roger Martin du Gard. Author of *Le testament du Père Leleu*, a farce staged in 1914 at the Vieux-Colombier, Martin du Gard played a key role in directing Copeau towards this line of research. Excited by Copeau's ideas, he imagined several scenarios, and in the middle of World War I, wrote his *Notes sur la Comédie de Tréteaux*:

I dream of a performance as natural as improvisation, but as finished as a fairy-tale. An audience avidly interested in current topics would come to relax and heartily laugh at the irresistible gags of living marionettes, which would be very familiar to the spectators. I dream of a performance which, with quick, precise strokes, would depict the tyrannical abuses of the age, the stupidity of fashionable lies, and the danger of certain daily conflicts. (Martin du Gard 1972: 820)

Martin du Gard had in mind a limited number of 'essential types': Hector and Carmen Punais (Bedbug), bourgeois wheeler-dealers; their son Jeannot, a would-be artist; Disert (Eloquent), the chatty lawyer, journalist and diplomat; Monsieur Tiède (Tepid), the learned professor; Monsieur Commissaire, policeman and judge or notary. On the other side, the lower classes: Fric (Dosh), the smart, cunning servant and his astute girlfriend Miette (Crumb); Falempin, the revolutionary mechanic; Miteux (Poor devil) and Cheminot (Vagabond), the two criminals, one sad and the other cheerful; then, Midinette, typist or seamstress, showgirl of modern times and finally Cul-terreux (Country bumpkin), the old, greedy peasant, etc. (Martin du Gard 1955: lxxvi–lxxvii).

Although he had probably not read Martin du Gard's notes, Copeau had the chance to look at his unfinished farces when he returned from New York in 1919 and abruptly swept away all his friend's aspirations: 'Everything you have attempted so far is too literary' (Martin du Gard 1972: 301). Responding to Martin du Gard's timid objections ('before your arrival, I had a few projects. Now you have wiped them out'), Copeau further clarifies his anti-literary plan:

> As a form of theatrical art, the *Comédie nouvelle* will have an *existence in itself*, and will thus be able to recover several subjects – all subjects . . . and adapt them. . . . This implies a rupture with current stage practices, as well as with our usual point of view as authors, with our methods and staging routines. We need to stop being authors who write for theatre. . . . We need to submit to certain conditions, obey, and let ourselves be dragged, *forced*. As a matter of fact, you are still separated from the stage, and so am I, until I can say: *there I go!* I will not be, in practice, within my creation: as soon as I determine its conditions, it will be independent of me. In other words, to make it clearer, I think that, supposing that this form is possible, the *Comédie Nouvelle*, as well as a new form of theatre, will exist before the actors, will be presented to them and exist before we can use it. (Martin du Gard 1972: 312–14)

The drafts of Martin du Gard's farces have not been transmitted to us, as the author himself destroyed them. However, it is highly likely that Copeau's harsh criticism of his friend's works actually hit the mark.

Although Copeau's disdain was ultimately beneficial to Martin du Gard, causing him to throw himself into writing *Les Thibault*, the novel for which he would go on to win the Nobel Prize, the episode remains pitiful. And even though Copeau was prompted to elaborate on the *Comédie nouvelle* by his opposition to Martin du Gard's *Comédie des tréteaux*, it should not be forgotten how long his idea of a new comedy existed only on paper. Perhaps if he had continued to discuss his ideas with Martin du Gard, who was an acute observer of society (as demonstrated by his masterpiece, the 1933 short story *Vieille France*), Copeau might have been able to put into practice the dialectical relationship between 'observation' and 'imagination', which he saw at the core of the technique of improvisation. Analysing the creative strategy on which his three children's games were based, Copeau wrote:

> This *identification* with a character is the first condition of an improvised creation. Each one is *always the same character*: a certain tone of voice, two or three gestures or attitudes, a rudimentary accessory to the costume, enough to make up the character's outward appearance and to suggest its personality. *Repetition of the same trait*. Then, everything that enriches this first rough outline comes from scrupulous observation of reality – manners, personalities, bad habits, idiosyncrasies, mannerisms – but all slightly magnified and parodied, always distorted in the same way. *Imagination* is added to *imitation* of the traits that are more and more fixed, parodied and almost fantastical. (Copeau 1990: 155)

Absorbed by the productions of his theatre, which reopened at the beginning of 1920, Copeau was eventually to abandon his dream of the *Comédie nouvelle*. The new professional troupe at the Vieux-Colombier was even more incompatible with the model of the 'brotherhood of farceurs' than the troupe of the early years had been. Copeau's research was now concentrated on the École du Vieux-Colombier. The common thread of improvisation did not lead to the definition of a formula intended as a new 'manner' of theatrical creation which could be traced back to the commedia dell'arte, but was rather deployed as mere 'pedagogical instrument in both the figurative exercises and the student's approach to an imaginary character' (Aliverti 1997: 13). This pedagogical instrument was supported by and connected to other practices, starting with basic mask work.

The notion of the *comédie nouvelle* – and its direct reference to the model of the commedia dell'arte – subsequently re-emerged in the experience of the Copiaus. 'Once in Burgundy, Copeau soon abandoned [the] idea of the *comédie improvisée*', orienting his work as a playwright towards 'a series of adaptations, in some cases inspired by the commedia dell'arte or by the works of Italian writers such as Ruzante and Goldoni.' Maria Ines Aliverti goes on to say that these adaptations, however, tended more towards the models of classic comedy than to 'an actual revival of the techniques of the commedia dell'arte, which would benefit some new dramatic forms' (Aliverti 1997:13).

Despite numerous contradictions, doubts and scruples – especially those dictated by his religious beliefs and, most importantly, by the kind of playwright that Copeau, almost against his will, still aspired to be, the material conditions of the company of the Copiaus – its being a troupe forced to perform a flexible, adaptable repertoire – did lead Copeau to develop certain elements of his longed-for *comédie nouvelle*. In Burgundy, Copeau's role most closely resembled that of an adapter, a *dramaturg* who outlines a dramaturgical structure without directly incorporating into his work the results of his company's improvisations. He revisited texts from the Vieux-Colombier repertoire, such as Molière's *Le Médecin malgré lui* and, apart from *Arlequin magicien*, inspired by Flaminio Scala's scenario *Il Cavadente*, mainly produced adaptations of other plays: in 1925 *Mirandoline*, after Goldoni's *The Mistress of the Inn*, which Copeau had staged at the Vieux-Colombier in 1923; still in 1925, *Le Cassis*, adapted from Lope de Rueda's *The Olives*; then in 1926 *L'Illusion* after *La Celestina*, embedded in a structure derived from Corneille's *Illusion comique* and finally, in 1927 *L'Anconitaine* from Ruzante's eponymous play.

These adaptations were certainly far from what he had declared in 1916: 'First, the characters, one by one, then, the scenarios. ... Soon, the characters develop entirely without me; they escape from me completely'. Copeau was never prepared to entirely submit to the creative play of his troupe, continuing to exercise full control over the performance, both as an omnipotent playwright and a (not so young) actor who jealously kept all the lead roles for himself (for example, Ruzante). When the Copiaus tried to produce their own performances, Copeau adopted an obstructive rather than a constructive approach.

Yet, upon closer examination, it seems clear that Copeau not only took into increasing consideration the actors he worked with, but also began to give more and more space to both the individual and the collective creations of his actors, especially in the prologues and the so-called *inductions*. This term was adopted by Copeau 'to highlight the prepara-tory and metatheatrical aspects of the classic comedy prologue' (Cuppone 2008: 347). According to the account of Aman Maistre, the *induction* consisted of

A preparatory action, with the curtains open, aimed at defining the place of the action by means of the scene performed there, at preparing the actors and the audience for mutual contact, and at gradually introducing the audience to the action, so as to avoid that sort of stupid, abrupt rupture created by the swag curtains and to pass from the Copiaus' existence to the actors' existence for the people who knew us. (Gontard 1974: 200)

As regards the stock characters or essential types, early characters such as Bitouille or Sébastien Congre disappeared as their creators, respectively Auguste Boverio and Léon Chancerel, returned to Paris, while others, such as Jean Bourguignon and Monsieur Oscar Knie (both created by Michel Saint-Denis) and Monsieur César (invented by Jean Bourguignon) strongly influenced the adaptations, even though they did not formally find a place in their fairly rigid structures.

Taking inspiration from the system of *generici* and jokes of the commedia dell'arte, Copeau employed the technique of merging different pieces from the exercises and the repertoire of the Copiaus in order to highlight the individual work of each actor. To this purpose, on the one hand he exploited the freedom given him by the complicated paratextual structure he had staged (for instance dances, *Le Lavoir*, the micro-sequences of acting by the masked actors – *zanni*); on the other, he developed specific narrative structures starting from pre-existing texts, such as *La Celestina*. (Aliverti 2017: n.p.)

This recycling strategy is particularly evident in mimed group performances: *Le Lavoir*, developed from an idea by Maïène (Copeau's daughter) and centred on the work of women at a wash house, was introduced as an *induction* in *L'Illusion*. Likewise, in *L'Anconitaine*, while Copeau's rewriting of Ruzante's praise of the countryside was clearly influenced by Jean Bourgignon's rambling speeches, the mime work developed by the Copiaus is directly included in the spectacular scenario. An example of this is the *induction* created by Jean Villard-Gilles and Aman Maistre enclosed between the two prologues opening the performance: a group scene of numerous characters on a square in Padua in the early morning. This scene was a great success in all the Copiaus tours. Problematically, the *Patron* – that is, Copeau – did not fully accept this success. Patrick Gaudart acutely observes:

Copeau attempted to organise the abundant material provided by his students. They represented a brute creative force, which Copeau could not find in himself any longer, but at the same time they were incapable of directing their efforts towards a specific goal, as they were dominated by impatience and by their great desire to show everybody what they could do. (Goudart 1997: 129)

When in March 1928, Copeau having returned from yet another extended period of absence, the young troupe presented its first independent production, *La Danse de la ville et des champs*, which is the first 'self-generated scenario', Copeau, who during the performance had seemed to greatly enjoy himself, destroyed the troupe's first immature creation with his harsh criticism, much as he had done to Martin Du Gard:

> Copeau deemed the ensemble of the Copiaus to be still incomplete. In his view, their increasing skills in group performance, body expression, mask and mime acting, must not result in autonomous and original theatrical creations; these are acceptable only within the boundaries of workshops and rehearsals, a work in progress aimed at a final all-encompassing creation which Copeau wanted to establish on new foundations and for a new audience. (Aliverti 2017)

Once again, Copeau was not entirely wrong. But at the same time it inevitably seems like a pitiful waste of work. The painful episode undermined the extremely fragile balance in the relationship between the Copiaus and their inspiration and leader. Nevertheless, he did write to them in the autumn of 1928: 'Pass me your notes, so that I can work on them' (Copeau 2017). His plan was to create scenarios centred on the jokes of Monsieur César and Monsieur Knie, intertwined with individual and group mime performances. Some months later, in May 1929, the troupe disbanded at Copeau's unilateral behest. Martin du Gard wrote him a harsh letter which remained in a drawer and was never sent:

> For the second time, I see a group of human beings, whom you promised – perhaps foolishly – to take care of, now abandoned, left to their fate and to chance, disappointed in you, despite everything you have done for them and your sacrifices; but disappointed anyway, because you let them glimpse a totally different future. And these days I have thought about the cruel consequences of your illusionist's skills, and about the fact that your way is paved with victims. (Martin du Gard 1972: 475–6)

This was how the experiments of the *comédie nouvelle* ended. Copeau was too intransigent with himself and his students, and at the same time incapable of constancy and perseverance, condemning himself not to reap the fruits of what he had abundantly sown. Yet, while he was in Paris – where quite unexpectedly he tried to obtain the directorship of the Comédie-Française at the time when the Copiaus were disbanded – Copeau had his friend Paul Albert Laurens paint a portrait of him.

He was not portrayed with a book, like Molière, his inspiring model, but with a mask in his hands, like Tristano Martinelli or Giovanni Gabrielli. It is the mask of the magician in *L'Illusion*, while in the background there are the costume and a drawing of the character Copeau himself had played. After all, Copeau decided to be portrayed with the visual symbols of a *comico dell'arte*.

Staging Gozzi
Meyerhold, Vakhtangov, Brecht, Besson

Franco Vazzoler

Meyerhold

When discussing Carlo Gozzi's popularity in the twentieth century, it is inevitable to start in Russia in the cultural atmosphere prevailing there between World War I and the era of the New Economic Policy in the 1920s. As summed up by Angelo Maria Ripellino, participants in the cultural life of that period 'loved carnivals, masks, dominoes, theatre dolls, the eighteenth century and Biedermeier-style tastes, Jean-Antoine Watteau, Pietro Longhi's Venice, pastorals, porcelain and Carlo Gozzi's fairy tales . . . generally favouring clown disguises and Pierrot stories'. Ripellino also mentions Vsevolod Meyerhold, who 'played Pierrot, a role which he had already performed in a comedy by Blok' and his 'Hoffmann disguises', in which 'he went by the name of Doctor Dapertutto' (Ripellino 1975: 439). 'Hoffmann disguises' consisted of two essential elements: on the one hand, dressing up and masquerades; on the other, fairy tales and fables.

Raissa Raskina's (2007: 343–55) retracing of Gozzi's growing popularity in the Russian artistic milieu starts with the passages which the art historian Pavel Muratov devoted to him in 1911 in his *Obrazy Italii* *(Images from Italy)*, in the chapter entitled 'Vek maski' ('The Century of the Mask'). The book was inspired by the work published by Vernon Lee in 1915 under the title *Italija. Izbrannye stranicy (Italy. Selected Pages)*. In Muratov's work, the Italian commedia are seen from a late Romantic perspective, Gozzi being regarded as an Italian Hoffmann. It is an idea which was prevalent throughout the nineteenth century in Germany, France and England and had a crucial influence on Meyerhold.

In a letter written in 1911 and referring to Muratov's book, Meyerhold defines Gozzi as 'the first Romantic, a precursor of Hoffmann and Maeterlinck' (Volkov 1929: II, 183), describing him as one of the forerunners of Romanticism and symbolism, whose theoretical works – especially the dramaturgy of Alexander Blok – had influenced him in the previous years, at the time when the Theatre-Studio on Povarskaya Street was active. In his manifesto-like article entitled 'Balagan' ('The Fairground Booth', published in the journal *Rec* in April 1912), Meyerhold hoped to modernise the repertoire by inviting new playwrights to use Gozzi's fairy tales as models. He was also inspired by the Russian symbolists' theoretical approach and encouraged playwrights to study excerpts from Cervantes, the dramas of Calderón, and the comedies of Tirso de Molina (Meyerhold 1962: 101–10).

By associating Gozzi with E. T. A. Hoffmann, Meyerhold defines 'theatricality' from an anti-realistic theoretical angle rather than an angle having anything to do with naturalism. This claim is further supported by considering the fairy-tale element of stories such as *Princess Brambilla*. In this regard, Meyerhold was influenced by Craig and his belief that, according to Hoffmann's story *Seltsame Leiden eines Theaterdirektors,* only a puppet company could perform the 'sublime fairy tale' of *L'Amore delle Tre Melarance* (*The Love of Three Oranges*).

Analisi riflessiva (*A Reflective Analysis*) was the first fairy tale Gozzi wrote and it took on the form of a manifesto. Meyerhold planned to stage it between the autumn of 1912 and the spring of 1913. Vladimir Solovyov and Konstantin Vogak took on the task of translating and adapting it. A critical account of the mise-en-scène of Gozzi's text contains the scenario of *The Love of Three Oranges*. Starting from the idea of creating a *divertissement,* in the style of the great opera and theatre traditions of the eighteenth century, Solovyov and Vogak aimed not at a literal or factual reconstruction of the text, but rather at reviving the legend of the commedia dell'arte. The project was never brought to fruition, nor did Meyerhold ever stage any of Gozzi's works, except for the 'fragment of a 'Chinese' commedia, modelled on Turandot' (Ripellino 1965: 168, which refers to Volkov 1929: 367–8) and the influence of Meyerhold's project on Prokofiev. However, Meyerhold's initial interest in *L'amore delle tre melarance* marked the beginning of a long period of theatrical work (Raskina 2007: 348) centred almost exclusively on the legend by Gozzi. This work was first documented in the journal *Ljubov' k trem apel'sinam. Zurnal Doktora Dapertutto* (*The Love of Three Oranges. Doctor Dapertutto's Journal*), published between January 1914 and 1916 (nine issues in all) and edited by Meyerhold. Using a pseudonym derived from Hoffmann's short story *Die Abenteur der Sylvester-Nacht* (*A New Year's Eve Adventure*), Meyerhold reaffirmed the connection between Hoffmann and Gozzi.

'A journal on history and topical issues' was how *Doctor Dapertutto's Journal* was described (Picon-Vallin 2002/2003: 286). Its circulation was very limited but it offered space for historical research and aesthetic and theoretical analysis of theatre, often reflecting intransigent positions and polemical activism, communicated by means of irony and parody. Furthermore, the research and analysis it offered were used in pedagogical courses for the artists attending the Studio which Meyerhold inaugurated in St Petersburg in 1913.

Gozzi's plays were translated as part of the project to produce an edited edition of his *Complete Works*: the *Reflective Analysis, Re cervo* (*The Stag King*) *La Donna serpent* (*The Serpent Woman*) and *Ragionamento ingenuo* (*Ingenuous Disquisition*); together with a number of critical studies on Gozzi and parodic-imitative texts such as the *Storia vera ma poco credibile* (*True but Not Very Credible Story*) (1915, n. 4–7). This story is claimed to be derived from the 'yellowed pages left by Count Carlo Gozzi to the editors of the journal', in particular from a prediction, according to which in the near future a group of strange people, in a northern country, would 'resuscitate' the commedia dell'arte (Picon Vallin 2002/2003: 284–6).

This renewed study was of crucial importance within the theoretical framework through which 'Meyerhold accomplished a second renaissance of the commedia dell'arte' (Gorchakov 1957: 67). This was implicit in his direction of Blok's *Balangànčik* (*The Fairground Booth*) – in a major production at the Theatre in Oficèrkaja Street (1906), as in the Hoffmannesque *Sarf Kolombiny* (*Columbine's Scarf*) at the Interlude House (1910) and in Solovyov's *Arlekin-chodàtaj svadeb* (*Harlequin Para Faun*). During the interval in the performance, which was based on two of Blok's plays and took place in the hall of the Tenishev Academy, 'a group of fake Chinese jugglers put on a performance in which the actors threw Gozzi's oranges and not Blok's black roses, to the audience' (Ripellino 1965: 173).

In the pages of the journal, the debate on the old 'contrast' between Gozzi and Goldoni in eighteenth-century Venice resurfaced. This led Meyerhold to interpret the whole history of theatre as a constant conflict between two opposing dramaturgical notions of theatre: on the one hand, a predominantly 'literary' theatre and, on the other, a 'theatrical' theatre. According to lectures in 1918 and 1919, Goldoni – towards whom he always felt 'acrimony' (Malcovati 1993: 15) – stands for the origin of psychological and realistic theatre, in which 'character' and 'real characters prevail' based on the 'fine texture of dialogue', and deploys the 'same literary stratagems used by novelists.' On the other hand, Gozzi exemplifies a form of theatre 'as a world of wonder and fairy-tale'. Therefore, as a result of the contrast between 'these two trends, eternally fighting for supremacy' (Meyerhold 2004: 29), stock characters and improvisation became symbols of theatrical-theatre. From a long-term perspective, as pointed out in a lecture delivered in 1928–1929, 'Carlo Gozzi became popular (for a certain period of time) not so much for bringing new life to the Italian commedia dell'arte – which was nearly dying because of Goldoni – but for making stock characters speak the language of his contemporaries' (Meyerhold 1993: 99).

This rivalry from the past resurfaced in the present: the first issue of the journal reported – not without sarcasm – on the recent performance of Goldoni's *La Locandiera* (*The Mistress of the Inn*) at the Moscow Art Theatre. A few months later, with equal disapproval, the editors of the journal wrote about the decision of Aleksandr Tairov's Kamerny Theatre to stage *Il Ventaglio* (*The Fan*) by the same author. They asked: 'Has the direction of the Kamerny perhaps decided to reject the cult of theatricality in favour of the theatre of psychologism proclaimed by the Moscow Art Theatre?' (Raskina 2007: 349).

As a matter of fact, besides the question of the eighteenth-century tradition of theatre masks – Meyerhold was actually arguing against the Art Theatre, which he had left in 1902 – the issues at stake were not only of a dramaturgical nature, but also concerned the education of the actor and in particular, the distinction between naturalistic and biomechanical training – for which, once again, Gozzi (not Goldoni) and the improvisations of the *comici* were used as models.

> In order to perform a play by Goldoni, actors had to spy on real life, as Goldoni himself used to do. On the contrary, to perform a play by Gozzi, the actors had to forget all of this, because traditional stock characters have rigidly fixed acting rules to follow. . . . On the stage, the actors had to walk as if they had just looked at themselves in the mirror. The whole system of our, and Gozzi's, concept of acting consists of actors uttering their lines as if they had just looked at themselves in the mirror. Gozzi's stock characters walk in a peculiar way, which is a skill, and this skill is innate in the actor. (Meyerhold 1993: 58–9)

Gozzi thus remained for Meyerhold merely a theoretical – though a crucial – point of reference, an example of that notion of 'abstract', 'imagined' theatre which he shared with those twentieth-century experimenters who were aiming at inventing a different theatre (Craig, Artaud, etc.).

Instead of *The Love of Three Oranges*, *Turandot* was staged by Theodore Komissarshevsky, also in 1914, but at the Nezlobin Theatre in Moscow. Komissarshevsky was the first to stage a work by Gozzi in a Russian theatre. He explicitly acknowledged his debt to Meyerhold's 'manner', although his espousal of that 'manner' or 'style' was only superficial, being, as he was, one of the most eclectic of Russian directors (Slonim 1961: 225).

Vakhtangov

The idea that there existed a connection between the theatricality of the commedia dell'arte (Gozzi) and Hoffmann remained influential in Russian theatre until at least Tairov's *Princess Brambilla*, which was performed on 4 May 1920 at the Kamerny Teatr in Moscow (the set was designed by Jakulov). With its atmosphere of 'performance-festival', characterised by the tones and rhythms of an 'unbridled Harlequinade' (Lenzi 2001: 127), the play established a link between Meyerhold and the *Turandot* produced by Yevgeny Vakhtangov at the Third Studio in 1929.

The performance of Vakhtangov's last work – he was still young at the time (born in 1883, he died of cancer at the age of 39) – took on the character of a momentous event. Not only did it mark the peak of his career, but it was also the starting point of a new perspective, which went beyond the principles of biomechanics, almost challenging Meyerhold – whom Vakhtangov greatly admired – in his own field.

'Fantastic realism' is the formula which Vakhtangov often discussed during rehearsals and to which he resorted in order to define the act of reviving Meyerhold's 'theatrical theatricality'. This implied 'associating – by carefully calibrating it - the interiority inherited by the method of Kostantín Sergèevič [Stanislavsky] with the loud theatricalism of Doctor Dapertutto' (Ripellino 1965: 248). This could be achieved by emphasising the theatricality of theatre and by exploiting the intimacy of a theatre with no more than 300 seats. It was not intended as a complete performance but as a workshop demonstration, as Vakhtangov, confined to bed, wrote in a letter read out by Zavadskij before the performance commenced:

> Dear teachers, old and young friends, you must believe me when I say that the form of today's performance is the only possible one for the Third Studio. This form is valid not only for the fairy tale of Turandot, but for all Gozzi's fairy tales. For Gozzi we sought a form which reflected the current trends of the Third Studio. This form required not only the narration of the plot of the fairy tale, but also some scenic devices which perhaps the audience will not notice, but which are absolutely necessary for the education of the actor. (Vakhtangov [1959] 1984: 157–8)

The translation by Osorgin (Mikhail Andreyevich Il'in, a well-known writer who was soon to emigrate to Paris) was faithful to the original, spurning any idea of updating the text (for instance, riddles with quizzes on current topics which had to be solved with the help of the audience: Gozzi's third riddle – the Lion of Venice – was replaced by Schiller's 'rainbow' riddle, which was more comprehensible for the Russian audience; this was the only case of substitution). This was because Vakhtangov 'believed that contemporaneity should not be sought in the lines or in the improvised moments of a play, but in the form of the performance, in its capacity to illustrate through theatrical stratagems' the Soviet reality existing in 1921 (Malcovati 1984: li). As reported by the protagonists of the time, (Vakhtangov 1923) and the memoirs of his student Nicolai Gorchakov (1957), contemporaneity emerged in the improvisations of the actors which they had developed throughout their study and training.

This meant that the crucial element of the work on Gozzi's text – although within the dynamic rhythm of the *ensemble* (essential in Vakhtangov's approach to directing) – were the relationships between the actors on the stage and between each actor and the audience. Hence the need for 'total freedom of improvisation', which resulted in a 'light, and almost vague, acting style', consisting of 'sudden passages' characterised by ironical and buffoonish tones as opposed to 'majestic waves of profound lyrical truth' (Lenzi 2001: 125). This interplay of contrasts was a characteristic feature of the *commedia dell'arte*, which had been assimilated by Gozzi. It was somehow symbolised by the 'round, central platform' of Nivinsky's final set which resembled a circus ring steeply raked towards the audience. It was as if the actors were 'on the deck of a ship', as Fedor Stepun explained:

> I don't know why, but it seems to me that the Third Studio performs Gozzi as if on the deck of a ship. Perhaps this depends on the raked platform, adorned with colourful curtains, or on the mast in the centre of the stage, or on the rope ladders – I don't know. What is certain is that the inexplicable feeling of being on the deck of a ship sadly upset me, while I was watching the merry performance of the merry, edifying fairy tale. ... Between the deck of a ship and the melody of an artistic soul there exists a deep spiritual affinity. (Malcovati 1984: liii)

Improvisation was used as a tool to 'demonstrate the so-called "attitude towards the character" ... continuously getting "into" and "out of" the role' (Lenzi 2001: 125). The actors trained 'on the spot' for the performance. To the rhythm of a popular song, they transformed first their clothes and then the stage with pieces of colourful material ('objects and rags swirled on the stage, various colours and pieces of fabric intertwined flying in the air before landing on the clothes or in the basket') (Malcovati 1984: li: the costumes were by N. P. Lamanova (1861–1941), fashion designer, who from 1901 also collaborated with Stanislavsky).

On Nivinsky's set theatre conventions were upheld too: stage extras, turned out as *zanni*, waved brightly-coloured banners until large letters making up the word 'Peking' appeared, creating a comical contrast to 'the most ordinary of Muscovite chairs' in the centre of the stage (Lenzi 2001: 125). These effects were later popularised by Brecht, who certainly took inspiration from this experience.

Of the points made by Vakhtangov during the workshop experiments and faithfully reported by Gorchakov (1957), many concerned the role which audiences played in the performances of the *comici dell'arte*, a role he was trying to imitate. Involving the audience was a crucial matter: the actors continually moved into the stalls, where the lights remained on, mocked latecomers and addressed them with double entendres. Drawing on Gozzi's scenario and clearly keeping in mind the dispute over the *Oranges*, the stock characters 'alternated frequently between comments on topical issues, and new performances in other theatres in Moscow theatres, between digs at critics and satirical barbs against bureaucratic attitudes or Western governments, much in the style of political meetings. . . . In the Divan Room, the procession of Turandot's slaves moved in a way which parodied Isadora Duncan's dancing. The characters of the Mandarins of the Royal Retinue were based, in cabaret style, on the cartoons and caricatures of Soviet satirical magazines' (Ripellino 1965: 238).

Another feature of the performance was that it was grotesque to an extent evocative of performances held in public squares, the fairground booth or the circus. Referring to the comparison he drew between Schiller and Gozzi (parallel to the comparison made by Meyerhold between Goldoni and Gozzi), Vakhtangov explains: 'It's not Schiller's way. . . . Schiller could never have imagined his play being performed in the open air, but Gozzi could. That's why it belongs more to Gozzi' (Gorchakov 1957: 102).

This rendered Vakhtangov's *Turandot* 'a festive theatre', i.e. 'a performance created and staged as a festival, which could express the joy of acting and, at the same time, convey its pure, unfathomable essence to the audience' (Lenzi 2001: 126). According to all the reports at the time, the audience was aware that 'the performance was a watershed, which went beyond realism to mark the triumph of theatricality and fairy-tale magic' (Cambiaghi 2006: 165).

Brecht – Besson

After Vakhtangov's *Turandot*, Gozzi became the symbol of a new directing style. In Italy, the staging of Strehler's *Il corvo* (*The Crow*) at the Piccolo

Teatro in Milan in 1948 (after the experiment of Goldoni's *Servitore/ Arlecchino*) was an attempt to revive Gozzi's ideas of interplay between stock characters, thus reinterpreting early twentieth-century experiments. It was produced by Marcello Moretti (Truffaldino) but did not make much of an impression in theatre circles. Silvio D'Amico expressed his disapproval on the grounds that it 'indulged in the tones reminiscent of the revue, or of popular circus' (Battistini 1980: 66; but see the reconstruction in Mazzocchi 2006). The directing approach which Strehler adopted for this performance consisted of staging the company (in this case a company of eighteenth-century *comici*) while it was performing the *commedia*. This idea was also used in the more successful *Arlecchino* by Goldoni – which was the basis for the study on Vakhtangov – starting from its third production.

It was Brecht, however, with his posthumously published (Brecht: 1967), *Turandot oder Der Kongreß der Weißwäscher* (*Turandot, or the Whitewashers' Congress*) (1953–1954), who revived Gozzi's fairy tale – in a manner much appreciated by Vakhtangov. According to Benno Besson 'Brecht was the only director . . . who was able to build a bridge between the 1920s and the 1950s' (Meldolesi and Olivi 1989: 235). During his years in Berlin, Brecht 'talked at length' with Besson about Gozzi's theatre (Besson 2001: 136). In this case, however, Brecht did not start from any idea of wanting to revive the theatricality of the commedia dell'arte. His starting point was Schiller's translation of the play, a German – rather than an Italian – 'classic', which he modified considerably. Brecht was aware of its peculiarity; he wrote in his *Work Diary* (13.9.1953), *Turandot* is 'clearly outside German literature and, as often happens to people who live alone, it does not look very solid'. (Brecht 1973: 1011).

In this *pièce*, which was to be his last, Brecht was certainly not interested in historical or philological reconstruction (Meyerhold), nor in reviving the 'myth' of improvisation from the commedia dell'arte (Vakhtangov). He was attracted by the stylised Oriental 'disguise' which allowed him to create an 'alienating' effect which he saw emanating from the burning issue of power (Brecht 1973: 1009), He had the East German workers' demonstrations of 17 June 1953 in mind. This notion of alienation was similarly used in other plays, such as *The Good Person of Szechwan* and *The Caucasian Chalk Circle*.

Common to both these plays and to *Turandot* is the fairy-tale element, coupled with the possibility of using metaphors to convey content. These are acted out in an imaginative, playful atmosphere, having been translated into the grotesqueness and irony of a buffoonish, puppet humour. On the other hand, the 'rapid change of scene', the 'aerial . . . constructions, poetically and realistically evocative' of the scenery and the 'fast . . . rhythm of acting' are all elements which can be traced back to Russian influence and which were laid down in the author's note included in the first edition.

In Brecht's reinterpretation, the main topic is the subjection of petit-bourgeois intellectuals to established power, an issue he had explored in his *Tui-Roman,* an unfinished satire on the intellectuals at the time of the Second German Empire and the Weimar Republic, on which he had worked in the mid-1930s. The satire was then developed into the *pièce,* acquiring a new meaning in the Berlin of the years after World War II. However, Brecht was inspired by Gozzi's dramatic fairy tales not only from a narrative point of view. He also borrowed the stock characters of *Turandot:* Tartaglia as Grand Chancellor, Pantalone as Secretary of the Emperor, Brighella as Master of the Pages, Truffaldino as Chief of the Eunuchs and the 'eight Chinese doctors on the sofa' (Gozzi 1994: 120), which he used to portray intellectuals. In addition to these, he borrowed many other characters, among which Gogher Gogh stands out: He is the bandit who wants to become Tui, in order to impose an authoritarian regime, based on police control (the Calaf of the situation, he will marry Turandot and possesses many of the same features as Hazdak in *The Caucasian Chalk Circle*).

Brecht's work was based far more on *Turandot* than on the *Tui-Roman,* even though he did not 'systematically overturn it' (Meldolesi and Olivi 1989: 126 n.). Above all, he introduced the narrative element into his handling of the social revolution spreading to the city and to the country at the same time, even though it is never visible. Only the echoes of it are heard on the stage (at and near the palace): Kai Ho leads the revolution but never appears on the stage – nor do the demonstrators – and the audience learns that the gunsmith transforms objects from the past into weapons but does not see how. According to Claudio Meldolesi and Laura Olivi, 'this not being there was also the point of view of the author of *Turandot,* a comedy in which absence is represented as the condition of the just. . . . The good is in what cannot be seen or in the choice of leaving' (Meldolesi and Olivi 1989: 132).

On the stage everything is presented as a game (a characteristic of Gozzi, reinterpreted through Russian models), both in a richly comic dialogue (not so common in Brecht's works) and in Turandot's (played by Carola Neher) capricious sentimentality at the moments in which the action on stage becomes more dramatically intense. Brecht himself never actually produced *Turandot.* It was first staged, many years after his death, on

1969 at the Schauspielhaus in Zurich and directed by Benno Besson and Horst Sagert, to music by Yehoshua Lakner. During his training at the Berliner Ensemble, Besson had collaborated with Brecht on *Turandot* and on a production of *Don Giovanni*, which he had adapted with Elisabeth Hauptmann (it is no accident that Brecht regarded Besson as the ideal director of the *pièce*) and which emphasised the arrogance of the protagonist's social class. *Turandot* and Besson's *Don Giovanni* shared the clown and puppet elements.

Therefore, from Brecht Besson learnt to be a 'poet-director' (as Meldolesi defined Brecht during his years in Berlin), in the spirit of the fairy tale, in which the comic element is seen as 'playful fluidity': This is the meeting point between Gozzi and Besson. In his Berlin years, Brecht was 'a fervent admirer' of Gozzi and spurred Besson on to 'consider the possibility of producing one of Gozzi's fairy tales' (Besson 2001: 136). A recurring element in Besson's productions – derived from Gozzi and Molière – is the court, considered as the symbol of a violent, absurd form of power, being both comic and tragic at any one time. The court is also the dramatic space in which – in the manner of Brecht – it is possible to develop on the one hand a plurality of voices and on the other a discourse on the relationship between characters and power.

It was through the influence of Brecht that most original aspects of Besson's revitalisation of Gozzi emerged: in 1971 in *The Stag King* at the Volksbühne in Berlin (which was staged again in 1994 at the Svenska Theatre in Helsinki) and in 1997 at the Comédie de Genève (in 1998 at the Palais de Chaillot in Paris). However, the most significant example is *The Green Bird*, staged in 1982 at the Comédie de Genève: Besson rewrote, in prose and in French, some parts which Gozzi had left for improvisation.

A new and original aspect of this play was the atmosphere of great *féerie* of the performance, to which Jean Marc Stelhé's set design and Werner Strub's masks made a crucial contribution. Its 'ironical sense of the marvellous' emphasised the 'comic alienation of the action', resulting in a 'multiplying of the festive attributes of the fairy tale and a tingeing of its rhythm with a subtle and threatening feeling of fear'. The acting was 'stylised to the extreme, lacking any psychological depth and almost exclusively reduced to mere bodily presence and meaningful rhythm'. It created a sort of 'gallery of embittered characters', on whose features the theatrical adaptation had worked very effectively – up to the point of turning Gozzi's *pièce* into a 'furious variation on egoism' (Macasdar and Tinterri 2006: 69–71).

'The criticism of egoism in the sense in which Gozzi understood it – as a dualism encompassing selfish behavior and actions dictated by altruism – has not been maintained'. This point is contained in a note to the text accompanying Besson's translation–adaptation, which clarifies in particular the changes the female characters had undergone in a new version which 'promotes self-love to the point of making it the indispensable source of love for others' (Besson 1985: 106).

In Besson's adaptation, Gozzi's text seems somehow to have been filtered through Brecht's last 'fairy tales': Smeraldina shares with Gruscha of *The Caucasian Chalk Circle* the same maternal animal instinct. Likewise, Pompea's egoism turns into virtue, echoing the character of Shen-Te in *The Good Person of Szechwan*. This is also a way of reinterpreting the conventional image of the commedia dell'arte, depriving it of reassuring conventions in order to find – in the writing of the improvised parts – 'the spicy, colourful and crude language' of original, improvised theatre. This unconventional revival of the commedia dell'arte – which was for Besson the revival of a 'lost tradition' (Besson 1985: 106) – is connected to the use of masks which he also adopted for performances of plays not written by Gozzi (for example in his productions of *Oedipus*). Far from traditional iconography, these masks were neutral, wiping out every individual feature of the character.

In this regard, Edoardo Sanguineti, who had long been familiar with Besson, wrote: 'If Besson deliberately chooses the masks, it is because he wants to emphasise, using provocative evidence, that a system of explicit falsification constitutes the basis of theatre' (Sanguineti 1985: 7–8). These words explain the reasons why he collaborated with Besson on the production of *Melarance* (2001), the 'disguise' written in *martelliani* (lines of fourteen syllables) but in modern language. It reinterpreted, from a strongly contemporary point of view, the metatheatrical suggestions contained in the story of the first act of Gozzi's *Analisi riflessiva* (the debate over the *larmoyant* (sentimental) theatre of Chiari and Goldoni was replaced by the debate over television).

In his introductory text, giving due consideration to Gozzi's historical position, Sanguineti spotlights the perception that *The Love of Three Oranges* is, historically, the 'funeral ceremony' of the commedia dell'arte and 'degradation' of the 'solemn archetype of the fairy tale'. In the eighteenth century, the Enlightenment marked the end of the fairy tale as myth and the beginning of the ideological age; myth and thus fairy tale were reduced to grotesque tragicomedy, even though some traces of both remained (Sanguineti 2001: 7–14). In the case under consideration here,

Besson did not work on Gozzi's text as a 'director-playwright' but he remained faithful to Sanguineti's 'disguise', hardly altering it, although the text was not entirely congenial to his taste. The aspects on which Besson was in disagreement were the representation of the feminine universe and the use of irony and parody (Besson 2001: 141). On the other hand, if there was something on which Besson and Sanguineti agreed completely, it was their receptiveness to Brecht's approach to using fairy tale and masks, without any intention of 'philological' restoration (Vazzoler 2007 and 2009: 109–50).

The play with Sanguineti's text was staged in Venice in July 2001, at the Teatro Verde dell'Isola di San Giorgio, during the theatre Biennale. In September of that year, almost simultaneously, Prokofiev's *Love of Three Oranges* was performed at the Malibran Theatre, as part of the programme of Teatro La Fenice. It was also directed by Besson (for both productions the sets were designed by Enzo Toffolutti), thus constituting, with Sanguineti's play, a sort 'diptych' (Winter 2007: 255–9), with a rich set of images (Capitta 2001: 89–93). The performance inevitably referred back – through Prokofiev's libretto and music to the Russian productions of Gozzi's works at the beginning of the nineteenth century (staged in Chicago in 1921 and inspired by Meyerhold's adaptation of 1914, in particular by its prologue and metatheatrical inserts). And, at the same time, Besson used Brecht as a 'great bridge'. Hence, if with Sanguineti's text Besson was faced with a contemporary reinterpretation with which he did not feel particularly comfortable, with Prokofiev he was dealing with the historical experience of theatre direction as in the nineteenth century.

Staging Goldoni
Reinhardt, Strehler

Erika Fischer-Lichte

Theatre within theatre . . . the hopping, leaping driving motor of the performance is Hermann Thimig's Truffaldino. The liveliness, the exuberance, the happy, light and hearty humour . . . falls over itself in a hundred somersaults of irrepressible merrymaking. All frolicking and running about that this role requires sees an unprecedented magnification here . . . How many nuances of feeling hungry, of sniffing at meals, of nibbling and licking plates. How it fits into the idea of a parodic staging when Hermann Thimig sits down on a painted chair. And then that fantastic preparation of macaroni, on which he pours sugar and cinnamon, salt and pepper, butter and tomato sauce. And finally that virtuosic show of pushing a thick strand of noodles into his mouth . . . Everything a success. A light, laughing evening.

(Norbert Falk, 3 November 1929, in Rühle 1988: I, 520 E-21)

Finally theatre, true theatre, theatre as we dream of it. No doubt it requires perfect skill on the part of the actors . . . But what is so charming about the performance is not skill but its authenticity, its radiant joy of life. Every gesture, every situation is stylized, polished and complete. And yet we get the impression that it is all happening for the first time, that it was decided on the spur of that moment and that we are the only ones who will ever get to see it. This return to commedia dell'arte is also an entrancing manifestation of the true nature of theatre. Harlequin's return is a triumph.

(Kott 1972: 50–2)

Reading these two reviews one could assume that they refer to one and the same production. One might imagine that while the first provides a concrete example, the second summarises the critic's and probably also the audience's overall impression of the performance. This, however, is not the case. The first is an account of Max Reinhardt's production (1924) of Carlo Goldoni's *The Servant of Two Masters*, while the second refers to Giorgio Strehler's staging of the same play, albeit not to its first (1947) but its third version (1956). This is not to say that the two productions were alike but that they both induced similar experiences – of presentness, sensuousness, revelry, joy of life and a general sense of happiness.

The similarities seem all the more surprising when we consider the differences between the two directors and their times. In the 1920s, Reinhardt (1873–1943) was a famous director celebrated across the globe. Since the beginning of the twentieth century he had striven to realise his idea that 'new life will arise out of the classics on stage: colour and music and greatness and splendour and merriment. The theatre will return to being a festive play which was its original meaning' (cited in Kahane 1928: 118–9). According to him, such a 'festive play' could only happen when the relationship between actors and spectators was redefined: 'Ever since I started to work at the theatre I have been pursued, and ultimately guided by one particular thought: bringing together the actors and spectators as close to one another as is physically possible' (Adler 1964: 43). To achieve this objective, and to put it to the test, Reinhardt set about constructing or renovating more than twenty theatres: tiny and convivial ones; intimate ones, such as the Kammerspiele; theatres for the masses in large-scale venues, such as exhibition and festival halls and arena stages as in a circus. He had plays performed in churches, on market places and out in the woods. After World War I, in 1919, he opened the Große Schauspielhaus in Berlin, built by the architect Hans Pölzig out of the existing Circus Schumann. Here Reinhardt for the first time realised his Theatre of the Five Thousand, a new people's theatre comprising spectators from all social classes and milieus. Reinhardt's most successful productions toured all over Europe and the United States and brought him international fame. In 1920 he resigned from all of his Berlin directorships and began to focus on the Salzburg Festival and on Vienna, where he had the Theater in der Josefstadt completely rebuilt after the model of the opera house La Fenice in Venice. It opened on 1 April 1924 with Reinhardt's production of *The Servant of Two Masters*. The same production marked his return to Berlin when he opened his new theatre, the Komödie, on 1 November 1924. Afterwards the production toured all over Europe. It was also shown at the Felsenreitschule at the Salzburg Festivals in 1926, 1930 and 1931. In 1939 Reinhardt restaged the play with young actors in Los Angeles, making some changes that adapted the production to new circumstances.

In 1947, two years after World War II had come to an end, Giorgio Strehler (1921–1997) founded his first theatre, the Piccolo Teatro in Milano, together with the director and theatre critic Paolo Grassi

(1919–1980). The Piccolo opened with Strehler's production of Maxim Gorky's *The Lower Depths*, followed by *The Servant of Two Masters*, which Strehler would restage several times over the next fifty years: the first production premiered on 24 July 1947, the second on 17 April 1952 at the Teatro Quirino in Rome and the third on 7 August 1956 at the Edinburgh Festival, which is the version to which Kott refers in the epigraph. The next version premiered on 10 July 1963 in the courtyard of the Villa Litta near Milan, followed on 24 June 1973 by one at the Villa Communale in Milan and another, opening on 4 October 1977, at the Théâtre de l'Odéon in Paris; on 14 May 1987 a new production was shown, once more in the Piccolo, followed by another premiere there on 30 October 1990. On the occasion of the 200th anniversary of Goldoni's death (1793) the play was restaged in 1992 at the Teatro Studio in Milan. The last production was staged in the Piccolo on 14 May 1997, a few months before Strehler's death. Of these ten productions, six were quite distinct from each other. The last version, the so-called 'edizione dell'Addio' is the one from 1987, even though Strehler revised it slightly on the occasion of the fiftieth anniversary of the Piccolo Teatro (14 May 1997).

Some of the differences between these six versions are decisive – in particular the Paris version from 1977 deviates from the other five in important ways. Nonetheless, it seems legitimate to regard them as versions instead of as six different productions, as certain artistic principles and some of the actor choices remained consistent throughout. Ferruccio Soleri played the part of Arlecchino from 1960 onwards. Initially, Soleri shared the role with the first Arlecchino actor, Marcello Moretti, who trained him for it. After Moretti passed away in 1962, since the version of 1963, Soleri was the only one to play the part.

Despite the enormous differences between the directors Reinhardt and Strehler as well as between the times in which they each initially staged Goldoni's play, there is a common reference point: the intention to 're-invent' theatre by taking recourse to commedia dell'arte. Since the beginning of the twentieth century, other prominent representatives of the avant-garde movements in different European countries, including Meyerhold, Vakhtangov, Tairov or Copeau, had also referred to commedia dell'arte in addition to theatre forms from the Far East, puppetry and fair booth spectacles of popular culture. They did so in order to 'restore' to theatre its 'original' sensuousness and physicality, and to turn it 'back' into a festival and a people's theatre that would unite actors and spectators in a community. However, while the popular traditions of their own respective regions were partly still alive, and Chinese and Japanese theatre forms could be witnessed on the occasion of guest tours – such as Kawakami Otojiro and his wife Sadda Yacco's visit at the beginning of the twentieth century – commedia dell'arte existed only as myth. Its tradition was lost and an immediate access therefore rendered impossible. All attempts to reconstruct it – e.g. through experiments with a particular set of stock characters, improvisation or special forms of body usage – thus cannot be seen as a return or revival but as a reinvention. In order to create or 'invent' a new theatre, they claimed to draw inspiration from the dead tradition of commedia dell'arte.

Such attempts were well known to Strehler. He was familiar with Copeau's work – whom he repeatedly invoked as his 'indirect master' – as well as with Reinhardt's. He had heard about Reinhardt's *The Servant of Two Masters* through 'a couple of reports, some stage photos and especially by speaking to actors, critics and others who had seen the performance in Vienna or elsewhere in Europe'. These materials inspired him while preparing his own production:

> I remember, for example, that someone told me about Harlequin's eating scene with Hermann Thimig, that scene in which Truffaldino eats the spaghetti. I don't know if the description was accurate in terms of the scene sequence but this 'theatrical fact' in its critical core corresponded with my own, as yet uncertain, undefined and almost frightening notion of Harlequin's hunger. Hunger as the foundation for the comic effect of a mask, its desperation, its hyperbolic and forever returning hunger, making it the force behind a human condition . . . This basic conception of my Harlequin still has its validity today and was a *direct* result of Reinhardt's poetic-critical intention. (Strehler 1977: 102)

Both Reinhardt and Strehler staged Goldoni's play in order to reflect on the constitutive elements and features of theatre – the relationship between actors and spectators, and the relationship between the actor and the role. Both made use of the principle of 'theatre within theatre', although Strehler did not introduce it before the version shown in Edinburgh (1956).

In Reinhardt's production, the emphasis is on the intertwining of both relationships – the fourth wall seemingly ceased to exist. This impression was brought about by the spatial arrangements (stage design: Oskar Laske and Karl Witzmann), the prologue or prelude (written by Hugo von Hofmannsthal), the changes in the set on the open stage and the songs directly addressing the audience (musical arrangements by Bernhard Paumgartner). The front section of the stage extended into the auditorium, bringing actors and spectators close to each other and allowing them to share one space. This impression was reinforced by the set of the first scene that seemed to extend the Venetian baroque auditorium onto the stage. The spectators could imagine being seated amidst the set. When after the sound of a gong the curtain rose too soon, it was clear that this was deliberate. There was still commotion on stage: 'Stagehands, Canaletto – dressed in Venetian style, carry around a great number of painted backdrops that smack of parody . . ., costumed actors show signs of anxiety, directors and inspectors clad in black with scripts in their hands walk around self-importantly – theatre within theatre' (Falk in Rühle 1988: 520). While all hurry to leave the stage Truffaldino remains, eager to address the audience. The others try to pull him away, each side arguing either for or against the need for such a welcome. One argument for it, articulated by a woman dressed as a man, centres on the relationship between actors and spectators:

> It is a folly to miss an opportunity to say something endearing to the audience, on whose goodwill we depend. Because there simply is that certain fluidity that we require, and if it fails to come about we are neither pretty nor appealing nor talented. But one must tell the audience that something will develop between it and us that can only be good if both parts become involved with each other; that every love affair starts looking sad when one party only takes and is unwilling to give. (Hofmannsthal 2006: 317)

When, finally, all agree that Truffaldino may address the audience, he doesn't know what to add: 'I have nothing to say to you. In their enthusiasm they [pointing at the others] have already beaten me to the punch. What you can take away from it is that we're all aspiring to win your goodwill – and to be deserving of it' (ibidem: 322).

Whatever changes were made to the set during the entire performance happened on the open stage itself. They were done by costumed stagehands and by the actors who were in costume but not in character, accompanied by music – mainly Mozart's, Haydn's and Richard Strauss' – played by the invisible orchestra on the balcony. The set changes can thus be described as pantomimes accompanied by music.

The music, the light, the colours of the different sets as well as of the costumes and the dynamic movements all contributed to a particular atmosphere emerging in the space. Spectators are never distinct from atmospheres, which spread out evenly throughout a space. Rather, they are immersed in it. Reinhardt was a master at creating atmospheres. When talking about Reinhardt's productions, the reviews usually mention the special atmosphere(s) of particular scenes or moments. Regarding *The*

Servant of Two Masters the most frequently mentioned atmosphere is that of festivity, merriment, joyfulness – 'joy of life' and 'happiness' are the terms that come up again and again in descriptions. The music as well as the movements with their special rhythms moreover directly affected the spectators' bodies, allowing them to lose themselves in each particular rhythm. In fact, the performance came into being out of the encounter between actors and spectators (Fischer-Lichte 2008), it exposed this special relationship and made the spectators perceive and enjoy it.

This special relationship is not to be understood independently of the relationship between actor or actress and their role or character. In fact, the dances, the pantomimes, the singing of arias and duets and, most of all, the lazzi directed the attention of the spectators toward the actors' art and craft. In particular, Hermann Thimig delighted the spectators with an abundance of such lazzi, as described in the review quoted in the epigraph. However, he was not the only reviewer. Another critic describes the scene between Pantalone and Dottore:

> The verbose Dottore (Gustav Waldau) tirelessly talks at the quiet, defenseless Pantalone (Hugo Thimy), making the latter topple over from the uninhibited assault of words, Dottore finally even leaning on the old man's legs pointing at the sky as if they were a lectern for him to continue his chatter. A monumental caricature of loquaciousness and its victim. (Falk in Rühle 1988: 511)

In all these cases, it is the art of acting that attracts the attention of the spectators rather than the qualities of the character that the actors are portraying. These qualities merely provide the point of departure, since at the centre of the performance are the actors and their art along with the special relationship that it establishes between them and the spectators.

This corresponds to the new name Reinhardt gave to his renovated Theater in der Josefstadt that was inaugurated with the production of *The Servant of Two Masters*: Die Schauspieler in der Josefstadt unter der Führung von Max Reinhardt (The actors in Josefstadt under the Director-ship of Max Reinhardt). The reflection on theatre through theatrical means and the self-reflection of theatre as performed here clearly aims to distinguish between production/*mise en scène* and performance: While the *staging* can be defined as the process of planning (including chance events and emergent phenomena in rehearsal), testing and determining strategies that aim at bringing forth the performance's materiality – spatiality, corporeality and tonality – as well as at exciting and directing the audience's attention, the *performance* comes into being out of the live encounter between actors and spectators. While the director is of utmost

importance for the process of staging, s/he vanishes in the actual performance, when all the responsibility falls to the actors and the spectators.
Reinhardt's production of *The Servant of Two Masters*, judging from
reviews and other reports, was performed as a reflection on this basic
premise of theatre. Through the staging itself the director foregrounds
the fact that he is not a part of the performance, in which everything
depends on the art of the actors and on the audience's responsiveness. This
encounter in the here and now allows spectators to experience emotions
such as happiness and the joy of life.

When after the end of fascism and World War II Giorgio Strehler began
to develop his first ideas for a production of Goldoni's play, he felt inspired
by what he knew about Reinhardt's staging even as he proceeded from a
rather different principle. While Reinhardt had not used masks for the
traditional 'masks' of the *commedia* – the *zanni* Arlecchino/Truffaldino
and Brighella, Pantalone and Dottore – Strehler employed them from the
very beginning. He understood masks to be constitutive of theatre, as
pointing back to its 'origin' and 'secret'. In his piece 'For Marcello
Moretti', written in 1962 as an obituary for his first Arlecchino actor, he
called the mask a 'mysterious, cruel instrument' which had always stirred a
'feeling of terror' in him:

> With the mask we arrive at the threshold of theatre's secret, the demons
> awaken once again, the unmoving, unchangeable faces that belong to the
> origin of the theatre. For example, it very quickly becomes evident that on
> stage the actor cannot touch the mask with a habitual gesture of his hands.
> (Hand to the forehead, finger over the eyes, covering the face with your
> hands, etc.) Such gestures then become absurd, inhuman, false. To find
> their means of expression again, the actor must learn to 'sketch' the gesture
> with his hands rather than doing it realistically. So the mask cannot
> support the concreteness of a real gesture. Masks are ritualistic. (Strehler
> 1977: 121)

Strehler raises two important points here. First, the mask defies any kind of
realistic psychological acting and, second, being ritualistic, it is endowed
with a transformative power that has a physical effect on the spectator
('feeling of terror'). Masks therefore presuppose and demand a particular
attitude from the actor and the spectator. In his first production of *The
Servant of Two Masters*, the actors playing the four masked roles used
'shoddy masks of cardboard and gauze that was pasted over it. We made
them new with our own hands every day. They were devilish masks,
uncomfortable, painful' (ibid. 120). Although the actors had considerable
difficulties in trying to 'befriend' these masks, they succeeded in developing

a 'marionette-like manner of movement' (Douël Dell'Agnola 1992: 38). For the second version Amleto Sartori, who 'out of the blue renewed the lost tradition of sixteenth to eighteenth century mask-making' (Strehler 1977: 122), manufactured 'half-masks', which were supposed to 'fit like a glove' (Sartori, in Strehler 1977: 122). They enabled the actors to discover the expressive means of the mask as they emerged, for instance, from the emphasis on the mouth and to invent completely new forms of movement. In this sense, the mask recreated the actor's body and demanded a new art of acting in which the particular corporeality and presence of the body outweighed its possible meanings.

Besides the masks, the introduction of the 'theatre within theatre' concept in the third version also drew the spectator's attention to the actors' art. The third version presented actors from a *commedia* company who performed on a piazza on the occasion of a festival. This idea remained constitutive up to the final version. It diverted the spectator's attention and interest from the dramatic characters and the plot even more than the first two versions and redirected them to the actors' work and their profession. However, it was not just the spectators who focussed on the acting: Actors who weren't performing could often be seen on stage observing their colleagues.

In the version I attended, which was more or less that of 1987, the wooden stage was lit by candles placed at the front. It was empty except for a white backdrop and white wings at both sides. Those actors and musicians who were not active on stage from time to time took a seat on the trunks containing the props and placed between the wings, or remained standing in order to watch the performance of their colleagues, on which they occasionally commented with a professional eye.

The 'theatre within theatre' concept was mainly used to mark transitions: the transition from the status of a visitor to that of a spectator and vice versa, or that of the actor to the dramatic character and vice versa. This concept makes it possible to repeatedly and expressly deal with spectatorship as a theme, whereby the spectator is confronted with the fundamental conditions and modes of watching. The performance opened as a kind of rite of passage that transformed the visitor into a spectator and was repeated after both intermissions. A white-haired man, bent with age, wearing spectacles, his dress resembling that of ordinary people from the eighteenth century, enters the auditorium from the left – he is the 'prompter' of the company. Mumbling incessantly and throwing remarks at the visitors, he shuffles to the stage and lights the candles. A warm, bright light spreads – the light which will eventually illuminate the set.

Initially, however, it only throws light on the white curtain that hides the stage from the eyes of the assembled, thus marking the curtain as a boundary and as an obstacle to their unimpeded view. The prompter, still mumbling, mounts the stage and raises the curtain: The light of the candles falls on the whole stage; the scene becomes visible; the visitors are transformed into spectators.

Throughout the performance spectators are time and again confronted with other spectators on stage. Actors who exit remain between the wings, push their masks back over their hair like sunglasses and watch. In the auditorium the spectators' interest is split. They can watch the actors in the scene or the ones in the wings watching their colleagues. They become witnesses to a very special mode of spectating, which may differ from their default one. Clearly, spectating here does not aim to attribute meanings to the perceived gestures, movements, words or sounds in order to constitute a story or a character. Rather, it is directed at the ways in which these physical manifestations are brought forth – at the specific rhythms with which the actors talk, sing or move; at the precision of their performance; at the volume and modulation of the voice; at the interaction, tempo, presence and dynamics – at what we would today call the performative qualities of acting.

The spectators on stage are critical but by no means cold. Rather, they are completely engaged in what they are perceiving. Spectatorship, it seems, requires a certain distance. Whether we watch from the auditorium or from the wings does not make much of a difference. What matters is that the spectators keep a certain distance which enables them to perceive *how* the actors perform on stage and to simultaneously become completely absorbed by *what* they are perceiving. This 'art' of spectatorship unites critique and enjoyment, i.e. two at first glance contradictory faculties, to acknowledge and appreciate the 'purity of gesture', the 'effortlessness of apparent improvisation', that is the actors' professionalism, and, at the same time, to let oneself be infected by their 'radiant joy of life', their 'drive to perform', their energy. This is the art of watching that the spectator can acquire during the performance, transforming him or her into a kind of 'ideal' spectator.

The transition from actor to character is also marked by a ritual of sorts. The players of Pantalone and Brighella, for instance, masks still pushed back over their hair, enter from the wings and move to the front of the stage, accompanied by trumpets and fanfare. The moment the musicians raise their instruments to their lips and play a short melody resembling a *leitmotif*, the actors very slowly and to the rhythm of the music pull their masks down over their faces – the transformation into the character is thus complete. In this context no need for special preparations or particular psychic dispositions arises. The transformation is brought about by the act of covering the face with the mask.

Accordingly, the reverse transformation happens through the movement of the actor's hand that pushes the mask back over his forehead and hair. The mask is transformative – pulling it on means undergoing a transformation.

At the end of the performance, when the spectators were already cheering and applauding, the players of the masked figures removed their masks. They did not simply push them back but took them off along with their wigs and held them in their hands. Now they were no longer actors playing roles and/or watching their colleagues at work but just themselves, the actors Ferruccio Soleri, Gianfranco Mauri, Giorgio Bongiovanni and Paolo Calabresi. They had played the role of actors who had taken the parts of Arlecchino, Brighella, Pantalone and Dottore in a performance of *The Servant of Two Masters* and had watched their colleagues at work whenever they were not part of a scene. At the end, the role-playing actor and the spectating actor were both revealed as dramatic figures brought together and related to each other in the person of Mauri or Bongiovanni.

As a matter of fact, it was possible in Strehler's as well as in Reinhardt's production not only to enjoy the lazzi, the art of the actors, i.e. their presence, the atmosphere, etc., but also to attribute meaning to it all. One might, for instance, interpret Arlecchino's/Truffaldino's movements and gestures as signs of his permanent and excessive hunger, which turns him into a carnivalesque figure. It is also conceivable to understand them as a social *gestus*, taking hunger as a marker for belonging to the lower classes: One might even construct a kind of opposition between Arlecchino/Truffaldino and Brighella on the one hand and Pantalone and Dottore on the other. While the first two frequently perform gestures on or with props that fulfill a certain purpose, the latter two mostly perform self-referential gestures, staging themselves for each other without any concrete results. Thus, the gestures could be interpreted with regard to the social status of the dramatic figures: The members of the lower classes work and produce, while the members of the bourgeoisie are focussed on their self-staging.

In Strehler's production, the lovers Clarice and Silvio as well as Beatrice and Florindo could in this sense be seen as representatives of courtly life. In the scenes of jealousy and love, Silvio and Clarice expressed their feelings through the operatic duet form. They stood at a certain distance and sang to each other or remained in an embrace. In both cases they displayed gestures characteristic of the traditional operatic code. Relating the lovers to the opera can be interpreted as a qualifier of their feelings and, at the same time, as a marker of their social status. Their feelings are so extraordinary that they are conceivable only in the artificial world of opera. Thus, the lovers' feelings are opposed to those of Arlecchino and Smeraldina. Since the lovers do not have to work in order to sustain themselves, they can be completely occupied by their feelings. Against this background, Strehler's production appears as a form of critical popular theatre.

Such interpretations are no doubt valid – and they are usually put forward belatedly, i.e. after the performance has ended. In their belatedness, they have nothing in common with the 'radiant joy of life', the incredible happiness felt by many spectators during the performance. Later interpretations remain incommensurable with these immediate experiences from which they proceed.

These are the experiences on which Reinhardt's as well as Strehler's productions focussed in their reflections on the basic conditions of theatre. Taking recourse to the myth of the commedia dell'arte here made perfect sense. For this myth relates to a physical, spontaneous theatre in which the performance emerged out of the improvisations of the actors in response to the behaviour of the spectators. Since it was used not to reconstruct or even to revive the commedia dell'arte but in order to reflect on the relationship between actor and role or character as well as on that between actors and spectators, it does not matter that this myth is exposed as such through the ongoing research on the *commedia*. Rather, the reference to the well-known myth allowed them to redefine theatre as a genuinely performative rather than a textual art. It was not the commedia dell'arte but merely its myth that came to life through these new forms of theatre created by Reinhardt and Strehler in a process that brought about a joy of life and happiness in the spectators.

23

Eduardo De Filippo and the Mask of Pulcinella

Teresa Megale

Eduardo De Filippo was almost seventy-three years old when he decided to put on the mask of Pulcinella once again. At least subconsciously, he wanted to save for posterity all he knew about this traditional stock character. The result was an extraordinary TV documentary called 'Pulcinella: Yesterday and Today' (1973). Directed by Paolo Heusch, the documentary was actually made in connection with *Saturday, Sunday, Monday*, directed by Franco Zeffirelli (31 October 1973, Old Vic Theatre in London). The purpose of the documentary was to explain and illustrate the character of Pulcinella in all its variations to the cast of English actors, which included Laurence Olivier, Joan Plowright and Frank Finlay. Through the medium of film, De Filippo was able to impart to these actors the 'secret' of Pulcinella's character, which lies at the heart of the theatrical culture of Naples and which is such an important part of the commedia dell'arte itself.

Towards the end of his life, De Filippo was, in this way, able to pass on the mask of Pulcinella to posterity. In doing so, he also unveiled the mystery of how to wear it, revealed the jargon used by the *comici* and showed how they expressed basic feelings. These were acted out in pairs, usually opposites: laughter and tears, heat and cold, love and hate, boldness and modesty, doubt and certainty. His performance in the film and his use of the black leather half mask of Pulcinella soon came to be regarded as legendary and was to make a vivid and lasting impression on generations to come. He also immortalised the *coppolone*, the squat, rounded, floppy conical hat, nicknamed the sugar-loaf hat, which reminded people of the 'tiny cap of dough' that Carlo Collodi placed on the head of Pinocchio, his recently invented marionette, which was shortly to become world renowned. In the course of the film, De Filippo switches in a matter of seconds from one emotional state to another, his gestures changing almost imperceptibly. The state the actor has in mind for the character at a particular instant is always perfectly clear and always played masterfully.

As De Filippo explains, Pulcinella is a responsive stock character, who feels intuitively what the actor wishes to communicate, absorbs it and transmits it to the audience. When the actor gives it the task of expressing a particular feeling, the mask, covering three quarters of the face, comes to life and takes on the flexibility necessary to perform its task. However, it is a fixed mask like any other and only the actor can bring it to life, bringing into play his art, his physical and emotional experience and his mimetic skill. Of special importance is the movement of his mouth which must correspond to that of the mask. Thus, the wrinkles on Eduardo's face – reflecting a richly expressive theatrical technique and a total mastery of mimetic and vocal skills – seem to become synchronised both physiognomically and artistically with the mask. With a few, carefully measured facial expressions, De Filippo transcends the boundaries of the possible and miraculously transmits the visible traces of an art of theatre which has not been lost, but has been kept alive and will be kept alive by future generations of actors.

Eduardo's portrayal of the character of Pulcinella in this film was not his first but was certainly his most distinguished. In the post-war period, the character had been reduced, in Salvatore Di Giacomo's words, to that of the *pazzariello* (fool) or to the marionette-like caricature immortalised by Totò in *L'oro di Napoli* (The Gold of Naples). De Filippo's efforts to revive Pulcinella inevitably tell us something about himself but were also aimed at renewing a tradition of acting practice which had become marginal and a theatrical world which, from its once dominant position, had receded into a niche characterised by a provincial, picturesque folkloric tradition. In his youth, he spent a lot of time working on Pulcinella, developing texts and scenarios for journals, producing translations and adaptations and performing in traditional theatres. These efforts culminated in 1954 in the inauguration of his Teatro San Ferdinando with a production of Antonio Petito's farce *'Palummella zompa e vola'* (Palummella Leaps and Flies) in the traditional acting style of the Teatro San Carlo (by Antonio Petito, performed by Compagnia Il Teatro di Eduardo with Titina De Filippo). De Filippo played the role of Pulcinella and produced the play in collaboration with Vittorio Viviani. In this farce, he sought reassuring refuge in the nineteenth-century theatrical tradition at a time when he was experiencing a crisis caused by the hostile reception of *La grande magia* (The Great Magic) in 1949 and trying to conceal a bout of writer's block (Meldolesi 1987: 57–87).

As a playwright, De Filippo regarded the character of Pulcinella as the hackneyed symbol of what had become a narrow, worn-out Neapolitan theatrical tradition. Like his father, Eduardo Scarpetta, before him, he intended to rid the theatre of improper figures, simplistic characterisations and the abuse of ideological tools. His purpose was to revive the tradition by strengthening its identity, attributing to it a new national force and placing it at the centre of the twentieth-century rediscovery of the commedia dell'arte. In Italy, this revival reached its spectacular climax in 1947 with Giorgio Strehler's splendid direction of Goldoni's *The Servant of Two Masters*. It was also fostered by the success, in 1950, of *Carosello napoletano* (Neapolitan Carousel), a play written and superbly directed by Ettore Giannini and featuring the dancer and choreographer Léonide Massine in the role of Antonio 'Pulcinella' Petito. As an actor, De Filippo, however, believed that the revival of Pulcinella did not indicate a mere return to a stereotyped Neapolitan theatrical culture. On the contrary, it was a sign of a correct re-evaluation of the theatrical and cultural system of Naples and, more generally, of southern Italy, as well as of a reconsideration of its symbolic value within the general revival of the *commedia dell'arte*. De Filippo was soon aware that Pulcinella played a crucial role not only in the renewal of Italian theatrical culture but also in the development of the emerging field of theatre studies, which predictably focused on the commedia dell'arte as its main object of attention and analysis.

In De Filippo's view, the revival of traditional theatre depended on the stock character. When he was in his fifties, after performing in the most important plays produced in the immediate aftermath of World War II, De Filippo turned his attention to nineteenth-century farce, the most important genre of the acting culture to which he felt he belonged. In this genre, he sought a solution to the crisis that tormented him and, perhaps unconsciously, a malicious way to surpass his brother Peppino in the theatrical genre in which he had always excelled. In the ten years from the beginning of the 1953–1954 season to the end of the 1961–1962 season, the stock character absorbed his attention, marked his return to Naples and was adopted as a symbol for his ambitious project of reconstructing and reopening the destroyed Teatro San Ferdinando. By offering Naples a modern theatre, De Filippo intended to restore the centrality of the art of theatre and have it act as a catalyst for the cultural revival of the city. The late eighteenth-century Teatro San Ferdinando, which had hosted performances of an older form of popular theatre embodied by Federico Stella, had been destroyed by American bombs during the war. Pulcinella became a symbol for its restoration: A mask was displayed in a prominent position in the elegant foyer and *Palummella zompa e vola* was chosen as the play to be performed on the evening on which the theatre was re-inaugurated. On the path to success, De Filippo was helped – in different yet complementary ways – by the international success of *Carosello napoletano* as well as by the centenary of the birth of his father, Scarpetta, whose *Miseria e nobiltà* De Filippo performed in October 1953 at the Teatro Eliseo in Rome. With Pulcinella's black half-mask as emblem, De Filippo's inaugural theatre program consisted of a repertoire of selected classic Neapolitan plays which clearly indicated his present artistic direction, which he had never really abandoned and to which he was now returning. It also indicated the importance of improvisation in his view of theatre, thus decidedly contributing to the re-evaluation of the commedia dell'arte in Italy. By reviving the stock character and faithfully restoring his infinite mimetic and expressive possibilities, De Filippo outlined a cultural strategy which could accelerate the establishment of a future national theatre – an idea which he entertained throughout his mature years but which never came to fruition.

On 22 January 1954, on the stage of the renovated Teatro San Ferdinando, the curtain rose for a performance of the farce *Palummella zompa e vola*, with a script by Antonio Petito. De Filippo's adaptation of Petito's comedies for Vincenzo Scarpetta's troupe in 1925 – the year that Scarpetta died – marked the beginning of De Filippo's career as a playwright.

Before the inauguration of the Teatro San Ferdinando, Eduardo received the mask of Pulcinella out of the hands of Salvatore de Muto (1876–1970), the last representative of the company of players of the Teatro San Carlo. De Muto had worn it since 1913, after inheriting it from Giuseppe De Martino, his immediate artistic predecessor. Almost eighty years old, de Muto-Pulcinella placed the black leather half-mask on the lean, gaunt and wrinkled face of the mature De Filippo with a solemnity reminiscent of an ancient ceremony of investiture. The mask had changed hands innumerable times since the era of the legendary, seventeenth-century actors. On Easter Sunday 1852, some hundred years before this latest hand-over, in a ceremony strong on symbols suggesting an initiatory rite, the mask is believed to have been handed over by Salvatore Petito to his son Antonio. As he was the writer of the farce which was performed on the inaugural night in the Teatro San Ferdinando and an acknowledged legend, he was regarded as spiritually present on stage that night. It was a true rite of passage: De Filippo was the performer chosen as the only one worthy of wearing the mask after the voluntary 'death' on stage of the previous holder. Thus the 'new' Pulcinella was born. It marked the start of De Filippo's total dedication to the Neapolitan comic theatrical tradition, of which the mask

was unmistakably the emblem, and proclaimed him heir to the artistic
tradition of the Teatro San Carlo, thus solving problems of legitimacy that
had long dogged him before (as expressed by Filumena's tears). As an
authentic man of the theatre, De Filippo was able to renew many familiar
aspects of the cultural legacy of Naples. He was also able to associate himself
with the development of new artistic and cultural contexts, in order to
reduce the dominance of tradition and give the city a new, fresh presence
within twentieth-century Italian theatrical culture. De Filippo questioned
tradition while developing it within his personal style as a playwright. He
followed Petito's text closely by performing Pulcinella in a sober, not
ungraceful way. It was the actor who modernised the text by condensing
its long stage history – not the reverse.

De Filippo's performance as Pulcinella at the premiere of Petito's farce
La Palummella on the occasion of the reopening of the Teatro San
Ferdinando received mixed and varied reviews. However, De Filippo was
able to overcome the prevailing prejudice associated with the character of
Pulcinella by soberly toning him down. Pulcinella stood for unrestrained
grossness and was seen by many as a symbol for Naples, a city of irredeemable *lazzaroni* (common people). The play was performed in the autumn
of the same year at the Eliseo in Rome with a totally different cast to that of
the premiere (Roma, Teatro Eliseo, 3 November 1954). Here, De Filippo
was again able to express his personal view of the stock character –
expressing his view had become both a desire and a need for him. The
character possessed an irresistible identity with considerable personal and
theatrical power, symbolising positive cultural and political values and
capable of influencing society in general. It is worth remembering that
shortly afterwards the company La Scarpettiana was formed, performing
from 1955 to 1960. Its aim was to revive the masterpieces of nineteenth-
century Neapolitan theatre (and the works of De Filippo's father) in the
restored Teatro San Fernando and stand for a different set of values than
the demagogic politics and economic exploitation pursued by the Naples-
based shipowner, Achille Lauro. At the end of the year De Filippo
demonstrated his developing interest in other forms of media, performing
Palummella for a radio programme called *Occhio magico*, which was
broadcasted every Friday night on the second national channel. With
other actors of his company, he recreated the 'immortal stock character
of Pulcinella' in Antonio Petito's comedy as a dancer. The critics said, he
did it 'soberly and effectively' (Raffaelli 1954: 16).

From 1954 onwards, dressed in Pulcinella's white garments, De Filippo
appeared both before live Italian audiences and to radio listeners. To the

critics he was no longer just the most prominent dramatic protagonist in his own plays, but also an actor in the great tradition of the commedia dell'arte. Pulcinella allowed him to go beyond dramatic writing and 'Pirandellism', finding a stable place in the cultural and expressive artistic context in which he had trained. It was almost as if Pulcinella had become his alter ego. Through the stock character, De Filippo drew on his prodigious mnemotechnical experience and on his extraordinary wealth of theatrical knowledge, thus preserving and immortalising the original seed of the tradition of Pulcinella – which otherwise would have been lost.

Following in the footsteps of Petrolini, Viviani and De Muto, De Filippo endeavored to assign new meanings to the ancient character of Pulcinella. In 1958 he adapted a classic from the nineteenth-century repertoire, Pasquale Altavilla's *Pulecenella che va' truvanno a fortuna soja pe' Napule* (Pulcinella seeks his fortune in Naples). It was staged on 2 October 1958 at the Piccolo Teatro in Milan and, on 13 November 1958, the opening performance in Naples was the start of the fourth season of the Scarpettiana company and featured Achille Millo in the role of Pulcinella. An elegant actor with flawless diction, Millo had worked almost exclusively in Italian, except for a brief radio performance in the Neapolitan dialect. In order to play this role, he studied to improve his Neapolitan and was assisted in this task by the singer and actress Marina Pagano, his partner in life and art. She was born and grew up in the poor neighbourhood of Sanità and could provide him with samples of authentic Neapolitan. During his tenure as director, the company became so successful that it was nominated to represent Italy at the International Festival of Nations in Paris, which took place on the first three days of June 1960 at the Théâtre Sarah Bernhardt. De Filippo also played the role of Jacobin Pulcinella in the film *Ferdinando I, re di Napoli* which was directed by Gianni Franciolini in 1958 and in which the stock character embodied the stereotype of the irreverent, mocking attitude towards authority.

In the four years between 1958 and 1962, De Filippo concentrated on writing *Il figlio di Pulcinella. Racconto moderno di una favola antica* (Pulcinella's Son: The Modern Tale of an Ancient Fable). This was particularly demanding for him, as it told the sad story of the end of the mask tradition, reflecting on the negative way in which the city was developing. In the story, Old Pulcinella tears the mask off the face of his son, who was born under a cabbage, like the original character in a fairy tale by Giovan Battista Basile, and was supposed to carry on the tradition from his father. Pulcinella's son has suddenly returned from America to a post-war world, inhabited by ruthless, unscrupulous politicians, torn by glaring inequalities and barely held together by a thin veil of fake democracy. This world has no longer any need for Pulcinella. He is merely its servile reflection and De Filippo sees no alternative to bitterly declaring his death on the stage.

Il figlio di Pulcinella, a play consisting of three acts on which De Filippo worked over a long period of time, was included in the collection *Cantata dei giorni dispari* (Cantata of the Odd-Numbered Days). It was written in 1958 but first performed on stage (in two parts and eighteen scenes) on 20 October 1962 by the company Il Teatro di Eduardo at the Teatro Quirino in Rome. It inspired numerous critical reviews and much polemical controversy. The underlying issue of the play is the conflict between generations and between social classes. At the end of act 3, John, Pulcinella's hitherto unknown son arrives from America, in the same way as cigarettes and rock music arrived from America after the war. By taking off his mask, Pulcinella symbolises the desire to change society and to rebel against a life of degradation and falsehood. Strangely enough, De Filippo left this comedy in a drawer for four years, putting it on stage only after a long period of hesitation. It premiered during the 1962–1963 season but was never performed again by De Filippo. However, he granted performing rights to others. Since *Il figlio di Pulcinella* marked the beginning of Luca De Filippo's theatrical career – this was his initiation as a stage actor in a leading role, after minor parts in *Miseria e nobiltà* (1955) and *Tre cazune fortunati* (Three Lucky Pairs of Trousers) (1959) – it is not inconceivable that the elder De Filippo consciously chose this work as a means of passing on his artistic legacy to his son, following the tradition of the *comici* transmitting their art from fathers to sons. It is not difficult to deduce that the comedy was written by De Filippo specifically for his son Luca and that Pulcinella is faced with the issue of paternity and of continuity – the secret of the mask on the one hand and trust in the future on the other. The comedy is imbued with the spirit of De Filippo's personal life in an effort to combine fantasy with reality. He uses dramatic citations ('the voice from inside' of the Lizard Woman, old Pulcinella leaning on the balcony of the baronial palace, like Pasquale Lojacono in *Questi fantasmi!*) and clear references to topical issues (the election campaign in which the old servant Pulcinella is involved). The philosophical framework of the play focuses on the possible role of the eternal stock character of Pulcinella in the new industrial world: The father's legacy is renounced and the stock character can live only by renewing himself, doing without the mask and concealing his true identity. Among the fiercest detractors of the comedy when it first appeared were Giorgio Prosperi, Renzo Tian, Nicola Chiaromonte and Bruno Schacherl. In contrast, Vito Pandolfi and Eligio Possenti were among its main advocates – however, they were isolated voices. The detractors described the play as 'a combination of Neapolitan theatre and historical symbolism along the Verhaeren-Mayakovsky line'; the advocates regarded it as an 'interesting and brilliant' work, a 'realistic fable' which could be compared with the creative work of De Sica and Zavattini or even of Chaplin.

While writing *Il figlio di Pulcinella*, De Filippo expressed his feelings of nostalgia for the original Pulcinella through the dining table ritual in *Sabato, domenica e lunedì* (1959) and by reference to the amateur performances of Raffele Priore, Rosa's brother-in-law, a bank clerk and a scrupulous guardian of tradition – starting from his costume, which must include 'the red woolen sweater, socks, the overalls'. This sense of nostalgia also emerges in De Filippo's production of his father Scarpetta's *Lu curaggio de nu pumpiero napulitano* (The Courage of a Neapolitan Fireman) (1974), in which Pulcinella was played by Tommaso Bianco. Furthermore, De Filippo incorporated elements of Pulcinella in his transposition of Shakespeare's *The Tempest* into an imaginary seventeenth-century Naples. This is especially evident in the character of Trinculo, his last effort, which he developed at Giulio Einaudi's request in 1983 (Megale 2009: 177–94). In the autumn of 1982, De Filippo took part in an experiment in collective writing – which eventually failed – based on the scenario *Le novantanove disgrazie di Pulcinella* (The Ninety-Nine Misfortunes of Pulcinella) with the students of the Sapienza University of Rome.

Il paese di Pulcinella (The City of Pulcinella) was the title of De Filippo's first collection of poems. It was dedicated to Pulcinella and published by Casella di Napoli in 1951. The collection contains the poem *O' paese e' Pulecenella*, written in 1949 and imbued with an implicit theatrical spirit. Significantly, the poem appeared in all subsequent collections. It was based on the idea that poetry has a special place in the creation of drama, a privileged place where the theatrical imagination can soar.

Eluding his father Scarpetta's approach to Pulcinella, and thus severing artistic ties with his family, De Filippo followed in Petiti's footsteps in his attempt to recover the original Pulcinella – a path also pursued by Petrolini, Leonide Massine and Ettore Giannini as well as by Igor Stravinsky in his 1920 ballet *Pulcinella*. De Filippo's courageous choices resulted in a contagious modern revival of the stock character. As further confirmation of the fact that theatre is an extraordinary machine producing transformations, reinventions and rewritings rather than just preserving original creations, De Filippo was not 'the last heir' to Pulcinella, although the term was used by the press and appeared on playbills. Thanks to De Filippo, master of essentiality and rigour, Pulcinella finally gained a central position in Italian culture and was performed by some of his followers – most eminently Carlo Cecchi, who wanted Marina Confalone in the role of Pulcinella for the production of Scarpetta's *Lu curaggio de nu pumpiere napulitano* in 1985. Confalone's performance was an unparalleled example of her exceptional, rare and multifaceted acting talent. Even cartoons were involved in the revival of the Pulcinella promoted by De Filippo. In 1973, the year in which the TV documentary was produced, Emanuele Luzzati and Giulio Gianini, extraordinary production designers and film directors, were nominated for an Academy Award for their animation film *Pulcinella*.

As regards music, in the early 1970s the Nuova Compagnia di Canto Popolare revived *Serenata di Pulcinella*, to the music of Domenico Cimarosa and sung by Peppe Barra, which remained in the repertoire of the group under Roberto De Simone. The Nuova Compagnia di Canto Popolare also staged *La fucilazione di Pulcinella* (The Shooting of Pulcinella); it was directed by Gennaro Magliulo and broadcasted on 7 August 1973 on RAI 2. The group's work on Pulcinella continued in numerous plays created by De Simone, who concentrated on retrieving the anthropological roots and the popular features of the stock character, for example, in *La Lucilla costante* (1982) and *Le 99 disgrazie di Pulcinella* (1994). A remarkable instance of the revival of Pulcinella can be found in the theatrical works of Lamberto Lambertini. In his *Signori, io sono il comico* (Gentlemen, I'm the comedian) in 1987, Lambertini directed Concetta and Peppe Barra in an outstanding scene dealing with feelings of jealousy between Colombina and Pulcinella, who had returned to earth from heaven because he still loved someone.

Among others, Maurizio Scaparro performed a memorable Pulcinella in a highly successful play in 1987, which was directed by Massimo Ranieri, using a text creatively adapted by Manlio Santanelli (see Santanelli 2005) from a film script by Roberto Rossellini and Jean Gruault. The piece was later (in 2008) brought to the screen with a script reworked by many hands (Rafael Azcona and Diego De Silva, besides Scaparro himself) under the overused and misleading title of *L'ultimo Pulcinella* (The Last Pulcinella) (2008). The story of the revival of Pulcinella started by De Filippo also includes the alienated Pulcinella played by Massimo Troisi in *Il viaggio di Capitan Fracassa* in 1990. It was directed by Ettore Scola and is the modern heir to Pulcinella's continuous, if alternative, legacy – its unstoppable and unpredictable cycle of life and death.

24

Dario Fo, Commedia dell'Arte and Political Theatre

Paolo Puppa

The story of the relationship between Dario Fo and the commedia dell'arte is a series of obsessive metaphors and personal myths. In 1987, Fo declared that 'commedia never died. I am still aware of its presence' (Fo 1991: 88). The open staging of his works in the 1950s–1960s incorporated old jokes in the tradition of silent films and variety shows, mixed with elements of circus, *pochade* and late Futurist and Absurdist-Surrealist nonsense, in line with the slapstick comedy style of the old-fashioned Italian actors' theatre. This long-standing tradition fosters his self-projection as a *cacciaballe* (con man) (Vescovo 2010b: 206) straight out of an authentic Bildungsroman. In his works, Fo assimilates jesters from the past and the raconteurs he met on the ferryboats plying their way across Lake Maggiore when he was young, as well as the ancestral relationship of the Rame family to the *scarrozzanti* (itinerant actors) of northern Lombardy. In this reinvention of the past, Fo freely associates the scenario of the commedia dell'arte with Ruzante, who further fuelled his deep aversion to any form of pedantry (Farrell 2000: 81–5).

The starting point of *Manuale minimo dell'attore* (*The Tricks of the Trade*) is the arrogance of those who have their texts reprinted in order to satisfy the supposed pressing requests from their admirers. However, he forgot that his faithful Franca kept all her husband's works – including the printed scripts – in online archives. Thus, he tears philologists to shreds, defining them as 'prejudiced ditherers and commentators ... learned nit-picking super-critics' and 'pompous snotty windbags' (Fo 1997: 248). Fo's aversion to pedantry is also evident in his parodying and debunking of higher genres and of official historiography, since the time of his early radio performances.

The political commitment of his theatre implies, first of all, an opposition to tragedy. Fo relates the comic genre to a perspective which is entirely typical of the Enlightenment, as it sanctions the mocking of all values and even of God himself (Fo 1990: 116–24). As a result, when he tackled different forms of theatre – such as in his treatment of the Moro case in 1978, where he incorporated a chorus and a fool straight out of epic theatre – he did not allow the script to be staged. However, he recycled the topic of the kidnapping of Moro in the farce *Clacson, trombette e pernacchi* (*Trumpets and Raspberries*), first performed in 1981 and based this time on the imaginary kidnapping of Gianni Agnelli (Farrell 2011: 151).

It is the *giullare* (jester) with whom Dario Fo is most fully identified, as was made clear in the statement announcing him as the winner of the Nobel prize in 1997. In an interview in 1970, the actor declared that '*giullari* were the actors of the people and performed a kind of newspaper-theatre against the official culture and established powers – both religious and secular' (Soriani 2007: 353). This role is emphasised and most systematically exemplified in *Mistero buffo* (*Comical Mystery*) which appeared in 1969. The play, however, focuses more on the skill of the *giullare* as raconteur rather than on his ability to sing and dance. Hence the idealised opposition of the medieval *hystrio* to authority – the result of a process of abstraction and simplification in a subversive sense which has never been supported by historical evidence and which can even lead to creative hypotheses on the origin of the word *giullare*. 'The word *giullare* comes from *ciullare*, which means "fucking with," both in the sense of mocking and of making love to' (Soriani 2007: 353). If it was the political content of the past that the scholars removed, it is necessary to uncover what has been censored out by the dominant culture.

The relationship between the *giullare* and Fo was illustrated further by his treatment of the figure of Harlequin ('Fo *is* today's Harlequin (at least after the death of Chaplin)': Cairns 1993: 261). Fo reinterpreted Harlequin by emphasising his at times brutal violence, often resulting in scatological gestures – for example, Tristano Martinelli defecating on stage in the middle of love scenes (Fo 1997: 68). While the actors of the *comédie italienne* exploited various modes – not only the comic, but also the tragic and the pastoral – Fo belongs to the tradition of the *giullare* (according to Martinelli, a 'buffoon almost more than actor'), rather than to the model of the versatile actor developed and practised by the commedia dell'arte (Taviani 1982: 350). From Martinelli, Fo derives solitary splendour more than a relationship with his fellow actors. The portrayal of this stock character is eminently supported by the hunger of the Zanni, depicted in a kind of phantasmagorical bulimia, in Ruzante's recollection, as the act of eating his own body and then feasting on a fly. Compared with Fo's version, Strehler's Harlequin in *The Servant of Two Masters* is characterised by a melancholic elegance of gestures (Zorzi 1990: 220). The aspect of the commedia dell'arte which Fo certainly does not respect is the violent disharmony of contrasts between the pathetic-melodramatic acting of the lovers and the ridiculous style of the *zanni*. Premiered on 18 October 1985 in Venice, the play on Harlequin (Fo 2011) anticipated the topics covered in *Tricks of the Trade* (I am referring to the DVD-script, based on the performance at Teatro Tenda in Rome on 1 December 1985, which is different from other versions). A few scenes from the play are sufficient to show that it is focused on the *capocomico*, although this time he does not deliver a monologue and is supported by eight stock characters, besides Franca Rame. Wearing only make-up, no mask, his costume features leaves recalling the 'savage man, the man of the forest' (Fo 2011). Taking his cue from the genre of history lessons characterising his most recent work, Fo holds forth on the asexual servant lacking appetite, as found in Goldoni. His Harlequin, by contrast, was a picaro, a 'desperate man who tries to survive in the only way he knows – through laughter' (interview in 1985, in Soriani 2007: 362). The first part of the play is an explosion of glorious obscenity, thanks to the phallus-obsessed Harlequin, passing, as usual, from the benevolently professorial mode of raconteur to the vulgar and multi-dialectal modes of the performer (as regards the expressive transformation of body and voice between the didactic prologues and the acts of the performance, see Puppa 2000). Thus, after drinking the magical potion, Harlequin waves his arms to cover his enormous phallus and goes on with his gags portraying the cat, the dog and the baby, until his phallus blows up when the women try to touch the baby. At the same time, he attacks politicians active in the 1980s. The same, simulated orgiastic atmosphere is further emphasised later, in the scene with the lock, based on the relationship between a key and a lock, allusively pointing to the sexual organs. Transgression is, actually, only verbal and quite distant from the model offered by Martinelli. Playing the role of Marcolfa and entrusted with delivering the prologue on the adventures of Isabella, Lorenzo the Magnificent and the courtesan Eleonora, Franca Rame gesticulates wildly while doing her personal parody of a talk show on sex by talking about men's prudery in a light-hearted, provocative tone. In the atmosphere of protest prevailing in 1968, Franca snatched the last issue which was still being discussed, the female question, which she explored in an ironically dialectical way – from *Tutta casa letto chiesa* (*All House, Bed and Church*) of 1977 to *Coppia aperta* (*Open Couple*) of 1983. In her not exceedingly burlesque speeches, Franca Rame played down the 'silly vamp' stereo-types – which had been associated with the roles she played at the start of her career – by tinging them with a sort of affected pathos, as in stories on partisan women or mothers of trade unionists killed by the mafia. Her fluctuating reputation received a boost from the play *Lo stupro* (*The Rape*), which marked the pinnacle of her career and was the only play which she wrote entirely by herself. It appeared in its definitive version in 1975, two years after she had actually been raped. The feeling of emptiness conveyed by the single chair on the stage is echoed by the extreme simplification of the plot as well as by the unusually succinct vocabulary. Franca Rame speaks consciously and exclusively in the present tense, almost as if she were the stepdaughter of Luigi Pirandello's *Six Characters in Search of an Author* who were, like her, condemned to be plunged at any moment into the vortex of a terrible experience.

At the end of the play on Harlequin, the piece *The Donkey and the Lion* contains references to the *Tale of a Tiger and Other Stories* (1979). In *Storia della tigre*, a poor wounded soldier – like a modern Philoctetes carrying out heroic deeds in the Chinese Revolution – is saved by a savage beast, which is then adopted by the population as a symbol of their struggle against bureaucrats and politicians. The soldier is dramatically transformed into the physiological incarnation of the animal by means of mighty roars, gargantuan meals and forced, unnatural, exclamatory grunts. The conclusion of *L'asino e il leone* of 1985, on the other hand, appears dull as the auditorium is gradually emptying.

Besides the primacy of laughter, transmitting political content requires the primacy of contemporaneity. In order to avoid 'dead theatre for dead people' (Fo 1997: 163), Fo gives authors this advice: 'attempt to write scripts that run the risk of upsetting entrenched power. In other words, get yourself thrown into jail every so often!' (Fo 1991: 123). This appears even more pressing in the years in which he used the stage as a court of history, a place of resistance against the dictatorships of the time. A typical example is *Guerra di popolo in Cile* (*The People's War in Chile*), which appeared in 1973 and in which a coup is staged in the auditorium, with fake police asking to see documents and pretending to arrest fake spectators. The grip of real panic dies away only after the deputy police superintendent sings the 'Internationale' into the microphone. The most striking example of this strategy, however, is *Morte accidentale di un anarchico* (*Accidental Death of an Anarchist*), written and produced in 1970 in the aftermath of the tragic events related to the Pinelli-Valpreda case. In other cases, unfortunately, the strategy proved detrimental to the dramaturgy, e.g. *Il diavolo con le zinne* (*The Devil with Boobs*), a play appearing in 1997 and dealing with magistrates and Di Pietro in an imaginary Renaissance setting; or *Marino libero! Marino è innocente* (*Free Marino! Marino is innocent*), a play with an ironically antiphrastic title, produced in 1997 in Pisa, in front of the prison where Adriano Sofri was held. *Morte accidentale di un anarchico*, however, was highly successful all over the world. In England six adaptations of the play appeared in just a few years, starting from the version of 1979 featuring Gavin Richards. He was not completely satisfied with the fool's blazing displays of bravura in the style of Fregoli, nor with the incredible liberties he took – in line with the carnival tradition of an upside-down world – by, for example, singing anarchical chants to the police, or throwing out of the window any commissioner who got in his way. Consequently, Richards transferred the political debate to an Anglophone context, with references to President Carter, Watergate, Anthony Blunt, Pinochet and Allende, so that 'there was a British focus'. The strong comic tone prompted one reviewer to say that 'the Brothers Marx, Karl and Groucho have been working in unison' (Lorch 2000: 151–2). Fo does not seem to appreciate 'solutions that are exclusively comic' (Lorch 2000: 155), because he felt that even with an inexhaustible repertoire of gags, the recent tragedy lying behind them should still be revealed. When the production of the play was resumed the following year, the critics resigned themselves to 'to put up with the politics' of the last part of the play as 'the price of the immense pleasure given by the previous two hours' (Lorch 2000: 153). These reviews, in which Fo is reduced to farce, seem paradoxical, especially if we consider his productions of Moliè-re's plays in 1990 at the Comédie Française, *Le Médecin malgré lui* and *Le Médecin volant*, mirroring a frenetic game which underlines the fairground origin of these scripts.

Dario Fo's career as an artist – now star of the media thanks to the Nobel prize after many years of being ostracised – follows the same ascending path as that of the commedia dell'arte stock characters in the past. They were often only able to achieve popularity through international tours and prestigious commissions from foreign courts and thus emancipate themselves from the image of street players. Another similar risk of losing access to the public was encountered by actors in the 1970s who were asked by activists of the same political orientation to prepare themselves for the struggle ahead. This risk was faced by Fo and Rame at a time of high tension and social conflict in Italy. In the 1963 play *Isabella, tre caravelle e un cacciaballe* (*Isabella, Three Sailing Ships and a Con Man*) – which belongs to the period of the light comedies – Fo hinted that officers carried out raids and other acts of violence to improve their social position. In 1964, in *Settimo: ruba un po' meno* (*Seventh Commandment: Steal a Bit Less No. 2*), he showed the police shooting at workmen but within the reassuring framework of satirical cabaret. In *La Signora è da buttare* (*Throw the Lady Out*) – a play performed in 1967 which marked his exit from commercial theatre – the politicisation is very evident. Punctuated by pop songs and icons of American consumerism, the justification of the assassination of John F. Kennedy is centred on the capitalist puppet, from which the marionettes who keep it alive emerge. Swinging on a trapeze between depths of depression and peaks of erotic rapture, Franca Rame, trained by the Colombaioni family who were involved in the production, seemed to imitate the prototype of Maddalena Marliani, the charming rope dancer for whom Carlo Goldoni created the character of Mirandolina. Harlequin as a jester is soon turned into an activist and a historian, as in the 1968 play *Grande Pantomima con bandiere e pupazzi piccoli e medi* (*Grand Pantomime with Flags and Small and Middle-Sized Puppets*), following the same approach as the Bread and Puppet Theatre. This play offers a documentary overview of Italy in the aftermath of World War II, characterised by the metamorphosis of the fascist monster into the clerical monster. In the course of development from Nuova Scena to La Comune, after the total break with the reformist circles of Arci (Italian Recreational and Cultural Association) and with the Italian communist party PCI, the stage becomes the place where fantasies of triumph are presented, such as the public confession of wrongdoings by those in power, which was already shown in *Accidental Death of an Anarchist*, but is now presented in a more compulsive way (Farrell 2001: 84–92). However, in *Non si paga! Non si paga!* the actor, avoiding the risks related to a one-dimensional character, wears different masks: of the Blunderer (the worker who belongs to the Italian Communist Party [PCI] by tradition), then of Harlequin (the incontinent who comes to enjoy the illegality of thefts) and of Scaramouche (the mask of the struggle: Meldolesi 1978:172).

A good example of the confusing political situation is the conflict between revisionist and revolutionary communism, between traitors of the people and heroes of original Marxism, the treatment of the subject matter oscillates between the irreverent and the celebratory. In the chaotic environment of the 'movement', the spectator alternates between being afraid and wanting to abandon the passive game of theatre and join the ongoing political struggle. The actors seem to be suspended between the urge to get involved in the struggle and the impulse to dramatise their protest. However, the cooperative structure and organisation of the company are not very compatible with Fo's individualistic charisma, as demonstrated by the way the one-man show, *Mistero Buffo* developed. It was originally conceived as a group performance but ended in a sneering

and extremely noisy state of solitude. Meanwhile, the performances generally were focused mainly on dramatising current debates on contemporary
social and economic issues, for instance, the exploitation of workers in
supermarkets in *Non si paga! Non si paga!* (*Can't Pay? Won't Pay!*) in 1974,
or the problem of drugs in *La Marjuana della mamma è la più bella*
(*Mother's Marijuana is the Best*) in 1976. Such performances were really
only a 'pretext' for mobilisation, reduced to agitprop, murals turned into
placards for use at the antimilitarist marches or the demonstrations for the
workers' rights in front of the factories.

On the other side of the Atlantic, theatre professionals offered different
political interpretations of the legend of the commedia dell'arte, turning
the stage into a sort of extension of the revolution. An interesting
example is that of two American troupes, the San Francisco Mime
Troupe and El Teatro Campesino who were active at the same time as
the Living Theatre. The San Francisco Mime Troupe was founded in
1959 by the dancer Ronnie Davis, who had studied abstract mime under
Étienne Decroux in Paris and was imbued with the spirit of West Coast
counterculture encompassing multimedia experimentation, electronic
rock music, pantomime and underground cinema. Since 1961, the
Troupe has focused on a form of on-the-road clownish counterculture,
by deploying exaggerated stock characters derived from the contemporary social context. This type of performance was held on a small stage
with live music and at the end one of the performers passed around a hat
to collect money from the audience. The performance also belonged to
outdoor happenings in public parks where the audience got involved. Its
features are those of a comic vaudeville minstrel show and were performed during the 1965 demonstrations for racial integration; originally,
however, they were part of a nineteenth-century form of entertainment,
performed by white actors who blackened their faces and did not conceal
any of their racial prejudices. This kind of mobile theatre had very scarce
resources at its disposal and seemed to have been born almost as a
response to Grotowski's concept of theatre. It was defined by Davis as
'guerrilla theatre' in 1966, in the *Tulane Drama Review*. The troupe got
involved in conflicts with the Black Panther Party, the most radical wing
of the Black liberation movement, and were influenced by the crisis of
American left-wing parties and the emergence of new theories on performance, but the core of the troupe remained together and evolved into
a multiracial outdoor cabaret, which is what they are today. Furthermore,
they were the first American troupe to stage Dario Fo's *Can't Pay? Won't
Pay!* in 1979.

El Teatro Campesino was originally composed of farm workers rather than professional actors. Founded in 1965 by Luis Valdez (a Chicano born to migrant farm worker parents, he studied at San Jose State University and trained at the San Francisco Mime Troupe), El Teatro Campesino actively participated in farm workers' strikes in southern California. The first performances were held in the fields and drew on varied traditions: Stock characters were mixed with Mexican folk humour and Mayan and Aztec sacred rituals were syncretically blended with Christian motifs derived from Spanish religious dramas. The troupe joined the protest marches, performing *actos*, i.e. short, satirical sketches directed against the landowners and the police supporting them on the backs of trucks and other improvised stages. These short acts gradually became longer; in 1968, the troupe produced *La Conquista de México*, performed by puppets and in 1970, *Vietnam Campesino*, focusing on independent civilisations wiped out by white people. In 1972, El Teatro Campesino toured Europe with *La carpa de los Rasquachis* (*The Tent of the Underdogs*). In this play, a wicked Harlequin – wearing masks of death and of evil landowners – wins over an enslaved, homeless Jesus, who is however destined to be finally resurrected from the dead. The English language clashes with the Spanish of the oppressed. The issues tackled included school, the war in Vietnam, people with indigenous roots and racism (Broyles-Gonzalez 1994).

Peter Schumann is another artist who comes to mind in connection with Dario Fo and the political theatre of the 1960s. A sculptor and painter, fascinated by the music of John Cage and the dance of Merce Cunningham, he trained in the artistic circles of Munich at the end of the 1950s. In 1961, he moved to the United States and in 1963 founded the troupe, Bread and Puppet. Images from the Bible were always at the centre of his picturesque productions, a fact that can be traced back to his roots in Silesia and to his Lutheran upbringing. Religion thus nurtured the mystic practice of sharing bread and garlic with the audience, conceived as a symbol of the utopia of peace (Bianchi 2001: 839) and echoed in the name of the troupe itself. In 1969, his *The Cry of the People for Meat*, written in the previous year, was staged in Italy. What delights the imagination of the audience is not only the decorative complexity of the troupe's appearance but also the overabundance of styles and symbols, while the combination of men and large puppets endows the parables with an atmosphere of estrangement and enchantment. The mix of the explosive energy of the images and their seemingly naïve, handcrafted quality results in an unusual blend of the pathetic and the grotesque, amalgamating both high and low forms of theatre culture, interspersed with crucial scenes and great,

reassuring endings. There is also a narrator-storyteller who organises
the story, commenting on the facts by holding up Brechtian signs and
introducing the various characters, who are often mannequins – either
supra-human or reduced to minimalist fetishes, as the godlike heads of
macabre animist figures. Typical examples include the monster with the tail
of a plane, referring to the bombing raids on Hanoi, surrounded by Old
and New Testament symbols and by red flags; or the giant tottering
puppets taking part in a festival in the country – who march in a picturesque parade, stopping briefly to deliver chants. The masks exemplify a sort
of relentless Manicheism, contrasting the capitalist villain – who is an object
of parody, although he oozes a sinister charm – and a predictably rebellious
Jesus, hero of a nativity scene, who is even transformed into a fish and
supported by a Vietnamese Madonna. This regressive form of theatre –
from and for the street – spread throughout Italy, before breaking up in
1970. It led to the development of various independent theatrical groups, as
well as to the fascinating solutions adopted by Eugenio Barba – his itinerant
icons of the so-called 'third theatre'.

As the world outside the stage changed with the increase in terrorism
causing destruction in public spaces, Fo's emphasis on the jester decreased.
Therefore, in *The Tricks of the Trade,* he distanced himself from his former
apodictic tones: 'I would not like this discussion on the minstrel in his
early period to give rise to misunderstanding. Some people might go off
with the idea that the minstrel was the symbol of never-ending revolt
against authority … a kind of full-time intellectual dedicated to the
cultural formation of the exploited classes' (Fo 1991: 85). We are certainly
far from the remarks made by the British scholar Allardyce Nicoll
regarding the politicisation of masks: 'Imagine what excellent comic business Harlequin might have devised had he been informed that he was "the
expression of the active protest against the force of the feudal—Catholic
reaction"'! (Nicoll 1963: 150). According to Nicoll, 'the true commedia
dell'arte shows not the slightest trace of social satire' (Nicoll 1963: 150)
and should be interpreted by looking at their musical intentions.

According to entries regarding myth in the *dictionnaire des idées reçues* of
the twentieth century, the popular and not the political aspect of the
commedia dell'arte can develop, revived by a combination of freedom
and people. If the improvisation of the stock characters results in interpretative anti-naturalism and abstract theatre – such as in Craig, Meyerhold,
Vakhtangov and Reinhardt – it drifts towards the child-centred approach
characterising the ludicrous fantasies of Théâtre de l'Oncle Sébastien. This
theatre was founded in 1935 by the theatre historian Léon Chancerel, who

was sympathetic to the circus projects associated with Dullin's and Jouvet's experiments on improvisation. However, behind their work, there is the figure of Copeau, who was obsessed with a desire to represent the vices and virtues of human comedy by using only a few masks and by depicting great feelings with small tricks. After he moved to Burgundy, he and his students, Les Copains, focused their attention on the social variant of childhood, namely the peasants. The ludicrous or extravagantly comic dimension of the commedia dell'arte determined a rhythmical-musical path which emerged very clearly in Italy in the mid-1950s, especially in small experimental theatres – such as Giovanni Poli's Commedia *degli* zanni in 1956. Poli's theatre was based on sound and gymnastic abstractions and on Alessandro Fersen's contemporary research. Founded in 1957 in Rome, Fersen's project started in the Studio di arti sceniche, a school for mimes, acrobats and actors, which made forays into the world of television between 1957 and 1959. In this project, Harlequins, Pierrots and Sganarellis appear strongly influenced by, on the one hand, Copeau's ideas filtered through Barrault and on the other, by a psycho-technical aesthetical approach of Jewish origin (Cuppone 2009). All this appears quite distant from the political claims which characterised the theatre on both sides of the Atlantic in 1968.

Nevertheless, Harlequin, the most popular character in the world of theatre apart from Hamlet, to the surprise of scholars continues to be the object of ideologically slanted interpretations. An interesting example is *I ventidue infortuni di Mor Arlecchino* (*Moor Harlequin's Twenty-Two Misfortunes*), written by Marco Martinelli and staged by Michele Sambin in 1993. Based on a scenario by Goldoni, it is set in a violent and racist end-of-millennium Milan; the protagonist is a Senegalese storyteller, a helpless *vu cumprà* (African street pedlar). Another example is Ariane Mnouchkine's *L'age d'or*, which premiered in 1975 and in which the stock character is transformed from an entrepreneur Pantalone into a modern Algerian immigrant in the uncertain world of the building industry. The use of the prototype of the *comédie italienne* – mixed with influences from the East and Ancient Greece and characterised by actors often being modelled as big and dreamlike puppets – all this, in Mnouchkine's hands, becomes a popular festival and, at the same time, poignant disenchantment when the festival is over (Picon-Vallin 2009). This is particularly evident in *Les Clowns*, a collective creation which appeared in 1969 and is considered to represent Mnouchkine's manifesto, exemplifying her idea of theatre as colourful and dazzling lighting of the stage on which the actors parade. Thus, politics appears compatible with musical rhythm, and her diptych is a combination of shared history and the tradition of popular theatre, as in the two French Revolution plays, La *Révolution doit s'arrêter à la perfection du bonheur-1789* in 1970–1971 and *La cité révolutionnaire est de ce monde-1793* in 1972–1973. A victim of financial boycotts by the government and of censuring, even by the left wing, Mnouchkine uses Molière as her principal model; in 1978 she even wrote and directed an epic film on his life. In the film, the mutual incompatibility between the theatre of revolution and the revolution in the theatre is emphasised by the contrast between the Court of Versailles and the poor players travelling through the provinces of France. In the penultimate scene, Molière, already ill, drags himself up in front of the mirror for his last performance in *Le malade imaginaire*, letting out occasional guttural cacophonies, almost symbolising the imminent release of a wounded animal spirit. Other terrified actors run up the staircase of an old palace, dragging his body with them, while the music of Purcell's *King Arthur* renders the scene even more frantic.

During her training, Mnouchkine attended the school founded in Paris in 1956 by Jacques Lecoq, whose central area of interest was movement of the body in space. His introduction to theatre had been through his collaboration in 1945 with Jean Dasté, Copeau's son-in-law. Lecoq worked in Italy for eight years starting in 1948. From 1949 to 1951 he taught in Padua in the school adjacent to the university, focusing on strategies to free the body and on physical actions, combining the Greek choir with the *commedia dell'arte*. At the same time Gianfranco De Bosio and Ludovico Zorzi rediscovered Ruzante (Meldolesi 1984: 422–9). Also in the same period, Lecoq met the sculptor and mask maker Amleto Sartori, who worked with Strehler. In 1953 Lecoq joined the group consisting of Franco Parenti, Giustino Durano and Fo, just in time to participate in their *Sani da legare* (*Fit to Be Tied*) in 1954, perfecting the pantomime of the intermezzi.

A painter and failed architect, Fo learnt from Lecoq's teachings how to exploit the defects of his lanky, clumsy body – similar to that of Jacques Tati – and his innate acrobatic skills, besides defining his idea of a theatre of situations, based on anti-naturalism, and distant from any psychological analysis of characters. Most importantly, Fo derived from Lecoq a repertoire of expressive, physiognomic gestures and sounds, as well as different – even silent – forms of laughter, which was extremely important for him, facial expressions being, in other words, the theatrical madness of the character. The *grammelot*, an accretion of the linguistic pastiche of the jester and of the stock character of the commedia dell'arte, was developed by Fo, starting with vocal exercises that his teacher gave to him during rehearsals. Once more, France proves to be crucial in this game of reciprocal influences, as the word 'grammelot' had already been used by Copeau's pupils to designate a preverbal kind of physical exercise consisting of mutterings.

In fact, it is possible to find common ground between politics and games. Vito Pandolfi, with Luigi Squarzina's help, proved it in *La fiera delle maschere* (*The Masks' Fair*) which he successfully performed in 1947, during the First World Festival of Youth and Students in Prague (Cuppone 2012), where, as Pandolfi himself stated, 'The Italian stock characters were modernised and seen from the point of view of class conflict, *servants against masters*' (Pandolfi 1990: 217). Amongst the simulacra, there was Pantalone impersonating Harry Tru(st)man (of Hiroshima) whose script ended with 'a mocking twirl on emptiness' (Squarzina 2005: 334–5). Once more, the mask of death and the death of the mask appear to become allies.

Commedia dell'Arte and Experimental Theatre

Mirella Schino

In order to consider the problematic subject of the commedia dell'arte in the second half of the twentieth century, it is best to begin with a text written in 1923, although this may, at a first glance, seem paradoxical. This very famous text was written by Edward Gordon Craig. In just a few lines, in what is a remarkable narrative *tour de force*, Craig relates a sequence of births. The first is that of Greek theatre ('Their Drama was triumphant . . . without contortions it passed away triumphantly'), the second that of church-theatre ('we shuddered because . . . dare we say it . . . the bleeding face and torn body of the Son was too much – too many such faces and bodies were brought to us to see – all torn bodies, all drawn mouths – all grief and pain – all – and the incense suffocated us'), which is followed by an escape into the open air ('We will go out – we try to find the door – we go out – we get out – fresh air – thank God') (Craig 1923: 5–7).

Later in Craig's text, while the spectators he describes are sitting in a relaxed mood in front of the doors of their homes, they see three figures appear on the wall in front of them. The figures are barely visible, to the point that the spectators feel the need to shield their eyes from the sun with their hands, to assure themselves that it is not a mirage or a simple shimmer of sunlight (here Craig seems almost to be describing a theatre of shadows). They conjure up frightening images but it is not clear why. The spectators remain indifferent and go back into the building. The thought of having seen familiar, tormented bodies and faces only crosses their minds for a second; they think it is impossible, it cannot be. It must have been a figment of the imagination, albeit a horrible one.

However, the following day the strange figures are still there, jumping and making gestures. People around them are laughing. Nothing could be more different from the bleeding face and the broken knees that were once central to liturgical drama. Yet in their sleep, when their eyes are far removed from these laughing, comic figures, the spectators dream of martyrs. For Craig, this is the moment of birth of the commedia dell'arte: when sneering, terrified spectators encounter actors who, despite being followed by the spectre of agony, are laughing all the time. Misery does not laugh. Only winners do.

If we think about the commedia dell'arte in early twentieth-century theatre, the first thing that strikes us is a feeling of obsession, transmitted from one person to another, from Europe to Russia and back again, so recurrent and intense that it ends by becoming mysterious. Craig's text reminds us of the quality – both literary and non-literary – of the debate on the commedia dell'arte which was sparked by the protagonists of the great theatre reformation in the early twentieth century. Interestingly enough, these reformers – despite being so diverse, geographically distant and often having contrasting tastes and interests – embarked on their journey to discover the commedia dell'arte with a marked sense of togetherness. They returned full of revolutionary ideas (politically and theatrically speaking), which they applied to the search for a deeper comic sense, a new aesthetic of performances, the technical skill of actors and the rediscovery of movement. Thus in the second half of the century, the continuing influence of the commedia dell'arte shaped many theatrical productions, some of which were nothing short of excellent. The original obsessiveness as well as the belief in being on the threshold of a new world had faded, become remote and obscure, but not disappeared. It was as if these ideals had sunk below ground.

While the commedia dell'arte has certainly influenced twentieth-century experimental theatre to a significant degree, its influence on theatre at the beginning of the century was much greater. The question then was how the most interesting characteristics could best be brought to the stage in a way that suited the modern age or, in other words, how best to build contemporary equivalents of such characteristics. It amounted to the observation and then the reconstruction of a tradition.

We could ask ourselves to what extent performances at the end of the century analysed the genre of commedia dell'arte through the filter of the discoveries made by theatre performers in the early part of the century. Although the meaning of many of their questions has become difficult to decipher with the passage of time, these questions must doubtless have had an influence, similar to the important studies carried out. Together, both have influenced theatrical practice by dispelling a great number of common misconceptions. The image of the commedia dell'arte as it appears on stage today – with reference to experimental rather than conventional theatre – is new and different. Not only do we have fixed types and masks and a dance-like agility, there is more. The genre has become grotesque, political, acrobatic and surreal, colourful and cruel. The renewed genre, with its darker side restored, has brought a surge of violence with it, in addition to the familiar laughter (for an Italian example of commedia dell'arte performance which is really different, violent, grotesque and condemnatory, see *Il ritorno di Scaramouche*, Poqueline and De Berardinis 1994).

Laughter and violence, when combined, form a very difficult duo. The term 'commedia dell'arte', in the context of experimental theatre at the end of the twentieth century and from the tangible point of view of performances, suggests a genre that possesses characteristics that are not only aesthetic and formal in nature. These characteristics have a natural tendency towards variability, perhaps due to shifts in the points of view of those researching questions such as whether the commedia dell'arte can be seen as folk theatre or not, as a by-product of carnival or not, etc. But most of all, what is changing is the opinion as to which characteristics should be regarded as central to the phenomenon of the commedia dell'arte: which characteristics are the real cornerstones of its influential position and 'meaning' and will save it for posterity as well. With the passage of time, we see different pairs of characteristics being dominant at a given time: laughter and politics, laughter and sensuality, laughter and dance, laughter and movement or laughter and hunger. Even the mask as an object or as the characteristics of a fixed type (the mask as character, so to speak) are influenced by the diversity of these combinations.

We will leave out of this discussion anything that might touch on the different 'methods' and teachings of the commedia dell'arte, from Jacques Lecoq to Antonio Fava, not to mention the numerous seminars which are constantly being held all over the world, in many theatres and universities. Nor will we explore or describe individual commedia dell'arte perform-ances. The borders of the genre are too porous to delineate, so that trying to do so leads to fallacious questions. Do performances by Ronconi, based on texts by Giovan Battista Andreini, belong to the genre? Andreini's parents were the most acclaimed couple of *comici dell'arte* and he became an illustrious *comico* himself, author of some of the most difficult works ever staged in the history of theatre. However, his works have little in common with other classics of the genre. Similarly, how to classify *Don Giovanni*, which, along with other works, was frequently presented by groups of *comici*?

Some of these performances can at least be grouped together in that they seek to reconstruct the genre, albeit in ways which range from the philo-logically accurate to the completely arbitrary. The most illustrious example of this first group is Giorgio Strehler's *Arlecchino servitore di due padroni,* which combines laughter and acrobatics. It is a very powerful combination, but the production offered much more than that. Created in 1947, it became the longest-running play in Italian theatre history, even surviving the death of its exceptional protagonist and first Harlequin, the great Marcello Moretti. He was replaced by Ferruccio Soleri who – at over eighty years of age – continues to play the part.

The cultural strategy adopted by Strehler in this production was to reclaim a genre which had not found favour in Italy since the end of the commedia dell'arte as a historical phenomenon. What is more, by taking it back it established a connection between the great international theatre innovators of the beginning of the century (who were particularly enamoured of the commedia dell'arte) and the budding Italian directors' theatre of the time, which was particularly inspired by Max Reinhardt's production of the same play. The connection to the commedia dell'arte had been blocked and forbidden by the fascist regime, so that Strehler's commedia dell'arte effectively made a political statement and embodied an act of protest against fascist theatre policies.

Strehler's acrobatic Harlequin was also an act of courage, in a different sense, because the debate on how to renew theatre in Italy in the first decades of the twentieth century and again after World War II had a distinctly literary flavour. When in 1932 Reinhardt featured a Harlequin-like *zanni* without a mask, dynamic and joyful in an almost brutal way, it was certainly appreciated on its tour through Italy, but with a touch of caution. In the very same period, Italian theatre was experiencing the beginning of what would later become a strident campaign in favour of a new theatre culture, more modern and more fascist, in short: moderate, strictly Italian and faithful to the text. Reinhardt's example was appreciated, although a few critics started using the Austrian director as an example to warn against the tendency – which many foreign theatre professionals had – of aspiring to authorship and of identifying the 'new theatre' envisaged by Craig with the omnipotence of the director.

Strehler, fifteen years later, did not follow in Reinhardt's 'arbitrary' footsteps of taking liberties with the text. Reinhardt had taken the text apart and reassembled it again and had introduced Mozart's music with sung passages and dancing stock characters. Yet, the very fact that he was staging the play in the style of the commedia dell'arte was, in itself, a clear sign of new times. This was because the fascination with the commedia dell'arte was not just one of the recurring themes in the new theatre of the early twentieth century. It was also one of the most widely known and, for many, one of the most obscure aspects of the paradoxical entity which was later called the 'great reformation', or, in Italy, 'direction'. At the time, Reinhardt's was the best and most successful of all the productions aiming to reconstruct the genre of commedia dell'arte. It was technically perfect, featured amazing actors and possessed an intrinsic artistic value which was not compromised by the will to entertain.

A second grouping of productions and performances in the late twentieth century relate to the commedia dell'arte by aiming to transpose and reuse its styles and techniques in order to reinvent the genre from a contemporary point of view. A major reference point for this movement was *L'âge d'or* by Ariane Mnouchkine and the Théâtre du Soleil (1975), based on a very different pair of characteristics than the one used by Strehler: 'laughter and hunger' instead of 'laughter and acrobatics'. Mnouchkine portrayed a cruel, contemporary hunger, not the ancient hunger of the seventeenth century, which had been sweetened by the passage of time. Hers was the contemporary hunger felt by the outcasts of our times. In the production, Harlequin was recast as an Algerian immigrant by the name of Abdallah who wore a cap and a black mask. Twenty years later, in 1993 in Italy, Marco Martinelli and Michele Sambin staged their *I ventidue infortuni di Mor Arlecchino* with a young actor, Mor Awa Niang, who was born in Senegal of a Griot family and had emigrated to Italy, playing the principal role of a black street vendor in contemporary Milan. He is kicked around by destiny and by history, as Martinelli describes it, just like his continent, Africa (for a beautiful analysis of his Senegalese Harlequin, see Martinelli 1993).

Such examples certainly belong to the most interesting attempts of using the strategies of the commedia dell'arte to describe contemporary reality. Ariane Mnouchkine explicitly started from Jacques Copeau's experimentations, reinventing the commedia dell'arte by creating new types.

'We theatre professionals, who are we really?' Mnouchkine asked herself this question after reflecting on the commedia dell'arte and on Copeau. Are we representatives of something past or are we announcing a future that is soon to come? She then answered: The commedia dell'arte is not an ancient form of theatre; it is theatre in its purest form. According to Mnouchkine, the commedia dell'arte offers us the opportunity to reflect on drama itself. Her analysis shows a creative embryo capable of generating complex characters quickly and effectively. The text of *L'âge d'or* – based on improvisations by the actors – was a collective act of creation after all.

From the very start, Mnouchkine operated by using Copeau as a reference point. On the other hand, Martinelli opted for a quiet reference to Brecht. These are clear, isolated points of reference, yet both of them actually refer – as we know – to a complicated labyrinth. The great reformation of early twentieth-century theatre is a paradoxical net, put together by personalities who were entirely different from one another, yet formed an ensemble which encompassed both obscure and well-known aesthetic, technical, existential and political currents. Within Copeau's reflections, Meyerhold's and Craig's thoughts played an important part, along with the entire Russian theatre of the revolutionary years.

Our last example of a late twentieth-century performance has little to do with the two major groups of experimental performances influenced by the commedia dell'arte genre that we have examined so far. It could be, at most, an example of the power of persistence: even very unpredictable theatre professionals have ended up eventually wearing the mask. In fact, the commedia dell'arte made a fleeting appearance in a theatre that is considered very distant from the genre – and certainly distant from the art of stage improvisation: the Odin Teatret. The production in question is *Talabot*, which premiered in 1987.

Talabot centred on the relationship between man and history. The protagonist was a character based on a living person, a Danish anthropologist by the name of Kirsten Hastrup. On an elliptical, enclosed stage, squeezed in between rows of spectators, appeared figures typical of the commedia dell'arte (such as Pantalone, the Captain and a small demon-like Harlequin named Trickster). They wore wooden masks that were anything but literal tributes to the commedia dell'arte and which even had been broken and glued back together and then artfully decorated to look like African masks. The actors wore costumes embellished with Mexican fabrics. They represented the 'hidden people', the humble people that the Danish anthropologist had studied as a part of his work on Icelandic folklore. They also embodied dead people, the dead people in our history, who share the same vital space as us, stamp on our feet, influence us and keep moving all around us. The Captain was Che Guevara and Pantalone was Artaud. It was a pretty picture. Masks represented beings halfway between ghosts and sprits as well as humble, 'hidden' figures typical of the commedia dell'arte. It was the survival of the dead. Odin's masks of the commedia dell'arte – representing people who are dead but who still live among us and guide us, without our being aware of the fact – have presented us with a precious clue or maybe just a question: Who do we, theatre professionals of the late twentieth century, think is behind those masks?

About twenty years before *Talabot* was first performed, a seminar was held at the Odin Theatre at which both Giovanni Poli and Dario Fo

participated. The year was 1968. For the occasion, an entire issue of the
Odin's periodical, *Teatrets Teori og Teknikk,* was dedicated to the commedia dell'arte. It featured texts from the seventeenth and eighteenth centuries and many texts from the twentieth century by authors ranging from
Niccolò Barbieri to Luigi Riccoboni and from Strehler to Fo. But most
importantly, it featured texts on – and by – Vsevolod Meyerhold, on
Nikolai Evreinov and on Yevgeny Vakhtangov.

The genre of the commedia dell'arte was, in terms of technique and
appearance, poles apart from the Odin and its reference points, but the
two could nevertheless share their perspectives. This was a legacy of the
great masters of early twentieth-century theatre. Behind the masks,
found in the most interesting performances and studies of the late
twentieth century, are the mysterious faces of the first great masters of
the century, the keepers of the secret. They imagined characters such as
Jacques Callot and figures from E. T. A. Hoffmann's short stories, and
they certainly were not unaware of the differences between Hoffmann
and the historical context of the commedia dell'arte. The relationship
between these contradictory entities and their historical context could
thus be compared to the relationship between mask and face, or between
a ghost and its shadow.

For us, what lies behind the mask is even more mysterious. The first
directors left their successors with many questions and very few answers.
The protagonists of the great reformation in theatre at the beginning
of the twentieth century have hardly earned the sympathies of the
following generations. Brilliant and innovative as they were, completely
focused on explaining their new theories and on practicing intensively a
new kind of pedagogy, they nevertheless left behind a – still unresolved –
secret. The commedia dell'arte is an intrinsic part of this uncertain and
mysterious legacy.

The essence of the commedia dell'arte, as described by Craig, lies in the
fact that it always operates at two levels. There are comic images by day
and the shadow of a tortured body with broken knees by night. There is
the laughter of the winners and the suffering of the martyrs. It is something
more complex and much more tormenting than a simple blend of the
tragic and the comic. Long before Craig, Hoffmann, in his *Princess
Brambilla,* described the commedia dell'arte's 'chronic dualism' as a form
of sickness and laughter with the irrepressible tendency to reconstruct the
unity of the human being. He created a character, Giglio Fava, who was
affected by this dualism and tormented by his dual existence as penniless
actor and Assyrian prince, as a tragic actor and a parrot. The character is

one of Meyerhold's starting points for his research on the grotesque. He would then go on to examine Gozzi through Hoffmann's eyes.

Maybe a glance at a performance that quickly became a legend will help our understanding here. In 1921, under the spell of chronic dualism, the young actors of Vakhtangov's troupe staged Gozzi's *Turandot*, dressed in formal evening wear. These were young revolutionary men, led by a communist director. They didn't tell stories about hunger, cold or death by influenza. They laughed and they sang and, in their formal evening wear, looked even more bizarre than they would have had they worn the Chinese Mandarin costumes originally envisioned for the play. Presenting a tale which spoke about torture, yet they narrated nothing. They became an oxymoron themselves.

In the early twentieth century, interest in the commedia dell'arte had the same effect as a bomb. It blew away the very foundations of the debate on the role of the author. Thus, new ways of moving and risk taking, new forms of interaction between actors were initiated, but most importantly, deliberations were undertaken and practices emerged which changed the face of theatre itself. The study of and thinking about the commedia dell'arte led to the discovery of the grotesque and the tragic power of laughter. It also revealed the possibility of overcoming the idea of the text providing the foundation and primary meaning of the performance. In addition, it assisted the development of the concept of an – at least partially – codified theatre and of dialogue with an emerging non-bourgeois theatre. Finally, it produced a manifestation of the strength of theatre, declaring it equal to and a possible alternative to faith in the church. The commedia dell'arte, considered from the perspective of the great reformation in theatre, represents a violent drive towards change, a deflagration.

This last aspect has certainly been lost over time, but some of the others have survived, more or less intact. If we think about the strength of Craig's words and research and that of his colleagues, what really surprises us is the fact that the commedia dell'arte has not been entirely consumed by them and that it is still present in the late twentieth century. It may only be a shadow or a ghost of its former self, but it is much more present than logic would dictate. Perhaps this also happened because, in the second part of the twentieth century, the debate on the commedia dell'arte was seen as one of the possible ways to interrogate the sphinx, the legacy of the great reformation.

Commedia dell'arte means pure form – as stated by Mnouchkine – because it represents the personification of an essence. We have talked about a visible level of permanence of the commedia dell'arte in the experimental forms of theatre of the late twentieth century – amounting to a reflection on the characteristics of the genre itself. We have also talked of a subliminal, invisible level – a presence, or influence, that transcends human awareness. Although most of the research on the first directors has been lost or interrupted by a lethal combination of wars and dictatorships, it is almost as if some of their demands have simply become invisible, even while there are still here, influencing us.

This underground level has another face, which might seem more obvious, but has just as many consequences. According to Craig, the commedia dell'arte is not just mask or improvisation. It is gesture above text. Craig put this to use to support his revolutionary vision of a theatre which he saw as being free from the tyranny of the word and of realism. It is well-known that the commedia dell'arte, is the idea of a theatre where people can go and *watch* a performance, rather than go and listen to a text; a theatre which is not based on the psychology of his characters, in which masks are not realistic representations, in which not even the stage and its surroundings are realistic nor magical. When the commedia had first won the interest of audiences throughout Europe, it had been poetic, artistic and it had been loved by the refined, by the cultured, by the courts. However, it was, at the same time, a popular form of theatre.

In his publication *The Mask*, Craig included unusual engravings of the commedia dell'arte, which, in the period between 1908 and 1929, appeared bizarre. They contrasted starkly with the graceful – although rather more affected – engravings of the French tradition from Maurice Sand onwards. This sparked off a 'rediscovery', so to speak, of Callot's *Balli di Sfessania*, which allowed the rediscovery of strange, contorted, painful, dual gestures which were much more suitable to express dualism than any written text. What is more, behind these unusual illustrations of the comici dell'arte, the shadow of Asia had appeared.

Almost every great director in the early twentieth century had been inspired (often for similar reasons) by both Asia and the commedia dell'arte. In their search for the foundations of a 'science of the actor', an obsession which would continue in the following decades, the great masters of the late twentieth century would follow the same road. The acting techniques and formalised gestures of classical Asian theatre forms comprise movements that are not normally encountered in everyday life. They involve a particular way of holding one's shoulders, stiffening one's neck and back, walking and resting one's feet on the ground. Eugenio Barba would later call this 'pre-expressive': a series of postures that makes the actor's body, in the eyes of the audience, more alive, interesting, and ready to spring in any direction, potentially multiplying the number of conveyable meanings.

In addition, from the very same group of subjects, an opposite branch of research emerged, namely the establishment and adaptation, in a methodological sense, of a 'physical' tradition of the commedia dell'arte. The result was somewhat fictive and invented. Nevertheless, this branch has had a certain importance in the last part of the century as well, especially with regard to the creation of new methods, seminars and forms of pedagogy. Regarding the most common technical matters, such as everyday stage improvisation in front of the audience or the creation of new stock characters, it should be mentioned that most practitioners in the twentieth century have tried their hands at it without achieving definitive results. No one was able to reinvent or bring the tradition of the commedia dell'arte back to life.

Only elements of it became influential, taking on a life of their own. 'Gesture, not text' is not a matter of well-trained bodies or of new kinds of agility. Nor is it about adorning space with lively physical activity. It means searching for the dual or 'knotted' gesture, the one that always refers to something else, the one that can speak even when the text cannot and that – unlike the text – can speak in divergent directions. This gesture reveals the ultimate, revolutionary essence of a comic theatre – something very different from a text which is comic and political at the same time. The manifestation of a revolt is not the same thing as the revolt itself. A revolutionary text can be important, but it is not the same thing as a theatre in revolt.

We can now consider the new image of the commedia dell'arte which has endured in twentieth century theatre: it, perhaps, has left the strongest mark as a whole. The person who has grasped its essentiality most directly is that unique man of theatre who is so inclined to creative explanations on the commedia dell'arte: Dario Fo. Clearly not interested in the absolute, source-supported, historical accuracy of the details he loves to talk about, he focused on their essence instead. To him, one thing was perfectly clear: commedia dell'arte does not merely mean mask or improvisation. It means freedom for the actor. For him, the actor thus becomes a jester. However, it is not Fo's jester we are talking about here. We are looking at what is perhaps the very DNA of twentieth-century theatre. What remains when all the styles, colours, fashions have faded and only pure form, the essence, survives. This pure form is that of the commedia dell'arte: live performance and revolt.

Summarising previous points, we can say that Craig and his contemporaries, including Copeau, Stanislavski, Meyerhold, Vakhtangov, Tairov, Reinhardt and many others, form the ranks of what is generally called the great reformation in theatre and what is called by us Italians 'the birth of the director'. Almost all of these theatre professionals were obsessed with the commedia dell'arte. It drove them towards change, towards the destruction of old habits and the creation of new ones. One of the roots of the radical transformation which they brought about came from their discovery of the potential of theatre, extracted from its history. According to Meyerhold, the history of theatre was a 'wonderland'– stretching from the Dionysian festivals and from Greek tragedy to the commedia dell'arte.

We know which aspects of the commedia dell'arte the great directors studied and from which aspects they drew their inspiration and the violent drive that cast them out of the mainstream of their era, out of the sphere characterised by moderate reforming impulses, consistency, decency, good acting and reverence towards the 'good practices' which plagued theatre in the early years of the century. A number of these directors achieved a deeper, albeit more concealed, resonance. In doing so, they acknowledged the inherently dual nature of theatre, for which the distance between voice and echo and between movement and gesture is crucial. The essential condition of the century is thus a chronic dualism, that is to say, the ability of the actor to appear as a living paradox and embody the non-verbal aspects of language (gesture, not text).

In the second decade of the century, the great Russian scholar Constantin Miklachevski identified the *non-bourgeois* character of the commedia dell'arte as its most important aspect, signifying nothing less than revolt. He provides perhaps the first truly historical interpretation of the commedia dell'arte, seen for the first time as the key episode of a history of theatre which is independent of literature and drama. But there is more. According to Miklachevski, the 'folk' character of the commedia dell'arte had nothing to do with the naivety and playfulness that it had been portrayed as during the period when it was under the influence of the French tradition started by Maurice Sand. It became something else, a phenomenon standing for opposition to the culture of the ruling classes. Miklachevski's commedia dell'arte is not naïve, it is *non-bourgeois*.

This was a fundamental discovery, but not in the literal sense, of course. Subsequent studies have drawn distinctions and reflected on the contribution of high culture to this unique theatrical phenomenon and on the fact that the commedia dell'arte is the result of a blend of skills performed at a highly refined artistic level and including comic abilities which would be more likely to be employed in a public square. Another topic of reflection was the fact that the *comici dell'arte* often welcomed artists who had defected from the ranks of the bourgeoisie. In this context, however, we are not asking if this 'non-bourgeois' character was an intentional form of opposition, nor whether the synthesis developed by the *comici* from forms of theatre performed in public square and borrowed from the refined techniques of the arts of the sixteenth and seventeenth centuries in fact made their theatre devoid of any subversive force.

The great discovery of twentieth-century scholars and theatre professionals was not of any anti-establishment quality, which would be fairly easy to delimit, or – arguably – to prove wrong. The great discovery centred on the nature of their theatre as being a parallel, *non-bourgeois*, different and foreign world which had to invent its own knowledge from scratch and which knew how to do so. Here, perhaps, we can find the truly innovative aspect of the relationship between the commedia dell'arte and the theatre of the late century, because the commedia dell'arte – among other things – has been perceived as the ghost of a birth out of nothingness. The great theatre professionals of the early century created their revolution on the basis of very solid technical foundations and a vast knowledge of theatre. They were in this sense rich. Many experimental theatres of the late twentieth century, on the other hand, started, in the same sense, from absolute poverty and even ignorance.

Studies on the commedia dell'arte and on theatre practice interacted with each other in the early twentieth century, in the second half of which an interesting pedagogical practice emerged and a few memorable performances took place, along with a number of further studies. These studies favoured the birth of a new awareness of the commedia dell'arte, seeing it primarily as a revolution (see in particular, Taviani 2007). We are not talking about a theatre that is consciously in opposition to a powerful establishment, nor about popular theatre. We are talking about revolt in our times and about a direction which is – more indirectly and more deeply – political and which emphasises the importance of forming groups, of intertwining life and work strategies, and of feeling like – and remaining – outsiders.

The importance of the actor arises not only from the fact that he is the keystone and the essence of scenic art, but also because he guarantees its vulnerability, fragility and imperfection - and thus its strength. Perhaps it is here that we find something really new and important. In the late twentieth century, the commedia dell'arte bequeathed to experimental theatre something basic and essential, namely that poverty is not necessarily an obstacle. It showed that it is possible to start from scratch, from technical ignorance and from poverty. By forming groups we can save ourselves from a hostile society.

During the vivid, combative, but now forgotten years which followed 1968, during the seventies and the slowly passing eighties, many, including the Odin Company, saw theatre as a form of rebellion, of escape from the conventions of political struggle. Rebellion is impossible for a single person on his own and perhaps also for groups when they are too numerous. A few, however, might just be the right number. In this regard the commedia dell'arte has been a friendly ghost – if not the provider of a vital boost to the desire to destroy and recreate – who can actually teach us something. For instance, that it is possible to gather in a group in order to invent new kinds of performance (among other things). Furthermore, that it possible to do this not only – as was quite common in the sixteenth or in the seventeenth century – in order to escape prostitution, hunger, a fool's costume, or to avoid debasing a profession by performing in the street or in the marketplaces.

Conclusion
Commedia dell'Arte and Cultural Heritage

Christopher B. Balme

The mythologisation of the *commedia* has gone through several stages beginning in the nineteenth century with Maurice Sand's *Masques et buffons* and consolidating in the first half of the twentieth century with practical experiments in Russia, France and finally Italy itself with the legendary Carlo Goldoni production by Giorgio Strehler. The outlines of the myth were well defined by Ferdinando Taviani and Mirella Schino in their 1982 book *Il segreto della commedia dell'arte*. Taviani proposes a series of oppositions that highlight the central differences between the mythical and the historical phenomena. The myth is based on the idea of a popular improvised theatre, where every evening a new play was created *ex nihilo* and the actors identified with one role for their whole performing lives. It was theatre of the marketplace and the street open to all; 'un teatro della pura immaginazione', a theatre of the pure imagination (Taviani 1987: 319). The material, historical reality was quite another thing. Scholarly research over the past twenty to thirty years has followed these dichotomies and focused on elucidating in great detail the historical as opposed to the mythical aspects of the phenomenon.

On the level of theatrical practice, we find a certain attachment to the mythical version, however, as it would seem to have greater popular appeal for audiences and artists alike. A number of charismatic Italian actors and pedagogues such as Carlo Boso, Antonio Fava and more recently Luciano Brogi (not to mention Dario Fo) have done much to disseminate via performances and above all workshops a notion of the commedia dell'arte that would seem to owe more to the myth than to history (at least in the historiographical sense). What this work has done is to gradually forge the idea of the commedia dell'arte as a specific Italian theatrical tradition with an unbroken heritage stretching back to the Renaissance. Following this logic, commedia dell'arte together with bel canto opera would be the two great contributions of Italy to the European theatrical heritage. This idea was given actual form in a proposal launched by Luciano Brogi in 2007 in which he and a number of influential *commedia* performers, pedagogues and scholars applied to the United Nations Educational, Scientific and Cultural Organization (UNESCO) for recognition of *commedia* as part of Italy's intangible cultural heritage.

In this chapter I examine the proposal in more detail. I argue that we need to see it both within specific Italian concerns and within wider processes of globalisation associated with networking and standardisation. In the final section I discuss the initiative in the context of recent theoretisations of cultural heritage, which have begun to explore discursive aporia underlying the concept of heritage itself. In this reading, recognition of *commedia* as part of Italy's intangible cultural heritage would mean creating yet another 'heritage zombie'.

In 2008 a 'video appeal' to UNESCO involving leading exponents of the commedia dell'arte was launched by Luciano Brogi and his non-profit organisation Scuola Addestramento Teatrale per Attori (SAT) based in Siena. Brogi had already launched another initiative, the *Incommedia.it* project, to create an archive of audiovisual material on the *commedia* for distribution both in Italy and in other countries. On the basis of this project SAT had obtained the status of a UNESCO-associated non-governmental organisation (NGO), thereby obtaining observer status. Brogi mobilised the *commedia* world to organise a common candidature for recognition as an Intangible Cultural Heritage of Italy.

But what does it mean to be recognised as part of a country's Intangible Cultural Heritage (ICH)? According to UNESCO this status refers to 'practices, representations, expressions, as well as the knowledge and skills, that communities, groups and, in some cases, individuals recognise as part of their cultural heritage' which are threatened by globalisation. They enjoy a special protected status to ensure continued transmission from generation to generation. The programme is based on a set of criteria, which emphasise:

> Oral traditions and expressions including language as a vehicle of the intangible cultural heritage; performing arts (such as traditional music, dance and theatre); social practices, rituals and festive events; knowledge and practices concerning nature and the universe; traditional craftsmanship. (UNESCOa)

Further important criteria include transmission of the ICH from generation to generation and constant recreation by communities and groups, particularly in response to their environment, through interaction with nature and their history. It should be proven that an ICH provides communities and groups with 'a sense of identity and continuity'; furthermore the ICH should promote respect for cultural diversity and human creativity, be compatible with international human rights and comply with the requirements of sustainable development.

With these criteria in mind, the *video-appello* compiled by Luciano Brogi focused on a triple claim: *Commedia* represents not just a national and European heritage but also a legacy for all humanity. The main message is conveyed by Titino Carrara at the beginning of the video:

> Commedia dell'arte workers, actors, directors, teachers, mask makers request that commedia dell'arte be acknowledged as national tradition and intangible cultural heritage of humanity based on the Convention of Unesco held in Paris, on October 17, 2003. They request the protection and promotion of commedia dell'arte as other countries are providing this to other important theatrical traditions. (Brogi 2008)

Other leading *commedia* figures lent their voices, including Antonio Fava, Carlo Boso, Claudia Contin, Ferrucio Soleri, Michele Casarin, Serena Sartori, Cristiano Roccamo, Giancarlo Dettori and Ferruccio Marotti. It is not surprising that these voices do not coalesce into a common chorus but articulate quite divergent aspects:

> It is a scandal that commedia dell'arte is not acknowledged as national heritage, first of all, but also as heritage of humanity. (Gianni de Luigi)
>
> We manage to spread (*divulgare*) commedia dell'arte abroad, but we cannot manage to establish commedia dell'arte and make it thrive in our own country. (Leonardo Petrillo)
>
> But the worst thing, the most outrageous thing is that we are not able to evaluate our own artistic quality. (Gianni de Luigi)
>
> Since the government is not doing much, let's try and motivate it. (Peppe Barra)
>
> When I tour abroad with these shows they often ask me, 'is this part of the Italian cultural heritage?' And I answer 'I think so' but we do not know if it is official. (Ferrucio Soleri)
>
> We do not feel an absolute need for it because we have such a bad, horrible example of commedia dell'arte everyday in politics, therefore we feel we do not need more of it. But maybe it is about time we eliminate bad commedia dell'arte so that the good one can live again. (Andrea Camilleri)
>
> (Brogi 2008)

These responses cover a variety of themes and reactions, most of them centring on the lack of interest in *commedia* in Italy itself, whether on the part of audiences or in terms of political, i.e. financial, support. An impression is conveyed of a tradition fighting for its survival but one that finds little support within the wider national community. While fighting for survival is certainly an important axiom with which to obtain recognition as an Intangible Cultural Heritage, it can also have the opposite effect of suggesting that *commedia* is little more than an invented tradition promoted by a number of aficionados. The protagonists appear to be fighting for acceptance in their own country, whereas France has provided official recognition and financial support for *commedia* groups based there. As Leonardo Petrillo states: Italy does not even have commedia dell'arte theatres in the cities like Rome, Venice or Naples, where the form was born and where the dialects constitute its language. Carlo Boso calls for the establishment of a research centre for commedia dell'arte and compares the lack of interest in Italy with the special status accorded to traditional Japanese forms such as Nô, Kyogen and Kabuki. Arlecchino performer Claudia Contin argues in a similar vein by pointing out that commedia dell'arte is probably the only European theatre form that can be compared with the great traditions from the Far East. The Japanese forms, including Bunraku puppet theatre, have all attained recognition as ICH traditions. The arguments also extend beyond the equation of national tradition to suggest that *commedia* played a central role in the origin of European theatre and even 'European culture in general' (Mario Gallo). It is also claimed that *commedia* is 'acknowledged as the foundations upon which modern theatre was built' (Beppe Barra). Antonio Fava and Ferruccio Marotti make the boldest claims. Fava considers *commedia* 'as a synonym of theatre' whereas Marotti equates *commedia* with the European project itself: 'I believe that in order to build a unified Europe, we remember that commedia dell'arte was one of the primordial moments of interaction among various nations. ... it is a cultural responsibility of a unified Europe' (Brogi 2008).

While there is no doubt that the commedia dell'arte was a European phenomenon in terms of its diffusion and long-term cultural impact, the cultural-political claim is more difficult to justify; it is perhaps a burden too heavy for Pantalone or even Arlecchino to carry. The argument runs that if the Italian government is not prepared to protect and promote the cultural heritage of commedia dell'arte then it should be made a responsibility for Europe. This argument, interesting though it might be in the context of a European research proposal, is counterproductive in terms of the criteria applicable to UNESCO Intangible Cultural Heritage, which emphasise regionality, particularity and community, not transnational cultural and historical impact.

The video was distributed by Luciano Brogi at the UNESCO meeting held in Sofia in February 2008. He attempted to enlist backing from the French and Italian delegations. The French were willing to support the initiative while the Italians expected an official application. On 28 March 2008 SAT submitted an official application to the UNESCO office of the Ministero dei Beni Culturali in the name of 'all those cultural workers of the commedia dell'arte, signatories or not'. Nothing more was heard about the application.

To this day Italy has successfully registered the following ICH cultural forms: Sardinian pastoral songs, Sicilian puppet theatre, traditional violin craftsmanship in Cremona, the Mediterranean diet, shoulder-borne pro-cessions and head-trained vines (*vite ad alberello*) of the community of Pantelleria. With the exception perhaps of the Mediterranean diet (which was a joint application by seven different communities), it is clear from this list, which privileges small communities and specific, locally rooted per-formance forms or cultural practices, that commedia dell'arte could not qualify for recognition. More interesting than the question of why it failed is the question why such an application was attempted in the first place and what this can tell us about the myth and legacy of the commedia dell'arte in the twenty-first century.

Luciano Brogi and his fellow supporters argued on the basis of myth rather than history. The comparison of *commedia* to traditional Japanese forms such as Kabuki or Bunraku meant ascribing to it an unbroken lineage and patterns of performative, intergenerational transmission that at best reach back three generations. Japanese Nô theatre can demonstrate that certain families and archives of performance knowledge reach back centuries in a more or less unbroken line. Nô theatre also underwent periods of refashioning, especially during the modernisation period in the late nineteenth century, but can still demonstrate long chains of inter-generational, family-based performance practice. The last century of com-media dell'arte, on the other hand, has been a continual process of refashioning and rejuvenation, as each new *commedia* teacher attempted to recreate the original form. And what is recreated? Because most of the prominent *commedia* exponents featured in the video are practitioners and pedagogues they practice and teach a form of clowning. While historical in appearance – the Arlecchino costume can indeed be found in sixteenth-century iconography – the actual corporeal practice is a mixture of entan-gled devices which are, even for experts, difficult to pin down in terms of their provenance. Because historical research has demonstrated that the historical practice was highly diverse, consisting of many genres and by no means restricted to the comic theatre of Pantalone, Arlecchino and Brighella, recent endeavours can be seen as an example of the 'invention of tradition' as proposed by Hobsbawm and Ranger (1983) in their famous eponymous collection of essays.

The grandiloquent claims made by the many voices on the video were clearly at odds with the highly particularistic criteria of the ICH programme. These voices were neither a community nor were they focused on one particular region. It is perhaps more fruitful to contextualise the initiative in line with its own claims rather than the requirements of the UNESCO programme.

Amongst the many policy documents produced by and for the ICH programme we find, not surprisingly, explicit mention of globalisation: 'Culture has thus, for the first time in the history of international law, found its place on the political agenda, out of a desire to humanize globalization' (UNESCOb: 12).

It could be argued that the Brogi initiative itself had less to do with mythologising the commedia dell'arte than with trying to place it within larger imperatives that we can see as part of globalisation in the senses of networking and standardisation. Globalisation can, as we know, mean many things. Recent theorist David Singh Grewal has argued in his book, *Network Power: The Social Dynamics of Globalization* that as a social and cultural process globalisation is dependent on standardisation: 'In areas as diverse as trade, media, legal procedures, industrial control, and perhaps even forms of thought, we are witnessing the emergence of international standards that enable us to coordinate our actions on a global scale' (Grewal 2008: 3). Grewal claims that the standards that enable such global coordination display 'network power'.

> The notion of network power consists in the joining of two ideas: first, that coordinating standards are more valuable when greater numbers of people use them, and second, that this dynamic – which I describe as a form of power – can lead to the progressive elimination of the alternatives over which otherwise free choice can effectively be exercised. . . . More precisely, certain versions of local practices, routines, and symbols are being catapulted onto a global stage and offered as a means by which we can gain access to one another. (Grewal 2008: 4)

If we apply this insight to the initiative by Brogi and associates then we can find both agreement and disagreement. The fact that a word such as 'commedia dell'arte' is recognisable all over the world suggests that a degree of global branding has been achieved. Branding always presupposes standardisation of some kind. This does not mean however that standardisation results inevitably in homogenisation, i.e. that only one form of performance is recognisable under this term. On the contrary. Theatre today is remarkable for the degree of diversity that can be sustained within this concept. To use Grewal's terms, 'the local practices, routines, and symbols' of Western theatre were 'catapulted onto a global stage and offered as a means by which we can gain access to one another'. But how and under what conditions did this come about? More importantly, how can a balance be found between the creation of a European, if not a global brand and the heterogeneity of the diverse practices themselves?

With his initiative, Brogi documented the contradictions of the paradoxical forces at work. Parallel to the application, Brogi convened on 12 April 2008 a national meeting of commedia dell'arte practitioners (Incontro Nazionale degli Operatori di commedia dell'arte) in Cotignola. This was probably the first national meeting of commedia dell'arte performers in Italy. Up until this point different performers and schools had worked largely independent of one another. The UNESCO application was used as a rallying point to overcome old rivalries and speak as one group. The idea of a national commedia dell'arte school was proposed and a national committee for commedia dell'arte pedagogy was formed. All this activity was designed to produce a collective body with which to negotiate with UNESCO, which had not recognised SAT as being empowered to speak for all commedia dell'arte performers and teachers. What this meeting demonstrated was the move towards better networking among the individuals and groups. Yet, according to Grewal's definition, they were implicitly moving towards standardisation. The practice of rendering *commedia* a teachable set of practices, its pedagogisation, is also testimony to the processes of standardisation on a level of performance practices. The networks of these schools and communities of practitioners is undeniable. Ironically, the cultural heritage movement, while emphasising cultural diversity, is itself a classic case of standardisation according to which a set of pre-existing norms is established to which all countries and cultures have to conform, at least on the discursive level.

The concept of cultural heritage is fundamentally paradoxical, as Gil-Manuel Hernàndez i Martí has argued in his article entitled 'The Deterritorialization of Cultural Heritage in a Globalized Modernity' (2006). He argues that the modern idea of cultural heritage already implies a high degree of hybridisation, quite at odds with its essentialist claims. It mixes elements rescued from the past with elements generated in the present, in order to ensure its future endurance, so that cultural heritage can be transmitted from generation to generation. Thus, cultural heritage is paradoxical because while it appears to be predicated on a 'tragic and nostalgic awareness of the ... past', yet it creates its objects out of the needs of the present. His conclusion is therefore that 'cultural heritage appears before us as a *zombie* or a living dead'. This heritage zombie, as he calls it, is a modern machine that is able to extract 'rich fluids in the form of political-identity legitimisation and potentially exploitable merchandising' (Hernàndez i Martí 2006: 103). He compares the heritage zombie to the replicants from the movie *Blade Runner* in whom artificial memories have been implanted: 'They are not personal memories, but memories that have been implanted and incorporated through the institutional process of patrimonialisation' (Hernàndez i Martí 2006: 104).

If we apply this provocative thesis to our consideration of commedia dell'arte and cultural heritage, then we must ask if the failed attempt to gain recognition as ICH was not actually a fortunate decision. If it had succeeded it would have meant turning *commedia* into a cultural heritage zombie, a replicant composed of diverse artificial memories and hybrid performance practices whose main function would have been to extract from the Italian government and/or the European Community funding which would ideally flow back to the creators of the zombie, the Dr Frankensteins of SAT and its supporters. Fortunately perhaps, the zombie was never born or created; it never got out of the laboratory.

The difference between *commedia* and those practices recognised as intangible cultural heritage can be identified in the fact that, while the latter probably have elements of the zombie in them, they are highly localised and unable to spread beyond the specific locale. Commedia dell'arte on the other hand is already ubiquitous, practised not just in Italy but in many other countries as well. In those multifarious locales it functions as a form of comedic theatre with brand recognition for Italy. There has been much effort on the part of scholars and practitioners alike to recreate or reinvent the commedia dell'arte over the past thirty or forty years. This process has been successful and perhaps it is even complete; so the question remains, where *commedia* goes from here: will the commedia dell'arte be turned into a heritage zombie for commercial as well as cultural-political reasons or will it evolve in its multifarious forms outside the prescriptions of cultural policy?

Whatever direction *commedia* takes, it remains situated in a productive dialectic between myth and history which energises practitioners and scholars alike. The history of the commedia dell'arte, its cultural heritage, is not just the question of the forms and practices it took in the sixteenth, seventeenth and eighteenth centuries when there existed a largely unbroken performance tradition. Its history extends into the process of mythologisation which already begins in the nineteenth century and attains a highly productive level of creative reinvention when the leading exponents of theatrical modernisation draw on its various legacies to 'retheatricalise' theatre. The cultural heritage of the commedia dell'arte is thus a complex combination of myth and history which defies the essentialist requirements of the ICH project.

Glossary

Album/a amicorum: an autograph book kept mostly by university students in which friends contributed images and texts; an important source of commedia dell'arte iconography.

argomento: plot outline in a scenario which describes the stage action in a summarised form or narrates what has happened before the stage action begins.

buffone/i: clown or jester; performer in courts, halls or piazzas who usually worked alone or with one partner.

cabotin (French): ham actor, but used by Vsevolod Meyerhold in a positive sense to refer to street performers.

canevas: outline of a *commedia* play; scenario.

canovaccio: cf. *canevas.*

capocomico, plural capocomici: head of an acting company.

comici: Italian actors, organised mainly in professional associations.

commedia/e: play/s of any kind, whether improvised or scripted; an umbrella term for all kinds of theatrical forms up to the beginning of the eighteenth century.

commedia erudita: sixteenth-century literary Italian comedies; a term used in contrast to improvised plays.

commedia all'improvviso: an alternative name for commedia dell'arte current in the seventeenth and eighteenth centuries that emphasises the improvised nature of the works.

compagnie di piacere: groups of young men who organised themselves to provide entertainment.

corrales: Spanish theatres built in courtyards, usually open air.

fantesca: female servant character.

giullare: (from. lat.) joculator; jester; juggler; late medieval and Renaissance itinerant performer.

guitto/guitti: poor itinerant performer/s.

improvviso: see *commedia all'improvviso.*

innamorati: stock characters of young lovers; *innamorata* (female); *innamorato* (male).

intermezzo/i: often lavish performances between the acts of plays, featuring music and dance.

lazzo/i: extended comic routine; also improvised embellishment by an actor.

mandafuora/i: a list of exits and entrances.

marivaudage: play in the refined, affected style of Pierre de Marivaux, often using *commedia* figures.

ossatura (**lit. backbone**): outline of the action.

personaggio/i: character/s, dramatis personae.

robba generica/generico: stock or set speech.

sacre rappresentazioni: late medieval religious plays in Italy.

scaletta: see *mandafuora*.

signorie: aristocratic patrons.

soggetto/i: subject matter of an extended scenario; storyline.

Théâtre Italien: the French name for the commedia dell'arte, often associated with resident troupes in Paris.

tipi fissi: lit. fixed types, meaning stock characters.

trionfi: early modern processional theatre involving spectacular scenes, loosely based on Roman victory processions.

Vecchio/i: older character, e.g. Pantalone or Dottore, usually father of the *innamorati*.

Zanni: comic servant character/s; masked.

zibaldone/i: an actor's notes and collection of texts.

Bibliography

Adler, Gusti (1964), *Max Reinhardt: Sein Leben* (Salzburg: Festungsverlag).

Alekseeva, Kira, *Iz vospominanij ob otče* (Archive of the family K. P. Fal'k (Baranovskoj) MHAT Museum).

Alekseev-Yakolev, A. Ya. (1948), *Russkie narodnye gul'yanya* (Moscow: Iskusstvo).

Aliverti, Maria Ines (1989), 'Per una iconografia della Commedia dell'Arte. A proposito di alcuni recenti studi', *Teatro e storia*, 4 (1), 71–88.

—— (1997), *Jacques Copeau* (Rome: Laterza).

—— (2009), 'Il percorso di un pedagogo, introduction to', in Maria Ines Aliverti (ed.), *Jacques Copeau, Artigiani di una tradizione vivente. L'attore e la pedagogia teatrale* (Florence: La Casa Usher), 9–88.

—— (2017), 'De la Bourgogne à l'Europe (1926–1929)', in Maria Ines Aliverti and Marco Consolini (eds.), *Jacques Copeau: Registres VII. Les années Copiaus (1925–1929)* (Paris: Gallimard), 367–417.

Allegri, Luigi (1990), *Teatro e spettacolo ne Medioevo* (Rome: Laterza).

Almeida, Maria João (2007), *O teatro de Goldoni no Portugal de Setecentos* (Lisbon: Impresa Nacional-Casa da Maoeda).

Andreini, Francesco (1987), *Le bravure del capitano Spavento* (Pisa: Giardini).

Andreini, Giovan Battista (1622), *La Ferinda* (Paris).

—— (1625), *Lo specchio. Composizione sacra e poetica, nella quale si rappresenta al vivo l'imagine della comedia, quanto vaga e deforme sia alhor che da comici virtuosi o viziosi rappresentata viene* (Paris: Callemont).

—— (1627), *La Campanaccia. Comedia piecevole, e ridicolosa, del Sig. Gio. Battista Andreini Comico Piacevole detto Lelio, Al Christianissimo Luigi XIII Re di Francia, e di Navarra [. . .]* (Venice: Angelo Salvadori).

—— (1991), 'La ferza. Ragionamento secondo contra l'accuse date alla Commedia (Paris 1625)', in Ferruccio Marotti and Giovanna Romei (eds.), *La commedia dell'arte e la società barocca. Vol. 2: La professione del teatro* (Rome: Bulzoni), 489–534.

Andreini, Isabella (2005), *Selected Poems of Isabella Andreini*, trans. by James Wyatt Cook (Lanham: Scarecrow Press).

Andrews, Richard (2004), 'Shakespeare and Italian Comedy', in Andrew Hadfield and Paul Hammond (eds.), *Shakespeare and Renaissance Europe* (London: Arden), 123–49.

Antonucci, Fausta and Arata, Stefano (1995), *La enjambre mala soy yo, el dulce panal mi obra. Veintinueve loas inéditas de Lope de Vega y otros dramaturgos del siglo xvi* (Seville: UNED University of Seville).

Apollonio, Mario (1930), *Storia della Commedia dell'Arte* (Rome: Augustea).

—— (1968), 'Prelezioni sulla Commedia dell'Arte', in *Contribuiti dell'istituto di filologia moderna. Serie storia del teatro* 1, 144–90.

—— (1971), 'Il duetto di Magnifico e Zanni alle origini dell'Arte', in Maria Teresa Muraro and Gianfranco Folena (eds.), *Studi sul teatro veneto fra Rinascimento ed età barocca* (Florence: Olschki), 193–222.

—— (1981), *Storia del teatro italiano. Vol. 2: Il Teatro del Cinquecento* (Florence: Sansoni).

Arcangeli, Alessandro (2004), *Passatempi rinascimentali. Storia culturale del divertimento in Europa (secoli XV-XVII)* (Rome: Carocci).

Arróniz, Othón (1969), *La influencia italiana en el nacimiento de la Comedia Española* (Madrid: Gredos).

Aslan, Odette and Bablet, Denis (1989), *Le Masque. Du Rite au Théâtre* (Paris: CNRS).

Avalle, D'Arco Silvio (1989), *Le maschere di Guglielmino. Strutture e motivi etnici nella cultura medievale* (Milan: Ricciardi).

Bader, A. L. (1935), 'The Modena Troupe in England', *Modern Language Notes*, 50, 367–9.

Barasch, Frances K. (2011), 'Hamlet versus Commedia dell'Arte', in Michele Marrapodi (ed.), *Shakespeare and Renaissance Literary Theories* (Farnham: Ashgate), 105–17.

Barbieri, Nicolò (1971), *La supplica. Discorso famigliare a quelli che trattano de' comici*, ed. by Ferdinando Taviani (Milan: Il Polfilo).

Barillari, Sonia Maura (2000), 'Il cappuccio e l'hurepiaus: Materiali per uno studio del lessico della maschera nel medioevo', in Alessandro Zironi, Rosanna Brusegan and Margherita Lecco (eds.), *Masca, maschera, masque, mask: testi e iconografia nelle culture medievali. L'immagine riflessa* (Alessandria: Edizioni dell'Orso), 19–39.

Baschet, Armand (1882), *Les comédiens italiens à la cour de France sous Charles IX, Henry IV et Louis XIII* (Paris: Plon).

Battistini, Fabio (1980), *Giorgio Strehler* (Rome: Gremese).

Baumbach, Gerda (2002), *Theaterkunst und Heilkunst. Studien zu Theater und Anthropologie* (Weimar: Böhlau Verlag).

Beaumont, Cyril W. (1926), *The History of Harlequin* (New York: Blom).

Beijer, Agne and Duchartre, Pierre-Louis (1981), *Le Recueil Fossard: La Commedia dell'Arte aux XVIe Siècle* (Paris: Librairie Théâtrale).

Belkin, A. A. (1975), *Russkie skomorokhi* (Moscow: Nauka).

Benedetti, Jean (1990), *Stanislavsky: His Life and Art* (London: Methuen).

Berkov, P. N. (1957), *Iz istorii russko-frantsuzkikh kul'turnykh svyazey* (Moscow: Iskusstvo).

Berman, Eugene, in *Strawinsky Festival correspondance 1971–1972*, Jerome Robbins Dance Collection, New York Public Library for the Performing Arts, (S)*MGZMC-Res 28 – folders 1–23.

Bernardi, Claudio (2000), 'Censura e promozione del teatro nella Controriforma', in Roberto Alonge and Guido Davico Bonino (eds.), *La nascita del teatro moderno. Cinquecento-Seicento.* Storia del teatro moderno e contemporaneo (Turin: Einaudi), 1023–42.

Besson, Benno (1985), *L'Oiseau vert, d'après Carlo Gozzi* (Lausanne: L'âge d'homme).

—— (2001), 'La comicità è una cosa seria', in Edoardo Sanguineti (ed.), *L'amore delle tre melarance. Un travestimento fiabesco dal canovaccio di Carlo Gozzi* (Genoa: Il melangolo), 136–46.

Besson, Benno and Toffolutti, Ezio (2007), 'Gozzi Inszenieren, ein Gespräch mit Benno Besson und Ezio Toffolutti', in Susanne Winter (ed.), *Il mondo e le sue favole. Sviluppi europei del teatro di Goldoni e Gozzi* (Rome: Edizioni di Storia e Letteratura), 253–57.

Bianchi, Ruggero (2001), 'Il teatro negli Stati Uniti: alla ricerca dell'innovazione permanente', in Roberto Alonge and Guido Davico Bonino (eds.), *Avanguardie e utopie del teatro. Il Novecento.* Storia del teatro moderno e contemporaneo (Turin: Einaudi), 773–856.

Boiteux, M. (1981), 'Les fêtes publiques dans l'environment du palais', *Le palais Farnèse*, vol. 1 (Rome: École Française de Rome), 613–56.

Bolaños Donoso, Piedad and Reyes Peña, Mercedes des los (1990), 'Presencia de comediantes en Lisboa (1580–1607)', in María Luisa Lobato (ed.), *Teatro del Siglo de Oro. Homenaje a Alberto Navarro González* (Kassel: Reichenberger).

Bragaglia, Anton Giulio (1953), *Pulcinella* (Rome: Casini).

Braudel, Fernand (1991), *Out of Italy: 1450–1650*, trans. by Sian Reynolds (Paris: Flammarion).

Brecht, Bertolt (1967), *Turandot oder Der Kongreß der Weißwäscher. Der Tui-Roman (Fragment)* (Frankfurt a. M.: Suhrkamp).

—— (1973), *Arbeitsjournal (1942–55), vol. 2* (Frankfurt a. M.: Suhrkamp).

Brenner, Clarence (1961), *The Théâtre Italien: Its Repertory 1716–1793* (Berkeley: University of California Press).

Brogi, Luciano (2008), 'Video-appello all'UNESCO'. <www.incommedia.org>

Brooks, William (1996), 'Louis XIV's Dismissal of the Italian Actors: The Episode of *La Fausse Prude*', *Modern Language Review*, 91 (4), 840–7.

Broyles-Gonzalez, Yolanda (1994), *Teatro Campesino. Theater in the Chicano Movement* (Austin: University of Texas Press).

Brunetti, Simona (2005), 'Viaggi di Alberto Naselli detto Zan Ganassa', in Umberto Artioli and Cristina Grazioli (eds.), *I Gonzaga e l'Impero. Itinerari dello spettacolo. Con una selezione di materiali dall'Archivio informatico Herla (1560–1630)* (Florence: Le Lettere), 329–42.

Burattelli, Claudia, Landolfi, Domenica and Zinanni, Anna (1993), *Comici dell'arte: Corrispondenze* (Florence: Le Lettere).

Burke, Peter (1997), *Varieties of Cultural History* (Cambridge: Polity Press).

Cairns, Christopher (1993), 'Dario Fo and the commedia dell'arte', in David J. George and Christopher J. Gossip (eds.), *Studies in the Commedia dell'Arte* (Cardiff: University of Wales Press), 247–65.

Calmo, Andrea (1996), *Il Travaglia. Comedia di Messer Andrea Calmo, nuovamente venuta in luce, molto piacevole et di varie lingue adornata, sotto bellissima invenzione. Al modo che la fo presentata dal detto autore nella città di Vinegia* (Padua: Antenore).

(2006), *Il Saltuzza* (Padua: Esedra).

Cambiaghi, Mariagabriella (2006), 'Carlo Gozzi e Evgenij Vachtangov: il volto fiabesco della teatralità', in Mariagabriella Cambiaghi (ed.), *Studi gozziani* (Milan: CUEM), 147–66.

Campardon, Emile (1970), *Les comédiens du Roi de la Troupe Italienne pendant les deux derniers siècles*, 2 vols. (Geneva: Slatkine Reprints).

Capitta, Gianfranco (2001), 'Una favola moderna al Malibran. Da un incontro con Benno Besson ed Ezio Toffolutti', in Sergej Prokofieff (ed.), *L'amour des trois oranges* (Venice: La Fenice).

Cascetta, Annamaria (1995), 'La *spiritual tragedia* e l'azione devota. Gli ambienti e le forme', in Annamaria Cascetta and Roberta Carpani (eds.), *La scena della gloria. Drammaturgia e spettacolo a Milano in età spagnola* (Milan: Vita e Pensiero), 115–218.

Casella, Alberto (1975), 'Buttafuori', in Silvio D'Amico (ed.), *Enciclopedia dello Spettacolo*. Vol. II. (Rome: Unione Editoriale), col. 1413.

Castagno, Paul (1994), *The Early Commedia dell'Arte 1550–1621: The Mannerist Context* (New York: Peter Lang).

Cecchini, Pier Maria (1991), 'Discorso sopra l'arte comica con il modo di ben recitare', in Ferruccio Marotti and Giovanna Romei (eds.), *La Professione del Teatro* La Commedia dell'Arte e la Società Barocca, vol. 2 (Rome: Bulzoni), 67–76.

Chaffee, Judith and Crick, Oliver (eds.) (2015), *The Routledge Companion to Commedia dell'Arte* (Abingdon: Routledge).

Chambers, Edmund K. (1923), *The Elizabethan Stage*, 4 vols. (Oxford: Clarendon Press).

Chiabò, Myriam and Doglio, Federico (1995), *I gesuiti e i primordi del teatro barocco in Europa* (Rome: Torre d'Orfeo Centro studi sul teatro medioevale e rinascimentale).

Chilton, Meredith (2001), *Harlequin Unmasked: The Commedia dell'Arte and Porcelain Sculpture* (New Haven: Yale University Press).

Clair, Jean (2004), *La grande parade: portrait de l'artiste en clown* (Paris: Gallimard).

Clarke, Jan (1992), 'The Expulsion of the Italians from the Hôtel de Bourgogne in 1697', *Seventeeth-Century French Studies*, 14(1), 97–117.

(2007), *The Guénégaud Theatre in Paris (1673–1680). Volume 3. The Demise of the Machine Play.* (Lewiston: Edwin Mellen Press).

Clubb, Louise (1989), *Italian Drama in Shakespeare's Time* (New Haven: Yale University Press).

Cooper, Douglas (2005), 'Picasso e la scena', in Gabriella Belli and Elisa Guzzo Vaccarino (eds.), *La danza delle avanguardie. Dipinti, scene e costumi da Degas a Picasso, da Matisse a Keith Haring* (Geneva: Skira).

Cope, Jackson I. (1984), *Dramaturgy of the Daemonic: Studies in Antigeneric Theatre from Ruzante to Grimaldi* (Baltimore: Johns Hopkins University Press).

Copeau, Jacques (1979), *Registres III. Les Registres du Vieux-Colombier*, ed. by Marie-Hélène Dasté and Suzanne Maistre-Saint-Denis (Paris: Gallimard).

—— (1990), *Copeau: texts on theatre*, ed. by John Rudlin and Norman H. Paul (London: Routledge).

—— (2009), *Jacques Copeau, Artigiani di una tradizione vivente. L'attore e la pedagogia teatrale*, ed. and trans. by Maria Ines Aliverti (Florence: La casa Usher).

—— (2017), *Jacques Copeau: Registres VII. Les années Copiaus (1925–1929)*, ed. by Maria Ines Aliverti and Marco Consolini (Paris: Gallimard).

Cotticelli, F., Goodrich, A., and Heck, Th. F. (eds.) (2001), *The commedia dell'arte in Naples: a bilingual edition of the 176 Casamarciano scenarios* (London: Scarecrow Press).

Courville, Xavier de (1967), *Luigi Riccoboni dit Lélio: Chef de troupe en Italie (1676–1715)* (Paris: Larche).

Cowling, Elizabeth and Mundy, Jennifer (1990), *On Classic Ground: Picasso, Léger, De Chirico and the New Classicism 1910–1930* (London: Tate Gallery).

Cracraft, James (2004), *The Petrine Revolution in Russian Culture* (Cambridge, MA: Harvard University Press).

Craig, Edward Gordon (1923), *Scene* (London: H. Milford Oxford University Press).

Croce, Benedetto (1933), 'Intorno alla Commedia dell'Arte', in *Poesia popolare e poesia d'arte. Studi sulla poesia italiana dal Tre al Cinquecento* (Rome: Laterza), 503–14.

—— (1934), *Saggi sulla letteratura italiana del Seicento* (Rome: Laterza).

Cruciani, Fabrizio (1983), *Teatro nel Rinascimento. Roma 1450–1550* (Rome: Bulzoni).

—— (1985), 'Percorsi critici verso la prima rappresentazione dell'Aminta', in Andrea Buzzoni (ed.), *Torquato Tasso tra letteratura, musica, teatro e arti figurative* (Bologna: Nuova Alfa), 179–92.

Cuppone, Roberto (1999), *CDA. Il mito della commedia dell'arte nell'Ottocento francese* (Rome: Bulzoni).

—— (2008), '"Moi je ne joue plus". L'Illusion de Jacques Copeau', *Teatro e Storia*, 22, 333–60.

—— (2009), *Alessandro Fersen e la Commedia dell'Arte. Tre commedie inedite di A. F.* (Rome: Aracne).

—— (2012), '"Servitù" o "fierezza"? Genesi della Fiera delle maschere di Vito Pandolfi', in Federica Natta (ed.), *Teatro e teatralità a Genova e in Liguria. Drammaturghi, registi, scenografi, impresari e organizzatori* (Bari: Pagina), 83–120.

Dahlberg, Gunilla (1992), *Komediantteatern i 1600-talets Stockholm* Stockholmsmonografier utgivna av Stockholms stad, 106 (Stockholm: Komitten for stockholmforsking).

D'Amico, Silvio (1936), *Storia del teatro italiano* (Milan: Valentino Bomi).

D'Ancona, Alessandro (1891), *Origini del teatro italiano*, 2 vols. (Turin: Loescher).

Davis, Charles and Varey, John E. (1997), *Los corrales de comedias y los hospitales de Madrid: 1574–1615. Estudio y documentos* (London: Tamesis Books).

De Filippo, Eduardo (2000–2007), *Teatro*, ed. by Nicola De Blasi and Paola Quarenghi (Milan: Mondadori).

De Maio, Romeo (1973), *Riforme e miti nella Chiesa del Cinquecento* (Naples: Guida).

De Ritis, Raffaele (2008), *Storia del circo, dagli acrobati egizi al Cirque du Soleil* (Rome: Bulzoni).

Décaudin, Michel and Apollinaire, Guillaume (1965–1966), *Oeuvres complètes de G. Apollinaire*, 4 vols. (Paris: Balland, Lecat).

Del Monaco, Francesco Maria (1969), 'In actores et spectatores comoediarum nostri temporis paraenesis (1621)', in Ferdinando Taviani (ed.), *La Fascinazione del Teatro* (Rome: Bulzoni), 184–222.

Di Bella, Sarah (ed.), (2012), *Pensée, pratiques et représentations de la discipline à l'âge moderne* (Paris: Classiques Garnier).

Di Simplicio, Oscar (2010), 'Demonologia', in Adriano Prosperi (ed.), *Dizionario storico dell'Inquisizione*, vol. 1 (Pisa: Edizioni della Normale), 465–7.

Dick, Kay (1960), *Pierrot: An Examination of the Pierrot Legend* (London: Hutchinson).

Diderot, Denis (1758), *Un Discours sur la poésie dramatique* (Amsterdam). Online at http://gallica.bnf.fr/ark:/12148/bpt6k70965g

Dieterich, Albrecht (1897), *Pulcinella. Pompejanische Wandbilder und römische Satyrspiele* (Leipzig: B. G. Teubner).

Dionisotti, Carlo (1967), *Geografia e storia della letteratura italiana* (Turin: Einaudi).

Doménech Rico, Fernando (2007), *Los Trufaldines y el teatro de los Caños del Peral. La commedia dell'arte en la España de Felipe V* (Madrid: Fundamentos).

Douël Dell'Agnola, Catherine (1992), *Gli spettacoli goldoniani di Giorgio Strehler: 1947–1991* (Rome: Bulzoni).

Driesen, Otto (1904), *Der Ursprung des Harlekin. Ein kulturgeschichtliches Problem* (Berlin: Duncker).

Duchartre, Pierre-Louis (1924), *La Comédie Italienne. L'improvisation, les canevas, vies, caractères, portraits, masques des illustres personnages de la Commedia dell'Arte* (Paris: Librairie de France).

Dullin, Charles (2005), *La ricerca degli dèi. Pedagogia di attore e professione del teatro* (Pisa: ETS).

Erenstein, Robert (1986), 'Claude Gillot e il Théâtre Italien', *Biblioteca Teatrale*, (2), 23–42.

Evans, Mark (2006), *Jaques Copeau* (London: Routledge).

Fabiano, Andrea (2007), 'Un exemple de transferts de dramaturgie et de savoirs théâtraux entre la commedia dell'arte et l'opera buffa: *Don Giovanni* de Da

Ponte et Mozart', in Andrea Fabiano (ed.), *À travers l'opéra: parcours anthropologiques et transferts dramaturgiques sur la scène théâtrale européenne du XVIIIe au XXe siècle* (Paris: Harmattan), 75–92.

Falavolti, Laura (1982), *Commedie dei comici dell'arte* (Turin: Utet).

Famintsyn, Aleksandr (1889), *Skomorokhi na Rusi* (St Petersburg: Tip. E. Armgol'da).

Fantappié, Francesca (2009), '"Angelina senese" alias Angela Signorini Nelli. Vita artistica di un'attrice nel Seicento italiano: dal Don Giovanni ai libertini', *Bullettino Senese di Storia Patria*, 116, 212–67.

Farrell, Dianne Ecklund (1980), 'Popular Prints in the Cultural History of Eighteenth-Century Russia' (PhD dissertation, University of Wisconsin).

Farrell, Joseph (2000), 'Fo and Ruzzante. Debts and Obligations', in Joseph Farrell and Antonio Scuderi (eds.), *Dario Fo: Stage, Text and Tradition* (Carbondale: Southern Illinois University Press), 80–100.

―― (2001), *Dario Fo and Franca Rame: Harlequins of the Revolution* (London: Methuen).

―― (2011), 'Dario Fo and the Moro Tragedy', in Anna Barsotti and Eva Marinai (eds.), *Dario Fo e Franca Rame, una vita per l'arte. Bozzetti, figure, scene pittoriche e teatrali* (Corazzano: Titivillus), 133–53.

Ferrari Barassi, Elena (1984), 'Feste, spettacoli in musica e danza nella Milano cinquecentesca', in Aldo Castellano (ed.), *La Lombardia spagnola*. Civiltà di Lombardia (Milan: Electa).

Ferrazzi, Marialuisa (2000), *Commedie e comici dell'arte italiani alla corte russa (1731–1738). La fenice dei teatri* (Rome: Bulzoni).

Ferrone, Siro (ed.) (1985), *Commedie dell'arte* 2 vols., vol. 2 (Milan: Mursia) 5–44.

―― (1993a), 'Epistolari carteggi corrispondenze. Storia materiale e invenzione artistica', in Claudia Burattelli, Domenica Landolfi and Anna Zinanni (eds.), *Comici dell'arte: Corrispondenze* (Florence: Le Lettere), 11–51.

―― ([1993b] 2001), *Attori, mercanti, corsari. La Commedia dell'Arte in Europa tra Cinque e Seicento* (Turin: Einaudi).

―― (2006), *Arlecchino. Vita e avventure di Tristano Martinelli attore* (Rome: Laterza).

―― (2008), 'La Commedia dell'Arte', in Luigi Allegri (ed.), *Breve storia del teatro per immagini* (Rome: Carocci), 106–11.

―― (2014), *La Commedia dell'Arte. Attrici e attori italiani in Europa (XVI-XVIII secolo)* (Turin: Einaudi).

Ferroni, Giulio (1989), 'L'ossessione del radoppiamento nella commedia dell'arte', in Domenico Pietropaolo (ed.), *The Science of Buffoonery: Theory and History of the Commedia dell'Arte* (Ottawa: Doverhouse), 135–47.

Fiaschini, Fabrizio (2001), 'Negotium diaboli. Approcci, valutazioni e ipotesi di ricerca intorno ai rapporti tra Chiesa post-tridentina e professionismo dello spettacolo', *Aprosiana: rivista annuale di studi di Barocchi*, 9, 309–28.

―― (2007), *L'incessabil agitazione. Giovan Battista Andreini tra professione teatrale, cultura letteraria e religione*. Biblioteca di drammaturgia, vol. 1. (Pisa: Giardini).

(2011), "'Ludus est necessarius": Pier Maria Cecchini e la "somma teologica" dei comici dell'Arte', in Stefano Mazzoni (ed.), *Studi di Storia dello spettacolo. Omaggio a Siro Ferrone* (Florence: Le Lettere), 115–36.

Filippi, Bruna (2001), *Il teatro degli argomenti. Gli scenari seicenteschi del teatro gesuitico romano. Catalogo analitico* (Rome: Institutum historicum).

(2010), 'Il corpo glorioso: il martire sulla scena gesuitica (XVII secolo)', in Ulf Birbaumer, Michael Hüttler, and Guido Di Palma (eds.), *Corps du théâtre / Il Corpo del Teatro. Organicité, contemporanéité, interculturalité / Organicità, contemporaneità, interculturalità* (Vienna: Verlag Lehner Hollitzer Wissenschaftsverlag), 141–50.

Fischer-Lichte, Erika (2008), *The Transformative Power of Performance: A New Aesthetics*, trans. Saskya Jain (London: Routledge).

Fletcher, Ifan Kyrle (1954), 'Italian Comedians in England in the Seventeenth Century', *Theatre Notebook*, 8 (4), 86–91.

Fo, Dario (1990), *Dialogo provocatorio sul comico, il tragico, la follia e la ragione* (Rome: Laterza).

(1991), *The Tricks of the Trade (Manuale minimo dell'attore)*, trans. by Joseph Farrell (London: Methuen).

(1997), *Manuale minimo dell'attore* (Turin: Einaudi).

(2011), *Arlecchino = Hellequin = Harlekin = Arlekin. Dialoghi originali* (Turin: Einaudi).

Foglia, Patrizia (2013), *Maschere. Dalla Commedia dell'Arte personaggi e costumi nella grafica tra Seicento e Novecent* (Busto Arsizio: Nomos).

Fokine, Michel (1961), *Memoires of a Ballet Master*, trans. by Vitale Fokine (Boston: Little, Brown and Co.).

Folena, Gianfranco (1983), 'L'italiano di Mozart nel concerto europeo del suo epistolario', in Gianfranco Folena (ed.), *L'Italiano in Europa. Esperienze linguistiche del Settecento* (Turin: Einaudi), 432–69.

Folengo, Teofilo (1997), *Baldus* (Turin: Utet).

Franciotti, Cesare (1969), 'Il giovane christiano, overo institutione de' giovani alla devotione (1611)', in Ferdinando Taviani (ed.), *La Fascinazione del Teatro* (Rome: Bulzoni), 166–79.

Franko, Mark (1994), *Dance As Text: Ideologies of the Baroque Body* (Cambridge: Cambridge University Press).

Franko, Mark and Richards, Annette (2000), 'Actualizing Absence: The Pastness of Performance', in *Acting On The Past: Historical Performance Across the Disciplines*, ed. by M. Franko and A. Richards (Hanover: Wesleyan University Press), 201–9

Freixe, Guy (2014), *La filiation Copeau, Lecoq, Mnouchkine. Une lignée théâtrale du jeu de l'acteur* (Lavérune: L'Entretemps).

Fumaroli, Marc (1990), *Eroi e oratori. Retorica e drammaturgia secentesche* (Bologna: Il mulino).

Gambelli, Delia (1993), *Arlecchino a Parigi. Vol. 1 : Dall'Inferno alla corte del Re Sole* (Rome: Bulzoni).

(1997), *Arlecchino a Parigi. Vol. 2 : Lo scenario di Domenico Biancolelli* (Rome: Bulzoni).

García García, Bernardo J. (1992–1993), 'La compañía de Ganassa en Madrid (1580–84). Tres nuevos documentos', *Journal of Hispanic Research* (1), 333–70.

Garzoni, Tomaso (1996), *La Piazza universale di tutte le professioni del mondo*, 2 vols. (Turin: Einaudi). Online at http://gallica.bnf.fr/ark:/12148/bpt6k77612

Gavrilovich, Donatella (2012), *Le arti e la danza. I coreografi russi e sovietici tra riforma e rivoluzione* (Rome: UniversItalia).

Gherardi, Evaristo (1700), *Le Théâtre Italien ou Le Recueil général de toutes les Comedies & Scenes Françoises jouées par les Comediens Italiennes du Roy* (Paris: Cusson et Witte). Online at http://gallica.bnf.fr/ark:/12148/bpt6k77612

Gignoux, Hubert (1984), *Histoire d'une famille théâtrale: Jacques Copeau – Léon Chancerel, les Comédiens-Routiers, La Décentralisation dramatique* (Lausanne: Editions de l'Aire).

Gontard, Denis (ed.) (1974), *Le Journal de bord des Copiaus (1924–1929)* (Paris: Seghers).

Gorchakov, Nikolai (1957), *Theatre in Soviet Russia*, trans. by Edgar Lehrman (New York: Columbia University Press).

Goudart, Patrick (1997), 'La produzione drammatica di Jacques Copeau e dei Copiaus in Borgogna (1924–1929). Appendix', in Maria Ines Aliverti (ed.), *Jacques Copeau* (Rome: Laterza).

Gozzi, Carlo (1994), *Fiabe teatrali*, ed. by Alberto Beniscelli (Milan: Garzanti).

Graminaeus, Dietrich (1587), *Beschreibung derer Fürstlicher Güligscher [e]tc Hochzeit / so [...] zu Düsseldorff mit grossen freuden / Fürstlichen Triumpf vnd herrligkeit gehalten worden* (Cologne). Online at http://reader.digitale-sammlungen.de/resolve/display/bsb11195691.html

Greenblatt, Stephen Jay (1980), *Renaissance Self-Fashioning: From More to Shakespeare* (Chicago: University of Chicago Press).

Grewal, David Singh (2008), *Network Power: The Social Dynamics of Globalization* (New Haven: Yale University Press).

Grewar, Andrew (1993), 'Shakespeare and the Actors of the Commedia dell'Arte', in David J. George and Christopher J. Gossip (eds.), *Studies in the Commedia dell'Arte* (Cardiff: University of Wales Press), 13–47.

Gros de Gasquet, Julia (2007), 'Rhétorique, théâtralité et corps actorial', *Dix-septième siècle*, 236 (3), 501–19.

Gruen, John (1986), 'Familiar Faces', *Dance Magazine*, March.

Guardenti, Renzo (1990), *Gli Italiani a parigi. La Comédie Italienne (1660–1697)*, 2 vols. (Rome: Bulzoni).

(1995), *Le fiere del teatro. Percorsi del teatro forain del primo Settecento. Con una scelta di commedie rappresentate alle Foires Saint-Germain e Saint-Laurent (1711–1715)* (Rome: Bulzoni).

(2002), 'The Iconography of the "Commedia dell'Arte": Figurative Recurrences and the Organization of the Repertory', in Christopher B.

Balme, Robert Erenstein, and Cesare Molinari (eds.), *European Theatre Iconography*. *Proceedings of the European Science Foundation Network (Mainz, 22–26 July 1998; Wassenaar, 21–25 July 1999, Poggio a Caiano, 20–23 July 2000)* (Rome: Bulzoni), 197–206.

(2004), 'Attrici in effigie', *Culture teatrali*, 10 (1), 55–71.

Guarino, Raimondo (1995), *Teatro e mutamenti. Rinascimento e spettacolo a Venezia* (Bologna: Il mulino).

Hansen, Günther (1984), *Formen der Commedia dell'Arte in Deutschland* (Emsdetten: Lechte).

Heed, Sven Åke (ed.) (2007), *Teater före 1800*. Ny svensk teaterhistorie, vol. 1 (Möklinta: Gidlungs förlag).

Henke, Robert (2002), *Performance and Literature in the Commedia dell'Arte* (Cambridge: Cambridge University Press).

(2007), 'Transporting Tragicomedy: Shakespeare and the Magical Pastoral of the Commedia dell'Arte', in Robert Henke and Eric Nicholson (eds.), *Transnational Exchange in Early Modern Theatre* (Aldershot: Ashgate), 19–34.

(2008), 'Border-crossing in the Commedia dell' Arte', in Robert Henke and Eric Nicholson (eds.), *Transnational Exchange in Early Modern Theater*. Studies in Performance and Early Modern Drama (Aldershot: Ashgate), 19–34.

Hernàndez i Martí, Gil-Manuel (2006), 'The Deterritorialization of Cultural Heritage in a Globalized Modernity', *Transfer: Journal of Contemporary Culture*, 1, 92–107.

Heywood, Thomas (1606), *The Second Part of If You Know Not Me, You Know Nobody* (London: printed by Thomas Purfoot, Jr., for Nathaniel Butter).

Hobsbawm, Eric J. and Ranger, Terence (eds.) (1983), *The Invention of Tradition* (Cambridge: Cambridge University Press).

Hofmannsthal, Hugo von (2006), *Dramen* 15. Sämtliche Werke. Kritische Ausgabe in 38 Bänden, vol. 18 (Frankfurt a. M.: S. Fischer).

Holberg, Ludvig (1970), 'Hexerie eller Blind Alarm', in Billeskov F. J. Jansen (ed.), *Værker i tolv bind*, vol. 5 (Copenhagen: Rosenkilde og Bagger).

Holm, Bent (1992), 'La Raccolta Fossard "di Copenaghen"', *Teatro e storia*, 7 (1), 73–97.

(1998), 'Harlequin, Holberg and the (In)visible Masks: Commedia dell'Arte in Eighteenth-Century Denmark', *Theatre Research International*, 23 (2), 159–66.

(2012), 'La discipline dialectique: La figure du fou dans le théâtre et la philosophie de Holberg', in Sarah Di Bella (ed.), *Pensée, pratiques et représentations de la discipline à l'âge moderne* (Paris: Garnier), 143–58.

(2013), 'L'identità comica. Il ruolo dell' italianità di Holberg e della danesizzazione di Goldoni nella formazione di un teatro nazionale danese', in Gert Sørensen (ed.), *L'Italia in Europa. Italia e Danimarca*. Analecta Romana Instituti Danici. Supplementa (Rome: Quasar).

Honolka, Kurt (1984), *Papageno. Emanuel Schikaneder. Der grosse Theatermann der Mozart-Zeit* (Salzburg: Residenz).

Hulfeld, Stefan (ed.) (2014), *Scenari più scelti d'istrioni. Italienisch-Deutsche Edition der einhundert Commedia all'improvviso-Szenarien aus der Sammlung Corsiniana* (Göttingen: V&R unipress).

Jansen, Reinhard (ed.) (2001), *Commedia dell'Arte. Fest der Komödianten: keramische Kostbarkeiten aus den Museen der Welt* (Stuttgart: Arnoldsche).

Jones, Louisa E. (1984), *Pierrot-Watteau. A Nineteenth-Century Myth* (Tübingen: G. Narr, Jean-Michael Place).

Kahane, Arthur (1928), *Tagebuch eines Dramaturgen* (Berlin: Bruno Cassirer Verlag).

Kallinikov, P. and Korneeva, I. (eds.) (1998), *Russkiy biograficheskiy slovar' v dvadtsati tomakh*, 12 vols. (Moscow: Terr).

Katritzky, M. A. (2006), *The Art of Commedia: A Study in the Commedia dell'Arte 1560–1620 with Special Reference to the Visual Records*. Internationale Forschungen zur Allgemeinen und Vergleichenden Literaturwissenschaft (Amsterdam: Rodopi).

——— (2007), *Women, Medicine and Theatre, 1500 – 1750: Literary Mountebanks and Performing Quacks*. Studies in Performance and Early Modern Drama, vol. 16 (Aldershot: Ashgate).

——— (2012), *Healing, Performance and Ceremony in the Writings of Three Early Modern Physicians: Hippolytus Guarinonius and the Brothers Felix and Thomas Platter*. History of Medicine in Context (Farnham: Ashgate).

——— (2015), 'The Images of the Commedia dell'Arte', in Judith Chaffee and Oliver Crick, (eds.), *The Routledge companion to Commedia dell'Arte* (Abingdon: Routledge), 284–99.

Kelly, Catriona (2009), *Petrushka: The Russian Carnival Puppet Theatre*. Cambridge Studies in Russian Literature (Cambridge: Cambridge University Press).

Koll, Alfred (ed.) (1980), *Diener zweier Herren – Erinnerungen an 1924* (Vienna: Museumsverein Josefstadt).

Kotar, S. L. and Gessler, J. E. (2011), *The Rise of the American Circus: 1717–1899* (Jefferson: McFarland).

Kott, Jan (1972), *Spektakel – Spektakel. Tendenzen des modernen Welttheaters* (Munich: Piper).

Krogh, Torben (1931), *Studier over Harlekinaden paa den danske Skueplads* (Copenhagen: Jespersen og Pios Forlag).

Kyd, Thomas (2009), *The Spanish Tragedy* (London: A. & C. Black).

La Rocca, Patrizia (1993), 'L' "unica e virtuliosa Ziralda". Ritratto di una ballerina pavana del XVI secolo', in Alessandro Pontremoli and Patrizia La Rocca (eds.), *La danza a Venezia nel Rinascimento* (Vincenza: Neri Pozza).

Lambranzi, Gregorio (1928), *New and Curious School of Theatrical Dancing* (with all the original plates by Johann Georg Puschner; translated by Derra de Moroda; edited with a preface by Cyril W. Beaumont) (London: C. W. Beaumont).

Lacan, Jacques (1992), *The Ethics of Psychoanalysis* (London: Routledge).

Långfors, Arthur and du Bus, Gervais (1914), *Le Roman de Fauvel* (Paris: Didot).

Lazzerini, Lucia (1982), 'Preistoria degli zanni. Mito e spettacolo nella coscienza popolare', in Istituto Nazionale di Studi sul Rinascimento (ed.), *Scienze, credenze occulte, livelli di cultura. Convegno internazionale di studi (Firenze, 26–30 giugno 1980)* (Florence: Olschki), 445–75.

Lea, K. M. (1928), 'Sir Aston Cokayne and the "Commedia dell'Arte"', *Modern Language Review*, 23, 47–51.

—— (1934), *Italian Popular Comedy: A Study in the Commedia dell'Arte, 1560–1620 with Special Reference to the English Stage* (Oxford: Clarendon Press).

Lenzi, Massimo (2001), 'Il Novecento russo: stili e sistemi', in Roberto Alonge and Guido Davico Bonino (eds.), *Avanguardie e utopie del teatro. Il Novecento*. Storia del teatro moderno e contemporaneo (Turin: Einaudi), 99–206.

Lestini, Riccardo (2010), 'Alla ricerca de un attore perduto: Francesco Manzani, Capitan Terremoto', *Commedia dell'arte: Annuario Internationale*, 3 (1), 63–94.

Leyva, Aurelia (1997), 'Juan Jorge Ganassa y los epígonos de la commedia dell'arte en España', in Maria Grazia Profeti (ed.), *Percorsi europei* (Florence: Alinea Editrice), 9–17.

Lo Gatto, Ettore (1954), 'La Commedia dell'arte in Russia', *Rivista di studi teatrali*, 9/10, 176–85.

Lombardi, Marco (1995), 'L'educazione del sovrano. Platonismo nello spettacolo francese del Seicento', in *Drammaturgia* 2, 14–47.

Lorch, Jennifer (2000), 'Morte accidentale in English', in Joseph Farrell and Antonio Scuderi (eds.), *Dario Fo. Stage, Text and Tradition* (Carbondale: Southern Illinois University Press), 143–60.

Lovarini, Emilio (1965), 'L'Alfabeto dei villani in pavano nuovamente edito ed illustrato', in Emilio Lovarini and Gianfranco Folena (eds.), *Studi sul Ruzzante e la letteratura pavana* (Padua: Antenore), 411–34.

Macasdar, Philippe and Tinterri, Alessandro (2006), *Viaggio in Italia di Benno Besson* (Perugia: Morlacchi).

MacNeil, Anne (1994), 'Music and the Life and Work of Isabella Andreini: Humanistic Attitudes toward Music, Poetry and Theater during the Late Sixteenth and Early Seventeenth Centuries' (PhD dissertation, University of Chicago).

—— (1995), 'The Divine Madness of Isabella Andreini', *Journal of the Royal Musical Association*, 120 (2), 195–215.

—— (2003), *Music and Women of the Commedia dell'Arte in the Late Sixteenth Century* (Oxford: Oxford University Press).

Magarshack, David (1975), *Stanislavsky: A Life* (Westport: Greenwood Press).

Majorana, Bernadette (1992), 'Un "gemino valor": mestiere e virtù dei comici dell'Arte nel primo Seicento', *Medioevo e Rinascimento*, 6 (3), 173–93.

—— (1994), 'Governo del corpo, governo dell'anima: Attori e spettatori nel teatro italiano del XVII secolo', in Paolo Prodi (ed.), *Disciplina dell'anima, disciplina del corpo e disciplina della società tra medioevo ed età moderna*. Annali dell'Istituto storico italo-germanico in Trento (Bologna: Il mulino), 437–90.

(1996a), 'Finzioni, imitazioni, azioni: donne e teatro', in Gabriella Zarri (ed.), *Donna, disciplina, creanza cristiana dal XV al XVII secolo. Studi e testi a stampa* (Rome: Edizioni di Storia e Letteratura), 121–39.

(1996b), 'Il pulpito e l'attrice. Il teatro nella predicazione di Paolo Segneri', *Fantasmi femminili nel castello dell'inconscio maschile. Atti del convegno internazionale, Torino, 8–9 marzo 1993* (Genoa: Costa & Nolan), 16–31.

(2000), 'La scena dell'eloquenza', in Roberto Alonge and Guido Davico Bonino (eds.), *La nascita del teatro moderno. Cinquecento-Seicento*. Storia del teatro moderno e contemporaneo (Turin: Einaudi), 1043–66.

Malaev-Babel, Andrei (ed.) (2011), *The Vakhtangov Sourcebook* (London: Routledge).

Malcovati, Fausto (1984), 'Introduction', in Evgenij B. Vachtangov (ed.), *Il sistema e l'eccezione* (Florence: La casa Usher).

(1988), Introduction, in K. Stanislavskij (ed.), *Il lavoro dell'attore sul personaggio* (Rome: Laterza).

(1993), Introduction, in Fausto Malcovati (ed.), *L'attore biomeccanico* (Milan: Ubulibri).

Mariti, Luciano (1978), *Commedia ridicolosa. Comici di professione, dilettanti, editoria teatrale nel seicento. Storia e testi*. Biblioteca teatrale, vol. 22 (Rome: Bulzoni).

(2007), 'Les Stratégies Éditoriales et les Lectures Sceniche de Giovan Battista Andreini, comico dell'arte', in Georges Forestier, Edric Caldicott and Claude Bourqui (eds.), *Le Parnasse du théâtre. Les recueils d'oeuvres complètes de théâtre au XVIIe siècle* (Paris: PUPS).

Marotti, Ferruccio and Romei, Giovanna (1991), *La professione del teatro. La commedia dell'Arte e la società barocca* (Rome: Bulzoni).

Martin, Isabelle (2002), *Le théâtre de la foire. Des tréteaux aux boulevards* (Oxford: Voltaire Foundation).

Martin, John (1930), 'Martha Graham Gives Dance Without Music', *The New York Times*, 9 January 1930. Online at www.loc.gov/resource/ ihas.200154262.0

Martin du Gard, Roger (1955), 'Souvenirs autobiographiques et littéraires', in *Œuvres complètes* (Paris: Gallimard).

(1972), 'Notes sur la "Comédie des tréteaux"', in Claude Sicard (ed.), *Correspondance Jacques Copeau–Roger Martin du Gard* (Paris: Gallimard).

Martinelli, Marco (1993), 'I ventidue infortuni di Mor Arlecchino', *Teatro e storia*, 15 (2), 309–14.

Martino, Alberto (2010), 'Fonti tedesche degli anni 1565–1615 per la storia della commedia dell'arte e per la costituzione di un repertorio dei lazzi dello zanni', in Alberto Martino and Fausto De Michele (eds.), *La ricezione della Commedia dell'Arte nell'Europa centrale 1568–1769: Storia, testi, iconografia* (Pisa: Serra), 13–68.

Martino, Alberto and De Michele, Fausto (2010), *La ricezione della Commedia dell'Arte nell'Europa centrale 1568–1769: Storia, testi, iconografia* (Pisa: Serra).

Maser, Edward A. (1968), *Gian Domenico Ferretti* (Florence: Marchi e Bertolli).

Massine, Léonide (1995), *La mia vita nel balletto*, ed. by Lorena Coppola (Naples: Fondazione Léonide Massine).

Mazouer, Charles (1986), 'Les Comédiens italiens dans les ballets au temps de Mazarin', in J. Serroy (ed.), *La France et l'Italie au temps de Mazarin (15e Colloque du C.M.R. 17)* (Grenoble: Presses Universitaires de Grenoble), 319–29.

—— (2006), *Molière et ses comédies-ballets*, Nouvelle Édition Revue et Corrigée (Paris: Honoré Champion).

Mazzocchi, Federica (2006), 'Il libero volo del "Corvo" di Strehler', in Mariagabriella Cambiaghi (ed.), *Studi gozziani* (Milan: CUEM), 241–52.

Mazzocchi, Federica and Bentoglio, Alberto (1997), *Giorgio Strehler e il suo teatro* (Rome: Bulzoni).

McKerrow, Ronald B. (ed.), (1958), *The Works of Thomas Nashe* (Oxford: Blackwell).

Megale, Teresa (2009), '"'O culore d' 'e parole". Il napoletano di Eduardo per Shakespeare', in Stefania Stefanelli (ed.), *Varietà dell'italiano nel teatro contemporaneo* (Pisa: Edizioni della Normale).

—— (2014), 'Per una drammaturgia nazionale delle maschere: Eduardo De Filippo e il teatro di e con Pulcinella', *Nuova Antologia*, 2272 (4), 255–66.

Meldolesi, Claudio (1978), *Su un comico in rivolta. Dario Fo il buffalo il bambino* (Rome: Bulzoni).

—— (1984), 'La microsocietà degli attori. Una storia di tre secoli e più', *Inchiesta*, 67, 102–11.

—— (1987), 'La trinità di Eduardo: scrittura d'attore, mondo dialettale e teatro nazionale', in Claudio Meldolesi (ed.), *La trinità di Eduardo: scrittura d'attore, mondo dialettale e teatro nazionale* (Rome: Bulzoni), 57–87.

Meldolesi, Claudio and Olivi, Laura (1989), *Brecht regista* (Bologna: Il Mulino).

Merlini, Domenico (1894), *Saggio di ricerche sulla satira contro il villano* (Turin: Loescher).

Meyerhold, Vsevolod (1962), *La rivoluzione teatrale* (Rome: Editori Riuniti).

—— (1969), 'Doctor Dapertutto 1908–1917', in Edward Braun (ed.), *Meyerhold on Theatre* (London: Methuen), 111–56.

—— (1993), *L'attore biomeccanico*, ed. by Fausto Malcovati (Milan: Ubulibri).

—— (2004), *1918. Lezioni di teatro* (Milan: Ubulibri).

—— (2009), *Écrits sur le théâtre. Tome II: 1917–1930* (Lausanne: L'Âge d'Homme).

Middleton, Thomas and Rowley, William (1653), *The Spanish Gypsy* (London).

Miklăsevskij, Konstantin (1981), *La Commedia dell'arte, o, Il teatro dei commedianti italiani nei secoli XVI, XVII e XVIII* (Venice: Marsilio).

Molière (1904), *Œuvres complètes*, vol. 8 (Paris: Garnier).

Molinari, Cesare (1985), *La Commedia dell'Arte* (Milan: Mondadori).

Mollica, Fabio (1989), *Il teatro possibile. Stanislavskij e il Primo Studio del Teatro d'Arte di Mosca* (Florence: La casa Usher).

Monaldini, Sergio (1996), 'Arlecchino figlio di Pulcinela e Colombina. Note sulla famiglia Biancolelli, tra Bologna e Parigi', *L'Archiginnasio: bollettino della Biblioteca comunale di Bologna*, 91, 83–161.

(2002), 'Servitù ridicolosa e mestiere. Carlo Cantù detto Buffetto ed il suo Cicalamento', *Maske und Kothurn*, 48(1–4), 91–116.

(2005), 'Teatro del principe e del cardinale. Sulla rilevanza culturale e sociale del teatro dell'arte', in F. Cazzola and R. Varese (eds.), *Cultura nell'età delle Legazioni* (Florence: Le Lettere), 371–405.

Mooser, Robert Aloys (1948), *Annales de la musique et des musiciens en Russie au XVIIIme siècle: Des Origines a la Mort de Pierre III*, 3 vols., vol. 1 (Geneva: Mont-Blanc).

Mulryne, J.R. (ed.) (2009), *Thomas Kyd. The Spanish Tragedy* (London: A. & C. Black).

Neri, Ferdinando (1913), *Scenario delle maschere in Arcadia* (Castello: Lapi).

Neuhuber, Christian (2011), 'Scene della Commedia dell'Arte usate come decorazione di interni. I rivestimenti delle pareti di J. B. A. Raunacher nel Castello Eggenberg a Graz', in Alberto Martino and Fausto De Michele (eds.), *La ricezione della Commedia dell'Arte nell'Europa centrale 1568–1769. Storia, testi, iconografia* (Pisa: Serra), 433–40.

Nicholson, Eric (1991), 'Il teatro immagini di lei', in Natalie Zemon Davis and Arlette Farge (eds.), *Storia delle donne in occidente. Dal rinascimento all'età moderna* (Rome: Laterza), 290–313.

Nicoll, Allardyce (1963), *The World of Harlequin* (Cambridge: Cambridge University Press).

(1980), *Il mondo di Arlecchino. Guida alla Commedia dell'Arte* (Milan: Bompiani).

Noe, Alfred (2011), 'Gli *affreschi* nel Castello di Böhmisch Krumau', in Alberto Martino and Fausto De Michele (eds.), *La ricezione della Commedia dell'Arte nell'Europa centrale 1568–1769. Storia, testi, iconografia* (Pisa: Serra), 427–31.

Nolhac, Pierre de and Solerti, Angelo (1890), *Il viaggio in Italia di Enrico III re di Francia e le feste a Venezia, Ferrara, Mantova e Torino* (Turin: L. Roux).

Nyström, Eiler (1918), *Den danske Komedies Oprindelse. Om Skuepladsen og Holberg* (Copenhagen: Gyldendalske Boghandel).

O'Brien, John (2004), *Harlequin Britain: Pantomime and Entertainment, 1690–1760* (Baltimore: Johns Hopkins University Press).

Ojeda Calvo, María del Valle (2004), 'Otro manuscrito inédito atribuible a Stefanelo Botarga y otras noticias documentales', *Criticón*, 92, 141–69.

(2007), *Stefanelo Botarga e Zan Ganassa: Scenari e zibaldoni di comici italiani nella Spagna del Cinquecento* (Rome: Bulzoni).

Ottonelli, Giovan Battista (1648), *Della christiana moderatione del theatro. Libro I, detto la qualità delle comedie* (Florence: Franceschini e Logi).

Padoan, Giorgio (1982), *La commedia rinascimentale veneta (1433–1565)* (Vicenza: Neri Pozza).

Pagani, Maria Pia (2007), *I mestieri di Pantalone. La fortuna della maschera tra Venezia e la Russia* (Costabissara: Angelo Colla Editore).

Pandolfi, Vito (1957–61), *La Commedia dell'Arte. Storia e testo*, 6 vols. (Florence: Sansoni).

(1990), 'Esperienze di vita teatrale', in Andrea Mancini (ed.), *Teatro da quattro soldi. Vito Pandolfi regista* (Bologna: Nouva Alfa), 203–25.

Peretts, V. N. (1917), *Italiyanskiya komedii i intermedii predstavlennaya pri dvore Imperatritsy Anny Ioannovny v 1733–1735 gg* (Petrograd: Imperatorskaya Akademiya Nauk).

(1923), 'Italiyanskaya intermediya 1730-kh godov, v stikhotvornom perevode', in *Starinnyy teatr v Rossii XVII–XVIII vv. Sbornik statey* (St Peterburg: Academia), 143–79.

Perrucci, Andrea (1961), *Dell'Arte Rappresentativa premeditata ed all'improvviso* (Florence: Sansoni).

Pesenti, Maria Chiara (1996), *Arlecchino e Gaer nel teatro dilettantesco russo del Settecento. Contatti e intersezioni in un repertorio teatrale* (Milan: Guerini e Associati).

(2006), 'Traditsii russkikh ustnykh narodnykh komediy i intermediy pervoy poloviny XVIII veka v rannem Russkom teatre', in *Osnovanie natsional'nogo teatra i sud'by Russkoy dramaturgii* (St Petersburg: Rossiyskaya Akademiya Nauk), 19–29.

Peters, Julie Stone (2000), *Theatre of the Book, 1480–1880: Print, Text, and Performance in Europe* (Oxford: Oxford University Press).

Picon-Vallin, Béatrice (1989), 'Les années 10 à Petersbourg. Meyerhold, La commedia dell'arte et Le Bal Masque', in Odette Aslan and Denis Bablet (eds.), *Le Masque. Du Rite au Théâtre* (Paris: CNRS), 147–58.

(2002/2003), 'La rivista di un praticante-ricercatore: "L'amore delle tre melarance" (Pietroburgo, 1913–1916)', *Culture teatrali*, 7/8, 283–8.

(2009), *Ariane Mnouchkine* (Arles: Actes sud).

Pineda, Juan de (1589), *Los treynta y cinco diálogos familiares de la Agricultura christiana* (Salamanca: Pedro de Arduça y Diego López).

Pirrotta, Nino (1975), *Li due Orfei. Da Poliziano a Monteverdi* (Turin: Einaudi).

(1984), 'Commedia dell'Arte and opera', *Music and Culture in Italy from the Middle Ages to the Baroque: A Collection of Essays* (Cambridge: Harvard University Press).

Pirrotta, Nino and Povoledo, Elena (1982), *Music and Theatre from Poliziano to Monteverdi* (Cambridge: Cambridge University Press).

Pontremoli, Alessandro (1995), 'La danza negli spettacoli dal Medioevo alla fine del Seicento', in Alberto Basso (ed.), *Musica in scena. Storia dello spettacolo musicale. Vol 5: L' arte della danza e del balletto* (Turin: Utet), 1–36.

(2005), *Intermedio spettacolare e danza teatrale a Milano fra Cinque e Seicento*, 2nd ed. (Milan: Euresis).

De Berardinis, Leo (1994), *Il ritorno di Scaramouche: di Jean Baptiste Poquelin e Leòn de Berardin* (Bologna: Fuori Thema).

Posner, Donald (1977), 'Jacques Callot and the Dances Called Sfessania', *The Art Bulletin*, 59 (2), 203–16.

Pozzi, Giovanni (1986), 'Occhi bassi', in Edgar Marsch and Giovanni Pozzi (eds.), *Thematologie des Kleinen* (Fribourg: Éditions Universitaires Fribourg Suisse), 161–211.

Pretini, Giancarlo (1988), *Antonio Franconi e la nascita del circo* (Udine: Trapezio).

Prodi, Paolo (ed.), (1994), *Disciplina dell'arnima, disciplina del corpo e disciplina della società tra medioevo ed età moderna.* Annali dell'Istiutio storico italo-germanico in Trento (Bologna: Il mulino).

Puppa, Paolo (2000), 'Tradition, Traditions and Dario Fo', in Joseph Farrell and Antonio Scuderi (eds.), *Dario Fo: Stage, Text and Tradition* (Carbondale: Southern Illinois University Press), 181–96.

Raffaelli, Filippo (1954), 'Occhio magico', *Radiocorriere*, 47 (16–17).

Rasi, Luigi (1897), *I Comici italiani*, 2 vols. (Florence: Bocca).

—— (1912), *Catalogo generale della raccolta drammatica italiana* (Florence: Landi).

Raskina, Raissa (2007), 'Carlo Gozzi e il "neo-romanticismo" teatrale nella Russia del primo Novecento', *Problemi di critica goldoniana*, 13, 343–55.

—— (2010), *Mejerchol'd e il dottor Dappertutto. Lo 'Studio' e la rivista 'L'amore delle tre melarance'* (Rome: Bulzoni).

Riccoboni, Luigi (1728), *Histoire du théâtre italien, depuis la décadence de la comédie Latine*, 2nd ed. 1730 (Paris: Cailleau).

—— (2009), 'Dell'arte rappresentativa', in Sarah Di Bella (ed.), *L'Expérience théâtrale dans l'oeuvre théorique de Luigi Riccoboni, suivie de la traduction et l'édition critique de dell'Arte Rappresentativa de Luigi Riccoboni* (Paris: Honoré Champion).

Ripellino, Angelo Maria (1965), *Il truco e l'anima* (Turin: Einaudi).

—— (1989), *Siate buffi!* (Rome: Bulzoni).

Robinson, Harlow (1986), 'Love for Three Operas: The Collaboration of Vsevolod Meyerhold and Sergei Prokofiev', *Russian Review*, 45 (3), 287–304.

Rosand, Ellen (1979), 'The Descending Tetrachord: An Emblem of Lament', *Musical Quarterly*, 65, 346–59.

Rudin, Bärbel (2000), *Venedig im Norden oder: Harlekin und die Buffonisten: "die hochfürstl. Braunsch.-Lüneb.-Wolfenbüttelschen Teutschen Hof-Acteurs" (1727 – 1732)* (Reichenbach i.V.: Neuberin-Museum) 149.

Rudnitsky, Kostantin (1988), *Russian and Soviet Theater 1905–1932*, ed. by Lesley Milne (London: Thames and Hudson).

Ruffini, Franco (2005), *Stanislavskij. Dal lavoro dell'attore al lavoro su di sé*, 2nd ed. (Rome: Laterza).

Rühle, Günther (1988), *Theater für die Republik im Spiegel der Kritik. 1917–1925*, vol. 1 (Frankfurt a. M.: S. Fischer-Verlag).

Sánchez Romeralo, Jaime (1990), 'El supuesto retorno de Ganasa a España', *Quaderni Ibero-Americani*, 67–68, 121–33.

Sand, Maurice (1860), *Masques et bouffons. (Comédie Italienne). Texte et dessins.* Préface par George Sand (Paris: Lévy).

Sanguineti, Edoardo (1985), 'Masque et choc', *Théâtre/Publique*, 69, 7–8.

—— (2001), *L'amore delle tre melarance* (Genova: Il melangolo).

Santanelli, Manlio (2005), *Teatro* (Rome: Bulzoni).

Sanz, Carmen and García García, Bernardo J. (1995), 'El "oficio de representar" en España y la influencia de la "commedia dell'arte"', *Cuadernos de Historia Moderna*, 16, 475–500.

Scafoglio, Domenico, Satriani, Lombardi and Maria, Luigi (1992), *Pulcinella: il mito e la storia* (Milan: Leonardo).

Scala, Flaminio and Andrews, Richard (2008), *The Commedia dell'Arte of Flaminio Scala: A Translation and Analysis of 30 Scenarios* (Lanham: Scarecrow Press).

Scherl, Adolf (2010), 'La Commedia dell'arte in Boemia', in Alberto Martino and Fausto di Michele (eds.), *La ricezione della commedia dell'arte nell'Europa centrale 1568–1769: storia, testi, iconografia* (Pisa: Fabrizio Serra), 145–57.

Schindler, Otto G. (2005a), 'Comici dell'arte bereisen Europa. Ein Abriss', in Otto G. Schindler, et al. (eds.), *Maske und Kothurn: Commedia dell'Arte.* Maske und Kothurn. Internationale Beiträge zur Theaterwissenschaft (Vienna: Böhlau), 7–17.

(2005b), 'Viaggi teatrali tra l'Inquisizione e il Sacco. Comici dell'Arte di Mantova alle corti degli Asburgo d'Austria', in Umberto Artioli and Cristina Grazioli (eds.), *I Gonzaga e l'Impero. Itinerari dello spettacolo. Con una selezione di materiali dell'Archivio Informatico Herla (1560–1630)* (Florence: Le Lettere), 107–60.

(2010), 'Comici dell'arte alle corti austriache degli Asburgo', in Alberto Martino and Fausto di Michele (eds.), *La ricezione della commedia dell'arte nell'Europa centrale 1568–1769: storia, testi, iconografia* (Pisa: Fabrizio Serra), 69–143.

Scott, Virginia (1990), *The Commedia dell'Arte in Paris, 1644–1697* (Charlottesville: University of Virginia Press).

(1992), 'Les Filles Errantes: Emancipated Women at the Comédie Italienne, 1683–1691', in Laurence Senelick (ed.), *Gender in Performance: The Presentation of Difference in the Performing Arts* (Hanover: University of New England Press), 101–16.

Segneri, Paolo (1687), *Il christiano instruito nella sua legge. Ragionamenti morali . . . Parte terza* (Venice: Baglioni).

Sentaurens, Jean (1984), *Séville et le théâtre de la fin du Moyen Âge à la fin du XVIIe siècle* (Bourdeaux: Université de Bourdeaux).

Serena, Alessandro (2008), *Storia del circo* (Milan: Mondadori).

Shakespeare, William (1997), *The Riverside Shakespeare*, 2nd ed., vol. 2 (Boston: Houghton Mifflin).

Shiryaev, Alexander (2009), *Master of Movement*, ed. by Birgit Beumers, Victor Bocharov and David Robinson, (Pordenone: Le Giornate del Cinema Muto).

Simoncini, Francesca (2011), 'Innamorate dell'Arte. Gli esordi teatrali di Barbara Flaminia', in Stefano Mazzoni (ed.), *Studi di storia dello spettacolo. Omaggio a Siro Ferrone* (Florence: Le Lettere), 106–14.

Slonim, Marc (1961), *Russian Theatre from the Empire to the Soviets* (New York: Collier Books).

Smith, Gretchen Elizabeth (2005), *The Performance of Male Nobility in Molière's Comédies-Ballets: Staging the Courtier* (Aldershot: Ashgate).

Smith, Winifred (1912), *The Commedia dell'Arte: A Study in Italian Popular Comedy* (New York: Columbia University Press).

Soriani, Simone (2007), *Dario Fo. Dalla commedia al monologo (1959–1969)* (Corazzano: Titivillus).

Sottili, Fabio (2008), 'Le "Arlecchinate" di Giovanni Domenico Ferretti e la committenza Sansedon', *Paragone Arte*, 49 (81), 32–54.

——— (2011), 'Non soltanto Arlecchini. Novità sulle tele teatrali di Ferretti e Gambacciani per Giovanni Sansedoni', *Paragone Arte*, 62 (98–99), 70–83.

Squarzina, Luigi (2005), *Il romanzo della regia. Duecento anni di trionfi e sconfitte* (Pisa: Pacini).

Stanislavski, Konstantin (1954–1961), *Sobranie socinenij*, 8 vols., vol. 8 (Moscow: Iskusstvo).

——— (1988), *Il lavoro dell'attore sul personaggio* (Rome: Laterza).

——— (2008), *My Life in Art* (London: Routledge).

——— (2010), *An Actor's Work on a Role*, trans. by Jean Benedetti (Abingdon: Routledge).

Starikova, L. M. (1989), 'Novye dokumenty o deyatel'nosti ital'yanskoy truppy v Rossii v 30-e gody XVIIIv. i russkom lyubitel'skom teatre ego vremeni', in *Pamyatniki kul'tury. Novye otkritiya 1988* (Moscow: Nauka), 80–92.

——— (1995), *Teatral'naya zhizn' Rossii v épokhy Anny Ioannovny. Dokumental'naya khronika 1730–1740 vyp. I* (Moscow: Radiks).

——— (2000), *Moskva starodavnyaya. Geroy zhizni i stseny* (Moscow: Artist-Rezhissyor-Teatr).

——— (2006), 'Na puti professionalizatsii (russkoe akterstvo do osnovaniya gosudarstvennogo teatra)', in *Osnovanie natsional'nogo teatra i sud'by russkoy dramaturgii* (St Petersburg: Rossiykaya Akademiya Nauk), 12–18.

Starobinski, Jean (1970), *Portrait de l'artiste en saltimbanque* (Geneva: Skira).

Stefani, Gianluca (2009), 'Iconografia dello spettacolo a Napoli nel Settecento. Napoli allo specchio: leggenda e abisso dell'Arte', in Francesco Cotticelli and Paologiovanni Maione (eds.), *Storia della musica e dello spettacolo a Napoli. Il Settecento* (Naples: Edizione Turchini), 356–82.

Sterling, Charles (1943), 'Early paintings of the Commedia dell'Arte in France', *The Metropolitan Museum of Art Bulletin*, 2 (1), 11–32.

Stoddart, Helen (2000), *Rings of Desire: Circus History and Representation* (Manchester: Manchester University Press).

Stokes, Adrian (1935), *To-Night the Ballet* (New York: Dutton).

Stoppato, Lorenzo (1887), *La commedia popolare in Italie* (Padua: Draghi).

Strehler, Giorgio (1977), *Für ein menschlicheres Theater. Geschriebene, gesprochene und verwirklichte Gedanken*, trans. by Sinah Kessler (Frankfurt a. M.: Suhrkamp).

Sulerzhitsky, L. A. *Notes on the Studio* (Archive of L.A. Sulerzhitsky, n. 6477/47, MHAT Museum).

Tamburini, Elena (2010), '"Commedia dell'arte": Indagini e percorsi intorno a un'ipotesi'. Online at http://drammaturgia.fupress.net/saggi/saggio.php?id=4644

Taviani, Ferdinando (1969), *La fascinazione del teatro*. Vol. 1 : La commedia dell'arte e la società Barocca (Rome: Bulzoni).

(1979), 'Cecchini, Pier Maria', *Dizionario Biografico degli Italiani*, vol. 17 (Rome: Istituto dell'Enciclopedia Italiana), 274–80.

(1980), 'Commedia dell'arte', in A. Attisani (ed.), *Enciclopedia del Teatro del Novecento* (Milan: Feltrinelli), 393–40.

(1982), 'Il segreto delle compagnie italiane note poi come commedia dell'arte', in Ferdinando Taviani and Mirella Schino (eds.), *Il segreto della commedia dell'arte* (Florence: La casa Usher), 297–488.

(1984), 'Bella d'Asia. Torquato Tasso, gli attori e l'immortalita', *Paragone Letteratura*, 25, 3–76.

(1986), 'Un vivo contrasto. Seminario su attrici e attori della Commedia dell'Arte', *Teatro e storia*, 1 (1), 25–75.

(1987), 'L'ingresso della Commedia dell'arte nella cultura del Cinquecento', in Fabrizio Cruciani and Daniele Seragnoli (eds.), *Il teatro italiano nel Rinascimento* (Bologna: Il Mulino), 319–45.

(2006), 'La minaccia di una fama divaricata', in Ferdinando Taviani (ed.), *Luigi Pirandello: Saggi e interventi* (Milan: Montadori), xiii–cii.

(2007), 'Il segreto delle compagnie italiane note poi come commedia dell'arte', in Ferdinando Taviani and Mirella Schino (eds.), *Il segreto della commedia dell'arte* (Florence: La casa Usher), 295–450.

Taviani, Ferdinando and Schino, Mirella ([1982] 2007), *Il segreto della Commedia dell'arte. La memoria delle compagnie italiane del XVI, XVII e XVIII secolo* (Florence: La casa Usher).

Tessari, Roberto (1981), *Commedia dell'Arte: La maschera e l'ombra* (Milan: Mursia).

(2013), *La Commedia dell'Arte* (Rome: Laterza).

Testaverde, Anna Maria (ed.), (2007), *I canovacci della Commedia dell'Arte* (Turin: Einaudi).

Teulon-Lardic, Sabine (2008), 'Arlequin, Gilles et Pierrot à l'opéra-comique. Résurgences de l'esprit de la Foire et de la Comédie-Italienne au XIXe siècle (1830–1887)', *Revue de Musicologie*, 94 (1), 91–137.

Théâtre du Soleil (ed.) (1975), 'Écrire une comédie de notre temps', in *L'Age d'or, première ébauche: texte programme* (Paris: Théâtre Ouvert Stock), 13–14.

Tomlinson, Robert James (1981), *Watteau et Marivaux. La fête galante* (Paris: Droz).

Toporkov, Vasily Osipovich (1979), *Stanislavski in Rehearsal. The Final Years* (New York: Theatre Arts Books).

Toschi, Paolo (1955), *Le origini del teatro italiano. Origini rituali della rappresentazione popolare in Italia* (Turin: Boringhieri).

Trautmann, Karl (1887), 'Italienische Schauspieler am bayrischen Hof', in Karl von Reinhardstöttner and Karl Trautmann (eds.), *Jahrbuch für Münchener Geschichte*, vol. 1 (Munich: Lindauersche Buchhandlung), 193–312.

Troiano, Massimo (1569), *Discorsi delli trionfi, apparati, e delle cose più notabile fatte nelle sontuose nozze dell'Illustrissimo et Eccellentissimo Sig. Duca*

Guglielmo, primo genito del generosissimo Alberto Quinto (Munich: A. Montano).

Ueltschi, Karin (2008), *La 'Mesnie Hellequin' en conte et en rime. Mémoire mythique et poétique de la recomposition* (Paris: Champion).

UNESCOa, 'What Is Intangible Cultural Heritage?' Online at www.unesco.org/culture/ich/en/what-is-intangible-heritage-00003

UNESCOb, 'Working Towards a Convention on Intangible Cultural Heritage'. Online at www.unesco.org/culture/ich/doc/src/01854-EN.pdf

Vakhtangov, Evgenij B. (1923), *Carlo Gozzi, Printsessa Turandot. Teatral'no-tragicheskaia kitaiskaia skazka v 5 aktakh* (Moscow: Gosizdat).

(1959), *Materialy i Stat'i* (Moscow: Vserossniskoe Teatral'noe Obščestvo).

(1984), *Il sistema e l'eccezione* (Florence: La casa Usher).

Valentin, Jean-Marie (1978), *Le théâtre des jésuites dans les pays de langue allemande (1554–1680). Salut des âmes et ordres des cités*, vol. 1 (Bern: Lang).

Van Buchel, Arnold (1900), 'Description de Paris par Arnold Van Buchel d'Utrecht', *Mémoires de la Société de l'histoire de Paris et de l'Ile-de-France* (Paris: H. Champion).

Van Norman Baer, Nancy (1987), *Bronislava Nijinska: A Dancer's Legacy* (San Francisco: The Fine Arts Museum of San Francisco).

Vazzoler, Franco (2007), 'Il "travestimento fiabesco e gozziano" di Edoardo Sanguineti: L'amore delle tre melarance per Benno Besson', *Problemi di critica goldoniana*, 13, 385–98.

(2009), *Il chierico e la scena* (Genoa: Il melangolo).

Vescovo, Piermario (1996), *Da Ruzante a Calmo. Tra 'signore commedie' e 'onorandissime stampe'* (Padua: Antenore).

(2002), 'L'orologio di Don Giovanni tra Bertati e Da Ponte', *Quaderns d'Italià*, 7, 177–86.

(2010a), '"Farvi sopra le parole", "Scenario", "ossatura", "canovaccio"', *Commedia dell'Arte/Annuario Internazionale*, 3, 95–116.

(2010b), 'Dario Fo e la (sua influenza sulla) commedia dell'arte', *Révue des études italiennes*, 56 (3–4), 199–214.

Vianello, Daniele (1999), 'Tra inferno e paradiso. Il "limbo" dei buffoni', *Biblioteca Teatrale*, 49–51, 13–80.

(2005), *L'arte del buffone. Maschere e spettacolo fra Italia e Baviera nel XVI secolo* (Rome: Bulzoni).

(2009), 'Maschere, commedie all'italiana e teatro dei gesuiti in area tedesca del XVI secolo', in Myriam Chiabò and Federico Doglio (eds.), *Fortuna europea della Commedia dell'Arte* (Rome: Centro studi sul teatro medioevale e rinascimentale), 235–57.

Vicentini, Claudio (2004), 'L'orizzonte dell'oratoria. Teoria, recitazione e dottrina dell'eloquenza nella cultura del Seicento', *Annali dell'Università di Napoli "L'Orientale". Sezione romanza*, 46 (2), 303–35.

Volkov, Nikolaj (1929), *Mejerchol'd*, vol. 2 (Moscow: Accedemia).

Vsevolodskiy-Gerngross (1929), *Istoriya russkogo teatra*, vol. 1 (Moscow: Tea-Kino-Pechat').

Wiles, David (1987), *Shakespeare's Clown. Actor and Text in the Elizabethan Playhouse* (Cambridge: Cambridge University Press).

Winter, Susanne (2007), 'Gozzi Inszenieren, ein Gespräch mit Benno Besson und Ezio Toffolutti', in Susanne Winter (ed.), *Il mondo e le sue favole. Sviluppi europei del teatro di Goldoni e Gozzi* (Rome: Edizioni di Storia e Letteratura), 253–58.

Yawney, Marshall James (1971), 'Early Russian Theatre and Commedia dell'Arte' (Master's thesis, University of British Columbia).

Zanlonghi, Giovanna (2002), *Teatri di formazione actio, parola e immagine nella scena gesuitica del Sei-Settecento a Milano* (Milan: Vita e Pensiero).

Zarri, Gabriella (2008), Introduction, in Gabriella Zarri (ed.), *L'età moderna. Storia della direzione spirituale*, vol. 3 (Brescia: Morcelliana), 5–53.

Zguta, Russell (1978), *Russian Minstrels: A History of the Skomorokhi* (Philadelphia: University of Pennsylvania).

Zorzi, Ludovico (1977), *Il teatro e la città* (Torino: Einaudi).

(1990), *L'attore, la commedia, il drammaturgo* (Turin: Einaudi).

(1967), Preface, in Ludovico Zorzi (ed.), *Ruzante Teatro* (Turin: Einaudi), vii–lxvii.

Further Reading

Cairns, Christopher (1993), 'Dario Fo and the Commedia dell'Arte', in David J. George and Christopher J. Gossip (eds.), *Studies in the Commedia dell'Arte* (Cardiff: University of Wales Press), 247–65.

Dick, Kay (1960), *Pierrot: An Examination of the Pierrot Legend* (London: Hutchinson).

Fava, Antonio (2004), *The Comic Mask in the Commedia dell'Arte: Actor Training, Improvisation and the Poetics of Survival* (Reggio Emilia: Ars Comica).

Fitzpatrick, Tim (1995), *The Relationship of Oral and Literate Performance Processes in the Commedia dell'Arte: Beyond the Improvisation/Memorization Divide* (Lewiston, Queenston, Lampeter: Edwin Mellen).

George, David J. and Gossip, Christopher J. (eds.) (1993), *Studies in the Commedia dell'Arte* (Cardiff: University of Wales Press).

Gordon, Mel (1983), *Lazzi: The Comic Routines of the Commedia dell'Arte* (New York: Performing Arts Research Publications).

Grantham, Barry (2000), *Playing Commedia: A Training Guide to Commedia Techniques* (London: Nick Hern Books).

Lawner, Lynne (1998), *Harlequin on the Moon: Commedia dell'Arte and Visual Arts* (New York: Abrams).

Murray, Simon David (2003), *Jacques Lecoq* (London: Routledge).

Rudlin, John (1994), *Commedia dell'Arte: An Actor's Handbook* (London: Routledge).

Rudlin, John and Crick, Olly (2001), *Commedia dell'Arte: A Handbook for Troupes* (London: Routledge).

Williams, David (ed.) (1994), *Collaborative Theatre: The Théâtre du Soleil Sourcebook* (London: Routledge).

Index

Manufactured by Amazon.ca
Bolton, ON